3   3 00246 1941

TX349 .R48 1
Riely, Elizabe
    The Chef's
Concise Dictio
Terms

D0428955

Companion

A Concise Dictionary
of Culinary Terms

Second Edition
Revised and Expanded

The Chef's Companion

A Concise Dictionary of Culinary Terms

Second Edition
Revised and Expanded

~

Elizabeth Riely

Illustrations by
David Miller

JOHN WILEY & SONS, INC.

New York   Chichester   Weinheim   Brisbane   Singapore   Toronto

This text is printed on acid-free paper. ☺

Copyright © 1996 by John Wiley & Sons, Inc. All rights reserved.

Published simultaneously in Canada.

No part of this publication may be reproduced, stored in a retrieval system or transmitted in any form or by any means, electronic, mechanical, photocopying, recording, scanning or otherwise, except as permitted under Sections 107 or 108 of the 1976 United States Copyright Act, without either the prior written permission of the Publisher, or authorization through payment of the appropriate per-copy fee to the Copyright Clearance Center, 222 Rosewood Drive, Danvers, MA 01923, (978) 750-8400, fax (978) 750-4744. Requests to the Publisher for permission should be addressed to the Permissions Department, John Wiley & Sons, Inc., 605 Third Avenue, New York, NY 10158-0012, (212) 850-6011, fax (212) 850-6008, E-Mail: PERMREQ@WILEY.COM.

This publication is designed to provide accurate and authoritative information in regard to the subject matter covered. It is sold with the understanding that the publisher is not engaged in rendering legal, accounting, or other professional services. If legal advice or other expert assistance is required, the services of a competent professional person should be sought.

6   7   8   9   10

Library of Congress Cataloging-in-Publication Data:

Riely, Elizabeth.
    The chef's companion: a concise dictionary of culinary terms /
Elizabeth Gawthrop Riely.—2nd ed.
        p.   cm.
    Includes bibliographical references.
    ISBN 0-471-28759-8
    1. Food—Dictionaries.   2. Cookery—Dictionaries.   I. Title.
TX349.R48   1996   96-15287
641'.03—dc20   CIP

For my Mother and Father

Preface

The culinary boom of the last twenty-five years has brought profound changes in the way we think about food in this country. Many foreign cuisines and ethnic styles of cooking, once little known, have gained great popularity. More and more people have become involved in food preparation either as a profession or as a pastime. This increased interest has led, in turn, to a greater appreciation of our own American regional cooking.

The Chef's Companion reflects these developments by bringing together information from a wide range of sources. The dictionary's scope is broad, serving the needs of home cooks as well as professional chefs, culinary students, restaurateurs, and foodservice managers. At the same time, its definitions are brief, pointed, and meant for quick reference in the kitchen.

As in the first edition, the book contains many entries for classic dishes and styles of preparation; cooking techniques and equipment; pastries and cheeses; foreign-language words for many foodstuffs (translated into English); and edible plants, animals, and fish not widely known. Some notable figures in the history of food and gastronomy are identified. Because wine is an integral part of gastronomy, many names and terms—major European wine regions and vineyards, grape varieties, and wine-making techniques—will be found here. There are also numerous entries for beers and liqueurs.

Entries for sauces, styles, and garnishes are listed by the particular name of each in its original language. For example, the entry for *poulet à la Marengo* will be found under *Marengo*, not under *poulet* or chicken, and the entry for *à la* explains its usage. Numerous cross references, in **bold-face** type, serve as signposts. To correct common errors, I have called attention to words that are often misspelled or misunderstood.

This second edition adds much fresh information to the European, Asian, Middle Eastern, and Latin American entries in the first edition. Travel abroad and new immigration has heightened our awareness of cultures once thought remote. Of the new material, many Asian culinary terms—Vietnamese, Thai, Korean, Cambodian, Pacific Rim—have found their way into these pages. Focusing on cultural traditions rather than political boundaries, the dictionary now has greater representation of the food of India, Persia, and Turkey. The book embraces Arab cooking along the coast of the Mediterranean from the Middle East to Morocco as well as more from the rest of Africa.

Continuing westward, this edition takes in many new terms from Latin America that reflect the cultural mix—Native-American, African, European—of the Caribbean Islands, Mexico, and South America. Similarly, American regional cooking, especially southern, is covered more fully. A few entries from the first edition seemed dated, so more recent styles take their place. And unusual or exotic foodstuffs available to us now as never before, particularly the ever-evolving cultivated varieties of fruits and vegetables, have entries.

The greatest change in this new edition is the inclusion of a phonetical guide. In parentheses after nearly every main entry in a foreign language, and sometimes those in English, this transcription tells readers how to pronounce words (and occasionally how not to *mis*pronounce them). In keeping with a concise dictionary, this guide aims to be clear and simple. Those looking for more subtlety can consult a specialized language dictionary or, better yet, a speaker of that language.

This dictionary makes no pretense to being all-inclusive. From the beginning it was intended to be concise. Words in English for very familiar foods or basic kitchen techniques (apple, beef, chop, etc.) have been omitted. Some readers will want more entries or greater detail. They may consult the works listed in the bibliography, which is updated and expanded from that in the first edition, or a comprehensive English dictionary. As the culinary boom continues, inevitably there are yet more terms that might be added to *The Chef's Companion*. I hope readers will let me know of those, along with any errors I have committed, to be amended in a future edition. Just as language and gastronomy continue to change, so too do books that define them.

Pronunciation Guide

Vowels:

A
a = short a as in "apple"
ah = a as in "fava"
ay = long a as in "bake"
ar = ar as in "carve"
aahr = ar as in "garni"
anh = nasal an as in "blanc" (also amh)

E
e or eh = short e as in "set"
ee = long e as in "leek"
eu = e as in "feu"
enh = nasal en as in "entrée" (first e; also emh)

I
i = short i as in "mix"
ī = long i as in "knife"
inh = nasal in as in "vin" (also imh)
ee = i as in "bistro"

O
o = short o as in "hot"
ō = long o as in "rosemary"

oh = o as in "pomme"
onh = nasal on as in "fond" (also omh)
eu = ö as in "Möhre"
ow = ao as in "bacalao"

U
u or uh = short u as in "butter"
oo = long u as in "tuna"
ü = French u as in "tu" or German ü as in "Küche"
unh = nasal un as in "aucun" (also umh)

Consonants:
g = hard g as in "gumbo"
j = hard j as in "juniper"
jh = soft j as in "julienne"
kh = gutteral ch as in "challah" or "Kuchen"
s = s as in "salad"
z = s as in "risotto"
ts = z or zz as in "pizza"

Rhythm and Stress:
Syllables in upper case show emphasis. Double dash (—) in some Turkish words denote an extra moment's pause.

This pronunciation guide aims for clarity and simplicity, using a minimum of diacritical marks. Some sounds foreign to English are difficult to render in phonetic transcription—for example, the French r as in "croissant"; the German ch as in "Küche"; the Vietnamese ng as in "gung." Some words sound just as they look and so have no transcription.

Readers should note that the phonetical guide tells how to say the term in the original language, not in common Americanized pronunciation (see **sauter, dim sum, Spätzle**).

Acknowledgments

I wish to thank many people who helped me with this second edition of *The Chef's Companion* along with those I named in the first a decade ago. The pronunciation guide new to this edition required an extraordinary amount of support, and people responded with remarkable generosity at every turn.

Loan Rothschild's experience in teaching languages was invaluable with Vietnamese terms. For Chinese, Nina Simonds and Cynthia Cheng gave me expert advice and assistance. Sam Rojanasuvan, of Amarin of Thailand restaurant in Newton, Massachusetts, answered my inquiries on Thai culinary terms with fortitude. Jae Chung and Sand Cho, of Jae's Cafe in Boston, kindly helped me with Korean. Makoto Takenaka of Boston College generously assisted with Japanese pronunciations.

John Akar contributed his first-hand knowledge of West African food. Mizrak Assefa, of the Red Sea restaurant in Boston, helped with Ethiopian terms. For Russian pronunciation, I relied on the expertise of Joyce Toomre; for Hungarian, Barbara Kuck. Azita Bina-Seibel and Gregory Pope, of Lala Rokh restaurant in Boston, guided me through Persian culinary tradition. Lucien Robert, of Maison Robert in Boston, helped with French pronunciation.

Catherine Van Orman, of Jessica's Biscuit in Newton, recommended cookbooks that gave me the information I sought. Zarela Martinez, of

Zarela's restaurant in Manhattan, aided me with Mayan words in Mexican cooking. Eli Alperovicz, of Za'atar's Oven in Brookline, Massachusetts, helped sort out the intricacies of Middle Eastern terms. Longteine de Monteiro, of the Elephant Walk in Somerville, Massachusetts, enlightened me about Cambodian cuisine. Doug Erb, of Bread & Circus market in Newton, responded to my questions on new varieties of greens. For seafood entries, Ken Coons, of New England Fisheries Development Association, provided detailed information.

Barry Girten and Sarah Boardman are valued friends who gave me general encouragement and specific suggestions, sometimes without even realizing it. Margaret Leibenstein, besides guiding me through Spanish and Mexican terms, graciously fielded many other queries. Once again, I thank members of the Culinary Historians of Boston for widening and deepening my knowledge of food.

Clifford A. Wright's profound understanding of Middle Eastern cooking and the Arabic language saved me from many errors, especially standardized spelling and linguistic changes as the culinary traveller crosses borders around the Mediterranean. Alice Arndt gave freely of her time and expertise, using her grasp of Turkish language and culture. Laxmi and Vivek Rao answered my questions on Indian food with precision, authority, and good humor.

To Professor Thomas S. Hansen of Wellesley College I owe special thanks far beyond his help with German and Scandinavian terminology. His experience with language textbooks and his discerning questions have significantly improved this dictionary. Alan and Olivia Bell read through the entire book, making numerous suggestions and queries that sharpened it, particularly on British food and French wine. I am greatly indebted to them for their connoisseurship of gastronomy.

At Van Nostrand Reinhold, I am grateful to Melissa A. Rosati for her belief in an expanded edition. Phyllis Dalton saved the day with her masterful word processing. Elaine Silverstein's editorial eye helped to shape the new edition, Jacqueline Martin and Joan Petrokofsky shepherded it along, and Andrea G. Mulligan at Benchmark Productions brought it forward ably. David Miller came through with last-minute help with his evocative drawings. My agent Susan Lescher has my continued thanks for her advice and support.

Finally, I wish to acknowledge my husband John Riely, whose refined taste in wine, food, and books has contributed so much to this one. My older son Christopher has readily shared his knowledge of French language and culture. I am grateful to him and to his brother Andrew for their cheerful patience throughout the remaking of *The Chef's Companion.*

The Chef's Companion

A Concise Dictionary
of Culinary Terms
Second Edition
Revised and Expanded

asperge

Aal (ahl) German for eel.

abadejo (ah-bah-DAY-hō) Spanish for fresh cod.

abaissage (a-bes-sajh) Rolling out pastry dough, in French.

abalone (a-bah-LŌ-nee) A **mollusk** whose large adductor muscle connecting its single shell is edible; used widely in Japanese and Chinese cooking, either fresh, dried, or canned; found throughout the Pacific Ocean, off the coast of California, and in the English Channel, where it is called ormer.

abatis (a-ba-tee) French for external poultry trimmings, such as wing tips, necks, and feet; sometimes used interchangeably with **abats** for giblets.

abats (a-bah) French for poultry giblets and meat offal; internal organs or variety meats, such as hearts, liver, sweetbreads, and gizzards; sometimes used interchangeably with **abatis**.

abbacchio (ah-BAH-kyō) Italian for a very young suckling lamb.

abgusht (ahb-GOOSHT) Stew in Persian cooking, usually of lamb and vegetables.

abricot (a-bree-kō) French for apricot.

absinthe (ab-sinht) A green liqueur flavored with **wormwood** leaves and **anise**; highly intoxicating and therefore outlawed in many countries.

abura (ah-boo-rah) Japanese for oil.

aburage Japanese for deep-fried **tōfu**.

acaçá (ah-ka-SAH) A Brazilian porridge of coconut milk and rice flour, molded, cooled, and sliced, to be served with sauces and stews; sometimes steamed in banana leaves; similar to **pirão.**

acarajé See **akkra.**

acciuga (ah-CHOO-gah) Italian for anchovy.

accra de morue (AH-krah deu mor-ü) Salt cod fritters from the French Caribbean eaten as an hors d'oeuvre; related to **akkra.**

aceite (ah-CHAY-tay) Spanish for oil.

aceituna (ah-chay-TOO-nah) Spanish for olive.

acetic acid The acid in vinegar that comes from a second fermentation of wine, beer, or cider.

aceto (ah-CHAY-tō) Italian for vinegar; *aceto balsamico* is a very fine vinegar, made in Modena, Italy, aged in special casks for a dark, mellow, subtle flavor.

aceto-dolce (ah-CHAY-tō DŌL-chay) A sweet-and-sour mixture of vegetables and fruits used in Italy as an **antipasto.**

achiote (ah-CHYŌ-tay) **Annatto** seeds used in Latin American cooking; the paste combines annatto with garlic, cumin, Mexican oregano, and citrus juice.

achar (ah-CHAHR) Pickle in Indian cuisine.

acidophilus milk Milk slightly soured with the *lactobacillus acidophilus* bacteria, which converts the lactose in milk to lactic acid, making it both easy to digest and healthful.

acidulated water Water to which a small amount of lemon juice or vinegar has been added; used to prevent fruits and vegetables from discoloring and to blanch certain foods, such as **sweetbreads.**

Acton, Eliza (1799–1859) A poet *manquée,* whose best-selling cookbook, *Modern Cookery for Private Families* (1845), is notable for its clear and well-organized directions to the middle-class housewife in preindustrial England.

ackee The pod of a tropical fruit that bursts open when ripe to expose the yellow flesh and black seeds; eaten for breakfast in Jamaica with salt fish.

adega (ah-DAY-gah) A wine cellar or storage space, usually above ground.

adobo (ah-DŌ-bō) Spanish for marinade; the word extends to the method of preparing meat or seafood in a marinade and to the dish itself; the Mexican version is hot with chilies, the Philippine pungent with vinegar.

adrak (ah-DRAHK) Fresh ginger root, in Indian cuisine.

adzuki See **azuki.**

aemono (ī-mō-nō) Japanese for salad or dressed mixtures.

agar-agar (ah-gar-ah-gar) An Oriental seaweed used by commercial food processors as a gelatin substitute in soups, sauces, jellies, and ice cream; it has a remarkable capacity for absorbing liquids—far greater than that of **gelatin** or **isinglass.**

age (ah-gay) Japanese for deep-fried.

aging A method of improving and maturing the flavor of a food, such as game, cheese, or wine, by allowing controlled chemical changes to take place over time.

agiter (a-jhee-tay) To stir, in French.

aglio (AH-lyō) Italian for garlic.

agneau (a-nyō) French for lamb.

agnello (ah-NYEL-lō) Italian for lamb.

agnolotti (ah-nyō-LOHT-tee) Stuffed squares of pasta, such as ravioli, with a meat filling, in Italian cooking.

agrio (ah-GREE-ō) Spanish for sour.

aguacate (ah-gwah-KAH-tay) Spanish for avocado.

aguardiente (ah-gwar-DYEN-tay) A very strong Spanish liqueur, similar to Italian **grappa** or French **marc.**

aiglefin (AY-gluh-FINH) French for haddock.

aigre (AY-gruh) French for sour, tart, bitter.

aiguillette (ay-gwee-yet) A thin strip of poultry cut lengthwise from the breast; also a strip of meat cut lengthwise with the grain; from French cuisine.

ail (ī) French for garlic

aïoli (ī-yō-lee) A garlic mayonnaise from French Provence, thick and strongly flavored, usually served with seafood; also spelled *aïlloli.*

airelle rouge (ay-rel roojh) French for cranberry.

aji (ah-jee) Japanese for horse mackerel; flavor.

ají (ah-HEE) Spanish for hot chili pepper; also refers to a dish in which hot peppers are a major ingredient, as _ají de gallina_.

ajilimogilli (ah-HEE-yee-MŌ-gee-yee) Puerto Rican pepper sauce served with pork and other meats.

ajo (AH-hō) Spanish for garlic; _ajo e ojo_ is an Italian dialect name for a spaghetti sauce of garlic sautéed in olive oil. See **aglio** and **olio**.

ajouter (a-jhoo-tay) To add an ingredient, in French.

akkra (AHK-rah) Caribbean dried pea or bean fritters, found with variations on several islands, descended from a Nigerian snack; Brazilian **acarajé**, black-eyed pea fritters served with a spicy shrimp sauce, are closely related.

akvavit (ahk-vah-VEET) A colorless Swedish liquor distilled from grain or potatoes and flavored variously, often with **caraway**; served very cold and drunk neat, often with beer, before or after the meal.

à la (ah lah) In the style of, the full phrase being _à la mode de;_ this term designates a specific garnish; often the _à la_ is assumed rather than stated, so that a dish such as _Sole à la bonne femme_, for instance, is usually contracted to _Sole bonne femme_. The same holds true for the Italian _alla_.

alaria (ah-LAHR-yah) Seaweed similar to **wakame**; mild in flavor, thick and crunchy in texture, usually dried and presoaked before it is cooked in soups.

albacore See **tuna**.

albigeoise, à l' (ah l'al-bee-jhwahz) In the style of Albi in southern France, that is, garnished with tomatoes, ham, and potato croquettes.

albóndigas (ahl-BOHN-dee-gahs) Spicy Spanish or Mexican meatballs made of pork, beef, etc.; also a dumpling.

Albuféra (al-BÜ-fayr-ah) A suprême sauce with meat glaze and pimento butter, named after the lagoon near Valencia in Spain; the garnish _à l'Albuféra_ consists of poultry stuffed with **risotto, truffles,** and **foie gras** with elaborate tartlets; also a small cake topped with chopped almonds; from classic French cuisine.

albumen (al-BYOO-men) The protein portion of egg white, comprising its greater part, which coagulates with heat; also found in milk, animal blood, plants, and seeds.

alcachofa (ahl-kah-CHŌ-fah.) Spanish for artichoke.

alcohol See **fermentation.**

al dente See **dente, al.**

ale English beer made from unroasted barley malt and hops, quickly top-fermented, and drunk fresh; usually stronger and more bitter than beer; varies in color from light to dark.

algérienne, à l' (ah l'al-jhayr-yen) Garnished with tomatoes braised in oil and sweet-potato croquettes, in French cuisine.

Ali-Bab The pseudonym of Henry Babinski, a French gourmand who, as an engineer on location and desperate for good food, taught himself to cook. His mammoth *Gastronome Pratique* (1928), which has since become a classic, shows that he learned very well.

alicot (al-ee-kō) Dish of duck or goose wings and giblets braised with **cèpes** and chestnuts; a dish from southwestern France.

alioli (ahl-YŌ-lee) Spanish for **aïoli.**

alla (ahl-lah) Italian for in the style of; see **à la.**

allemande (al-leh-mahnd) Veal **velouté** reduced with white wine and mushroom essence, flavored with lemon juice, and bound with egg yolks; *sauce allemande,* which means "German sauce," is a basic classical sauce in French cuisine.

allspice A spice made from the berries of the Jamaica pepper tree, dried and ground, which tastes like a combination of cloves, nutmeg, and cinnamon (hence its name); used in sweet and savory cooking.

allumette (al-lü-met) A "match-stick" strip of puff pastry with either a sweet or savory filling or garnish; also potatoes, peeled and cut into matchstick-sized strips; from French cuisine.

almeja (ahl-MAY-hah.) Spanish for clam.

almendra (ahl-MEN-drah) Spanish for almond; in Portuguese, *amêndoa.*

almond paste See **marzipan.**

almuerzo (ahl-MWAYR-thō, ahl-MWAYR-sō) Spanish for lunch.

alose (a-lōz) French for shad.

Aloxe-Corton (a-lox kor-tonh)   A village in Burgundy that produces excellent red and white wines and has some of the most celebrated **Côte d'Or** and **Côte de Beaune** vineyards.

aloyau (al-wah-yō)   French for sirloin.

Alsace (al-sas)   A province in northeastern France along the Rhine, whose German and French cuisine reflects its political history; famous for its **foie gras, charcuterie,** ducks, wine, and many other specialties.

alsacienne, à l' (ah l'al-sas-syen)   Garnished with sauerkraut and potatoes, ham, or sausages, or with other Alsatian specialties in French cuisine.

Altenburger (AHL-ten-boor-ger)   A soft, uncooked German cheese made from goats' milk or goats' and cows' milk mixed; has a delicate white mold on the exterior and a creamy, smooth, flavorful interior.

Alto Adige (AHL-tō AH-dee-jay)   A valley in northeastern Tirolean Italy around Bolzano, which exports a large quantity of good wines, both red and white, across the border to Austria.

alu (AH-loo)   Potato in Indian cuisine; also spelled *aloo.*

alum (AL-um)   A colorless crystalline salt used to keep the crisp texture of fruits and vegetables, especially in pickles; an ingredient in baking powder.

am (ahm)   Mango in Indian cuisine. Dried green mango is *amchoor,* often powdered for use as a souring agent like **tamarind** or lemon juice.

amai (ah-mī)   Japanese for sweet.

amalgamer (a-mal-ga-may)   To mix, blend, or combine ingredients, in French.

amandine (a-manh-deen)   French for garnished with almonds; often misspelled *almondine.*

amaranth (a-mah-ranth)   A green vegetable related to spinach and similar in flavor, much used in Asian cooking; one type is all green, another has red stems and markings on the leaves.

amardine (ah-mar-DEEN)   Middle Eastern dried apricot paste, in sheet form.

amaretto (ah-mah-RET-tō)   Italian for **macaroon.**

ambrosia   Food of the gods that, in Greek mythology, they ate with nectar; a Southern fruit dessert, often citrus, topped with grated coconut.

amêijoas na cataplana   (ah-may-JHŌ-ahs nah kah-tah-PLAH-nah) Portuguese stew of cockles with **chouriço,** tomatoes, garlic, and peppers, from the Algarve.

amêndoin   (ah-men-DŌ-in)   Peanut, a staple in Brazilian cooking, from *amêndoa,* the Portuguese word for almond.

américaine, à l'   (ah l'a-mayr-ee-ken)   In French cuisine, garnished with sliced lobster tail and truffles; also, a dish of lobster sautéed with olive oil and tomato in the style of Provence; often confused with **armoricaine.**

amiral, à l'   (ah l'a-mee-ral)   A classic French fish garnish of mussels, oysters, crayfish, and mushrooms in **sauce normande,** enriched with crayfish butter.

amontillado   (ah-mon-tee-YAH-dō)   A Spanish **sherry,** literally in the **Montilla** style, usually somewhat darker and older than a **fino**; the term is sometimes loosely used to mean a medium sherry.

amoroso   (ah-mor-Ō-sō)   A kind of **oloroso** sherry, sweetened and darkened.

amuse-gueule   (a-müz-geul)   French slang for cocktail appetizer, "taste tickler"; *amuse-bouche* is more polite.

anadama   An American yeast bread made from white flour with cornmeal and molasses.

anago   (ah-nah-gō)   Japanese for conger eel.

Anaheim chili   See **güero.**

ananas   (a-na-na, a-na-NAS)   French and German for pineapple.

ancho   (AHN-chō)   A deep red chili pepper, fairly mild in flavor and dried rather than fresh, about five inches long and three inches wide.

anchois   (anh-shwah)   French for anchovy.

anchovy   A small silvery fish, sometimes broiled or fried fresh like a **sardine,** but most often salted and canned; sometimes used in **whitebait.**

ancienne, à l'   (ah l'anh-syen)   In French cuisine, various preparations, often fricasséed and garnished in the old-fashioned style; usually a mixture such as cocks' combs and truffles; there are classic recipes for braised beef rump and chicken *à l'ancienne.*

andalouse, à l' (ah l'anh-da-looz)   In French cuisine, garnished with tomatoes, sweet red peppers, eggplant, and sometimes rice **pilaf** and **chipolata** sausages or ham.

andouille (anh-doo-yuh)   A French sausage made from pork **chitterlings** and **tripe,** sliced and served cold as an hors d'oeuvre.

andouillette (anh-doo-yet)   A French sausage similar to **andouille** but made from the small intestine rather than the large; the many varieties are sold poached, then grilled before serving hot with strong mustard.

angel food cake   A sponge cake made with stiffly beaten egg whites but no yolks, producing a light and airy texture and white color.

angel hair   See **capelli d'angelo.**

angelica   An herb of the parsley family used for medicinal and culinary purposes; it flavors several liqueurs and confections and often imparts a green color.

angels on horseback   Oysters wrapped in bacon, skewered, grilled, and served on buttered toast fingers; a favorite hors d'oeuvre or **savory** in England.

anglaise, à l' (ah l'anh-glez)   In French cuisine, English style—that is, plainly boiled or roasted, or coated with an egg-and-breadcrumb batter and deep-fried.

angler   See **monkfish.**

angostura bitters   See **bitters.**

anguille (anh-gwee)   French for eel; *anguila* in Spanish; *anguilla* in Italian.

animelles (a-nee-mel)   The French culinary term for testicles of animals, especially rams; *animelles* are less popular in Europe today than formerly but still common in the Middle East; in Italy, *animelle* means sweetbreads.

anise (A-nis)   An herb of Mediterranean origin, highly regarded by the ancient Greeks and Romans, that tastes like licorice and is used in many parts of the world; its potent seeds flavor several liqueurs as well as cheeses, pastries, and confections; not to be confused with **fennel.**

aniseed   See **anise.**

anitra (ah-NEE-trah)   Italian for duck; wild duck, *anitra selvatica.*

Anjou (anh-jhoo)   A northwest central region of France, around Angers and Saumur, known for its wines, both still and sparkling, and for excellent poultry, fish from the Loire, and produce, especially pears; **Curnonsky,** the great gastronome, came from Anjou and praised its cuisine and wine in his writings.

Anna, pommes   See **pommes Anna.**

annatto (a-NAT-tō)   A red dye from the fruit of a South American tree, used to color cheese, butter, and confectionery.

antipasto   In Italian, literally "before the pasta," an *antipasto* is an appetizer or starter; *antipasti,* like *hors d'oeuvres variés,* exist in great variety and profusion.

anversoise, à l' (ah l'anh-vayr-swahz)   In the style of Anvers (now Antwerp), that is, garnished with **hops** in cream.

aonegi (ah-ō-nay-gee)   Japanese green onion.

apéritif (a-payr-ee-teef)   A drink, usually alcoholic, taken before the meal to stimulate the appetite.

Apfel   German for apple; *Apfelstrudel* is thin **strudel** dough filled with apples, white raisins, and spices—a very popular dessert in Germany and Austria.

aphrodisiac   A food or drink that arouses the sexual appetite.

Apicius (a-PEE-syus)   The name of three ancient Romans celebrated for their gluttony, with which their name has become synonymous; a cookbook written by one of them survives in two manuscripts, both ninth-century translations.

aporeado de tasajo (ah-por-ay-AH-dō day tah-SAH-hō)   Cuban salt-dried beef hash in a spicy vegetable sauce.

appareil (a-paarh-ray)   French for a mixture of ingredients ready for use in a preparation, such as an *appareil à biscuit.*

appellation contrôlée (a-pel-a-syonh conh-trō-lay)   Two words found on French wine labels, designating a particular wine by its place of origin, grape variety, or district tradition; this control, used for the best French wines, was established in 1935 to guarantee that the wine is what its label claims it to be, and it is strictly enforced by French law. Similar attempts have been made to certify cheese, both by type and by origin. Sometimes abbreviated to AC or AOC.

appellation d'origine (a-pel-a-syonh d'ohr-ee-jheen)   The name of a wine, giving its geographic location, be it a château, vineyard, town, river valley, or general region; strictly regulated by French law.

Appenzell (AP-pen-tsel)   A Swiss whole-milk cows' cheese made in large wheels, cured, and washed in a brine with white wine and spices, which impart their flavor; the cheese is pale straw-colored with some holes and a yellow-brown rind; similar to **Emmental,** it is firm, buttery, yet piquant.

apple butter   A preserve of chopped apples cooked slowly for a long time, usually with sugar, cider, and spices, until reduced to a thick, dark spread.

applejack   Brandy distilled from fermented cider; **Calvados** is one type.

apple pandowdy   See **pandowdy.**

apple schnitz   Dried apple slices, much used in Pennsylvania German cooking for such dishes as apple pie and *Schnitz un Gnepp* (apple and smoked ham stew with dumplings).

aquavit   See **akvavit.**

Arabian coffee   Coffee ground to a powder, spiced with cardamom, cloves, or even saffron, and drunk without sugar or milk; in Arab countries, the ceremony of its preparation and service is symbolic of hospitality.

arabic   See **gum arabic.**

arabica (ah-rah-BEE-kah)   A type of coffee tree grown at high altitudes, low yielding but producing the best quality of coffee; see also **robusta.**

arachide (a-ra-sheed)   French for peanut.

aragosta (ah-rah-GOS-tah)   Italian for lobster.

arak (AR-ak)   A Middle Eastern liqueur made from various plants; strong and anise-flavored.

arame (ah-rah-may)   Asian seaweed, strong in flavor; usually dried, reconstituted, cooked, and seasoned with lemon juice or soy sauce, for salads.

arància (ah-RAHN-syah)   Italian for orange.

Arborio rice (ar-BOR-yō)   Short, fat-grained Italian rice that is perfect for **risotto** and similar moist rice dishes.

Arbroath smokies (AR-brōth)   In Scottish cooking, small haddock that are gutted, salted, and smoked but not split until broiling before serving.

archiduc, à l' (ah l'aahr-shee-dük)   In French cooking, seasoned with paprika and blended with cream.

ardennaise, à l' (ah l'aahr-den-nez)   In the style of Ardennes, that is, with juniper berries, small game birds, and pork.

arenque (ah-REN-kay)   Spanish for herring.

Argenteuil (aahr-jhenh-toy)   Garnished with asparagus; named for a region in northern France where the best asparagus is grown.

arhar dal   See **dal.**

aringa (ah-REEN-gah)   Italian for herring.

arista (ah-REES-tah)   Italian for roast loin of pork.

arlésienne, à l' (ah l'aahr-lay-zyen)   Garnished with eggplant and tomato, cooked in oil with fried onion rings; there are other French garnishes by this name, and all contain tomatoes.

Armagnac (aahr-ma-nyak)   A famous brandy from Gascony, in south-western France, which can be compared to **Cognac;** it is dry, smooth, dark, and aromatic.

armoricaine, à l' (ah l'aahr-mohr-ee-ken)   In French cuisine, lobster in the Breton style, after the ancient Roman name for Brittany and often confused with **à l'américaine;** the sliced lobster is sautéed in olive oil with tomato.

aromatic   A plant, such as an herb or spice, that gives off a pleasing scent and is used to flavor food or drink.

arrack   See **arak.**

arroser (a-rōz-ay)   To baste or moisten, in French cooking.

arrowroot   A powdered flour from the root of a tropical plant of the same name, used as a flour or thickener; in cooking it remains clear when mixed with other foods, rather than turning cloudy, and is easily digested.

arroz (ah-RŌTH, ah-RŌS)   Spanish for rice; when cooked and combined with other foods it makes dishes such as *arroz con pollo,* rice with chicken; **arroz a la milanesa,** not the Italian **risotto,** but a Cuban-style dish made with long-grain rice cooked with onion and various seasonings.

arsella (ar-ZEL-lah)   Italian for mussel.

artichaut (aahr-tee-shō) French for artichoke, both the *globe artichoke*, a favorite French vegetable, and the **Jerusalem artichoke.**

arugula (ah-ROO-guh-lah) Italian for rocket, a salad herb with peppery, piguant flavor, newly popular in the United States.

asado (ah-SAH-dō) Spanish for roasted or broiled.

asafetida (a-sah-FEH-ti-dah) A spice derived from resinous plant gum that, when used in small quantities, imparts an interesting onion flavor but is offensively rank in larger amounts; favored by the ancient Romans, today used in southern Indian vegetarian dishes and pickles.

asam manis (ah-sahm mah-nis) Indonesian for sweet and sour.

asciutta See under **pasta.**

ash (ahsh) Persian for soup.

Asiago d'Allevo (ah-SYAH-gō d'ah-LAY-vō) A scalded-curd cheese usually made from skimmed evening and whole morning cows' milk and aged up to two years; the large wheels have a thin brownish rind and a smooth pale paste with holes; other Asiago cheeses from Vicenza, Italy, are used mainly as table cheeses.

Asian pear A fruit distantly related to the familiar pear; it looks like a round, firm apple with a yellow, brownish, or green skin; although faint in flavor, it holds its crisp, firm texture well in cooking.

aspartame (AS-par-taym) A new artificial sweetener, much sweeter than sugar; not suitable for cooking or use with acids.

asperge (as-payrjh) French for asparagus.

aspic A clear jelly made from meat or vegetable stock and gelatin, strained, cleared, and chilled; used to dress savory foods of all kinds by covering them in a mold or surrounding them, chopped into cubes, as a garnish; also used for sweet dishes, based on a fruit juice and gelatin aspic.

assaisonner (a-sez-onh-nay) In French, to season; *assaisonnement* means seasoning, condiment, or dressing.

Assam (AH-sahm) A tea, from the province in northern India of the same name, which is strong and pungent in character and often blended with milder teas.

Asti Spumanti (AHS-tee spoo-MAHN-tee) A sweet sparkling white wine from the town of Asti in the Piedmont region of northern Italy.

Asturias (ah-stoo-REE-ahs)   A strong, sharp-flavored cheese from northern Spain.

aşure (ah-SHOO-ray)   "Noah's pudding," in Turkish cuisine, made of hulled wheat, chickpeas, nuts, and dried fruit, of religious significance to Muslims.

ataïf (ah-TAY-if)   Arab pancakes, either sweet with nuts and syrup or savory with cheese; the filling is put on half of the round, folded in two, and deep-fried.

atemoya (a-teh-MOY-ah)   A fruit cross between the **cherimoya** and sugar apple that looks like a strange, melting artichoke; the creamy smooth flesh is sweet, rich, and custardlike, with dark flat seeds.

athénienne, à l' (ah l'atay-nyen)   In French cuisine, garnished with onion, eggplant, tomato, and sweet red pepper fried in olive oil.

atole (ah-TŌ-lay)   In Mexican cooking, a thin gruel drink varying widely but usually made from cornmeal; it can be flavored with sugar and fruit or chocolate or with chili.

atr (AH-tahr)   Arabic for sugar syrup, often scented with orange- or rosewater, used in desserts and pastries.

attereau (a-tay-rō)   In French, a metal skewer on which sweet or savory food is threaded, breadcrumbed, and deep-fried.

aubergine (ō-bayr-jheen)   French for eggplant.

Auflauf (OWF-lowf)   German for **soufflé.**

Aufschnitt (OWF-shnit)   A variety of thinly sliced cold meats and sausages sold in German delicatessens; cold cuts.

aurore, à l' (ah l'ohr-ohr)   In French cuisine, **béchamel** sauce colored pink with a small amount of tomato purée; "dawn" implies rosy hue.

Auslese (OWS-lay-zeh)   A superior German wine made from particularly ripe and fine grapes specially picked at harvest and pressed separately from the other grapes, making a sweeter and more expensive wine. See also **Trockenbeerenauslese.**

Ausone, Château (sha-tō ō-zohn)   A famous and very fine Bordeaux wine from St.-Émilion, a first-growth vineyard.

Auster (OW-stayr)   German for oyster.

Auvergne (ō-VAYR-nyeh)   A mountainous region in central France known for its relatively simple, straightforward, robust cooking; the

Auvergne is renowned for its fine cheeses, **charcuterie,** vegetables and fruits, nuts, wild mushrooms, lamb, and freshwater fish.

aveline (av-leen)   French for hazelnut, **filbert.**

avgolemono (av-gō-LAY-mō-nō)   A Greek soup made from egg yolks and lemon juice, combined with chicken stock and rice, that is very popular in the Balkans; also a sauce made from egg yolks and lemon juice.

ayam (ah-yam)   In Indonesian, chicken; *soto ayam,* chicken soup, which can be a main course served with rice, delicate or very spicy; *kelia ayam,* a chicken curry from Sumatra; *ayam panggang bumbu besengek,* roasted and grilled chicken in coconut sauce.

azafran (ah-thah-FRAHN)   Spanish for saffron.

azeite (ah-ZAY-tay)   Portuguese for olive.

azúcar (ah-THOO-kar, ah-SOO-kar)   Spanish for sugar.

azuki (ah-zoo-kee)   A dried bean, russet with a white line at the eye, used widely in Japan and prized for its sweet flavor; *azuki* flour is used in confections and puddings in Japan and China.

Bacchus

ba mee (bah mee) Thai for egg noodles.

baba A yeast cake, sometimes with raisins, that is baked in a special cylindrical mold and soaked with syrup and rum or sometimes **Kirsch;** supposedly named by Stanislaus I. Lesczyinski, King of Poland, when he steeped a **Kugelhopf** in rum and named it after Ali Baba.

baba ghanoush (BAH-bah gah-NOOSH) Middle Eastern purée of eggplant with **tahini,** lemon juice, olive oil, and garlic; spelled variously.

Babinski, Henry See **Ali-Bab.**

babka (BAHB-kah) Polish cake, savory or sweet, related to **baba.**

bacalao a la vizcaina (bah-kah-LOW ah lah vees-KĪ-nah) Salt cod pieces soaked, fried in oil with onions, garlic, tomatoes, and red peppers, then layered and baked; originally from the Spanish Basque region but popular in Cuba.

bacalhau (bah-kah-LOW) Portuguese for salt cod; the Spanish spelling is *bacalao.*

Bacchus The Roman god of wine; Dionysus in Greek mythology.

backen (BAHK-en) To bake in German.

Backhün, Backhändl (BAHK-hün, -HEN-del) Chicken rolled in breadcrumbs, then fried; a German dish.

Backobst (BAHK-ōbst) Dried fruit in German.

Backpflaume (BAHK-pflow-meh) German for prune.

badaam (bah-DAHM) Almond in Indian cooking; the Turkish is *badem.*

Baden (BAH-den) A province in southwest Germany containing the **Schwarzwald** (Black Forest) and many vineyards, producing mostly white wines.

bagel An unsweetened yeast bread, traditionally eggless, shaped like a doughnut, cooked first in boiling water, then baked; often eaten with **lox** and cream cheese.

bagna caôda (BAH-nyah KOW-dah) Italian "hot sauce"; Piedmont dialect term for *bagna cauda,* a sauce of garlic and anchovies in oil and butter, served warm with raw vegetables.

baguette (ba-get) A long cylindrical loaf of French white bread, literally a "stick."

bai cai (bī-tsī) Chinese bok choy, literally "white cabbage," a vegetable with thick white stems and long, narrow, chardlike leaves, often used in stir-fried dishes.

bai horapa (BĪ hor-ra-pah) Thai for **basil,** the variety familiar in the United States and Europe, used in Thailand as a vegetable and flavoring for curries; *bai horapa mangluk,* lemon basil, with paler leaves, for soups and salads; *bai horapa grapao,* another variety with reddish-purple, narrower leaves, cooked in meat and fish dishes.

baigan (BĪ-gahn) Eggplant in Indian cooking.

bain-marie (binh ma-ree) French for a container of warm water in which a smaller pot or pots rest, to provide slow, even heat and protect the contents from overheating; a hot-water bath used on the stove or in the oven; a double boiler is a type of bain-marie.

ba jiao (ba jow) Chinese star anise (literally, "eight points"); this seed from the magnolia family flavors marinades and slowly cooked dishes; although anise flavored, it is no relation to **fennel.**

bake To cook food by surrounding it with hot, dry air in an oven or on hot stones or metal.

bake blind To bake a pastry shell unfilled; the dough is pricked with the tines of a fork, fitted with grease-proof paper, filled with dried beans or rice as a weight, and partially baked.

baked Alaska Ice cream set on sponge cake, the whole masked with meringue, and quickly browned in a hot oven; the air bubbles insulate the ice cream from the heat.

bakers' cheese Pasteurized skimmed-milk cows' cheese used by bakers in the United States; it is similar to cottage cheese but smoother, softer, and sourer.

baking powder A leavening agent for bread and pastry; when moistened, it produces carbon dioxide to aerate and lighten dough. There are many types, each combining alkaline and acidic material. In double-acting baking powder, the chemical action occurs twice, first when moistened and second when heated.

baking soda Bicarbonate of soda; a leavening agent similar to **baking powder** but used with an acid such as sour milk.

baklava (BAHK-lah-vah) A Middle Eastern sweet pastry made of extremely thin sheets of **phyllo** dough layered with chopped nuts and honey syrup, baked with butter and oil, and cut into diamonds.

balachan, blachan (BLAH-kan) A Malaysian condiment of fermented shrimp or other seafood with chilies; salty and pungent, it is an acquired taste; spelled variously.

ballotine, ballottine (bal-ō-teen) In French cuisine, a large piece of meat, often poultry or occasionally fish, which is boned, possibly stuffed, rolled or shaped, braised or roasted, and served hot or cold; **ballotine** is often confused with **galantine,** which is poached and served cold with its own jelly; also known as **dodine.**

baloney See **mortadella.**

balouza (bah-LOO-zah) A Middle Eastern pudding made of cornstarch, flavored with orange- or rosewater and textured with chopped nuts.

balsamella (bal-zah-MEL-lah) **Béchamel** sauce in Italian.

balsam pear See **bitter melon.**

balsamic vinegar See under **aceto.**

balut (bah-loot) A fertilized duck egg nearly ready to hatch; considered a great delicacy to Filipinos and some Malaysians, but an acquired taste to others.

bamboo A tropical treelike grass whose young shoots are eaten raw, freshly boiled, or canned in the Orient.

bami goreng See under **nasi.**

bamia (BAH-myah) Arabic for **okra;** the Turkish word is *bamya,* the Greek *bamies.*

banana leaves   See **la chuoi.**

banane (ba-nan)   Banana in French.

Banbury cake   A cake from Oxfordshire, England, of oval flaky pastry filled with currants, lemon peel, and spices.

banger   British slang for sausage that is filled with ground pork and breadcrumbs.

banh (bahn)   Vietnamese for dough or cake.

banh can (bahn kang)   "Silver dollars cakes," from a batter of rice and yellow mung bean, filled with scallions and dried and fresh shrimp; from Vietnam.

banh cuon (bahn koon)   Vietnamese rolled dumplings with shallots, cucumber, bean sprouts, and mint.

banh hoi thit nuong (bahn hoy tit noong)   Marinated grilled pork strips with noodle cakes, a classic Vietnamese dish.

banh trang (bahn trang)   Rice paper, in Vietnamese cuisine, made of cooked rice processed into paper-thin rounds and dried; it is moistened and chewed as a flatbread, or filled and fried as a crisp snack.

banh xeo (bahn SAY-ō)   Happy cakes; Vietnamese pancakes made of rice flour, with various fillings.

banku (BAHN-koo)   Cornmeal dumpling, like **sadza;** from Ghana.

banlay (bahn-lī)   Cambodian for vegetables.

bannock (BAN-nuk)   A traditional Scottish cake of barley, wheat, or oatmeal; large and round, varying widely according to region.

bào (bow)   Chinese for abalone.

baobab (BAY-ō-bab)   A central African tree with a very thick trunk; its fruit, called monkey bread, is eaten fresh and made into a refreshing, healthful drink, while its edible leaves are dried and powdered.

bap   A small round loaf of soft white bread, eaten in Scotland and parts of England for breakfast.

bap (bahp)   Korean for cooked rice, a medium-length grain of sticky rice.

bar (baahr)   Sea bass in French.

baraquille (baahr-a-keel)   French for a triangular stuffed pastry hors d'oeuvre.

barbabiètola (baahr-bah-BYAY-tō-lah)   Italian for beet root; the tops are **biètola.**

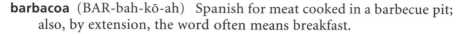

barbacoa (BAR-bah-kō-ah) Spanish for meat cooked in a barbecue pit; also, by extension, the word often means breakfast.

Barbaresco (bar-bah-RES-kō) A renowned red wine from the Italian Piedmont; produced from the **Nebbiolo** grape.

barbecue, barbeque A method of cooking marinated food on a grill or spit over a slow and smoky hardwood, charcoal, or briquette fire; the name also extends to marinades and social gatherings at such cookouts.

barberry A shrub whose berries are pickled or ripened and made into various preserves, syrup, and wine; red in color, high in acid; also called Oregon grapes.

barbue (baahr-bü) French for **brill.**

bard To tie extra fat, usually bacon, around fish, poultry, or meat to baste it while cooking. The barding fat is usually removed before serving.

Bardolino (baahr-dō-LEE-nō) A popular red wine made in northern Italy; fruity, light, best drunk young.

barfi (BAHR-fee) An Indian milk sweetmeat made with nuts and often decorated with edible silver leaf; also spelled *burfi.*

barigoule, à la (ah lah baahr-ee-gool) In French cuisine, artichokes blanched, trimmed, stuffed with **duxelles,** wrapped in bacon, braised in white wine, and served with a reduction of the cooking broth.

Bar-le-Duc (baahr-leu-dük) A red currant preserve whose name comes from the town in the French Lorraine where it is made.

barley An ancient and hardy grain grown in most climates, but today a staple only in the Middle East. In the modern world barley is used mostly for animal feed and for malt for brewing and distilling; only a small proportion is used for soup, cereal, and bread.

Barolo (bah-RŌ-lō) An Italian red wine from the Piedmont, south of Turin, made from the **Nebbiolo** grape; deep, full-bodied, and slow-maturing, it is an exceptional wine.

baron In England, a double sirloin of beef roasted for ceremonial occasions; in France, the saddle and two legs of lamb or mutton.

barquette (baahr-ket) In French cuisine, a boat-shaped pastry shell filled and baked as an hors d'oeuvre or sweet; the name sometimes applies to vegetable cases for stuffing, such as zucchini.

Barsac (baahr-sak)   An area within the **Sauternes** district of Bordeaux that produces a white dessert wine that is sweet and fruity.

basbousa (baz-BOO-zah)   A Middle Eastern baked pudding made with semolina, yogurt, and nuts.

basil (BA-zel, BAY-zel)   A pungent herb from the mint family used extensively in Mediterranean cooking; the basis of **pesto** sauce.

basilico (bah-ZEE-lee-kō)   Italian for **basil.**

basmati rice (baz-MAH-tee)   A high-quality, long-grain rice with an aromatic, nutty flavor that grows in the Himalayan foothills; excellent for **pullao**, **pilaf**, and **biryani** dishes as well as plain steamed rice.

basquaise, à la (ah lah bas-kez)   With tomatoes, peppers, Bayonne ham, **cèpes,** or rice characteristic of Basque cooking.

bass   A name for many fish, not necessarily related, some of which are separately entered under their individual names.

baste   To moisten during cooking by spooning liquid over food, in order to prevent toughness.

bastilla (bs-TEE-yah)   Pigeon pie, the traditional dish of Morocco; the best known version, which comes from Fez, is a large pie of squab or chicken on the bottom, in an egg, lemon, and onion sauce sweetened with almonds, all enclosed in thin layers of **warqa** pastry covered with cinnamon and sugar; one of the glories of Moroccan cuisine. Also spelled *bisteeya, pastilla,* and *bstilla.*

bâtarde (ba-taahrd)   A French sauce of white **roux** with water, bound with egg yolks, with butter and lemon juice added; called "bastard" for its indirect relationship to other classic sauces.

Bâtard-Montrachet (ba-taahr monh-ra-shay)   A vineyard in Burgundy producing an excellent white wine; small in volume but dry, flavorful, and possessing a fine bouquet, it is made entirely from **Chardonnay** grapes.

batata (bah-TAH-tah)   Sweet potato in Spanish and Portuguese.

batinjan (BAHT-in-jahn)   Arabic for eggplant; often spelled *badhinjan.*

bâton, bâtonnet (ba-tonh, ba-tonh-nay)   French for shaped like a "stick"; vegetables such as potatoes cut in this manner are generally larger than **allumettes** or **julienne.**

batter   A liquid mixture of flour and milk or water before it is spooned, poured, or dipped for cooking; it can be thick or thin but when no longer liquid it becomes **dough.**

batter bread   See **spoon bread.**

batterie de cuisine   (ba-tay-ree deu kwee-zeen)   French for kitchen utensils.

battuto   (bah-TOOT-tō)   In Italian cooking, a base for soups and stews consisting of diced onion, garlic, celery, and herbs, cooked in oil or pork fat, to which the rest is added; after the *battuto* is cooked it becomes a **soffrito.**

baudroie   (bō-dwah)   French for monkfish.

Bauernsuppe   (BOW-ayrn-ZOOP-eh)   In German cooking, a peasant soup of vegetables, legumes, and bacon; the adjective *bauern* means peasant or country-style.

Baumkuchen   (BOWM-koo-khen)   A German traditional, Christmas cake, baked in many layers to resemble the rings of a tree trunk, and iced with barklike chocolate.

Bavarian cream   A cold custard pudding, often molded into peaks, made from gelatin, eggs, whipped cream, and various sweet flavorings.

bavarois   (ba-vaahr-wah)   In French cuisine, **Bavarian cream,** but not to be confused with the *bavaroise* drink of sweetened tea enriched with egg yolks and milk and perhaps flavored with citrus.

bavette   (ba-vet)   French for tip of sirloin; flank steak.

bay   An herb from the laurel family whose dried leaves are an ingredient of the **bouquet garni** and whose leaves and berries have many medicinal uses; symbolic of intellectual achievement or victory.

bayerisch   (BĪ-rish)   Bavarian, of the southern region of Germany around Munich; also *bayrisch.*

Bayonne   (bī-yohn)   A town in the French Pyrenees famous for its fine cured hams.

bay poum   (bī-puhm)   Cambodian molded fried rice with pork, chicken, and onions.

bean curd   See **tōfu.**

bean sprout   The germinated seed pod of a leguminous plant whose nutritional value is between that of a seed and a vegetable; bean sprouts are eaten fresh or lightly cooked and are appreciated for their crisp texture.

bean threads   See **fěn sī.**

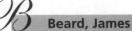

Beard, James (1903–85) American foodwriter whose many cookbooks, encouragement of home-grown chefs, and general ebullience, did much to raise the status of American food.

béarnaise (bayr-nez) A sauce of the warm emulsion type in classic French cuisine; wine vinegar is reduced with shallots and tarragon, then cooled; egg yolks and butter are beaten in and the mixture is strained and finished with chopped tarragon and perhaps chervil; served primarily with grilled meat, fowl, and eggs; one of the classic sauces.

Beaufort (bō-fohr) A whole-milk cows' cheese from the French Savoy; similar to **Gruyère** and available year-round.

Beauharnais, à la (ah lah bō-aahr-nay) A classical French garnish for **tournedos** made of stuffed mushrooms, artichoke hearts, **château potatoes,** and *Beauharnais* sauce (**béarnaise** with puréed tarragon).

Beaujolais (bō-jhō-lay) A region in southern Burgundy producing a popular red wine from the Gamay grape; pleasant, fruity, and light, best served cool and drunk young; *Beaujolais Nouveau* is new Beaujolais wine bottled immediately after fermentation; very light, fruity, and pleasant; a marketing phenomenon.

Beaulieu (bō-lyeu) A vineyard in the Napa Valley producing some of the best California wines, especially their **Cabernet** Sauvignon.

Beaune (bōn) A city in Burgundy and the center of its wine trade; see **Côte d'Or.**

bécasse (bay-kas) French for woodcock; the Italian word is *beccaccia.*

bec fin (bek finh) A French slang term for a connoisseur of fine food.

béchamel (bay-sha-mel) In French cuisine, a basic white sauce of milk stirred into a **roux** and thickened; one of the "mother" sauces.

bêche de mer See **sea cucumber.**

beef Stroganoff Strips of beef sautéed with chopped onions and mushrooms, thickened with sour cream; an American dish.

beef Wellington Fillet topped with **duxelles,** wrapped in puff pastry, and baked.

beer Any beverage made by the action of yeast on an infusion of malted cereal, brewed, flavored with hops, and fermented.

Beerenauslese (BAYR-en-ows-lay-zeh) A celebrated German wine made from overripe berries selected individually from specially chosen bunches of grapes; a sweet, fruity, intense wine of extraordinary flavor and expense.

Beetensuppe (BAY-ten-ZOOP-eh) German for **borsch.**

Beeton, Isabella (1836–1865) An English journalist and author of *The Book of Household Management,* which appeared in England in a women's magazine published by her husband (1859–61) and then in book form (1861), with a tremendous and lasting influence; the large scope of Mrs. Beeton's book on domestic economy included estimates of cost, quantities, and preparation times.

beid (bīd) Arabic for egg dishes; *beid bi lamoun,* **avgolemono.**

beignet (beh-nyay) French for food dipped in batter and fried in deep fat.

Bei jīng kǎo yā (bay jing kow yah) Peking duck: an elaborate and famous dish made from specially reared ducks; the skin of the bird is inflated with air to dry the skin, then smeared with a honey mixture and hung for a long time to dry again; it is then roasted until crisp, the skin removed to be served separately, and the meat shredded; skin and meat are served together with sliced scallions and cucumbers all rolled up in pancakes spread with soybean sauce and eaten with the fingers.

beijos de anjo (BAY-jhōs day AHN-jhō) "Angel's kisses," rich eggy little cakes in syrup, popular in Brazil.

Beilagen (BĪ-lah-gen) German for accompanying dishes, such as vegetables or salad.

belegtes Brot (beh-LAYG-tes brōt) German for sandwich, usually open-faced.

Belgian endive A specially cultivated chicory whose leaves are cut off and shielded from the light, so that new pale yellow leaves grow back in their characteristic cigar shape; used fresh in salads or braised in various preparations; this curious new vegetable was discovered in the last century near Brussels, where it is mostly grown today during fall and winter; also called *witloof.*

bell pepper See **pepper (sweet bell).**

Belon oysters (beu-lonh) Choice oysters from the river of the same name in Brittany.

Bel Paese (bel pah-AY-say) A semisoft, mild, uncooked Italian cheese made from whole cows' milk; it is produced on a large scale and is very popular.

Bénédictine A liqueur originally made by the monks of that order in Fécamp, Normandy, based on **Cognac** and flavored with many herbs and plants; B & B is a drier combination of Bénédictine and brandy.

benne seeds (BEN-nee) **Sesame** seeds, brought from Africa with the slave trade and used especially in the African-American cooking of South Carolina, often to symbolize happiness.

Bercy (bayr-see) A classic French fish sauce of white wine and fish **fumet** reduced with shallots and finished with butter and parsley; also made with meat glaze and beef marrow for grilled meat.

berbere (BUHR-buhr-ray) Ethiopian hot mixture of herbs and spices used in northeastern Africa; includes cumin, cloves, cardamom, fenugreek, coriander, chilies, ginger, garlic, onion, basil, and mint.

bergamot A bitter, pear-shaped orange whose skin is used for its essential oil in **Earl Grey tea** and perfume-making; also the name of a pear and a type of mint.

Bergkäse (BAYRG-kay-zeh) A hard yellow cheese from the Bavarian Alps; this is really a generic name for various cooked pressed cheeses from the region.

Berliner Weisse (bayr-LIN-er VĪ-seh) A pale, tart German ale made from wheat and low in alcohol; often drunk with a dash of raspberry syrup for refreshment.

Bernkastel (BAYRN-kast-el) A town in the Moselle region of West Germany with some of the region's best vineyards, all estate-bottled wines.

besan (BAY-sahn) Chickpea flour in Indian cooking.

betingan See **batinjan.**

betterave (bet-rav) French for beetroot.

beurre blanc (beuhr blanhk) A French sauce of white wine and shallots reduced, thickened with butter, and served warm with seafood, poultry, or vegetables.

beurre Chivry (beuhr shee-vree) A French compound butter flavored with parsley, tarragon, chives, and shallots.

beurre manié (beuhr ma-nyay) In French cooking, flour and butter, usually in equal proportion, kneaded together into a paste to thicken sauces and gravies; the flour can be browned or not.

beurre noir (beuhr nwaahr) A French sauce of butter cooked until brown, often flavored with chopped parsley, capers, and vinegar; served with fish or brains.

bhajia (BAH-jah) Vegetables stir-fried and highly spiced, in Indian cuisine.

bharta (BAHR-tah) Indian roasted and mashed vegetable dishes.

bhendi (BAYN-dee) Okra in Indian cooking.

Bhudda rice See **com chay.**

bialy (bee-AH-lee) A wheat roll topped with onion flakes, in the Jewish American tradition; named after the city of Bialystok in Poland.

biber (bee-BAYR) Turkish for sweet peppers.

bibimbap (bee-BEEM-bahp) A Korean dish, a mixture of rice and stir-fried beef strips, **gochu jang,** bean sprouts, scallions, seaweed, sesame seeds, and a fried egg, all cooked together in a **tukbaege;** made in many variations.

bicarbonate of soda See **baking soda.**

bicchiere (bee-KYAYR-ay) In Italian, a measuring glass roughly equivalent to one cup.

bien cuit (byinh kwee) French for well done, as for steak.

Bierwurst (BEER-voorst) A fat German sausage of pork, pork fat, and beef, dark reddish brown in color.

biètola (BYAY-tō-lah) Italian for Swiss chard.

bigarade (bee-ga-rad) In French cuisine, a classic brown sauce for roast duck made of caramelized sugar, lemon and orange juice, stock, and **demi-glace,** with blanched zest.

bigos (BEE-gosh) A Polish hunter's stew of sauerkraut with sausages, bacon, mushrooms, red wine, and meat (usually venison).

bilberry A small berry similar to the blueberry but usually smaller and tarter, with the same silvery cast; used for pies, jams, etc.; native to Europe, especially Northern Europe.

Billy Bi (BEE-lee BEE) French mussel soup with cream and white wine, originally created for a customer at Maxim's without the mussels themselves, but now usually served with them.

bind To hold together by means of a **liaison.**

Bingen (BING-en) A wine town of Hessia, West Germany, overlooking the Rhine and Nahe Rivers, producing excellent white wines.

bird's nest See **yen wo.**

bird's nest fryer A hinged double wire basket for deep-frying straw-potato nests to be filled with other food, such as peas.

birmuelos (beer-MWAY-lōs) Deep-fried little cakes, sometimes shaped like doughnuts, made with **matzo** meal during Passover; either savory with potato or sweet with honey; also spelled *bemuelos*; Sephardic in origin.

Birne (BEER-neh) German for pear.

biryani (beer-YAH-nee) In Indian cooking, a substantial and spicy rice dish, variously prepared, similar to **pilaf,** but richer, layered with meat or fish and vegetables.

Bischofsbrot (BEE-shofs-brōt) An Austrian cake containing dried fruit and chocolate drops.

biscuit A small flat cake, usually round and unsweetened, originally double-baked (see **zwieback**), hence its name; the term now covers a wide variety of small cakes and breads.

biscuit de Savoie (bees-kwee deu sa-vwah) A sponge cake from the French Savoy, often baked in a **brioche parisienne** mold and served with fruit.

biscuits à la cuillère (bees-kwee ah lah kwee-yayr) French ladyfingers; so named because before the invention of the pastry bag they were shaped by dropping the dough from a spoon.

biscuit tortoni See **tortoni.**

bishop A mulled wine drink, often made with port or Champagne, flavored with orange and lemon, cinnamon, clove, and other spices; a traditional drink in England and northern Europe.

Biskote (bees-KŌ-teh) German for ladyfinger.

Bismarck herring Herring that are marinated in vinegar, filleted and split, seasoned with onion, and eaten with sour cream.

bisque A thick soup purée, often made from shellfish, to which the pulverized shells are added. Originally a poultry or game soup, *bisque* has gradually come to mean a purée, thickened perhaps with cream.

bistec de palomilla (bees-TEK day pal-ō-MEE-yah) Steak first pounded thin, marinated, and fried in oil, then topped with chopped fried onions and parsley; very popular in Cuba.

bisteeya See **bastilla.**

bistro (bee-strō) Small informal French restaurant, often family-owned. Bistros became popular in Paris during World War II; the name's derivation from the shouts of Russian soldiers demanding quick service is apocryphal.

bitter melon A gourd vegetable, quite sour in flavor, with a ridged rind resembling a furrowed cucumber, used in Malaysian and Oriental cooking. Also called *balsam pear.*

bitter orange See **Seville orange.**

bitters A liquid, usually alcoholic, steeped with aromatic herbs and roots and used as a tonic or as a flavoring for alcoholic drinks.

Bitto A cows' milk cheese from Sondrio in Italy, which is aged from two months to three years and used as a table or grating cheese; it is popular in Italy sprinkled on top of **polenta** with butter.

bivalve A **mollusk** with two hinged shells, such as a clam, mussel, or oyster.

bizcochos borachos (beeth-KŌ-chōth bor-AH-chōth) Spanish sponge cakes sugared, splashed with wine, and sprinkled with cinnamon.

black bass A freshwater fish of several varieties, both smallmouth and largemouth, with firm, lean meat; suitable for most kinds of cooking.

black bean A common bean variety, black, shiny, and sweet; this dried bean is a staple food in Central and South America, especially in rice dishes, stews, **frijoles** refritos, and in the southern United States, as in black bean soup.

black butter See **beurre noir.**

black-eyed pea A white pea with a black eye, brought to the southern United States from Africa in the seventeenth century with the slave trade; a favorite bean in African-American cooking, either fresh or dried, and an essential ingredient in dishes such as **hoppin' John;** also called cowpea. See also **doù zhī.**

Black Forest See **Schwarzwald.**

black pepper See **pepper (black).**

black pudding See **blood sausage.**

black sea bass A small mid-Atlantic warm-weather fish; its lean, delicate white flesh is suitable for most cooking methods and is widely used in Chinese cuisine.

blackstrap Dark, heavy, strong **molasses** originally made in the West Indies and considered low-quality but nutritious and flavorful for certain uses.

blakhan In Indonesian cooking, a salty and pungent shrimp paste, related to the Philippine **balachan** and other Oriental fermented fish condiments.

blanc (blanhk) French for "white"; also cooking stock or **court bouillon** in which certain foods, such as artichokes, are cooked *au blanc* to retain their color; it usually includes a little flour mixed with water; lemon juice and butter or oil are sometimes included.

blanc de blancs A white French Champagne wine made from white grapes.

blanch To immerse vegetables, fruit, or meat in boiling water briefly, then plunge into cold water to stop cooking; this technique is used to firm or soften flesh, to set color, to peel off skin, or to remove raw flavor.

blancmange (bluh-manhjh) A medieval or older jellied mixture originally made of pulverized almonds and veal stock, spiced and sweetened; *blancmange* has changed over the centuries into a kind of pudding or custard.

blanquette (blanh-ket) A French stew of veal, chicken, or lamb braised in stock, thickened with egg yolks and cream, and garnished with mushrooms and small white onions; the sauce is always white.

blé (blay) French for wheat.

blending Mixing wines of different qualities or origins to produce a better wine or to give consistency; usually an honorable practice but sometimes unscrupulous.

blette (blet) French for Swiss chard.

bleu In French, very rare, as for steak; rarer than à point.

bleu, au A French method of preparing trout or other fish whereby the fish is killed immediately before being plunged into a boiling **court bouillon** with vinegar, which turns the skin bluish and curls the body of the fish.

Bleu d'Auvergne (BLEU d'ō-VAYR-nyeh) A whole-milk cows' cheese made in several areas in the French Auvergne; it is a soft, unpressed blue cheese with a distinctive flavor.

blind Huhn (blint HOON) A German casserole of beans, vegetables, dried apples, and bacon.

blini (BLEE-nee) Russian pancakes, usually of buckwheat flour, often served with sour cream and caviar.

blintz Pancake of Eastern European origin cooked on one side, filled with cottage or similar cheese, and topped with apple or another fruit, folded over and fried.

bloater In English cooking, inshore herring that are lightly salted and smoked, then gutted only just before serving.

Blockwurst (BLOHK-voorst) A German sausage of beef and pork, similar to salami.

blond de veau (BLONH deu VŌ) In French cuisine, white veal stock; *blond de volaille* means clear chicken stock.

blondir (blonh-deer) In French, to cook lightly in fat.

blood orange One of several varieties of the sweet orange with crimson flesh and juice; the skin may be flecked or blushed with red or purple, and the flavor can be like raspberry.

blood sausage A sausage colored black and flavored with blood and diced pork fat from fresh-killed pigs.

blue cheese Cheese injected with a mold such as *Penicillium roqueforti* (from **Roquefort,** the oldest cheese of the genre), which gives the cheese its characteristic flavor and blue-green veining; there are many varieties, some of which are individually noted. *Bleu cheese* is incorrect.

blue crab A variety of **crab** found on the Chesapeake Bay, eastern Atlantic, and Gulf coastlines, best appreciated in the form of **soft-shell crab.**

bluefish A voracious fish found off the North American East coast and in the Mediterranean; its oily and flavorful flesh takes well to assertive seasonings and accompaniments; best for baking, broiling, and smoking.

Blue Point A species of oyster found off the coast of Long Island, usually served raw.

Blumenkohl (BLOO-men-kōl) German for cauliflower.

Blutwurst (BLOOT-voorst) German for **blood sausage.**

bo bohng (bah buhng) Rice noodles with sautéed beef and onions, cucumbers, bean sprouts, herbs, and greens, a Vietnamese dish.

bocadito (bō-kah-DEE-tō) Spanish for "little mouthful," tiny sandwich served as an appetizer.

Bock (bohk) A strong Bavarian beer, usually dark.

bodega (bō-DAY-gah) A Spanish wine cellar or store.

boeuf à la bourguignonne See **bourguignonne, à la.**

bogavante (bō-gah-VAHN-tah) Spanish for large-clawed lobster.

Bohne (BŌ-neh) German for bean.

boil To cook in liquid at or above the boiling point (100° Celsius, 212° Fahrenheit), when liquid bubbles and evaporates into steam; a rolling boil is a vigorous boil.

boiled dinner See **New England boiled dinner.**

bok choy See **bai cai.**

bola (BŌ-lah) Portuguese for dough, pie, cake or dumpling; *bolo,* a meatball.

boletus (bō-LEE-tus) A genus of wild mushroom of which the bolete, **cèpe,** or **porcino,** as it is variously known, is best known and most prized; with a thick fleshy cap and stem, the **cèpe** grows in chestnut and oak woods from June to November and is eaten fresh and dried; not to be confused with other species.

boliche mechado (bō-LEE-chay meh-CHAH-dō) Cuban beef pot roast stuffed with ham and braised in a marinade flavored with **Seville orange** juice.

bollito (bōl-LEE-tō) Italian for boiled; refers especially to mixed boiled meats.

bologna See **mortadella.**

bolognese, alla See **ragù alla bolognese.**

Bombay duck An Indian fish (*bombil*) that is dried and used to flavor curry dishes.

bombe (bomhb) In French cuisine, ice cream that is layered and packed into a special mold, originally shaped like a bomb.

bonbon (BONH-bonh) French for candy, sweet.

boniato (bō-NYAH-tō) A sweet potato with white rather than orange flesh, much used in Caribbean cooking, and sometimes confusingly called a "Florida yam"; *boniatillo* is a rich dessert of the puréed root dusted with cinnamon.

bonito (bō-NEE-tō) A small member of the tuna family; often used in Japanese cooking, dried, salted, or flaked.

bonne femme, à la (ah lah bon fam) "In the style of the good woman or wife," in a simple home style, often accompanied by small onions and mushrooms, in a white wine sauce flavored with lemon juice.

bo nhung dam (boh nyung yam) Vietnamese version of **Mongolian hot pot:** sliced beef poached in flavored broth, then rolled up in a lettuce leaf with onion and ginger, served with **nuoc mam** dipping sauce.

boquerón (bō-kayr-ŌN) Spanish for anchovy or whitebait.

borage (BOR-aj) An herb, Mediterranean in origin, used to flavor vegetables and beverages; its flowers are made into fritters, its young leaves are used in salads, and its mature leaves are cooked like spinach and finely chopped.

Bordeaux A seaport city and capital of the Gironde on the Garonne River in southwest France; the Bordeaux region is famous for the large quantity of red and white wine it produces, some of it very fine.

bordelaise, à la (ah lah bohr-de-lez) In French cuisine, garnished with a reduction sauce of red or white wine with bone marrow and chopped parsley; with **cèpes** added; with **mirepoix;** or a garnish of artichokes and potatoes.

börek (BEU-rek) In Turkish cuisine, a very thin pastry filled with savory or sweet stuffing, folded or rolled up, and fried or baked.

borlotto bean (bor-LOHT-tō) A common bean variety, usually dried; this splotched brown bean is especially popular in Italy where it is cooked to a creamy purée or added to soups.

borracha, salsa (bor-RAH-chah) Literally "drunken sauce"; made with **pasilla** chilies, orange juice, onion, and tequila; a Mexican sauce.

borsch, borscht A Polish and Russian soup based on fresh beets (which impart their vibrant color), meat broth, and winter vegetables, and often flavored with **kvass;** the soup varies widely but is always served with sour cream; traditional for Christmas Eve, without meat.

Boston baked beans Navy beans flavored with molasses and salt pork and baked in an earthenware pot; originally prepared on Saturday and cooked in a communal oven to allow Puritan housewives to observe the Sabbath—hence Boston's nickname of Bean Town.

Boston brown bread A traditional accompaniment to **Boston baked beans,** this rye bread is flavored with molasses and often contains whole wheat and cornmeal; the dark sweet bread is steamed, usually in baking powder tins.

bot gao (bo gow) Vietnamese for rice flour, a staple made from ground white rice. See also **glutinous rice.**

botifarra (bō-tee-FAHR-rah) Spanish for **blood sausage.**

Botrytis cinerea See **noble rot.**

bottarga (bō-TAHR-gah) Roe of tuna or grey mullet dried, pressed, salted, similar to **tarama;** eaten with toast, egg, or pasta in Italian and Mediterranean cooking.

bottom round   See **round.**

bouchée   (boo-shay)   A small puff-pastry savory, in French literally a "mouthful," filled variously.

boucher   (boo-shay)   French for butcher.

bouchon   (boo-shonh)   French for cork.

boudin noir   (boo-dinh nwaahr)   French for **blood sausage.**

bouillabaisse   (boo-yah-bes)   This famous specialty from Marseilles, originally a hearty fisherman's stew, is made from a wide variety of native fish and shellfish and flavored with saffron; the exact recipe is hotly disputed.

bouillir   (boo-yeer)   In French, to boil.

bouillon   (boo-yonh)   In French cooking, stock or broth that forms the basis of soups and sauces; it can be made from vegetables, poultry, or meat boiled in water, depending on its use, and need not contain gelatin.

boulage   (boo-lajh)   In French cooking, shaping the dough in baking.

boulanger   (boo-lanh-jhay)   French for baker; *boulangerie*, bakery.

boulangère, à la   (ah lah boo-lanh-jhayr)   In French cuisine, garnished with braised onion and potato, originally cooked in the baker's oven.

boule-de-neige   (BOOL deu NEJH)   A French dessert pastry resembling snowballs (hence the name), of round cakes dipped in whipped cream; made in individual servings.

bouquet   (boo-kay)   In French, the aroma of wine, which gives it much of its character and charm.

bouquet garni   (boo-kay gaahr-nee)   In French cooking, a bunch of herbs tied together in a small bundle for flavoring a dish as it cooks and removed before serving; it usually includes parsley, thyme, and bay leaf, among other herbs.

bouquetière, à la   (ah lah BOO-keh-TYAYR)   In French cuisine, "in the style of the flower girl"; meat garnished with vegetables that are arranged in bouquets.

bourbon   American whiskey distilled from a mash that is at least 51% corn; sour mash bourbon contains some old mash to help start fermentation; named for Bourbon County, Kentucky.

bourgeoise, à la   (ah lah boor-jhwahz)   Braised meat garnished with carrots, onions, and diced bacon.

Bourgogne (BOOR-GŌ-nyeh) French for **Burgundy.**

bourguignonne, à la (ah lah boor-gee-nyon) In French cuisine, served with a red wine sauce garnished with mushrooms, small onions, and diced bacon.

bourride (boo-reed) A fish stew from Provence, similar to **bouill-abaisse,** served on a **croûte,** and flavored with **aïoli.**

bo vien (boh veen) Vietnamese beef meatball soup.

boysenberry A hybrid cultivar of the blackberry that tastes like a raspberry, developed early in this century and named after an American, Rudolf Boysen.

bo xao ot (boh sow EU) In Vietnamese cooking, marinated sliced beef stir-fried with bell peppers.

braciola (brah-CHYŌ-lah) Italian for cutlet or chop.

braewat (bray-WAHT) Moroccan small pastry triangle parcels filled variously, baked, and served warm; savory or sweet.

Brägenwurst (BRAY-gen-voorst) German smoked sausage of pig's brains, oats, flour, and onions; long and thin.

brains Usually from a calf or lamb, brains should first be blanched in **acidulated water,** then poached in a **court bouillon** or fried in butter; often served with **beurre noir** or **noisette.**

braise To cook in a small amount of flavored liquid in a tightly covered pan over low heat.

bran The thin brown outer covering of the wheat grain, which is removed during the refining of white flour; although bran is not absorbed into the body during digestion, its fiber, usually eaten in baked goods and breakfast cereal, is beneficial.

brandade (branh-dad) A salt-cod dish from Provence in which cod is pounded with olive oil, milk, and garlic into a thick, flavorful purée and served with **croûtes;** the name derives from the Provençal word for stirred; see also **morue.**

brandy A spirit distilled from wine (types of brandy are separately entered).

brasato (brah-ZAH-tō) Italian for braised.

brasserie (brah-sayr-ee) Informal French restaurant open long hours, serving a variety of fare including beer.

Braten (BRAH-ten) In German, a cut of meat roasted in the oven or braised on the stove.

Brathering (BRAHT-hayr-ing)   German for herring that is grilled or floured and fried, then pickled in a boiled vinegar marinade; usually served cold.

Bratwurst (BRAHT-voorst)   A German sausage of spiced pork, fried or grilled; very popular.

Braunschweiger (BROWN-shvīg-er)   German liver sausage.

brawn   See **head cheese.**

Brazil nut   The nut of a tall tree indigenous to the Amazon and growing mostly in the wild. The woody pod, looking something like a coconut, contains up to twenty seeds whose segments fit together in their husks; the nut is white, creamy, and high in fat. The tree grows only in Brazil and, curiously, almost all of the nuts are exported.

breadfruit   The fruit of a tree native to the Pacific; large, round, and starchy, it is eaten boiled or baked; sometimes confused with its blander-tasting relative, jackfruit.

bread pudding   Simple dessert of stale bread dipped in milk, egg, sugar, and flavorings, and baked.

bread sauce   An English sauce of milk cooked with onions and cloves and thickened with breadcrumbs; served with poultry and game.

bream   Several different species of fish, including the excellent Mediterranean **gilthead** and the American **porgy.**

bresaola (bres-ah-Ō-lah)   Dried salt beef sliced from the fillet, served as an **antipasto;** a specialty of northern Lombardy in Italy.

Bresse (bres)   A region in southern Burgundy famous for its excellent chickens and for its blue cheese, *Bleu de Bresse.*

Bretagne (BREH-TAN-yuh)   A province in northwest France noted for its fresh- and saltwater fish and shellfish, cider, and many other foods.

bretonne, à la (ah lah breh-TON)   In French cooking, garnished with fresh white haricot beans.

brewer's yeast   See **yeast.**

brick   A scalded-curd, surface-ripened whole-milk cows' cheese first made in Wisconsin; it is shaped in bricks and also weighted with bricks during pressing, hence its name; the taste and texture is between that of **Cheddar** and **Liederkranz.**

brider (bree-day)   To truss in French.

Brie (bree)   A soft uncooked cows' milk cheese from the region of the same name east of Paris; made in large flat discs, this cheese, with its white, surface-ripened rind and smooth buttery interior, is made similarly to **Camembert** and is renowned for its fine aroma and taste.

brik (breek) A Tunisian type of pastry, in very thin sheets like **phyllo,** a variation on the Moroccan **braewat;** stuffed, deep-fried, and served at once.

brill A member of the **flounder** family.

Brillat-Savarin, Jean Anthelme (1755–1826) (bree-ya sa-va-rinh) A French lawyer and magistrate who is remembered today for his great treatise on gastronomy, *The Physiology of Taste,* published in 1825.

brinjal (BRIN-jawl) Eggplant in Indian cooking.

brio (PREE-oo) Thai for sour.

brioche (bree-OSH) A French cake or pastry made from a rich yeast dough containing butter and eggs, often baked in a characteristic fluted mold with a smaller knob on top (*brioche parisienne*), as well as in various other shapes and sizes.

brisket A cut of beef from the lower forequarter, between the foreshanks and short plate; usually braised or cured for **corned beef.**

brisling The sprat, a small fish similar to the **herring.**

Brittany See **Bretagne.**

broa (BRŌ-ah) Spanish for cornbread.

broad bean See **fava.**

broccoli rabe A cousin of broccoli cultivated for its branches and leaves as well as flowerets and especially for its bitter, assertive flavor; it is best eaten not raw, but sautéed, braised, or steamed and served with strongly flavored foods, especially Mediterranean. Also called *rapini* and *broccoli raab.*

broche, à la (ah lah BRŌSH) French for spit-roasted.

brochet (brō-shay) French for **pike.**

brochette (brō-shet) French for a skewer for grilling pieces of food.

brodo (BRŌ-dō) Italian for broth or bouillon; *brodo ristretto* is consommé.

broil To cook under or over direct intense heat.

Brolio (BRŌ-lyō) A celebrated and ancient vineyard in the Italian Chianti district in Tuscany; the wine is robust and long-lived.

bronzino (brohn-ZEE-nō) Italian for sea bass.

Bröschen (BREUS-shen) German for sweetbreads.

Brot (brōt) German for bread.

brou (broo) A French liqueur made from walnut husks.

brouillé (broo-yay) French for scrambled.

Brouilly (broo-yee) A wine-producing district in Beaujolais with one of the best wines of that type.

brown To cook by high heat, causing the surface of the food to turn dark and imparting a richer, cooked flavor; browning affects the outside of the food only, leaving the inside moist; it can be achieved by sautéing, frying, grilling, or broiling; see also **caramel.**

brown betty An American pudding made of sliced fruit thickened with breadcrumbs, sweetened, and baked; usually made with apples.

brown sauce See **espagnole.**

brown sugar Refined sugar with a thin coating of **molasses;** not to be confused with raw, unrefined sugar.

brûlé (brü-lay) French for burned or flamed, as in **crème brûlée.**

brunoise (brün-wahz) In French cuisine, a mixture of vegetables cut into small dice and cooked slowly in butter for soups, sauces, etc.; **bâtonnets** cut across into cubes make brunoise.

Brunswick stew A southern American stew originally made with squirrel or whatever game was available, but now mostly made with chicken and a variety of vegetables.

bruschetta (broos-KET-tah) Bread slices toasted, rubbed with garlic, and dribbled with new green olive oil; a specialty of Rome.

brut (broot) Very dry Champagne to which virtually no sugar has been added; drier than "extra dry."

bruxelloise, à la (ah lah brük-sel-wahz) In French cuisine, garnished with Brussels sprouts, braised endives, and **château potatoes** and served with a Madeira sauce.

bstilla See **bastilla.**

Bual (boo-WAL) A type of **Madeira,** golden in color and quite sweet, now usually drunk as a dessert wine; the name comes from the particular grape variety.

bubble and squeak In Britain, fried cabbage and mash, that is, potatoes.

bûche de Noël (BÜSH deu NŌ-EL)   Literally yule log; the traditional French **gâteau** for Christmas, made of **génoise** and **buttercream** and decorated to look like a log.

buckwheat flour   Not a true cereal, buckwheat flour is made from dry fruit seeds of the plant; most popular in Russia (see **blini**), buckwheat is made into pancakes and special breads (sometimes mixed with wheat) but mostly used for fodder; also called *saracen wheat* or *saracen corn.*

budín (boo-DEEN)   Spanish for pudding; the Italian word is *budino.*

bue (BOO-ay)   Italian for beef; the Spanish word is *buey.*

buffalo fish   A freshwater American fish with sweet, white, lean flesh; a type of sucker, the buffalo is similar to **carp** and versatile in cooking.

bülbül yuvası (BUHL-buhl YOO-vah—seu)   "Bird's nest," a Turkish pastry made of paper-thin dough filled with pistachios, coiled, baked, and served in syrup.

bulghur   Cracked wheat, hulled and parboiled, originally Persian; this nutty-textured cereal is ground in different grades for various dishes such as **tabbouleh, kibbeh,** and **pilaf;** also spelled *bulgur* and *burghul.*

bulgogi (BOOL-gō-gee)   Korean barbecue of marinated beef, or, less commonly, chicken or squid, cooked over a wood fire or, more recently, a gas grill.

bullabesa (BOO-yah-BAY-sah)   Fish stew of Catalonia; a cousin of **bouillabaisse.**

bumbu (bum-boo)   Indonesian sauce, usually a spicy peanut sauce, as for **saté.**

bun bo hue (buhn boh hway)   Popular Vietnamese soup with beef, pork, **lemongrass,** shrimp paste, and noodles.

bundi (BOON-dee)   An Indian sweet; **besan** batter is poured through a sieve and deep-fried, sometimes then pressed into a ball, and served in a hot syrup.

Bündnerfleisch (BÜNT-ner-flīsh)   Swiss cured, dried beef sliced very thin.

buñuelo (boo-NWAY-lō)   Spanish for fritter.

burdock   A large plant whose leaves, young shoots, and roots are used for food and drink; much favored in Japan, where it is known as *gobo.*

burghul See **bulghur.**

burgoo (BUR-goo) A thick stew, originally a porridge for sailors, later containing many different meats and vegetables and thickened with okra; associated with the southern United States and Kentucky.

Burgos (BOOR-gōs) A fresh ewes' milk cheese, from the Spanish province of the same name; mild, soft, and pleasant, often served for dessert; the rindless discs weigh approximately three pounds.

Burgundy A province southeast of Paris, famous for its red and white wines; **Beaujolais, Chablis, Pouilly-Fuissé,** and those of the **Côte d'Or,** separately entered, are the best known; Bourgogne in French.

burnet An herb whose leaves, which taste like cucumber, are used to flavor salads, cool drinks, vinegar, and sauces.

burrida (boor-REE-dah) A fish stew from Genoa, a cousin of **bourride.**

burrito (boor-REE-tō) A **taco** of wheat rather than maize (**tortilla**), folded to enclose a filling.

burro (BOO-rō) Italian for butter.

Busserl (BOO-sehrl) Small round sweet pastries, literally "kiss" in German.

butaniku Japanese for pork.

butifarra (boo-tee-FAR-rah) A Spanish sausage of pork with white wine and spices.

butter bean Lima bean.

buttercream A mixture of butter, sugar, and egg yolks or custard, flavored in a wide variety of ways and used to ice or garnish dessert pastries and cakes.

butterfly To cut open but not quite through and spread apart (as with butterfly wings), especially for a piece of meat or fish.

buttermilk The residue from churned butter, containing the milk casein, which has a slightly sour flavor; buttermilk is easily digested and is often used with baking soda for breads and pastries; now usually cultured skim milk.

chèvre

Cabernet (ka-bayr-nay)   A grape variety that partly makes up red Bordeaux wines and many of the world's best clarets; *Cabernet Sauvignon,* higher in tannin, is slower maturing and longer lasting than *Cabernet; Cabernet Franc* is more productive.

Cabernet Rosé d'Anjou (ka-bayr-nay rō-zay d'anh-jhoo)   A rosé wine, of the *Cabernet Franc* grape, from the Loire Valley of France.

cabillaud (ka-bee-yō)   French for fresh cod; see also **morue.**

cabinet   See **Kabinett.**

cabra (KAH-brah)   Spanish for goat.

Cabrales (kah-BRAH-lays)   A blue-veined cheese from northern Spain; usually made from goats' milk but sometimes from cows' and sheep's milk; earthy, pungent, yet mellow in flavor; sometimes called *Picón.*

cabrito (kah-BREE-tō)   Spanish for kid.

cacao (kah-KOW)   A tree from whose seeds, fermented, roasted, and ground, come chocolate and cocoa; native to South America, it now grows in many tropical countries around the globe.

cacciagione (ka-chah-JŌ-nay)   Italian for game.

cacciatora (ka-chah-TOR-ah)   Italian for hunter's style: in a sauce of mushrooms, onions, tomatoes, and herbs with wine.

cacik (JAH-jeuk.)   A Turkish dish of sliced cucumbers in yogurt with garlic, mint, dill, perhaps olive oil.

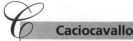

Caciocavallo (KA-chō-kah-VAHL-lō) A whole-milk cows' cheese, spindle-shaped and tied with string, from southern Italy; made by the spun-curd method. Table cheeses are aged for two months, grating cheeses up to twelve, and their flavor ranges from delicate and sweet to more pungent with age; this pale straw-colored cheese is used for eating and cooking and is sometimes smoked.

cactus pear See **prickly pear.**

Caen, à la mode de (KANH, ah l'ah MŌD deu) A classic French preparation for **tripe** in which blanched squares of tripe are slowly braised with onions, carrots, leeks, blanched ox feet, herbs, garlic, brandy, and white wine; it is cooked for twelve hours in a **hermetically sealed marmite.**

Caerphilly (kayr-FIL-lee) A cows' milk cheese, mild, crumbly, moist, and slightly sour; the traditional lunch of the Welsh coal miners, it is now mostly made in western England rather than Wales.

Caesar salad Romaine lettuce with croûtons, coddled eggs, and grated Parmesan cheese in an olive oil vinaigrette flavored with garlic and Worcestershire sauce; anchovies are often added; created in 1924 by Caesar Cardini, an Italian restaurateur in Tijuana.

café French for coffee, coffee bean, coffee shop or bar; *un café,* a small black coffee; *café au lait,* a large coffee with hot milk; *café crème,* a small coffee with cream; *café brûlot,* coffee with burnt brandy; *faux café,* decaffeinated; *café complet,* continental breakfast.

caffè Italian for coffee; *caffè e latte* (caffelatte), half coffee, half hot milk; see also **espresso** and **cappuccino.**

Cahors (ka-OHR) A fine red wine from the city of the same name in Toulouse, France, made from the **Malbec** grape; very dark red, slow maturing, long lasting.

cai juan (tsī juan) Chinese for egg roll; a square crêpelike wrapper made from an egg, flour, and water batter, usually stuffed with pork, cabbage, or other vegetables, rolled up, and deep-fried or steamed, or sometimes shredded for garnishing; the egg roll, very popular in Cantonese-American cooking, is thicker and less elegant than the **spring roll** and should not be confused with it.

caille (kī) French for quail.

Cajun Originally, this term pertained to the French Canadian settlers in Louisiana, a corruption of Acadia (from the colony of Acadia in southeastern Canada); Cajun cooking combines French methods with rural southern ingredients and a strong African influence and is often confused with **Creole; gumbo** and **jambalaya** are typical dishes of this unique cuisine.

cake comb   See **pastry comb.**

calabacita (KAHL-ah-bah-SEE-tah)   Spanish for zucchini.

calabash   See **passion fruit.**

calabaza (kal-ah-BAH-sah)   Large hard-skinned winter squash with orange flesh, native to the Americas and much used in South and Latin American cooking; similar to pumpkin, Hubbard, and butternut squashes, which can be substituted for it.

calamari (kal-ah-MAHR-ee)   Italian for squid.

Caldaro (kal-DAHR-ō)   A town in the Italian Tirol that produces a number of light and pleasant red and white wines.

calderada (kahl-dayr-AH-dah)   A thick Galician fish stew similar to **bouillabaisse.**

caldereta (kahl-dayr-AY-tah)   A Spanish meat or fish stew, whose name derives from the cauldron or pot in which it is cooked.

caldo (KAL-dō)   Italian for hot; in Spanish and Portuguese, *caldo* means broth.

caldo verte (kal-dō VAYR-tay)   Potato and cabbage or kale soup, widely popular in Portuguese cooking.

caliente (kahl-YEN-tay)   Spanish for hot.

Californian chili   See **guëro.**

callaloo (KAL-lah-loo)   In Caribbean cooking, the leafy green tops of the **taro** plant, cooked into a spicy vegetable stew with okra, eggplant, tomatoes, onions, garlic, chilies, herbs, salt pork or other meat, coconut milk, and sometimes crab; a popular and variable native dish related to **Creole** crab **gumbo;** also spelled *calalou* and *callilu.*

calmar (kal-maahr)   French for squid.

calsones (kal-sō-nays)   Sephardic pasta, like cheese ravioli.

Calvados (KAL-vah-dōs)   Apple brandy from the department of the same name in Normandy.

calzone (kal-ZŌ-nay)   A turnover made of pizza dough and stuffed with various savory fillings, usually in individual portions; originally from Naples and now popular in the United States; literally, "pant leg."

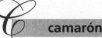

camarón (kah-mah-RŌN)   Spanish for shrimp.

Cambridge sauce   A mayonnaiselike sauce of hard-boiled egg yolks, anchovies, capers, herbs, mustard, vinegar, and oil, finished with chopped parsley.

Camembert (ka-memh-bayr)   A cows' milk cheese, soft and creamy with a white mold rind; from the town of the same name in Normandy; neither cooked nor pressed, this rich cheese in four-inch rounds is very popular and famous and, at its best—farmhouse cheese from unpasteurized milk—superb.

camote (kah-MŌ-tay)   Spanish for sweet potato.

campagnola (kahm-pah-NYŌ-lah)   Italian for country style, usually with onions and tomatoes.

canapé (ka-na-pay)   A small piece of bread spread or garnished with savory food and served as an hors d'oeuvre, originally French.

canard sauvage (ka-naahr sō-vajh)   French for wild duck.

caneton (ka-neh-tonh)   French for duckling.

cangrejo (kahn-GRAY-hō)   Spanish for crab.

canh bap su (kan bop shoo)   Cabbage roll soup in pork or chicken stock, from Vietnam.

canh chua ca (kan tchyoo kah) Sweet and sour fish soup, hot with chilies, sour with tamarind, from Vietnam.

canja (KAHN-jhah)   Clear chicken soup with rice, very popular in Brazil.

canola oil   Rapeseed oil, neutral in flavor and with a high burning point; low in saturated fats but with poly- and monosaturated fats; also called *colza*.

canneberge (kan-bayrjh)   French for cranberry.

cannèlla (kah-NEL-lah)   Italian for cinnamon; the French word is *cannelle*.

cannellini (kan-nel-LEE-nee)   Italian for white kidney beans.

cannelloni (kan-nel-LŌ-nee)   Italian pasta squares usually boiled, stuffed, rolled, and baked in a sauce.

cannoli (kan-NŌ-lee)   Italian pastry tubes or horns filled with ricotta cheese, chocolate, and candied citron.

Cantal (kanh-tal)   A cows' milk cheese from the French **Auvergne,** uncooked, pressed, and cured for three months; similar to **Cheddar,** this ancient cheese, known by the Romans, is cylindrical in shape with a nutty, full flavor.

cantaloupe   See **muskmelon.**

Cantenac (kanh-teh-nak)   A town in the **Médoc** region of France that produces several excellent clarets.

Cape gooseberry   Small golden or orange berry from South America in a fragile husklike covering similar to that of its cousin the **tomatillo;** the colorful flesh is dense, sweet, tart, and slightly bitter; the husk lends itself to decoration.

capeado (kah-pay-AH-dō)   In Spanish cooking, dipped in batter and fried.

capelli d'angelo (kah-PEL-lee D'AHN-jeh-lō)   Angel hair pasta; the thinnest pasta, almost too fine to cut by hand. This pasta has recently become popular with the health-conscious, putting a new twist on the old riddle: which weighs less, a pound of angel hair or a pound of macaroni?

caper   The bud or young fruit of a climbing plant, native to Africa and the Mediterranean, which is pickled to make a condiment; nasturtium buds or seeds are sometimes substituted.

capitolade (ka-pee-tō-lad)   In French cuisine, cooked chicken or other food, chopped and served in a sauce; a kind of chicken hash.

capitone (kah-pee-TŌ-nay)   Italian for large conger eel.

capon   A castrated male chicken, whose flesh is well fattened (it gains up to ten pounds in as many months). Capon is prepared like chicken, although its flesh has a distinctive taste of its own.

caponata (kah-pō-NAH-tah)   A Sicilian vegetable salad of fried eggplant, onions, olives, anchovies, capers, and tomatoes.

cappelletti (kap-pel-LET-tee)   Small squares of pasta stuffed and shaped like little hats, hence their name; very similar to **tortellini.**

cappone (ka-PŌ-nay)   Italian for capon.

cappuccino (ka-poo-CHEE-nō)   **Espresso** coffee with hot frothy milk, often dusted with cocoa powder or cinnamon.

capretto (kah-PRET-tō)   Italian for kid.

capsicum   See **chili.**

carambola   (kar-ahm-BŌ-lah)   A fruit (commonly referred to as star fruit), native to Malaysia and pale yellow when ripe, with five pointed ridges around the central core. It comes in sweet or sour varieties and is star-shaped when sliced across.

caramel   Sugar dissolved in water and cooked to a rich dark brown color; caramelized sugar is used in candy, desserts, stocks, and sauces.

caraway   An herb in the parsley family whose pungent seeds are used in making cheese, bread, and pastry, and whose milder leaves are used in cooking; a staple seasoning in German and Hungarian cuisine; often confused with **cumin.**

carbonada   (kar-bō-NAH-dah)   A beef stew from Argentina combining apples, pears, tomatoes, onions, and potatoes; *carbonada criolla*, a stew of beef, yellow winter squash, corn, and peaches, sometimes served in a squash shell.

carbonara, alla   (ahl-lah kar-bō-NAR-ah)   An Italian spaghetti sauce with bacon, eggs, Parmesan cheese, and (usually) cream.

carbonnade à la flammande   (kaahr-bō-nad ah lah fla-manhd)   A Belgian beef stew from Flanders flavored with bacon, onions, and a little brown sugar, and simmered in beer. The term *carbonnade* originally referred to meat cooked over charcoal.

carciòfo   (kar-CHŌ-fō)   Italian for artichoke.

cardamom   A spice of the ginger family whose pungent seeds are dried and used in Oriental, Indian, and Middle Eastern cooking.

cardinal, à la   (ah lah kaahr-dee-nal)   A French fish garnish of **béchamel** sauce flavored with truffle essence, lobster butter and slices, and cayenne pepper; *cardinal* sometimes refers to a brilliant red dessert sauce of puréed raspberries, strained and sweetened.

cardoon   A vegetable cultivated for its stalks and tender leaves; closely related to the artichoke, although it looks different.

Carême, Antonin   (anh-tō-ninh kaahr-em) (1784–1833)   A French chef who, by organizing the workings of the professional kitchen and thus grand classical cuisine, is regarded as its founder; Carême worked for many great patrons, but his fame rests mostly on his erudite books; see also **pièce montée** and **sauce.**

cari   (ka-ree)   French for curry.

ca-ri ga (ka-ree ga)   Classic Vietnamese chicken stew with curry and coconut milk.

carmine   A red dye used for food coloring, obtained from the female cochineal insect.

carne (KAR-nay)   Italian and Spanish for meat.

carne de res (KAR-nay day RAYS)   Spanish for beef.

carnero (kar-NAYR-ō)   Spanish for lamb or mutton.

carob   An evergreen tree whose pods are eaten both fresh and dried; high in sugar and protein, carob is used for confectionery (often as a chocolate substitute) and in pharmaceuticals and animal feed; carob may be the biblical locusts—a mistranslation of locust bean—that St. John ate in the dessert.

carp   A freshwater fish found in Asian, European, and American waters which, unless farmed, tends to live in muddy water; it is cooked and used in many ways, including **gefilte fish.**

carpaccio (kar-PAH-chō)   Very thin slices of raw beef fillet served with mustard sauce, mayonnaise, or olive oil and lemon juice; created by Arrigo Cipriani, of Harry's Bar in Venice, in 1961.

carrageen, carragheen   Commonly known as "Irish moss," really a seaweed that grows wild along the north Atlantic shore; the red plant is eaten fresh or dried, when it is bleached almost white; used in sweet and savory dishes and as an excellent source of gelatin.

carré d'agneau (kaahr-ay d'a-nyō)   French for loin or rack of lamb; *carré*, literally "square," can also mean best end of neck, sometimes of veal or pork as well as lamb or mutton.

carrottes à la Vichy (ka-roht ah lah vee-shee)   Sliced carrots cooked, if possible, in Vichy mineral water, with butter, a little sugar, and salt until glazed, and garnished with chopped parsley.

carte (kaahrt)   French for menu; *carte des vins*, wine list; *à la carte*, with items individually priced.

casaba   A large winter melon or **muskmelon** with yellow ribbed skin and very pale flesh.

casalinga (kah-zah-LEENG-ah)   Italian for homemade.

cascabel (kahs-kah-BEL)   A small, round, dried chili pepper with a smooth reddish-brown skin, about one inch across and fairly hot; its name (literally, rattlesnake) refers to its rattle.

cashew A kidney-shaped nut of an Amazonian tree much favored in South American, Indian, and Asian cooking; the nut is attached to an apple-like false fruit; wine, vinegar, and liqueur are made from the cashew.

casing The intestinal membrane that is cleaned and stuffed with sausage forcemeat; a synthetic tubing used similarly.

cassareep **Cassava** juice reduced, sweetened, and spiced, used as a seasoning in Guyanan cooking.

cassata (kah-SAH-tah) An Italian dessert of ice cream molded in contrastingly colored layers with candied fruits soaked in liqueur; also a rich chocolate dessert from Sicily combining layers of sponge cake and ricotta with candied fruits.

cassava See **tapioca.**

cassia A type of cinnamon often confused with cinnamon proper when sold in powdered form, as in the United States; cassia is reddish brown, cinnamon a lighter tan.

cassis (ka-sees) French for black currant; a liqueur made from black currants is called *crème de cassis* and it is used alone or mixed to make apéritifs such as *Kir*—white wine colored with a few drops of *cassis*—or *Kir royale,* made with **Champagne.**

cassoulet (ka-soo-lay) A French stew of dried haricot beans baked with various meats (usually pork and mutton), preserved goose or duck, onions, etc., in an earthenware pot; from the **Languedoc** region.

castagna (kah-STAH-nyah) Italian for **chestnut.**

caster sugar British for confectioner's sugar; also spelled *castor sugar.*

catalane, à la (ah lah ka-ta-lan) In French cooking, garnished with sautéed eggplant and rice **pilaf,** and sometimes also with tomatoes.

catfish A fresh- and saltwater fish with a slick, scaleless skin, sharp, poisonous spines, and "whiskers" (hence its name); the catfish is very popular in the southern United States where it is increasingly farmed; cooked in various ways, especially deep-fried, usually pan-dressed, steaked, or filleted.

caudle A hot, spiced drink, often including wine or ale, with a cereal base; a favorite cold-weather beverage in England and Scotland.

caul The thin, fatty membrane, like netted lace, from a pig's or sheep's intestines; used to contain and cover **pâtés,** roasts, etc.; the fat melts away during cooking.

causa azulada (KOW-sah ah-soo-LAH-dah) In South American cooking, a large potato cake made with blue potatoes, giving a striking color, filled with Swiss chard, peppers, and olives.

causa a la limeña (KOW-sah ah lah lee-MAY-nyah) In South American cooking, a large potato cake filled with vegetables, meat, or seafood; cut in wedges for serving and garnished generously.

cave (kav) French for wine cellar.

caviar Sturgeon roe, ranging in color from pearl grey to light brown, from the Caspian Sea and rivers leading to it. *Malossol* caviar means "lightly salted" in Russian, regardless of the type of sturgeon, and so is considered fresh. The largest caviar is *beluga*, with grey eggs; *sevruga*, with darker smaller eggs, also has fine flavor and is in greater supply; *osietr* is gold-brown; *pausnaya* is pressed caviar from roe damaged or too small for higher grades, but can be delicious; *sterlet caviar* is the legendary "gold" caviar of the tsars, now extremely rare. Pasteurizing makes caviar less perishable. Substitutes for true caviar are lumpfish, whitefish, and salmon roe. See also **bottarga** and **taramosalata.** Good-quality caviar is now produced in the American Northwest.

cavolfiore (kah-vōl-FYOR-ay) Italian for cauliflower.

cavolo (KAH-vō-lō) Italian for cabbage.

cayenne pepper Red chili pepper, dried and ground fine; in Mexico this pepper, about three inches long, is widely available fresh year-round.

cazuela (kah-THWAY-lah, kah-SWAY-lah) Spanish for earthenware casserole.

cebiche (say-VEE-shay) Raw fish or shellfish marinated in citrus juice (usually lime) and seasonings but not cooked by heat; also spelled *seviche* and often confused with **escabeche;** from Peru and South America.

cebolla (thay-BŌ-lah, say-BŌ-lah) Spanish for onion.

Cebreto (thay-BRAY-tō) A blue-veined Spanish cheese with a creamy texture and yellow rind.

ceci (CHAY-chee) Italian for chickpeas, garbanzo beans.

celeriac (seh-LER-ee-ak) Celery root—a variety of celery cultivated for its fat, knobby root rather than its stalks; best when peeled and shredded for salads and hors d'oeuvres.

cellophane noodles See **fěn sī.**

cena (CHAY-nah, THAY-nah) Italian and Spanish for supper.

cèpe (sep)   See **boletus.**

cerdo (THAYR-dō, SAYR-dō)   Spanish for pork.

cerfeuil (sayr-foy)   French for chervil.

cerise (sayr-eez)   French for cherry.

çerkez tavuğu (chayr-KES tah-woo)   "Circassian chicken," poached chicken pieces in a rich spicy sauce of crushed walnuts and oil tinted red with paprika, usually served at room temperature; a classical Turkish dish popular throughout the Middle East that, because of the legendary beauty of Circassian women, supposedly evokes the splendor of the Turkish harem.

cervelas (sayr-vel-ah)   A French sausage of pork meat and fat (and formerly brains), flavored with garlic; also called *saucisson de Paris;* some nouvelle cuisine seafood sausages are called *cervelas.*

cervelles (sayr-vel)   French for brains.

cerveza (thayr-VAY-thah, sayr-VAY-sah)   Spanish for beer.

cèrvo (CHAYR-vō)   Italian for venison.

cetriòlo (chay-tree-Ō-lō)   Italian for cucumber.

cévenole, à la (ah lah say-ve-nōl)   With wild mushrooms and chestnuts, characteristic of the mountainous Cévennes region of the French Languedoc.

cha (chya)   Vietnamese for rolls; *cha ram,* shrimp rolls in rice wrappers deep-fried; *cha gio,* pork and crab spring rolls sold widely as a snack and also served with **nuoc mam** dipping sauce.

cha (chah)   Cambodian for stir-fried.

Chabichou (sha-bee-shoo)   A goats' milk cheese from Poitou, France, small and conical or cylindrical in shape, soft and mild in flavor; also called *Chabi.*

Chablis (sha-blee)   A small town and its environs in Burgundy, southeast of Paris, producing a well-known white wine of the same name from the **Chardonnay** grape; dry, clean, "flinty," pale-colored, it can vary widely in quality; in other countries, the term *Chablis* has little meaning.

chafing dish   A metal pan or dish heated from below with a flame, hot coals, or electricity, for warming or cooking food; from the French word *chauffer,* to heat.

chah   Tea in India.

chai tom (chaee tohm)   A Vietnamese dish of chopped shrimp with pork and scallions pressed around sugar cane skewers, steamed, grilled, and eaten with lettuce and mint, and served with **nuoc mam** dipping sauce.

chakchouka   See **shakshouka.**

challah (KHAH-lah)   Traditional Jewish Sabbath bread, made with yeast, oil, water, egg yolks, and honey, and baked in a braided loaf; for holidays it is often baked in a braided knot or spiral with raisins.

chalupa (chah-LOO-pah)   In Mexican cooking, a boat-shaped **tortilla,** stuffed variously.

Chambertin (shamh-bayr-tinh)   A vineyard in the **Côte d'Or** producing exceptional red Burgundy; ancient and celebrated, it is well worth its expense; Alexandre Dumas, who was not a wine drinker, wrote that "nothing makes the future look so rosy as to contemplate it through a glass of Chambertin."

Chambolle-Musigny (cham-bōl mü-zee-nyee)   A village in the **Côte d'Or** of Burgundy that produces delicate, aromatic, and excellent red wines.

chambrer (shamh-bray)   In French, to bring wines up from the cellar to allow them to rise to room temperature before serving.

Champagne (SHAMH-PAN-yeh)   Sparkling white wine from the French region of Champagne, northeast of Paris, by law strictly delineated; made by the "classic" or "traditional" method of fermentation in the bottle. Properly speaking, only such wine should be called *Champagne,* although the term is used loosely (especially in the United States) for sparkling white wine made by this or another method.

champagne grapes   Very small red grapes clustered in large bunches; sweet in flavor but best used for garnishes; developed in California.

champignon (shamh-pee-nyon)   French for mushroom.

chanfana (shahn-FAH-nah)   In Portuguese cooking, a robust lamb or kid stew with red wine.

channa (CHAN-nah)   Chickpea, in Indian cooking.

chanterelle (shanh-teu-rel)   French name for a wild mushroom, yellow and trumpet-shaped with a ruffled edge; before being used in cooking, *chanterelles* are heated with salt in a covered pan to disgorge their liquid and then drained.

Chantilly (shanh-tee-yee)   French sauce of whipped cream, sweetened and sometimes flavored with vanilla or liqueur; also **hollandaise** or **mayonnaise** with whipped cream folded in at the last minute; a kind of **mousseline.**

chǎo (tsow)   To stir-fry in Chinese.

chap   The lower cheek or jaw of a pig.

chapati (chah-PAH-tee)   An Indian wholewheat flatbread cooked on a griddle, then turned over (or out on coals) to puff up; *roti* is another name; also spelled *chappati* or *chapatti.*

chapelure (sha-peh-lür)   French for brown breadcrumbs.

chapon (sha-ponh)   French for a heel of bread rubbed with garlic and olive oil; can be either rubbed along the rim of the salad bowl to impart its flavor or added to the salad itself; not necessarily removed before serving; *chapon* also means **capon.**

chaptalization   A method of adding sugar to grape juice before fermentation, especially in bad years in cooler climates, to enable wine to reach minimum alcoholic content; a process not necessarily but often abused. Named for Chaptal, a French chemist (and Napoleon's Minister of Agriculture).

char   A member of the **trout** and **salmon** family; the Arctic char is particularly good for eating.

charcuterie (shaahr-kü-tayr-ree)   In French cuisine, the art of preparing meat, especially pork; the meat specialties, such as sausages, ham, **rillettes, galantines,** and **pâtés,** made in a French butcher's shop.

charcutière (shaahr-kü-tyayr)   In French cooking, sauce **Robert** with julienne of gherkins added just before serving; served primarily with grilled pork chops and other meats.

Chardonnay   A grape variety from which many excellent white wines are made.

charentais (shaahr-enh-tay)   A sweet and succulent French melon with yellow-green, ribbed skin and orange flesh.

charlotte (shaahr-loht)   A classic dessert, originally an apple compote in a pail-shaped mold lined with buttered bread and served hot. **Carême** elevated this to **Bavarian cream** in a ladyfinger-lined mold to make *charlotte russe.* A *charlotte royale* replaces the ladyfingers with sponge cake cut into many thin layers sandwiched with jam; in a further elaboration, *charlotte royale à l'ancienne,* thin layers of jelly roll line a shallow mold filled with Bavarian cream.

charmoula   See **sharmoula**.

Charolais   (shaahr-ō-lay)   French cattle fed on grass rather than grain (as in the United States), producing the lean but flavorful beef favored in France; also a **chèvre** from the *Charolais* region of Burgundy.

charoset   See **haroset**.

Chartreuse   (shaahr-treuz)   A liqueur made by Carthusian monks, originally in Grenoble but now largely in Voiron, France, and Tarragona, Spain; the liqueur comes in two types, yellow and green, the latter being higher proof.

Chassagne-Montrachet   (SHAS-SAN-yeh MONH-RA-SHAY)   A **commune** in the southern **Côte d'Or** producing outstanding white wines and very good reds.

Chasselas   (shas-seu-lah)   French name for a white grape variety, producing a light and fruity wine; although it does not make the best wines, it is valued for its hardiness and productivity and cultivated extensively, especially in Switzerland.

chasseur   (shas-seur)   A classic French sauce of sliced sautéed mushrooms and shallots reduced with white wine, enriched with **demi-glace** and butter, and finished with chopped parsley; *chasseur* is the French word for hunter.

châtaigne   See **marron**.

chestnut   See **marron**.

château-bottled   Wine bottled where it was produced by the vineyard owner, especially in Bordeaux; this term ensures authenticity, if not quality, from the better vineyards; a statement such as *"Mise en bouteilles au Domaine"* or *". . . par le Propriétaire"* should be on the main wine label.

chateaubriand, châteaubriant   (sha-tō-bree-anh)   In French cooking, beef cut from the middle of the fillet, grilled, and garnished with **château potatoes** and **béarnaise sauce**; *chateaubriand sauce* is a reduction of white wine, shallots, herbs, and mushrooms, with **demi-glace** and butter added. Also a triple-crème cheese from Normandy.

Châteauneuf-du-Pape   A famous red wine from the village of the same name in the Rhône Valley, near Avignon, the site of the French pope's summer home in the fourteenth century.

chatni   (CHAHT-nee)   Chutney; in Indian cooking the word means "pulverized"; a condiment, originally created to accompany Indian curries, of fruit and spices cooked with vinegar and sugar as a preservative; much loved by the English and anglicized into chutney.

chaud-froid (shō-fwah) French for poultry, game, or meat that is cooked but served cold, usually covered with aspic or a special sauce and highly garnished.

chaurice (shō-REES) A highly spiced **Cajun** sausage, related to **chorizo.**

chausson aux pommes (shō-sonh ō pohm) Apple turnover, in French.

Chavignol (sha-vee-nyōl) A small, soft French goats' milk cheese from Sancerre.

chayote (chī-Ō-tay) A vegetable of the melon and gourd family, with a prickly ribbed skin and pear shape; native to Mexico and the Antilles, it is often used in Spanish and Caribbean cooking and is prepared in a wide variety of ways; also called *custard marrow, mirliton,* and *christophine.*

Cheddar A whole-milk cows' cheese, originally from Somerset, England, in which the curd is scalded, pressed, and aged; this style is made in factories the world over, while true farmhouse Cheddar, made with unpasteurized milk, wrapped in cloth, and matured for six months to two years, is one of the great cheeses; the technique called *cheddaring* is a combination of milling and turning the curd.

chef de cuisine French for executive chef.

chef de partie French for section chef, such as *saucier* or **pâtissier.**

chelo (CHAY-lō) In Persian cooking, plain rice, as opposed to **polo.**

chemiser (sheu-mee-say) In French, to coat a mold with aspic, ice cream, or some other lining; *en chemise,* literally "in a shirt," means any food in a coating, such as potatoes in their jackets or ice cream covered with a thin brittle layer of chocolate.

Chenin Blanc (cheu-ninh blanhk) A French grape variety from which excellent white wine is made.

chenna See **paneer.**

cherimoya (chay-ri-MOY-ah) A tropical South American tree of the custard apple family with large green-skinned fruit; after peeling the smooth or scaly skin, the interior pulp is eaten raw and unsweetened; its taste is somewhere between that of the pineapple and the strawberry.

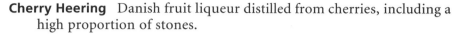

Cherry Heering   Danish fruit liqueur distilled from cherries, including a high proportion of stones.

cherrystone clam   See **quahog.**

chervil   An herb of the parsley family, originating in Russia and the Middle East and known from ancient times; its delicate flavor, slightly aniselike, is lost in stewing and drying, so it is best used fresh.

Cheshire   An English cows' milk cheese, cooked, hard-pressed, and aged, made in red (with **annatto**), white (uncolored), and blue; a venerable cheese that cannot be made elsewhere because of the special salty Cheshire pastureland; called *Chester* on the continent.

Chester   See **Cheshire.**

chestnut   See **marron.**

cheveux d'ange   (she-veu d'anjh)   French for angel hair pasta, the thinnest **vermicelli.** See also **capelli d'angelo.**

chèvre   (SHEV-ruh)   French for goat; by extension, goats' milk cheese that, properly speaking, is soft and fresh, uncooked and unpressed; specific *chèvre* cheeses are individually entered.

chevreuil   (shev-roy)   French for venison; roebuck.

Chevrotin   (shev-rō-tinh)   A French cheese of goats' milk, or occasionally a mixture of goats' and cows' milk, from Savoy; the cheese is uncooked, pressed, and shaped in a small disc.

Chianti   (kee-AHN-tee)   A red Italian table wine, ranging from pleasant to exceptional; very popular abroad as well as in its native Tuscany; *Chianti Classico* is particularly distinguished; Chianti bottles, or *fiaschi*, are shipped in their familiar woven-straw coverings.

Chiaretto   (kyah-RET-tō)   An Italian rosé wine produced near Lake Garda; light, fresh, and agreeable; *Chiarello* is virtually the same wine.

chicharrones   (chee-chah-RŌ-nays)   Spanish for pork cracklings.

chicken-fried steak   Steak dipped in batter and fried crisp like chicken; a African-American specialty.

chicken Kiev   Boned chicken breast rolled up to enclose an herb-flavored butter, egg-and-breadcrumbed, and deep-fried; the delicious butter has been known to squirt out on the unwary diner.

chicken paprikash   See **paprikás csirke.**

chicken steak A cut of beef from the **chuck,** in small individual portions with a characteristic white streak down the center.

chicken Tetrazzini Strips of cooked chicken and spaghetti in a cream sauce flavored with sherry and Parmesan, *gratiné;* named for the Italian coloratura soprano Luisa Tetrazzini.

chickpea A round legume, often dried, used extensively in Mediterranean, Middle Eastern, Indian, and Mexican cooking; an important ingredient in **couscous, hummus,** and many soups and stews.

chicory A group of related plants—including **Belgian endive, radicchio, escarole,** wild chicory (the roots of the latter are roasted and used to flavor coffee), and a bitter green often called curly endive or frisée, which is cooked or used in salads.

chiffonnade (shee-fohn-nad) In French cuisine, leaf vegetables sliced into very thin strips, particularly lettuce and **sorrel** shredded and sautéed in butter.

chilaquiles (chee-lah-KEE-lays) In Mexican cooking, **tortillas** layered with beans, ham, chicken, tomato sauce, and cheese.

Child, Lydia Maria (1802–80) An American abolitionist and author whose cookbook, *The American Frugal Housewife* (1829), gained wide popularity due to its common sense and directness.

chili The fruit of the pepper plant, from the *Capsicum* family, ranging in its many varieties from mild to fiery hot; the pungency is concentrated in the white tissue attached to the seeds, which should be handled with care. Originating in South America, chili peppers are used in many cuisines the world over; in common usage the word *chili* implies hot peppers. No relation to **black pepper,** an error first made by Columbus, who thought the chilies in the West Indies were the black pepper of the Indies. The plural of the Spanish word *chile* is *chiles;* the English spelling is either *chili* or *chilli,* with the plural *chilies* or *chillies*—a source of much confusion.

chili con carne A Mexican-American dish of beef highly seasoned with chili peppers and other spices and herbs; there are many variations, the subject of considerable controversy.

chilindrón, a la See under **pollo.**

chili powder Dried crushed chili peppers with other dried spices and herbs, including onion, garlic, cumin, cloves, coriander, and oregano.

chinchin   Round sweet doughballs, deep-fried, served at celebrations; from West Africa.

Chincoteague (CHINK-uh-tig)   Species of oyster from the Chesapeake Bay region, closely related to the **Blue Point.**

chine (chīn)   To separate the backbone from the ribs of a roast to make carving easier.

Chinese anise   See **ba jiao.**

Chinese beans   "Yard-long" beans, also called asparagus beans; bright green in color when cooked.

Chinese black beans   See **doù zhī.**

Chinese gooseberry   See **kiwi.**

Chinese parsley   See **coriander.**

Chinese sausages   Sausages usually of pork meat and fat, spiced and dried, and reddish in color; sometimes pork liver or even duck liver sausages are available in Chinese groceries in the United States.

chinois (shee-nwah)   French for a fine-mesh conical sieve shaped like a coolie hat—hence its name.

chinook   See **salmon.**

chipolata (chee-pō-LAH-tah)   A small Spanish sausage flavored with chives; in classical French cuisine the term designates a garnish of the sausages with braised chestnuts, diced pork, and glazed onions and carrots.

chipotle (chi-PŌT-lay)   A brownish-red chili pepper with wrinkled skin; dried, smoked, and often canned, this chili is very hot and has a distinctive smoky flavor.

chiqueter (sheek-tay)   To flute the edges of pastry with the fingertips, in French.

chitterlings, chitlins   The small intestines of pigs, scrubbed clean, boiled, and served with hot sauce; popular in Black and southern American cooking.

chive   An herb of the onion family, whose tall thin leaves delicately flavor savory foods.

chlodnik (KLOD-nik)   In Polish cooking, a cold summer soup of beet greens and roots, cucumbers, and onions, flavored with herbs, vinegar, and **kvass,** and garnished with sour cream; a warm-weather variety of **borsch.**

choclo (CHŌ-klō) Sweet corn in South America.

chocolate Product of cocoa tree beans after they have been fermented, roasted, shelled, and ground to produce chocolate liquor. Cocoa butter can be removed from the liquor to make **cocoa.** After refining (see **conch**) for high-quality chocolate, the various types are unsweetened chocolate, containing only chocolate liquor and cocoa butter, used for cooking; bittersweet chocolate, with a small amount of sugar added; semisweet chocolate, with more sugar than in bittersweet; sweet chocolate; milk chocolate, with milk solids to soften the chocolate flavor. Other flavorings can be added, but the more fat added other than cocoa butter, the cheaper the grade. See also **white chocolate.**

cholent (KHŌ-lent) **Brisket** with potatoes, lima beans, and pearl barley, slowly cooked overnight to be ready for the Jewish Sabbath.

chongos (CHONG-ōs) A Spanish custard with lemon and cinnamon.

chorek (SHŌ-rek) Sweet yeast bun, eaten for tea or toasted for breakfast in the Middle East.

chorizo (chor-EE-sō) A spicy sausage used in Spanish and Caribbean cooking, made of pork meat and fat and flavored with garlic and spices; the Portuguese is *chouriço.*

Choron (shohr-onh) In classical French cuisine, **béarnaise** sauce colored pink with a little tomato purée.

chou (shoo) French for cabbage.

chouchi (choo-chee) Cambodian fish dish with coconut milk, chilies, garlic, lemongrass, and peanuts.

choucroute (shoo-kroot) French for **sauerkraut;** *choucroute garnie* **à l'alsacienne** is a favorite French dish.

chou farci (shoo faahr-see) French for stuffed cabbage.

chou-fleur (shoo fleur) French for cauliflower.

chouriço See **chorizo.**

choux de Bruxelles (shoo deu brüks-el) French for Brussels sprouts.

choux pastry See **pâte à choux.**

chow-chow A Chinese-American vegetable pickle flavored with mustard; the original Chinese condiment consisted of orange peel in a thick syrup, flavored with ginger and other spices.

cochon (kō-shonh)   French for pig; the culinary term, like that in English, is *porc*.

cocido (kō-THEE-dō, kō-SEE-dō)   Spanish for stew; also means cooked, as opposed to fresh; *cozido* is an elaborate Brazilian stew.

cock-a-leekie   A Scottish soup made from chicken broth, leeks, and sometimes prunes and pieces of chicken.

cocoa   The remaining nibs in chocolate manufacture after the chocolate butter is liquefied; the pods of the **cacao** tree are fermented, roasted, and ground until the chocolate butter is liquefied, leaving the nibs, which are then powdered to make cocoa. Cocoa is thus much lower in fat than chocolate proper. See also **chocolate.**

cocotte (kō-KOT)   French for casserole; a cooking pot with a closely fitted lid for slow braising or stewing.

cod   A fish with great historic importance for its economic value in centuries past and an essential part of the triangle that supported the slave trade. Cod meat is lean, firm, white, and mild, with a large flake, suitable fresh for diverse cooking methods and with many flavors. Salted, smoked, or dried, it can be preserved for long periods; as *morue*, **brandade**, *bacalao*, *bacalhau*, **lutefisk,** and **finnan haddie** it is often preferred to fresh cod. Haddock, hake, and pollock are members of the cod family.

...da di bue (KŌ-dah dee BOO-ay)   Oxtail in Italian.

...dorniz (kō-DOR-neeth)   Spanish for quail.

...ur à la crème (KEUR ah lah KREM)   A cream-cheese dessert from provincial France in which heavy cream and cream cheese are combined and molded in a heart-shaped form that allows the whey to drain off, then turned out and garnished with strawberries or other berries.

...ac (kō-nyak)   Brandy, blended and aged, from the French town of the same name in the Charentes district north of Bordeaux.

... (kwinh)   French for quince.

...eau (kwonh-trō)   A colorless orange-flavored French liqueur, formerly called Triple Sec White **Curaçao.**

...)   Spanish for cabbage.

...à la (ah lah kōl-bayr)   In classic French cuisine, fish dipped in breadcrumbed, and fried; *Colbert* butter is a chicken or meat made of butter, chopped parsley, and perhaps tarragon.

chowder   A thick soup, made from various foodstuffs; the word comes from the french *chaudière*, the iron cauldron in which it was cooked, which, in turn, derives from the Latin word for "warm." Today, chowder is usually made of seafood or perhaps vegetables, with a milk base.

christophine   See **chayote.**

chuck   Cut of beef from the forequarter, between the neck and shoulder, usually best for stewing or braising.

chud (choot)   Thai for clear soup.

chuleta (choo-LAY-tah)   Spanish for chop.

chūn juǎn (tswin juan)   Spring roll; a thin, round pastry wrapper made from flour and water, stuffed with various fillings, such as shrimp, pork, and black mushrooms, wrapped up, and deep-fried to a golden brown; this authentic Chinese food is served at the spring festival to celebrate the Chinese New Year, and its elegant appearance is said "to resemble a bar of gold"; not to be confused with **cai juan.**

chuno   See **papa seca.**

chupe (CHOO-pay)   Chowder, usually of seafood, in South American cooking.

churrasco (shoor-RAHS-kō)   Charcoal-grilled meat, originally from Portugal and very popular in Brazil; restaurants that serve it are called *churrasqueirias.*

churro (CHOOR-rō)   Spanish for doughnut.

chutney   See **chatni.**

ciboulette (see-boo-let)   French for chives.

cicely, sweet cicely   A fragrant herb of the parsley family little used today, whose anise-flavored leaves and seeds contribute to salads and **bouquets garnis.**

cider   Apple juice, or sometimes another fruit juice, either fermented or not. In the United States, sweet cider is unfermented, while hard cider is slightly alcoholic; in Europe, fermented cider can range widely in alcoholic content and is often sparkling. Cider can also be made into apple brandy or vinegar and is often used in cooking in any of its many forms.

cigala (thee-GAH-lah)   Spanish for saltwater **crayfish,** a small lobster; the British call it a Dublin Bay prawn, the French *langoustine*, the Italian *scampo.*

cilantro (see-LAHN-trō)   Spanish for fresh **coriander** leaf.

cilièga (chee-LYAY-gah)   Italian for cherry.

Cincho (theen-CHŌ)   A ewes' milk cheese, from Spain; hard and pungent, similar to **Villalón.**

cinnamon   A spice from the dried bark of an evergreen tree indigenous to Asia and used since the Egyptians (third millennium B.C.); cinnamon was one of the most desirable Eastern spices from ancient to medieval times, but is now mainly relegated to flavoring desserts, at least in the West. Cinnamon is often confused with its close relative **cassia,** especially in powdered form.

cioccolata (chōk-kō-LAH-tah)   Italian for chocolate.

cioppino (chō-PEE-nō)   A fisherman's stew, often made with tomatoes; originally the *ciuppin* of Genoa, by way of San Francisco, where it is a favorite.

cipolla (chee-PŌL-lah)   Italian for onion.

Circassian chicken   See **çerkez tavuğu.**

cisco (SIS-kō)   A North American lake **whitefish**, usually smoked.

ciseler (see-zeh-lay)   In French, to cut into julienne strips or shred as for a **chiffonnade;** to score a whole fish to hasten cooking.

citron   A fruit of the citrus family, resembling a large, lumpy lemon; cultivated for its thick rind, which is candied or pressed; its oil is used in making liqueurs, perfume, and medicine.

citron (see-tronh)   French for lemon; *citron vert* means lime.

civet (see-vay)   A French stew of furred game, cooked with red wine, onions, mushrooms, and **lardons,** and thickened with the animal's blood.

civette (see-vet)   French for chives.

clabber   Buttermilk—soured, thickened milk that has not yet separated.

clafouti (kla-foo-tee)   A French pudding from Limousin made of small fruit, such as cherries or plums, with a thick egg batter poured over and baked.

clam   A saltwater bivalve **mollusk** in many varieties, generally divided into hard-shell (see **quahog**), which are eaten raw or cooked, and soft-shell, usually eaten cooked.

Clamart, à la (ah lah kla-maahr)   In French cuisine, garnished with peas.

clambake   See **New England clambake.**

claret   The British term for red **Bordeaux** wine.

clarified butter   Butter that has been heated to separate the impurities, thus allowing their easy removal; butter so treated has a higher burning point and clearer color but less flavor; also called drawn butter.

clarify   To remove all impurities from stock or jelly (usually with egg white) or from fat.

classed or **classified growth**   Wine, especially from the Fren Bordeaux, that has been officially ranked, usually by Classification of 1855 for Médoc. At that time, the best vine and estates were ranked *Cru Classé* ("Classed Growth"), incl the five official Growths—*Premier Cru* (First Growth) t *Cinquième Cru* (Fifth Growth)—and various lower rankings. *Cru Exceptionnel, Cru Bourgeois Supérieur,* and *Cru Bourgeoi* latter were often fine wines and not "inferior" at all in sense.) Since only Médoc and Sauternes were included i Classification, many excellent wines were omitted altoge

clementine   A hybrid produced by crossing the orange wit ine; small, sweet, and seedless.

clos (klō)   A specific vineyard, usually one of distinction, *Vougeot* of the **Côte d'Or** in Burgundy.

clotted cream   Cream skimmed from scalded milk an until it thickens; a specialty of Devonshire, Englan

cloud ear   See **yún ěr.**

clou de girofle (KLOO deu JHEE-RŌF-leh)   Clove;

clove   The dried bud of an east Indian evergre ancient times and a desirable commodity in th the name derives from the Latin word for na

club steak   A cut of beef from the **loin** between tion; tender and flavorful, it is the same as

cobbler   A deep-dish fruit pie with a thick top resembles cobblestones.

cocada (kō-KAH-dah)   Spanish for cocon

cochineal   See **carmine.**

cochino (kō-CHEE-nō)   Spanish for pig

Colby An American variety of Cheddar cheese; a washed-curd cheese, originally from Colby, Wisconsin.

colcannon An Irish peasant dish of cabbage, potatoes, leeks, and milk, traditionally eaten at Halloween with a "treasure," such as a ring, coin, thimble, or button, hidden within.

colère, en (enh kō-layr) In French cooking, fish, usually whiting, cooked with its tail in its mouth, giving it a so-called "angry" look; often dipped in egg, breadcrumbed, and deep-fried, and served *à la française*, with a tomato sauce.

coliflor (kō-lee-flor) Spanish for cauliflower.

colin (kō-linh) French for hake.

collage (kō-lahjh) French for **fining.**

collard, collard greens A type of cabbage whose leaves do not form a head; highly nutritious and able to withstand very hot and very cold temperatures; it is a favorite country vegetable in the southern United States but needs long, slow cooking.

collé (kō-lay) In French, with gelatin added.

collop A slice of meat; an old British term that has been used variously but now usually means a **scallop** of meat or fish.

colza See **canola oil.**

comal (kō-MAL) A Mexican cast-iron griddle or earthenware plate for making **tortillas.**

com chay (kohm chī) "Bhudda rice," cooked with coconut milk, ginger, and soy sauce; a Vietnamese vegetarian dish served on holidays.

comida (kō-MEE-dah) Spanish for meal, usually meaning lunch.

comino (kō-MEE-nō) Spanish for cumin.

commis (komh-mee) French for apprentice.

commune (komh-mün) French for a township or village and its surrounding land; frequently used to describe wine-producing regions.

composé(e) (komh-pō-say) A French term describing a salad that is arranged or composed in its serving dish or plate, rather than tossed.

compote (komh-PŌT) In French, a dish of fresh or dried fruit stewed slowly in syrup to keep its shape, often flavored with liqueur and spices and served cold.

compound butter   Butter combined with other seasonings such as herbs, shallots, and wine.

concasser (konh-kas-say)   In French cooking, to pound in a mortar or chop roughly; often applied to tomatoes that have been peeled, seeded, and chopped for sauce; _concassé_ is the adjective.

conch (konk)   A gastropod mollusk usually eaten in chowder or salad, mostly in Florida and the Caribbean. Conch (pronounced konch) is also the name of the curved trough, resembling the shell, in which refined chocolate particles are churned with **cocoa** butter to a smooth liquid; this process, essential to high-quality melting chocolate, is called _conching._

conchiglia (kon-KEE-lyah)   Italian for shellfish; pasta in the shape of a conch shell.

concombre (KONH-KOMH-bruh)   French for cucumber.

Condé (konh-day)   In French cuisine, with rice; also a pastry strip covered with almond icing and many other sweet or savory dishes, often with rice.

condensed milk   Milk with its water content reduced by slightly more than half, sterilized, homogenized, and canned; sweetened condensed milk has sugar added as a preservative and may not be sterilized; both types taste sweeter than regular milk.

condiment   Relish, pickle, or seasoning, highly aromatic, that accompanies food at the table and stimulates the appetite.

conejo (kon-AY-hō)   Spanish for rabbit.

confectioners' sugar   Powdered white sugar, not crystallized like superfine sugar, useful for its ability to dissolve quickly.

confectionery   The art of sugar working or candy making.

confiserie (konh-fee-seh-ree)   French for confectionery, confectioner's shop; _confiseur_ means confectioner in French.

confit (konh-fee)   Pork, goose, duck, or other meat, cooked and preserved in its own fat; a specialty of Gascony in southwestern France; also fruits and vegetables cooked and preserved in a brandy or liquor syrup.

confiture (konh-fee-tür)   French for preserve, jam.

cōng (tson)   Chinese for scallion; _yáng cōng_ (literally, "Occidental scallion") means onion.

congrí oriental (kon-gree or-yen-tal) Popular dish of red beans and rice from eastern Cuba, where the red bean rather than black predominates.

coniglio (kō-NEE-lyō) Italian for rabbit.

consommé (konh-somh-may) French for clear broth; meat, chicken, game, or fish stock flavored with vegetables, strained, reduced, and usually clarified.

coo coo Ball of steamed cornmeal and okra, sliced and served with **callaloo,** from Barbados.

copeaux en chocolat (kō-pō enh shō-kō-la) French for chocolate shavings.

çorba (CHOR-bah) Turkish for soup; the Persian is *shourba.*

corvina (kor-VEE-nah) Spanish for bass.

coq au vin (kōk ō vinh) In French cooking, chicken cut up and braised with onions, mushrooms, and **lardoons** in red wine.

coquillage (kō-kee-yajh) French for shellfish.

coquille de (kō-kee deu) French for served in a scallop shell.

coquille Saint-Jacques (kō-kee sinh-jhak) French for scallop; the apostle St. James wore the shell as his emblem. Also the name of a creamy scallop dish.

coral Lobster roe, which turns red when cooked; used for sauces and butters.

coratèlla (kor-ah-TEL-lah) Italian for organ meats.

cordero (kor-DAYR-ō) Spanish for lamb; a suckling or milk-fed lamb is *cordero lechazo* or *lechal.*

Cordon Bleu The "blue ribbon" awarded to outstanding women chefs, a tradition going back to a story, perhaps apocryphal, of Madame de Pompadour and Louis XV; the name also designates a dish of chicken or veal scallops cooked with cheese and ham, which came from the Cordon Bleu cooking school in Paris in the early twentieth century.

coriander An herb valued both for its dried seeds and fresh leaves; used extensively in Oriental, Indian, and Spanish cooking; the Spanish word for fresh coriander is **cilantro.**

corn A new-world grain from Central America, upon which the pre-Columbian cultures were founded; still the main food crop on the

American continent (in the United States indirectly, through live-stock and dairy feed). Columbus brought corn, or maize, to the Old World, where it has slowly gained acceptance. Corn, of which there are countless varieties, cannot sow itself and is therefore unknown in the wild. In Europe, corn is the generic name for whatever grain is dominant in a particular area. See also **polenta.**

corned beef   Salted and spiced brisket of beef, the traditional ingredient of **New England boiled dinner.** "Corned" means granulated; hence, corning means to preserve with salt.

cornet (kohr-NAY)   In French, a horn-shaped pastry stuffed with sweetened whipped cream; a slice of meat, such as ham, rolled into a cone and often filled, for a garnish or hors d'oeuvre.

corn flour   British term for **cornstarch.**

Cornish hen   See **Rock Cornish game hen.**

Cornish pasty (PAS-tee, not PAYS-tee)   A pastry turnover enclosing a meat and potato filling; originally from Cornwall.

corn pone   Cornmeal dough shaped into ovals and deep-fried or baked; a southern American bread served with butter and sometimes **pot liquor;** the word *pone* is of American Indian origin.

corn salad   See **lamb's lettuce.**

cornstarch   Very fine white flour milled from corn; used as a thickening agent for sauces and sometimes for baking; used extensively in Chinese cooking; sometimes called corn flour.

Corton (kohr-tonh)   Excellent red and white wines from the village of Aloxe-Corton in the Côte de Beaune region of Burgundy.

corvina (kor-VEE-nah) Spanish for bass.

cos   Romaine lettuce.

coscetto (kō-SHET-tō)   Italian for leg of lamb.

còscia (KŌ-shah)   Italian for thigh, as of chicken; leg, as of lamb.

cosciotto, coscetto (kō-SHOT-tō; kō-SHET-tō)   Italian for leg of lamb; haunch.

costata (kō-STAH-tah)   Italian for rib or chop.

costoletta, cotoletta (kō-stō-LET-tah, kō-tō-LET-tah)   Italian for chop or cutlet; *costilla* is Spanish for chop or cutlet.

côte (kōt)   French for rib or chop.

cotechino (kō-teh-KEE-nō)   In Italian cooking, a large fresh sausage made with pork meat and rind and seasoned with nutmeg and cloves; sometimes delicate, sometimes very spicy.

Côte de Beaune   See **Côte d'Or.**

Côte de Nuits   See **Côte d'Or.**

Côte d'Or (kōt d'ohr)   A narrow strip of hillside along the Saône River valley in Burgundy, southeast of Paris, comprising the *Côte de Dijon* in the uppermost part, the *Côte de Nuits* in the middle, and the *Côte de Beaune* in the southernmost part; in the latter two most of the greatest French wines are produced, hence the meaning of its name, "golden slope."

côtelette (kōt-let)   French for cutlet.

Côte Rôtie (kōt rō-tee)   A famous red wine from steep slopes overlooking the Rhône River in France.

Côtes de Provence (kōt deu prō-venhs)   Red, white, and rosé wines produced on the southern coast of France between Nice and Marseilles; light, pleasant, fairly inexpensive, and popular.

Côtes du Rhône (kōt dü rōn)   Pleasant but undistinguished wines, mostly red, from the Rhône Valley between Vienne and Avignon in France; the finer wines of the region are sold under more specific **appellations.**

cotriade (kō-tree-ad)   A fish soup from Brittany.

cottage cheese   Fresh lumpy cheese made from skimmed pasteurized cows' milk in which the curds are washed; its taste is bland and slightly acid, lending itself to various flavorings; also used in salads and cheesecake and with fruit; it is high in protein but low in fat.

còtto (KOHT-tō)   Italian for cooked.

coulibiac   See **kulibyaka.**

coulis (koo-lee)   An old French culinary term of some confusion; originally the strained juices from cooked meat, then a purée of chicken, game, or fish; now it usually means a **bisque,** thick sauce, or purée, such as tomato or berry.

Coulommiers (koo-lohm-myay)   A whole-milk cows' cheese from **Brie,** east of Paris, usually eaten fresh but sometimes molded and aged like Brie; shaped in wheels smaller than Brie, with a white rind flora; the interior is creamy white and increasingly flavorful with age.

country style spareribs A cut of pork—the backbones from the shoulder end of pork loin, cooked like breast **spareribs.**

courge (koorjh) French for marrow, squash.

courgette (koor-JHET) British for zucchini.

couronne, en (enh koor-on) French for in the shape of a crown; in a ring.

court bouillon (koor boo-yonh) In French cuisine, flavored, acidulated stock for cooking food, primarily fish, but also vegetables and meat.

couscous (koos-koos) The quintessential dish of Morocco, Algeria, and Tunisia prepared variously but usually consisting of **semolina** pasta steamed on top of a special two-part pot over meat and vegetable **tajins** cooked below, served all together with a hot sauce. Also the name for the little rounds of **semolina** that go into it; the special pot is called a *couscoussière.*

couverture (koo-vayr-tür) High-grade chocolate used especially for coating and ornamental work; it is semisweet and high in cocoa butter, giving it a glossy surface.

cozza (KOT-zah) Italian for mussel.

crab A large and varied family of clawed crustaceans with delicate white meat; all true crabs are edible, and some of them are separately entered.

crackling The crisp brown skin of pork or sometimes poultry with all its fat rendered; sometimes baked into breads.

crapaudine, à la (ah lah kra-pō-deen) Poultry, especially small birds, trussed to look like toad (*crapaud* in French).

crayfish A crustacean with many species, usually freshwater, varying widely in size but most often smaller than a lobster; these "dainties of the first order," as Audubon called them, are prized delicacies in many cuisines but largely ignored in the United States, except for the **Creole** and **Cajun** cooking of Louisiana. The freshwater crayfish is sometimes called crawfish or (in French) *écrevisse;* the saltwater crayfish is also called crawfish, rock or spiny lobster, *langouste, langoustine* (in French), Dublin Bay prawn (in Britain), Norway lobster, and *scampo* (in Italy). There is considerable confusion among these terms.

cream The fatty part of milk, which rises to the surface unless homogenized. Single cream is 45 percent butterfat, measured by the percentage of dry matter rather than volume; double cream is 60 percent butterfat; triple cream is 75 percent. In cheesemaking, additional cream must sometimes be added to the milk to bring it up to the degree of butterfat required.

cream cheese Fresh unripened whole-milk cows' cheese, with a high fat content (varying with different types); in the United States this cheese is usually factory made, with stabilizers added to keep the whey from draining further, but there are many versions throughout the world.

cream puff pastry See **pâte à choux.**

Crécy, à la (ah lah kray-see) With carrots; from the town of the same name, where the finest French carrots were grown.

crema (KRAY-mah) Spanish for custard, cream.

crémant (kray-manh) French wine term for a lightly sparkling wine.

crème à l'anglaise (krem ah l'anh-glez) French for custard.

crème brûlée (krem brü-lay) French for a rich custard topped with a brittle layer of sugar (usually brown sugar), caramelized under the broiler just before serving.

crème Chantilly See **Chantilly.**

crème chiboust (krem shee-boost) **Crème pâtissière** lightened with **Italian meringue,** usually stabilized with a little gelatin.

crème fraîche (krem fresh) French for heavy cream with a lactic culture introduced; the culture acts as a preservative and gives a characteristic tangy flavor; see also **fleurette.**

crème pâtissière (krem pa-tee-syayr) French for pastry cream—a custard of eggs, flour, milk, and sugar used to fill cream puffs, line tarts underneath fruit, and garnish various pastries.

crème pralinée (krem pra-lee-nay) **Crème pâtissière** flavored with powdered **praline;** used to fill **Paris-Brest** and other French pastries.

crème renversée (krem renh-vayr-say) A French custard baked in a caramel-lined mold, chilled, and inverted for serving.

cremini (kre-MEE-nee) A variety of cultivated white mushroom with fuller flavor and earthier texture; the singular is *cremino*; a **portobello** is a fully mature *cremino*.

Creole In Louisiana, food cooked in the Creole style usually begins with sautéed tomatoes, onions, celery, and sweet peppers, and often includes rice; it combines the many local influences—French, Spanish, African and Indian—in a unique way; see also **Cajun.** In classic French cuisine, *à la créole* designates a dish garnished with rice and containing sweet peppers, onion, and tomatoes cooked in oil.

crêpe (krep)   A pancake made thin, light, and surprisingly strong from the eggy batter; invariably stuffed, spread, or served with moist mixtures, either savory or sweet.

crêpes Suzette (krep sü-zet)   **Crêpes** heated in a chafing dish at table with a sauce of orange juice and zest, butter, and orange-flavored liqueur, and flambéed.

crépinette (kray-pee-net)   A small French sausage wrapped in **caul** rather than casing, usually made of pork, and occasionally truffled; *crépine* is pig's **caul.**

Crescenza   See **Stracchino.**

crespella (kres-PEL-lah)   An Italian pancake, usually stuffed like a **crêpe.**

crevette (kreh-vet)   French for shrimp.

croaker   A large family of fish, sometimes called drum, found mostly in temperate western Atlantic waters; it is named for the noise it makes during spawning season; croaker is excellent in various culinary preparations but should not be eaten raw.

croissant (kwah-sanh)   A light yeast-dough pastry layered like puff pastry, rolled into a "crescent" shape, sometimes stuffed, and baked; an indispensable part of the French breakfast. In 1686 the bakers of Budapest heard the Turks tunneling into the city by night and sounded the alarm. The grateful city gave them the privilege of making this pastry, whose shape comes from the emblem on the Ottoman flag.

croquembouche (krōk-emh-boosh)   French bite-size cream puffs piled high into a pyramid and cemented together with sugar glaze or caramel; other pastries and fruits arranged in a highly ornamented pile.

croque monsieur (krōk muh-syeu)   The French version of a grilled ham and cheese sandwich, often cooked in a special device; a *croque madame* is a cheese and chicken and fried egg sandwich.

croqueta (krō-KAY-tah)   Spanish for croquette.

croquette (krō-ket)   Chopped meat or vegetables bound with a sauce, crumbed, and fried into a crisp, brown cylindrical shape; originally French.

cròsta, crostata, crostatina (KRŌ-stah, krō-STAH-tah, krō-stah-TEE-nah) Italian for crust, pie, tart.

crostacei (krō-STAH-chay) Italian for shellfish.

crostino (krō-STEE-nō) Italian **croûton** or **croûte**; a small piece of toast.

Crottin de Chavignol (krō-tinh deu sha-vee-nyōl) A French goats' milk cheese from Berry; semihard to hard, shaped in very small discs; aging brings out its goaty flavor, an acquired taste that is favored by connoisseurs; *crottin* literally means "dung."

croustade (kroo-stad) French for hollowed bread or pastry that serves as a base for a savory purée or ragoût.

croûte (kroot) French for crust, shell, or piece of bread or dough used in various savory preparations; *en croûte* means encased in pastry.

croûton (kroo-tonh) French for a small piece of bread or dough used for garnish; sautéed bread cubes.

crown roast Loin of pork or two loins of lamb from the rib section, tied into a crown, trimmed, and roasted; the ends of the rib bones are often decorated with paper frills, the center filled with a vegetable or starch stuffing.

cru (krü) French for growth; that is, a specific vineyard and its wine; a vineyard of superior quality. See also **classed growth.**

crudités (krü-dee-tay) Raw food, usually vegetables, eaten before a meal to assuage hunger and stimulate appetite.

crudo (KROO-dō) Italian and Spanish for raw, fresh.

crumble British dessert of juicy raw fruit topped with crumbly pastry and baked.

crustacean A class of arthropods, mostly water-dwelling, with a hard shell; includes all members of the **lobster, shrimp, crayfish,** and **crab** families.

cruzado (kroo-SAH-dō) "Cross-breed" soup of beef, chicken, or fish and vegetables in broth, in many variations, from Venezuela.

cú (tsoo) Chinese for vinegar.

cua rang muoi (kooah rang mooee) A Vietnamese dish of crabs fried with garlic and onion; sometimes called "salt and pepper crab."

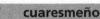

cuaresmeño (kwah-res-MAY-nyō)   A green chili pepper sometimes confused with the **jalapeño,** but actually darker, rounder, hotter, and less flavorful.

cu cai hu (koo kaee hoo)   Preserved cabbage in Vietnamese cooking.

cube   To cut food into cubes about ½ inch across; larger than **dice** or **mirepoix.**

cuisse (kwees)   French for drumstick; *cuisseau* means leg, usually of veal.

cuissot (kwee-sō)   French for haunch of venison or boar.

culotte (kü-loht)   French for rump of beef.

Cumberland sauce   Red-currant jelly dissolved with port and flavored with shallots, orange zest, and mustard—a traditional British accompaniment to ham, venison, and other game.

cumin (KUH-min)   A pungent spice made from the dried and ground seeds of the cumin plant; a relative of parsley, cumin is used in Mexican, North African, Middle Eastern, and Asian cooking, especially curries. The seeds look like those of **caraway,** and European languages often confuse the two spices despite their different tastes.

cuore (KWOHR-ay)   Italian for heart.

Curaçao (kyoor-a-SOW)   A liqueur made from the dried peel of the green sour oranges found on the island of Curaçao in the Dutch Antilles; **Cointreau, triple sec,** and **Grand Marnier** are similar to Curaçao.

curd   The solid residue of coagulated milk that separates from liquid whey after acidification in the cheesemaking process.

cure   To age a food product, such as cheese, wine, fish, or meat, in order to preserve it by methods such as drying, salting, or smoking.

curly endive   See **chicory.**

Curnonsky   The pen name of French gastronome, journalist, and food critic Maurice-Edmond Sailland (1872–1956); he encouraged interest in regional French cuisine and the development of the restaurant as we know it.

currant   Small berry, juicy, tart, and high in pectin, used in savory and sweet cooking, especially in Northern Europe. Of its three colors, red, black, and white, the red is most common, black (**cassis**) is larger in size and muskier in flavor than the translucent red, and white (actually colorless) is milder. Since the bush is host to white pine blister rot, its cultivation and sale is limited in some states.

curry   A mixture of spices widely used in Indian cooking for thousands of years, originally as a preservative. Ground on a special stone, the particular spices vary according to individual taste, a specific dish, or regional preferences (those of the south tend to be hotter). The **masala**, or spice mixture, can be either wet (in which case it is ground with vinegar, coconut milk, or water and must be used immediately) or dry (in which case it is ground to a powder that can be kept for a while). The many spices (most entered separately) include turmeric, cumin, coriander, fenugreek, fennel seed, saffron, mace, nutmeg, cardamom, clove, cinnamon, poppy and sesame seeds, tamarind, onion, garlic, and chilies. See also **garam.**

curry leaf   An Asian plant whose leaves, fresh and dried, are widely used in the cooking of southern India.

custard   Milk and egg mixture cooked gently (below boiling to avoid curdling) on the stove or in the oven.

custard apple   A general term for various tropical fruits, including the **cherimoya.**

custard marrow   See **chayote.**

cut in   To mix particles of fat, such as butter or lard, throughout flour with two knives or a pastry blender.

cutlet   A **scallop** of meat—usually a slice from the leg and preferably from one muscle.

cuvée (kü-vay)   French for a particular blend, lot, or batch of wine.

cygne (SEE-nyuh)   French for swan, made from **pâte à choux** and filled with **crème Chantilly.**

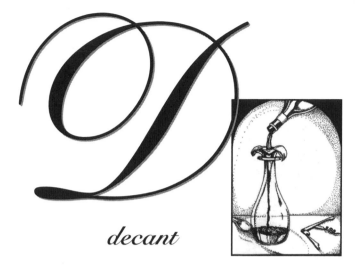

decant

dab See **flounder.**

dacquoise (da-KWAHZ) A French pastry made of **meringue** combined with finely ground nuts, baked in discs, and filled with flavored whipped cream or buttercream and often fresh berries.

daging (dah-ging) Indonesian and Malaysian for beef; *semur daging* is slices of cooked beef in gingered soy sauce.

daikon (dī-kon) A large radish used extensively in Japanese cooking, either in raw or cooked form.

daiquirí A cocktail of white rum and lime juice, named for the town in eastern Cuba; Hemingway's favorite drink.

daizu (dī-zoo) Dried soybeans.

dak jim (tahk chim) Korean chicken stew marinated and simmered with seasonings and vegetables.

dal In Indian cooking, legumes of all sorts; *arhal dal,* lentils.

dalchini (dahl-CHEE-nee) Cinnamon or cassia, in Indian cooking.

dam bay (dahm bī) Cambodian for cooked rice.

Dampfnudeln (DAHMPF-noo-deln) German yeast dumplings sweetened and served with fruit.

dàn (dahn) Chinese for egg.

Danablu (DAH-nah-bleu) A Danish blue cheese of whole raw cows' milk, made in the **Roquefort** style.

dandelion   Familiar weed whose young leaves when cultivated contribute a pleasant bitterness to salads, braises, and sautés; see also **pissenlit.**

Danish pastry   A yeast pastry filled with nuts, fruit, custard, or cheese, and iced; originally from Denmark, but much traveled since.

Daõ   (dow)   Red and white table wines produced in the Daõ river valley in the town of Viseu in Portugal; they are full-bodied, deep in color, and made from the same grape varieties as **port.**

dariole   (daahr-yōl)   French for a cylindrical mold, usually small; also a cake baked in such a mold.

Darjeeling   A variety of tea from the Indian province of the same name.

darne   (daahrn)   French for fish steak; a thick cross section of fish.

dasheen   See **taro.**

dashi   (dah-shee)   Japanese fish stock made of dried bonito and seaweed; used extensively in Japanese cooking.

dàttero   (DAT-tayr-ō)   Italian for date.

daube, en   (enh dōb)   In French cooking, meat, usually beef, slowly braised in red wine and seasonings; stew; a *daubière* is a tight-lidded casserole for cooking *daubes,* originally with indentations in the lid for charcoal.

Daumont, à la   (ah lah dō-monh)   In French cooking, a large fish garnished with quenelles, roe, mushrooms, and crayfish, served with **Nantua sauce.**

dauphine, à la   (ah lah dō-feen)   In French cooking, potato purée mixed with **pâte à choux** and deep-fried in balls or piped shapes.

dauphinoise   (dō-feen-WAZ)   In French cooking, in the style of Dauphiné, potatoes *à la dauphinoise* are sliced and baked with milk, egg yolk, nutmeg, **Gruyère,** and garlic.

daurade   (dō-rad)   French for gilthead **bream;** *dorade* is another type of bream.

David, Elizabeth   (1913–92)   English foodwriter whose early evocative books on Mediterranean food, published in the 1950s, helped to bring England out of post-war food-rationing attitudes about cooking. Her later books, such as *English Bread and Yeast Cookery* (1977), became more scholarly.

débourbage (day-boor-bajh) French for clearing of the sediment from newly pressed grape juice, especially white, by allowing it to settle for twenty-four hours before starting fermentation; this technique must be closely controlled.

debrecziner (deh-breh-zeen-er) A Hungarian sausage similar to a **Frankfurter** but spicier and coarser in texture.

decant To transfer wine from bottle to carafe or decanter, in order to remove sediment before serving; decanting is practiced primarily with old red wines, whose bottles are held against the light of a candle to show sediment as it first appears.

découper (day-koo-pay) In French, to cut up, to carve.

dee la Thai for sesame seeds.

deep-fry To cook food immersed in a large amount of hot fat, thus sealing the outside while keeping the inside moist.

déglacer (day-gla-say) In French, to deglaze by dissolving, with wine, stock, or other liquid, the sediment left in the pan after meat, poultry, or fish has been cooked in a small amount of fat.

dégorger (day-gohr-jhay) In French, to soak a food, such as sweetbreads, in cold water in order to cleanse it; also an important final step in making Champagne, whereby the sediment is removed from the bottle before the **dosage** and final cork are added.

dégraisser (day-gres-say) In French, to remove grease from the surface of liquid, by skimming, or from a large piece of meat, by scraping or cutting.

dégustation (day-gü-sta-syonh) French for tasting or sampling.

Deidesheim (DĪ-des-hīm) A town in the German Palatinate producing excellent white wines, mostly Rieslings, with full body, fine bouquet, and varying sweetness.

Delmonico A boneless cut of beef from the rib section, roasted or cut into steaks; also called Spencer steak.

Demeltorte (DAY-mel-tor-teh) A pastry filled with candied fruit, from Demel's Café in Vienna.

demerara sugar (deh-meh-RAHR-ah) Partially refined raw cane sugar, naturally light brown in color from the molasses and similar to light brown sugar.

demi, demie (deu-mee) French for half.

demi-deuil, à la (ah lah deu-mee doy)   In French cooking, poultry and other pale-colored foods garnished with truffles to resemble "half-mourning"; with poultry, the truffle slices are slipped between the skin and breast meat.

demi-feuilletage See **rognures.**

demi-glace (deu-mee glas)   In French cuisine, brown sauce reduced by half—nearly to a glaze—with veal stock.

demijohn   A large, narrow-necked wine bottle or jug of varying size, sometimes in a wicker or straw jacket; from the French *Dame Jeanne.*

demi-sec (deu-mee sek)   A French term for Champagne and sparkling white wines denoting them as sweet, even though the literal meaning is "half-dry"; this is the sweetest category of Champagne.

demi-sel (deu-mee sel)   Soft, fresh, whole-milk cows' cheese from Normandy, in a small square.

Demi-Suisse See **Petit-Suisse.**

dendê (DEN-day)   Palm oil, orange in color, that is strong in flavor and characteristic of Brazilian cooking. Because dendê is hard to digest and highly saturated, other fats are often substituted outside Brazil.

dénerver (day-nayr-vay)   In French, to remove gristle, tendons, membrane, etc., from meat.

denjang (DEN-jahng)   Korean for soybean paste, a staple seasoning.

denominazione controllata (day-nō-mee-na-TSYŌ-nay con-trō-LAH-tah)   The Italian equivalent of **appellation contrôlée;** recently implemented.

dente, al (al DEN-tay)   In Italian, literally, to the bite; refers to pasta or vegetables cooked only until firm and crunchy, not soft and overdone.

dépecer (day-peh-say)   In French, to cut up, to carve.

deposit See **sediment.**

dépouiller (day-poo-yay)   In French, to skim the fat or scum from the surface of a sauce or stock.

Derby or **Derbyshire** (DAR-bee-shur)   English cows' milk cheese, uncooked and hard, pale and mild, made in large flat rounds by a method similar to that of **Cheddar; Sage Derby** is flavored and colored with the herb.

desayuno (day-sī-YOO-nō)   Spanish for breakfast.

deshebrar (day-sheh-BRAR)   In Spanish, to shred.

désosser (day-sohs-say)   In French, to bone.

détrempe (day-tremhp)   In French, dough of flour and water in which a layer of butter is encased in the making of **pâte feuilletée.**

Devonshire cream   See **clotted cream.**

dhania (DUH-nyah)   **Coriander** in Indian cuisine.

dhansak (DAHN-sahk)   Substantial Indian Parsi dish of meat or chicken, vegetables, lentils, and blended and dry **masala,** served at festival meals with rice and accompaniments.

diable, à la (ah lah DYA-bleh)   In French cooking, deviled—food, usually meat or poultry, spiced with mustard, vinegar, or hot seasoning, coated with breadcrumbs, and grilled; *sauce diable* is **demi-glace** with white wine or vinegar and cayenne pepper.

diablotins (dya-blō-tinh)   In French, cheese-flavored **croûtes** or **choux** for garnishing soup.

dice   Small squares of food, technically smaller than a cube.

dicke Bohnen mit Rauchfleisch (DI-keh BŌ-nen mit ROWKH-flīsh)   A Westphalian dish of broad beans with bacon and smoked pork belly.

dieppoise, à la (ah lah dyep-pwaz)   In French cuisine, saltwater fish garnished with mussels and crayfish in a white-wine reduction sauce.

diffa (DEE-fah)   A Moroccan banquet, where abundance is the hallmark of hospitality: very many dishes (but actually no waste).

Dijon (dee-jhonh) The capital of Burgundy; Dijon mustard has a white-wine base; *à la dijonnaise* means with a mustard-flavored sauce.

dill   An herb whose seeds and leaves flavor sweet and savory foods, especially in northern and eastern European countries; in the United States it is commonly used with vinegar for pickling cucumbers.

dím sàm (dem shim)   In Chinese cooking, small dishes, such as various dumplings, fried shrimp balls, spareribs, or fried spring rolls, eaten for snacks during the day; served in restaurants specializing in these dishes, which are from Canton; commonly spelled *dim sum,* it means "little heart."

dim sum   See **dím sàm.**

dinde (dinhd)   French for turkey hen; *dindon* is a cock, *dindonneau* a young turkey.

Dionysus See **Bacchus.**

dip Thai for raw, half-cooked.

diplomat pudding In British cooking, a molded dessert of ladyfingers soaked with candied fruit in liqueur or brandy and layered alternately with custard; diplomat sauce is **sauce normande** with lobster butter, garnished with diced lobster and truffles.

dirty rice Rice and beans dish from the southern United States, with chicken gizzards and livers that, along with garlic, onions, and peppers, give the rice its "dirty" appearance.

disossato (dee-sohs-SAH-tō) Italian for boned.

djaj (djaj) Arabic for chicken; in Moroccan cooking, one classic chicken **tajin** is *djaj emshmel,* with preserved lemons, olives, onions, and spices; another is *djaj masquid bil beid,* chicken with eggs, lemons, and olives.

Dobostorte (DŌ-bōsh-tor-teh) Thin layers of sponge cake spread with chocolate cream, stacked, and glazed with hot caramel; created by the Austrian *pâtissier* Josef Dobos.

dodine See **ballotine.**

doigts de Fatma (DWAH de FAHT-mah) "The fingers of Fatima," Mohammed's daughter; a Tunisian appetizer of meat, cheese, etc., wrapped in **malsouka.**

dolce (DŌL-chay) Italian for sweet; the plural, *i dolci,* means desserts.

Dolcelatte (DŌL-che-LAH-tay) An Italian mild blue-veined cheese, a younger and sweeter type of **Gorgonzola.**

Dolcetto (dōl-CHET-tō) A grape variety, grown in Piedmont, used in Italian red wines; soft and early maturing.

dolmasi (dōl-MAH-see.) In Turkish cooking, stuffed leaves or other vegetables; usually a blanched grape leaf filled with rice and ground lamb and braised in stock, oil, and lemon juice; the Persian is *dolmeh,* the Greek *dolmathes.*

dom yam gung (tohm yam guhng) Thai for shrimp in broth with chilies, **lemongrass,** lime juice, and citrus leaves; very popular.

domaine (dō-men) French vineyards comprising a single property, whether or not they are contiguous; in Bordeaux and Provence, the word means *château;* the German word is *Domaene.*

domates (dō-MAH-tays) Turkish for tomatoes.

Dom Perignon (domh payr-ee-nyonh) A Benedictine monk, cellar-master at the Abbey of Hautvilliers, whom tradition credits with the invention of the process for making Champagne; now the brand name of the best wine produced by Moët et Chandon.

donburi (don-boo-ree) In Japanese cooking, a bowl of rice topped with a mixture of leftovers.

döner kebab (deu-NAYR keh-BAHB.) See **kebab.**

dong (dohng) To pickle in Thai; *pak dong,* pickled vegetables.

dōng gū (dohng goo) Chinese dried black mushrooms with a strong smoky flavor.

Doppelbock (DOHP-pel-BOHK) Extra strong German **Bock** beer.

dorage (dō-rajh) See **dorure.**

dorato (dor-RAH-tō) In Italian cooking, dipped in egg batter and fried to a golden color.

dorée (do-ray) French for **John Dory** or *Saint-Pierre.*

Doria (dor-yah) In classical French cuisine, a garnish for fish of cucumbers that are shaped into small ovals and simmered in butter.

Dorsch German for cod.

dorure (dor-ür) In French cooking, egg wash for "gilding" pastry, made by beating together egg or egg yolk and a little water and brushing a thin layer on the surface of the pastry to color during baking.

dosa (DŌ-sah) Indian pancake of rice flour and ground lentils, sometimes eaten with chutney and spicy potatoes, when it is *dosa masala,* from southern India.

dosage (dō-zajh) French for sugar syrup added to bottled wine after the *dégorgement* (during the Champagne process), the amount of which determines the degree of sweetness of the finished wine.

dòu (dō) Chinese for bean.

double boiler See **bain-marie.**

Double Gloucester Cows' milk cheese with a rich, mellow flavor, dense, almost waxy texture, and deep yellow color from **annatto** dye, made in large flat rounds; so named because this English cheese, made from the whole milk of two milkings of the Gloucester cow, is twice as large as **Single Gloucester.**

dòu fu (dō foo)   Chinese for bean curd or **tōfu;** the Chinese *dòu fu* is drier and firmer than the Japanese **tōfu.**

dough   Flour or meal mixed with water, milk, or other liquid, for making bread or pastry.

Douro Valley (DOOR-ō)   River valley in Portugal where **port** is made.

doux, douce (doo, doos)   Sweet; as a wine term it implies sweetening by an agent rather than by nature.

dòu zhī (dō seu)   Chinese black beans; *chǐzhī* is black bean sauce, made from fermented black beans, which are rinsed and chopped before being added to sauces.

Dover sole   See **sole.**

dovi (DOR-vee)   Peanuts in the cooking of Zimbabwe; *huku ne dovi*, a chicken and peanut stew, with onions, tomatoes, and mushrooms; *nhopi dovi*, puréed pumpkin with peanut sauce, either hot or cold, sweet or savory.

dragée (dra-jhay)   French for sugar-coated almond; sugarplum.

dragoncello (drag-on-CHEL-lō)   Italian for tarragon.

Drambuie (drahm-BOO-ee)   A Scottish liqueur made from **Scotch malt whisky** flavored with heather honey.

drawn   Refers to a whole fish scaled and gutted but with head and fins left on; also, a bird with its insides removed.

drawn butter   See **clarified butter.**

dredge   To coat food with a dry ingredient such as flour, cornmeal, or breadcrumbs, shaking off the excess.

drum   See **croaker.**

dry   Wine term meaning not sweet.

dua (yooah)   Vietnamese for coconut; *nuoc cot dua*, unsweetened coconut milk.

Dubarry, à la (ah lah dü-baahr-ee)   In French cuisine, garnished with cauliflower shaped into balls, coated with Mornay sauce, and glazed with **château potatoes.**

Dublin Bay prawn   British term for saltwater **crayfish;** the French *langoustine*, the Italian *scampo,* the Norway lobster.

duchesse, à la (ah lah dü-shes) In French cuisine, potatoes boiled and puréed with eggs and butter and often piped as a garnish or border; a *duchesse* is a small cream puff stuffed with savory purée, coated with a **chaud-froid** sauce, and served as an hors d'oeuvre.

duck sauce See **suan mei jiāng.**

Dugléré (dü-glay-ray) Sole poached and served in a sauce of tomatoes, shallots, herbs, and white wine reduced and finished with cream; named for the famous eighteenth-century French chef, Dugléré.

düğün çorbası (dun CHOR-bah—seu) "Wedding soup," a Turkish dish of mutton soup with beaten egg yolks, lemon, and paprika.

dukkah (DOO-kah) In Egyptian cooking, a dry mixture of crushed nuts and spices, such as hazelnuts with coriander, cumin, and sesame seeds, eaten with bread dipped in olive oil, for breakfast or a snack.

dulce (DOOL-thay, DOOL-say) Spanish for sweet.

dulse A coarse but edible seaweed from the North Atlantic, especially around Britain, used mostly for its gelatin.

Dumas, Alexandre, père (1802–70) (dü-mah) A prolific French dramatist and novelist (*The Three Musketeers*) and author of the *Grand Dictionnaire de Cuisine*, published posthumously; Waverly Root has called him "an author more picturesque than accurate," and his dictionary indeed makes for lively reading.

dumpling A round lump of dough steamed on top of a savory soup or stew, or stuffed and baked with a sweet fruit filling; the variety is infinite.

Dundee cake (dun-DEE) A rich fruit cake topped with almonds, from Scotland.

Dungeness crab Pacific rock crab, very popular, weighing up to four pounds.

dunkeles Bier (DOON-keh-les BEER) German for dark beer.

Dunlop A Scottish cows' milk cheese, similar to **Cheddar** but moister, softer, and blander.

dünsten (DÜN-sten) In Germany, to steam, to stew.

durazno (doo-RAHTH-nō, doo-RAHS-nō) Spanish for peach.

durian (DOOR-yan) The fruit of a Malaysian tree with prickly rind and edible pulp and seeds; its highly offensive smell keeps most

Westerners from tasting its flesh, considered exquisite by its advocates.

Dürkheim (DÜRK-hīm)   A town in the Rhine valley producing a very large amount of red and white wine, most unremarkable.

durra   See **sorghum.**

durum wheat (DOOR-um)   The hardest species of **wheat,** usually made into **semolina** flour.

dust   Finely broken tea leaves, inferior in grade, yielding a quick, strong brew.

Dutch oven   A large, heavy cast-iron or metal kettle with a close-fitting lid, used for cooking stews, pot roasts, etc.; originally, coals could be put on top to heat food from above as well as from below.

duxelles (dük-zel)   In French cooking, finely chopped mushrooms and shallots slowly cooked in butter to form a thick, dark paste that is used for seasoning sauces, as a spread for toast, and in other preparations; often said to be the invention of **La Varenne,** who worked for the Marquis d'Uxelles, but the story is probably apocryphal since he gives no such recipe in his books.

écrevisse

Earl Grey tea A China black tea flavored with oil of **bergamot,** popular as an afternoon tea.

eau de vie (ō deu vie) French for fruit brandy, literally "water of life," often called *alcool blanc* ("white alcohol"); colorless *eau de vie* retains its clarity because it is aged in crockery rather than wood, unlike most brandies. Alsace, Germany, and Switzerland produce many *eaux de vie,* flavored with a wide variety of fruits, **Kirschwasser** being the best known.

ebi (eb-ee) Japanese for shrimp; in Indonesia, dried shrimp, used as a side dish or garnish.

Eccles cake (EK-kuhls) A small traditional cake, originally from Lancashire, England, of puff pastry filled with currants and sprinkled with sugar.

échalote (ay-shal-loht) French for shallot.

échaudé (ay-shō-day) French for pastry whose dough is first poached in water, then baked in the oven.

éclair (ay-klayr) **Choux pastry** piped into finger shapes and filled with flavored cream; originally French.

écrevisse (AY-kreh-VEES) French for freshwater **crayfish.**

Edam (EE-dum) A round yellow Dutch cheese from the town of the same name, made of partly skimmed cows' milk and slowly fermented; the finished cheese is coated with linseed oil and, if for export, covered with red wax.

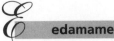

edamame (ay-dah-mah-may)   In Japan, fresh soybeans in the pod.

Edelfäule (AY-dehl-FOY-leh)   German for **noble rot.**

eel   A snakelike fish that migrates from the ocean to tidelands and rivers in spring; eel tastes best taken from fast-moving rather than brackish water and killed soon before eating; a rich and fatty fish, eel is excellent smoked, stewed, jellied, baked, and grilled; its shape may account for its unpopularity in the United States, but until the eighteenth century it was considered a delicacy in England and still is in many countries.

Eger (AY-ger)   A town in Hungary that produces two famous red wines, *Egri Bikavér* ("bull's blood") and *Egri Kadarka;* both are full-bodied, deep in color, and slow-maturing.

egg-and-breadcrumb   To dip food into beaten egg and then into breadcrumbs before frying to give it a crisp coating.

eggnog   A nutritious milk punch made of milk, egg yolks, sugar, spices (such as nutmeg), and usually some kind of liquor.

egg roll   See **cai juan.**

eggah   See **ijja.**

égrappage (ay-grap-pajh)   French term for the process of removing stems from grapes before pressing, thus reducing the **tannin** content of the wine.

egushi (ay-GOO-shee)   An African word for pumpkin or sesame seeds.

Ei, Eier (Ī, Ī-er)   German for egg, eggs.

eingelegt (ĪN-ge-laygt)   German for pickled, marinated, preserved.

eingemacht (ĪN-geh-mahkt)   German for pickled, preserved, bottled, canned; also preserves, jam, pickles.

Eintopf (ĪN-tohpf)   German for "one-dish" stew or meal containing various meats and vegetables and possibly even fish.

Eis (ĪS)   German for ice, ice cream.

Eisbein (ĪS-bīn)   German for pickled pork hocks, usually accompanied by mashed potatoes and sauerkraut.

Eiswein (ĪS-vīn)   German for wine made from very ripe grapes caught by an early hard frost and only partially frozen because of their high sugar content.

ekmek (ek-mek) Turkish for bread.

elaichi (ay-LĪ-chee) **Cardamom** in Indian cooking.

elder A shrub whose cream-colored flowers are delicious in fruit compotes and fritters, and whose deep purple berries contribute to fruit soups, jellies, homemade wines, and the liqueur **sambuca.**

elote (ay-LŌ-tay) Corn in Mexican cooking.

Eltville A town in the Rheingau region of West Germany producing many consistently good white wines.

émincé (ay-minh-say) In French, thinly sliced cooked meat, usually left over, covered with sauce and reheated.

Emmental, Emmentaler (EM-men-tahl) A whole-milk cows' cheese from German-speaking Switzerland; the cheese is cooked, pressed, and shaped into large wheels with a hard, light brown rind and golden interior with large holes; its taste is mellow, rich, and nutty, excellent for eating or cooking, the quintessential Swiss cheese; incorrectly spelled Emmenthal or Emmenthaler.

empanada, empanadilla (em-pah-NAH-dah, em-pah-nah-DEE-yah) A pie or tart with various savory fillings, originally from Galicia in Spain; *empanar* means to breadcrumb.

empandita (em-pahn-DEE-tah) A Spanish pastry turnover whose shape—square, round, triangular, or rectangular—indicates the specific type of filling, such as meat, seafood, or vegetable.

emshmel With preserved lemons and olives, a Moroccan term.

emulsion A stable liquid mixture in which one liquid is suspended in tiny globules throughout another, as with egg yolks in oil or butter for **mayonnaise** or **hollandaise** sauce.

enchilada (en-chee-LAH-dah) In Mexican cooking, a **tortilla,** fried and filled variously, often with meat, chilies, or cheese.

endive See **Belgian endive.**

enokidake (eh-nō-kee-dah-kay) Japanese wild mushrooms with long, thin stems and tiny caps, either white or tan; the stems should be trimmed before using these mushrooms fresh in salads or cooked in soup, stir-fried, or in **tempura** dishes; mild in flavor, they are available fresh or canned.

enrollada (en-rō-YAH-dah) Spanish for rolled.

ensalada (en-thah-LAH-dah, en-sah-LAH-dah)   Spanish for salad.

Ente (EN-tay)   German for duck.

Entrammes   See **Port-Salut.**

entrecôte (ENH-treh-KŌT)   In French, steak cut from between the ribs.

entrecuisse (ENH-treh-KWEES)   French for thigh or second joint of poultry and game birds, as opposed to drumstick (*cuisse*).

Entre-Deux-Mers (ENH-treh DEU-MAYR)   A region "between two rivers," the Dordogne and Garonne, in Bordeaux, that produces a large quantity of wine; those using the name *Entre-Deux-Mers* are dry white wines, some of them exceptional.

entrée (enh-tray)   In the United States, this word today usually means the main course, but in France it retains its original meaning of first course.

entremeses (en-treh-MAY-ses)   Spanish for appetizers, hors d'oeuvre.

entremets (ENH-treh-MAY)   In French, literally "between courses," this vague term can denote side dishes, such as vegetables and salads, and desserts served after the cheese course.

entremettier (ENH-treh-MET-TYAY)   French for vegetable cook.

épaule (ay-pōl)   French for shoulder.

epazote (ay-pah-ZŌ-tay)   A wild herb with strong flavor that can be an acquired taste; used in Latin American cooking, especially legume dishes to reduce flatulence and for tea.

éperlan (ay-payr-lanh)   French for smelt.

épice (ay-pees)   French for spice.

Epicurus   A Greek philosopher who espoused the pursuit of pleasure, often interpreted as indulgence in luxury and sensual pleasure; an epicure, with regard to food, can mean either a gastronome or a voluptuary.

épigramme (ay-pee-gram)   In French cooking, a preparation of lamb in which a cutlet or chop and a slice of breast are dipped in egg and breadcrumbs and fried or grilled.

épinard (ay-pee-naahr)   French for spinach.

éplucher (ay-plü-shay)   In French, to peel; *épluchoir* is a paring knife.

éponger (ay-ponh-jhay)   In French, to drain vegetables cooked in water or oil on towels.

Erbsen (AYRB-sen)   German for peas, usually dried and split.

Erdapfel (AYRD-ap-fel)   German for potato, especially in southern Germany and Austria. See also **Kartoffel.**

Erdbeere (AYRD-bayr-eh)   German for strawberry.

escabeche (eth-kah-BAY-chay, es-kah-BAY-shay)   Spanish and Portuguese for cooked fish, sometimes poultry, marinated in vinegar or wine (which pickles it) and other seasonings; served cold in the earthenware container in which it was pickled; often confused with **cebiche.**

escalibada (eth-KAH-lee-BAH-dah)   Spanish for mixed vegetables—sweet peppers, eggplants, tomatoes, and onions—grilled over charcoal; from Catalan.

escalope (es-ka-lōp)   French for scallop of meat or fish; a thin slice possibly flattened by pounding.

escargot (es-kaahr-gō)   Snail.

escarole (es-kaahr-ōl)   A type of chicory with broader, less delicate leaves and a more bitter taste than lettuce; excellent for winter salads.

Escoffier, Auguste (1847–1935) (es-kohf-fyay)   A great French chef who codified classical French cuisine with *Le Guide Culinaire* and other books. Escoffier, who worked with the great hôtelier César Ritz at the London Savoy, Connaught, and Carlton hotels, and the Ritz in both London and Paris, improved the organization and working conditions of the professional kitchen.

eshkeneh Shirazi   Persian yogurt soup with onions, walnuts, and **fenugreek,** from the city of Shiraz.

espadon (es-pa-donh)   French for swordfish.

espagnole (es-pa-nyōl)   A basic brown sauce that serves as the basis for many others in classic cuisine; made from brown **roux,** brown stock, browned **mirepoix,** tomato purée, and herbs cooked together slowly, skimmed, and strained.

espazato (es-pah-SAH-tō)   A Mexican perennial herb with a strong flavor, sometimes called "stink weed."

espresso (es-PRES-sō)   Strong Italian coffee made with a special machine that forces steam through the coffee grounds; see **caffè.**

essence   A concentrated substance, usually volatile, extracted by distillation, infusion, or other means, such as fish essence, coffee essence, vanilla extract; see also **extract.**

estate-bottled   see **château-bottled.**

estilo de, estilo al (eth-TEE-lō deu)   Spanish for in the style of, **à la.**

estofado (eth-tō-FAH-dō, es-tō-FAH-dō)   Spanish for stew.

estouffade (es-too-fad)   In French, a dish cooked by the **étouffer** method; also a brown stock used to dilute sauces and moisten braised dishes.

estragon (es-tra-gonh)   French for tarragon.

estufa   See **Madeira.**

étamine (ay-ta-meen)   In French, a cloth for straining stocks, sauces, etc.; see **tamis.**

étouffer, étuver (ay-too-fay)   A French method of cooking food slowly in a tightly closed pan with little or no liquid; *estouffade* refers to the dish itself.

evaporated milk   Milk with its water content reduced by half and sterilized; this causes it to taste caramelized, but no sugar is actually added.

extract   Concentrated stock, juice, or solution produced by boiling and clarification (as for vegetables, fish, poultry, game, and meat, when the extract may be reduced to a jelly or *glace*) or by distillation (as for fruits, seeds, or leaves, such as vanilla, almond, rosewater, and peppermint essence). Fish extract is usually called **fumet.**

eye of round   See **round.**

fennel

fabada asturiana (fah-BAH-dah ah-thtoo-RYAH-nah) A hearty Spanish peasant stew of dried **fava** or white beans cooked slowly with salt pork, ham, sausages, and onions.

fagioli (fah-JŌ-lee) Italian for beans, usually white *haricot* or kidney beans; *fagiolini* are green string beans.

faisan (fay-sanh) French for pheasant; the Spanish term *faisán* sometimes includes other game birds.

faisinjan See **fesenjan.**

falafel, felafel (fah-LAH-fel) Dried **fava** beans or **chickpeas** minced, spiced, shaped into balls, and deep fried; this Egyptian dish is eaten throughout the Middle East with slight variations; also called *ta'amia.*

falooda (fah-LOO-dah) Refreshing sweet drink made from various starches such as tapioca or cornflour noodles, with **agar-agar** and **sharbat;** served with curry or for dessert in Indian cuisine.

fàn (fahn) Chinese for rice; *bai fàn,* plain rice, *chăo fàn,* fried rice, and *zhōu fàn,* congee rice.

fannings Tea made from broken leaves, yielding a quick, strong brew.

farce (faahrs) French for stuffing, forcemeat; *farci* means a stuffed dish, such as cabbage, breast of veal, or flank steak stuffed and braised.

farcito (fahr-SEE-tō) Italian for stuffed.

farfalle (fahr-FAL-lay) "Butterfly"-shaped pasta.

farfel (FAHR-fel)   In Jewish cooking, egg dough grated, dried, and cooked in soup as a garnish.

farina (fah-REE-nah)   Italian for flour; *farina* is also a grade of wheat finer than **semolina.**

farinaceous   Made of flour or meal; from cereal grains, starchy.

Farmer, Fannie Merritt (1857–1915)   A cooking teacher and author of *The Boston Cooking School Cook Book* (1896), which achieved great and lasting popularity; its main innovation was precise measurements for ingredients, but Farmer has been blamed, perhaps unfairly, as "the maiden aunt of home economics."

farmer cheese   Cheese made from whole or partly skimmed cows' milk, similar to **cottage cheese.**

farofa (fah-RŌ-fah)   A mixture of **dendê,** onion, **manioc** meal, and chile peppers, all browned in a pan and used for stuffings and side dishes in Brazilian cuisine.

Fasnacht, Fastnacht (FAHS-nahkt, FAHST-nahkt)   A potato doughnut deep-fried in pork fat; the diamond-shaped yeast pastry, Pennsylvania German in origin, is traditionally eaten on Shrove Tuesday (*Fastnacht* in German), to use up the fat before Lent.

fasulye (fah-SOO-lyah)   Turkish for beans; *fasulye pilaki,* dried white beans stewed with onions.

fatta (FAH-tah)   An Egyptian soup of leftover sacrificial lamb, ritually eaten 70 days after Ramadan as part of a feast; lamb soup with rice and herbs is poured over toasted bread.

fatto in casa (FAHT-tō een KAH-zah)   Italian for homemade.

fattoush (fah-TOOSH)   A Syrian salad, like **panzanella,** of **pita** toasted and soaked with chopped cucumber, tomatoes, onions, and herbs, with lemon juice and olive oil.

fava (FAH-vah)   Broad or faba bean, of Mediterranean origin; important as a nutritional component of the diet and as a rotation crop; fava beans can be eaten raw, cooked fresh, or dried, and though esteemed for their distinct flavor in the Mediterranean are largely ignored in the United States.

fegato (fay-GAH-tō)   Italian for liver; *fegatelli* means pork liver; *fegatini* means chicken livers.

feijão (fay-JHOW)   Portuguese for beans or legumes.

feijoa (fay-YŌ-ah)   A fruit native to South America and now grown commercially in New Zealand; deep green with a white pulp, it is eaten fresh in salads or made into preserves.

feijoada (fay-JHWAH-dah)   A robust Brazilian dish halfway between a soup and a stew, made of pork trimmings, sausage, beef, **black beans,** rice, and **manioc** meal, seasoned with peppers and garnished with oranges.

Feingebäck (FĪN-geh-bek.)   German for pastry.

fennel   A vegetable, herb, and spice in many varieties whose bulb, stems, leaves, and seeds are edible; anise-flavored, it is favored in Mediterranean countries where it originated; Italians call the bulb *finocchio,* the English refer to it as Florence fennel; it is no relation to Chinese anise (see **ba jiao**). American markets often mislabel it as **anise.**

fenouil (feh-NOO-ee)   French for fennel; *au fenouil* means grilled over dried wild fennel stalks.

fĕn sī (fen seu)   Cellophane or translucent noodles made from mung beans, softened in a liquid before being used in Chinese cuisine.

fenugreek   A leguminous plant from western Asia whose slightly bitter leaves are consumed fresh in salads and whose celery-flavored seeds are eaten by people and cattle; usually added to curries, fenugreek is eaten mostly in India, the Near East, and Northern and East Africa; in the United States it is used as the main flavoring in imitation maple syrup.

fermentation   A chemical process in the making of bread, cheese, wine, beer, and other foods, in which yeast, mold, or bacteria act upon sugar and bring about a transformation.

fermière, à la (ah lah fayr-myayr)   In French cooking, in the style of the farmer's wife; with mixed vegetables.

ferri, ai (ī FAYR-ree)   Italian for grilled over an open fire; also *ferri alla griglia.*

fesenjan (FES-in-jahn)   A classic Persian dish of duck or chicken pieces fried and served in a sauce of ground walnuts and pomegranate juice.

Feta (FAY-tah)   A goats' or ewes' milk cheese from Greece, pressed, then cured in brine or its own salted whey; crumbly, salty, white, and rindless, it is often used in salads and cooking; generic feta is increasingly made with cows' milk or a mixture of cows' and goats' milk, especially by large commercial producers outside Greece.

fetta (FET-tah) Italian for slice, fillet.

fettucine (fet-too-CHEE-nee) Long, flat thin strips or "ribbons" of egg pasta; this is the Roman and southern Italian name for **tagliatelle,** almost the same, but slightly narrower and thicker.

feuilletage (FOY-eh-TAJH) French for puff pastry, **pâte feuilletée.**

fiambre (FYAHM-bray) Spanish and Portuguese for cooked cold food.

fiasco (FYAHS-kō) Italian for a flask or wine bottle, thin and round-bottomed, with a woven straw covering for strength and support; the plural is *fiaschi*; Chianti has the most familiar *fiasco.*

fico (FEE-kō) Italian for fig.

fiddlehead The young shoots of certain ferns, such as bracken, harvested in spring as they unfurl, at which time they resemble violin ("fiddle") heads.

Figeac, Château (fee-jhak) A large and fine vineyard from **Saint-Émilion** in Bordeaux; several lesser-known vineyards nearby have *Figeac* as part of their names.

fila (FEE-lah) Arabic for **phyllo.**

filbert A cultivated hazelnut, so called because the nuts ripen around St. Philbert's Day, August 22; used in confectionery and hazelnut butter.

filé powder (FEE-lay) Dried ground sassafras leaves used to thicken **gumbos** in **Creole** cooking; added at table, not before, and (properly) instead of **okra.**

filet (fee-lay) French for fillet; a boneless cut or slice of meat, poultry, or fish, especially beef tenderloin; **filet mignon,** a small, boneless, tender slice of beef from the thick end of the **tenderloin.**

filfil mihshi (FIL-fil MEE-shee) A Tunisian dish of sweet peppers stuffed with ground lamb, onions, eggs, and seasonings, then lightly battered and fried in oil.

filo See **phyllo.**

financière, à la (ah lah fee-nanh-syayr) In French cuisine, "banker's style," that is, expensive: meat or poultry garnished with cocks' combs and kidneys, sweetbreads, mushrooms, olives, and truffles; sometimes these ingredients are encased in **vol-au-vent** pastry.

fines herbes (feen ayrb) A mixture of chopped herbs such as parsley, chervil, tarragon, and chives used to flavor omelets, salads, chops, etc.; occasionally the term means chopped parsley alone.

fining The process of clarifying wine by adding various substances and removing sediment.

finnan haddie Smoked haddock; originally from the Scottish town of Findon, hence the name.

fino (FEE-nō) Pale, light, dry sherry, generally used as an apéritif and considered the best type of sherry.

finocchio (fee-NŌK-kyō) Italian for **fennel.**

Fior di Latte (fyor dee LAHT-tay) A cows' milk cheese of the spun-curd type, similar to **Mozzarella;** originally from southern Italy.

fiorentina, bistecca alla (bee-STEK-kah ah-lah fyor-en-TEE-nah) In Italian cooking, a T-bone steak charcoal-grilled in the Florentine style—rare and plain but moistened after grilling with a few drops of olive oil.

fiori di zucca (fyor-ee dee TZOOK-kah) Italian for squash blossoms dipped in batter and fried.

Fior Sardo (fyor SAR-dō) A whole, raw ewes' milk cheese—the original Sardinian **Pecorino** and still produced in Sardinia; this Italian cheese is good for the table when young and excellent for grating when mature.

firm-ball stage Sugar syrup that has reached a temperature of 243° F. (117° C.) and that forms a firm ball between the fingers when immersed in cold water.

firni (FEER-nee) Indian dessert pudding of ground rice cooked in milk, usually with cardamom and nuts.

first-growth wine See **classed growth.**

Fisher, M.F.K. (Mary Frances Kennedy, 1908–92) American foodwriter whose books, stories, and translation of **Brillat-Savarin** elevated the genre: "our three basic needs, for food and security and love are so mixed and mingled and entwined that we cannot straightly think of one without the others."

five-spice powder See **wu hsiang fun.**

flageolet (fla-jhō-lay) French for a small pale green bean, fresh or dried, similar to the **haricot** or kidney bean.

flamande, à la (ah lah fla-manhd)   In French cuisine, garnished with braised cabbage, carrots, turnips, sliced pork belly, sausage, and potatoes.

flambé (flamh-bay)   The French word for flamed; used to describe food that is ignited with a small amount of heated liquor poured over it, the burning alcohol enveloping the dish in flames.

flameado (flah-may-AH-dō)   Spanish for **flambé.**

flan   An open tart made in a ring mold, usually filled with custard, either sweet or savory; in Spanish, *flan* is a caramel cream custard, a very popular dessert.

flank   A cut of beef from the lower hindquarter that, well trimmed, is true **London broil.**

flatbrød (FLAT-breud)   "Flatbread," very thin and crisp, traditionally made in Norway of rye, barley, and wheat flours.

flatfish   Any saltwater fish with both eyes on one side of the head; this includes **sole, flounder, turbot, halibut,** and **plaice.**

Fleisch (flīsh)   German for meat.

Fleischkäse (FLĪSH-kay-zeh)   German for meat loaf.

flétan (flay-tanh)   French for halibut.

fleurette (fleur-et)   French sweet cream that has not been cultered with lactic acid to make **crème fraîche.**

fleuron (fleur-onh)   French for a small ornament, such as a crescent, cut from flaky pastry to garnish hot food.

floating island   See **île flottante.**

flor   In Spanish, literally "flower," it is the name for the yeast that naturally forms after fermentation on Spanish **fino** and **amontillado** sherries and on those of other countries by inoculation, and which greatly improves the wine.

Florence fennel   See **fennel.**

florentine, à la (ah lah flohr-enh-teen)   In French cuisine, with spinach; a garnish, especially for eggs and fish, of a bed of spinach; the whole dish is often masked with **Mornay** sauce. Also a confection of butter, sugar, honey, cream, candied orange zest, and almonds cooked to the soft-ball stage; mounds are baked and coated on the bottom with chocolate.

flounder A flatfish member of the **sole** family in many varieties, including plaice, brill, halibut, sanddab, turbot, and so-called gray, lemon, rock, and petrale sole. The flounder's shape is rounder than that of sole and though an excellent fish for eating, many of the names under which it is marketed are merely intended to make it more attractive to the consumer.

flour Finely milled meal of grain, usually meaning wheat. Flour can be steel-ground in huge industrial machines, that destroy some nutritional value and eliminates the germ, or stone-ground by the old traditional method that preserves the germ and uses less heat. Bolting, or sifting, determines texture. All-purpose flour contains both hard (high-gluten) and soft (low-gluten) wheats; bread flour (high-gluten) is best for yeast breads; cake or pastry flour (fine-textured, low gluten) is best for cakes and cookies. See also **wheat, gluten, self-rising flour;** non-wheat grains are separately entered.

flummery In British cooking, an oatmeal or custard pudding, thick and sweet; in the United States, it has come to mean a fruit pudding thickened with cornstarch.

flute To make a grooved or furrowed pattern in certain fruits and vegetables, especially mushrooms, or in the edges of a pie crust; also the name of a Champagne glass shaped in a deep slender cone.

focaccia (fō-KAH-chah) A flat, round Italian peasant bread flavored with sage and **pancetta** and originally baked on hot stones on the hearth; with its new-found American popularity, there are many other flavorings.

foie gras (fwah grah) In French cuisine, the enlarged livers of force-fed geese and ducks, especially the geese of Toulouse and Strasbourg.

fold To combine a frothy light substance, such as beaten egg whites or cream, with a heavier one by using a gentle circular motion, in order not to lose air and reduce volume and lightness.

Folle Blanche (fōl blanhsh) A French grape variety yielding a pale, light, clean, and acidic wine, productive but vulnerable; also called *Picpoul* in the Armagnac country, where it produces an excellent brandy but a mediocre table wine.

foncer (fonh-say) In French, to line a cake or pie tin; **pâte brisée** and **pâte sucrée** are types of *pâte à foncer*.

fond, fonds de cuisine (fonh) See **stock.**

fondant (fonh-danh)   French for an icing mixture used as a coating in confectionery and pastry.

fond d'artichaut (fonh d'aahr-tee-chō)   French for artichoke heart.

fondre, faire (FAYR FONH-dreh)   In French, to "melt" vegetables, especially onions, leeks, and garlic, by cooking them very gently until softened.

fondue (fonh-dü)   From the French word for melted, *fondue* has several meanings: in Switzerland, it refers to Swiss cheese, melted with white wine and seasonings in a special earthenware pot over a flame, for dipping bread cubes into; *fondue bourguignonne* is cubes of raw beef speared and cooked in a pot of oil heated over a flame, then eaten with various sauces; in French cooking, it refers to minced vegetables, such as tomatoes, cooked in butter or oil until they disintegrate; also a dish of eggs scrambled with melted cheese and butter.

fonduta (fohn-DOO-tah)   An Italian dish of melted **Fontina** cheese with eggs, butter, milk, sliced truffles, and white pepper; from the Piedmont region.

Fontal (fohn-TAL)   A pasteurized whole-milk cows' cheese from northern Italy and eastern France, similar to **Fontina** but without its distinction.

Fontina (fohn-TEE-nah)   Raw whole-milk cows' cheese, semicooked and pressed, originally from the Italian Aosta Valley near the Swiss border; it is pale yellow with a brown crust, about one foot across (in wheels), firm but creamy, mild yet nutty; true Fontina is a fine cheese, but there are many inferior imitations.

foo foo   Mashed plantain dumpling, boiled or perhaps fried, served with stews and sauces in the Caribbean; sometimes made from other starchy vegetables; also spelled *fou fou*.

foogath (FOO-gath)   An Indian vegetable dish cooked with coconut.

fool   In British cooking, a purée of fruit, such as rhubarb or gooseberry, mixed with cream; the word apparently does not come from the French *foulé,* meaning crushed, but is akin to the English folly or **trifle**.

forcemeat   Stuffing.

Forelle (for-EL-leh)   German for trout.

forestière, à la (ah lah for-es-tyayr) In French cuisine, garnished with sautéed morels or other mushrooms, diced bacon, and diced potatoes sautéed in butter.

formaggio (for-MAJ-jō) Italian for cheese.

fortified Refers to wines (such as port, sherry, and Madeira) that have had brandy or another spirit added to them before bottling, thus strengthening their alcohol content.

fouet (foo-ay) French for whisk; *fouetté* means whisked.

four, au (ō FOOR) French for baked in the oven.

Fourme d'Ambert (foorm d'amh-bayr) Tall cylindrical cheese from the French Auvergne, made from raw, partly skimmed cows' milk; it is creamy, with blue veins and a dry rind.

fourrage (foor-rajh) In French, filling or stuffing, as for pastry.

fragola (FRAH-gō-lah) Italian for strawberry; *fragoline di bosco* are wild strawberries.

frais, fraîche (fray, fresh) French for fresh.

fraisage (freh-zajh) French for a technique for kneading dough by smearing it across the workboard with the heel of the hand and then regathering it.

fraise (frez) French for strawberry; *fraises des bois* are wild strawberries.

framboise (frahm-bwaz) French for raspberry.

frambuesa (frahm-BWAY-sah) Spanish for raspberry.

française, à la (ah lah franh-sez) In the French style, used very broadly.

Franconia A wine-producing region of West Germany in the upper Main Valley around Würzburg; its white wines, of Sylvaner and Riesling varieties, are bottled in the characteristic squat flat-sided green flagons called *Bocksbeutels.*

frangipane (franh-jhee-pan) In French cooking, a type of **choux pastry,** originally Italian; *frangipane* cream is a **crème patissière** flavored with almonds.

Frankfurter (FRAHNK-foor-ter) A German sausage from which the hot dog is descended.

frappé (frap-pay) French for chilled; iced; surrounded by crushed ice.

Frascati, à la (ah lah fra-SKAH-tee) A classical French garnish of sliced **foie gras,** truffles, fluted mushroom caps, asparagus, and **duchesse** potato crescents, with veal stock; also a pleasant dry white wine produced in the town of the same name near Rome.

freddo (FRED-dō) Italian for cold.

fresa (FRAY-thah) Spanish for strawberry.

fresco (FRES-kō) Italian and Spanish for fresh.

Fresno chili In Mexican cooking, a small cone-shaped chili pepper, fairly hot in flavor.

friandise (free-anh-deez) French for **petits four** or small confection.

fricassée (free-kas-say) A French stew of white meat, usually poultry or veal, in a white sauce, such as **blanquette.**

Friese (FREE-seh) A whole or partly skimmed cows' milk cheese from the Netherlands, uncooked and very hard; it is spiced with cloves and cumin, giving it a strong flavor.

frijoles (free-HŌ-lays) Spanish for beans; in Mexican cooking, *frijoles negros,* black beans; *frijoles refritos,* refried beans—that is, beans that are boiled, mashed, and fried with **piquín** chilies for filling tacos, etc.

Frikadellen (freek-ah-DEL-en) German meatballs of beef, breadcrumbs, and egg, often served cold.

frío (FREE-ō) Spanish for cold.

frire (freer) In French, to fry; *frit* means fried; *friture,* fried food or frying.

frisée See **chicory.**

frita (FREE-tah) Spanish for fritter; in Cuba, fritas are little hamburgers in buns topped with shoestring potatoes, a popular fast food.

frito (FREE-tō) Spanish for fried; *fritura,* fried food.

frittata (free-TAH-tah) Italian for an open-faced omelet.

frittèlla (free-TEL-lah) Italian for fritter.

fritter Food, either savory or sweet, dipped into batter and deep-fried.

fritto misto (FREE-tō MEES-tō) Italian for mixed food, deep-fried in batter; can be very elaborate and include a wide variety, such as meat, offal, and vegetables served together.

fritura (free-TOO-rah) Spanish for fritter.

frizzante (freet-ZAHN-tay) An Italian wine term meaning slightly sparkling or effervescent, due to some additional fermentation in the bottle.

froid (fwah) French for cold.

fromage (frō-majh) French for cheese; *fromager* means to add grated cheese, usually **Gruyère** or **Parmesan,** to a sauce, dough, or stuffing, or to sprinkle it on top of food for browning in the oven.

fromage de tête de porc French for **head cheese,** pork brawn.

Frucht (frookht) German for fruit.

fructose The form of sugar found in many plants, especially fruits, and also in honey; fructose tastes sweeter than sucrose and contains half as many calories but is not necessarily more healthful or "natural" than other forms of sugar, especially when crystallized.

Frühlingsuppe (FRÜ-ling-zoo-peh) A German soup of spring vegetables in meat stock.

Frühstück (FRÜ-stük) German for breakfast.

fruits de mer (FWEE deu MAYR) French for seafood, usually shellfish.

frumenty (FROO-men-tee) A porridge of oatmeal or wheat berries and milk with raisins, sugar, and spices—a traditional old English Christmas food; spelled variously.

fruta bomba (FROO-tah BOHM-bah) Spanish for **papaya.**

frutta fresca de stagione (FROOT-tah FRES-kah day stah-JŌ-nay) Italian for fresh seasonal fruit.

frutti di mare (FROOT-tee dee MAH-ray) Italian for seafood, usually shellfish.

fry To cook in hot fat, either a large (see **deep-fry**) or small (see **sauter**) amount.

fuki (foo-kee) Japanese for coltsfoot, a vegetable similar to celery.

ful medames (FOOL meh-DAH-mes) Brown **fava** beans cooked in olive oil with garlic, lemon, and parsley, and served with hard-boiled eggs; an ancient dish that has become the national dish of Egypt.

Füllung (FÜ-luhng) German for stuffing.

fumé (fü-may) French for smoked.

fumet (fü-may) In French cuisine, a concentrated liquid that gives flavor and body to stocks and sauces; made by completely reducing stock that may contain wine; see also **essence** and **extract.**

fungo (FUHN-gō) Italian for mushroom; the plural is *funghi.*

furai (foo-rī) In Japanese, to fry.

fusilli (foo-ZEE-lee) Thin, spiral-shaped pasta.

fusion cuisine Style of cooking that combines the traditions of two or more disparate regions, such as French and Chinese (in Cambodian cuisine, for instance), or Polynesian, Chinese, and Spanish (in Philippine). As chefs become familiar with techniques and ingredients from different parts of the world or combine them in their own heritage, this style becomes more popular. The danger, however, is that the culinary distinctions become not fused but confused, the roots neither recognized nor appreciated.

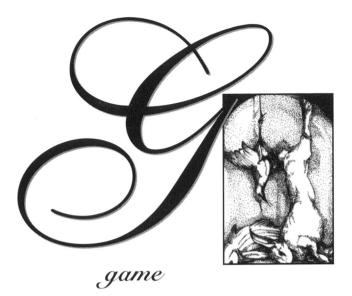

game

ga nuong cam (ga nyoong kahm) In Vietnamese cuisine, chicken in a spicy marinade, grilled or roasted.

gado-gado (gah-dō-gah-dō) Indonesian mixed vegetable salad, usually with **bumbu.**

gaeng (gang) Thai for curry paste; *gaeng ped*, hot curry paste; *gaeng mussaman*, a spicy Muslim curry of beef or chicken, with coconut milk and peanuts; *gaeng ped neua*, red beef curry, with coconut milk, citrus leaves, and spices.

gai (gī) Thai for chicken; *gai lae pet*, poultry; *gai tua*, chicken in peanut sauce; *gai yang*, marinated grilled chicken in a garlicky piquant sauce.

galangal (gah-LAHNG-ahl) A rhizome of the ginger family used in southeast Asian cooking, especially in Malaysia and Indonesia; there are two types, greater and lesser, and "lesser" galangal is more important in cooking.

galantine (gal-anh-teen) In French cuisine, boned poultry, or occasionally fish or meat, stuffed, rolled or shaped, poached in gelatin stock, and served cold surrounded by its own aspic; often confused with **ballotine,** which is similar in construction but braised or roasted and served either hot or cold.

galette (gal-et) A thin broad French cake usually of flaky pastry or **feuilletage;** *Galette des Rois* is the Twelfth Night cake, baked with a bean and perhaps other emblems to symbolize good fortune for the finder; its shape and decoration vary according to the traditions of particular French regions.

gallina (gah-LEE-nah)   Spanish for hen.

galumblee (gah-lump-lee)   Thai for cabbage.

Gamay (ga-may)   A grape variety that yields an especially excellent red wine in Beaujolais; also grown in Burgundy and California.

gamba (GAHM-bah)   Spanish for shrimp.

gambero (gam-BAY-rō)   Italian for shrimp; *gamberetti* are small shrimp; *gamberi di fiume* are freshwater crayfish.

game   Wild animals, either furred, feathered, or finned, that are pursued for sport and whose flesh is edible; except for fish, game is often hung and marinated in vinegar or wine and oil to break down tough muscular tissue and develop flavor.

Gammelost (GAM-meh-lohst)   A Norwegian blue cheese made from skimmed cows' milk with interior and exterior molds; apparently the Vikings made this cheese.

gammon   British for ham; the bottom part of a side of bacon.

ganache (ga-nash)   A rich chocolate icing or filling for French pastry, made of semisweet chocolate melted with heavy cream, that sets when cool.

gandules (gahn-DOO-lays)   A Spanish name for the Caribbean staple legume also called *congo, gunga,* or pigeon peas.

ga nuong cam (gah nyoong kahm)   Vietnamese dish of chicken in a spicy marinade, grilled or roasted.

Gans (gahns)   German for goose; *Gansleber* is goose liver.

garam (GAAHR-um.)   Hot, warm in Indian cooking; *garam masala* is a mixture of ground spices—such as cinnamon, cloves, cardamom, cumin, nutmeg, coriander, and black peppercorns—that is sprinkled over a dish just before serving.

garbanzo (gar-BAHN-sō)   Spanish for **chickpea.**

garbure (gaahr-bür)   A thick soup from Béarn in France, varying widely but usually containing cabbage, beans, potatoes, vegetables, and pork, sausage, or ham; usually served with toasted bread.

garde manger (gaahrd manh-jhay)   French for a pantry or cold storage area for foodstuffs where the cold buffet in a hotel dining room is prepared; the *chef garde manger* oversees this area and is responsible for **pâtés,** salads, **galantines, chaud-froids,** etc., and for fancy display garniture.

garganelli (gar-gah-NEL-lee)   Homemade Italian macaroni made with egg pasta, rolled with a comblike tool.

gargoulette des émirs (gaahr-goo-let days ay-meer)   A Tunisian dish of lamb and seasonings sealed in an amphora-shaped clay pot and slowly baked in a fire; the pot is broken before serving. An old celebratory dish.

gari (GAH-ree)   Coarse cassava powder in Nigerian cooking; *gari foto* combines tomatoes, onions, chilies, and egg with *gari* in a kind of **risotto; manioc** meal.

Garibaldi   In classic French cuisine, a **demi-glace** sauce seasoned with mustard, cayenne, garlic, and anchovy butter.

garlic   An herb of the allium family widely used in Eastern, Middle Eastern, and Latin cooking, but disdained by Anglo-Saxons until quite recently; aside from its odor, which is strongest when chopped raw and disappears with gentle slow cooking, garlic has many healthful properties recognized by the ancients.

garlic chives   A member of the allium family, with long flat leaves with garlicky flavor, used as a garnish, and white flowers, also edible.

garnacha   See **sope.**

Garnele (GAHR-neh-leh)   German for shrimp, prawn.

garni (gaahr-nee)   French for garnished.

garnish   An edible trimming or embellishment added to a dish, usually enhancing its flavor as well as visual appeal; in classic cuisine the name of the dish, such as *Sole à la florentine* or *Sole florentine,* designates its particular garnish; care must be given to choose appropriate garnishes; see also **à la.**

garniture (gaahr-nee-tür)   **Garnish.**

gasconne, sauce (sōs gas-kohn)   In French cuisine, veal velouté with white wine, herbs, and anchovy butter; *gasconne* sometimes means flavored with Armagnac.

gastronomy   The science and art of fine food and drink; the connoisseurship of the culinary arts.

gâteau (ga-tō)   French for cake; the plural is **gâteaux.**

gâteau Saint-Honoré (ga-tō sinh-tohn-ohr-ay)   A French pastry dessert of a crown of **choux** puffs on a **pâte brisée** base filled with **crème pastissière** lightened with beaten egg whites, the whole topped with caramel; Saint Honoré is the patron saint of bakers.

Gattinara (gat-tee-NAH-rah) A fine Italian red wine, from the **Nebbiolo** grape, produced near Lake Maggiore in the Piedmont; big, slow-maturing, and long-lasting.

gaufre (GŌ-fruh) French for waffle; *pommes gaufrette* are potato chips cut like waffles in a **mandoline.**

gauloise, à la (ah lah gōl-wahz) A French garnish for clear soup made of cocks' combs and kidneys.

gayette (gī-yet) A sausage from Provence of pork liver and bacon wrapped in **caul** and baked.

gazpacho (gahth-PAH-chō, gahs-PAH-chō) A light, refreshing but thick peasant soup from Andalusia in Spain, made of tomatoes, garlic, olive oil, and vinegar, and sometimes breadcrumbs, mashed together and thinned with ice water; *gazpacho* is traditionally served with a garnish of diced fresh vegetables, hard-boiled eggs, and croûtons, with many regional variations.

Gebäck (geh-BEK) German for pastry; *gebacken* means baked.

gebraten (geh-BRAH-ten) German for roasted.

gebunden (geh-BUHN-den) German for thickened.

gedämpft (geh-DEMPFT) German for steamed.

gefilte fish (geh-FIL-teh) In Jewish cooking, balls of mashed fish, onion, **matzo** meal, egg, and spices cooked variously; originally, the fish mixture was stuffed back into the skin of the fish.

Geflügel (geh-FLÜ-gel) German for poultry.

gefüllt (geh-FÜLT) German for filled, stuffed.

Geisenheim (GĪS-en-hīm) A town in the Rheingau region of Germany known for its excellent Rieslings and for its outstanding wine school.

gekocht (geh-KOKHT) German for cooked.

gelatin, gelatine A glutinous substance found in animal bones, cartilage, and tendons which, when dissolved in water, heated, and chilled, turns to jelly.

gelato (jeh-LAH-tō) Italian for ice cream or water ice; a *gelateria* is an ice cream parlor.

gelée, en (enh jheh-lay) French for in aspic.

gemischt (geh-MEESHT) German for mixed.

Gemüse (geh-MÜ-seh) German for vegetables.

Gênes, pain de See **pain.**

genevoise (jheh-neh-vwahz) A classic French sauce of salmon stock reduced with red wine and herbs and flavored with anchovy butter.

genièvre (JHEH-NYEV-ruh) French for juniper berry; also, gin that is flavored with the berry; the Italian is *ginepro*.

génoise (jhay-nwahz) In French cuisine, a basic sponge cake made with well-beaten eggs to produce a dry, light base for buttercream icings, petits fours, lining for molds, and various other elaborate pastries.

genovese, alla (ah-lah jeh-nō-VAY-say) In the style of Genoa, the northwestern maritime city in Liguria, Italy, whose cuisine stresses fresh herbs, vegetables, and seafood.

geräuchert (geh-ROY-shayrt) German for smoked.

German sauce See **allemande.**

geschabt (geh-SHAHBT) German for ground, grated, scraped.

geschmort (geh-SHMOHRT) German for pot-roasted, stewed.

Gevrey Chambertin (jhay-vray shamh-bayr-tinh) A **commune** in the **Côte d'Or** producing extraordinary Burgundy wines, including first-growth and **grand cru** vineyards, most of which carry the name of **Chambertin** as part of their title.

Gewächs (geh-VEX) German for growth or **cru,** usually meaning an estate-bottled wine.

Gewürz (geh-VÜRTS) German for spice, condiment, seasoning.

Gewürztraminer (geh-VÜRTS-tra-MEE-ner) A grape variety producing a spicy and refreshing white wine quite unusual in quality; planted widely in Alsace, also in Germany, the Tyrol, and California.

ghee (gee) Clarified butter; in India, *ghee* is usually made of buffalo butter. *Vanaspati ghee,* vegetable *ghee*—hydrogenated cooking fat, for everyday use; *usli ghee,* pure fat or butter.

gherkin A small cucumber—the young specimen of certain varieties—used especially for pickling and garnishing.

ghiaccio (GYAH-chō) Italian for ice; *ghiacciato* means iced.

giardiniera, alla (ah-lah jar-dee-NYAY-rah) With mixed sliced vegetables, in Italian cooking.

gibier (jhee-byay) French for game.

giblets   The heart, liver, gizzard, neck, wing tips, feet, leg ends, and sometimes cocks' combs and kidneys of poultry, cooked separately in stocks and stews; goose and duck livers, as special delicacies, are not considered giblets.

gigot   (jhee-gō)   French for leg of mutton; *gigot d'agneau,* leg of lamb; *manche à gigot,* a special attachment to the *gigot* bone that facilitates carving.

gique   (jheek)   French for haunch of venison or boar.

gilthead   A type of sea bream from the Mediterranean, with a gold spot on each side of the head; its fine, firm, white flesh is excellent grilled over fennel stalks and in numerous other aromatic preparations.

gingembre   (JHINH-JHENH-bruh)   French for ginger.

ginger   The rhizome of a plant native to tropical Asia and used as a spice fresh, preserved, or dried and ground; pervasive in Far and Middle Eastern cooking, important dried in medieval European cooking, it is enjoying a new popularity used fresh in America cooking.

gingerbread   A cake flavored with ginger (and often with other spices) and molasses; also a cookie cut into imaginative shapes and decorated.

ginkgo nut   The seed or nut of a tree native to China and considered a delicacy in the Orient; eaten raw or cooked, it is high in starch.

ginnan   Japanese for **ginkgo nut.**

giorno, del   (del JOR-nō)   Italian for of the day, *du jour* in French.

giri   (gee-ree)   A cut, or stroke, of the knife, in Japanese; used with another word.

girolle   (jhee-rōl)   See **chanterelle.**

gîte à la noix   (jheet ah lah nwah)   **Silverside** of beef.

Gjetost   (gyeh-TOHST)   A cheese made in Norway from leftover goats' milk whey that is boiled down for some hours; the milk sugar caramelizes and produces a rich brown color and sweet flavor; shaped in a brick, it can be soft or hard and, strictly speaking, is not a cheese.

glaçage   (gla-sahjh)   French for browning or glazing; see **glaze.**

glace   (glas)   French for ice cream; cake icing; see **extract;** *glacé* means glazed, iced.

glacier   (gla-syay)   French for Ice cream maker—usually a pastry cook in a large kitchen.

glassato (glah-SAH-tō)   Italian for glazed.

Glasse, Hannah (1708–70)   Author of *The Art of Cookery, Made Plain and Easy* (1747), a bestseller for a century despite Dr. Johnson's remark that "Women can spin very well; but they cannot make a good book of cookery." The clarity of her writing ensured her posthumous popularity among servants and mistresses alike.

glaze   To give a shiny appearance to various preparations both hot and cold in one of several ways: to brown meat in its own stock in the oven or under the **salamander;** to brush extract over meat or other food; to coat chilled food with aspic jelly; to cover fish or eggs in a light sauce; to coat hot vegetables with a butter sauce with a little sugar; to coat sweets with sprinkled sugar or strained jam and caramelize them quickly under intense heat; to ice confections.

glögg (gleug)   Swedish hot spiced wine with **akvavit** or brandy, almonds, and raisins.

Gloucester   See **Double Gloucester** and **Single Gloucester.**

glucose   Natural sugar, found in fruit and other foods, which is easily absorbed by the body.

Glühwein (GLÜ-vīn)   German for mulled wine.

gluten   A substance formed when certain flours, especially hard wheat, are combined with water and yeast into an elastic dough, which rises due to trapped air bubbles produced by the yeast; if dough is put under running water or well chewed, the starch is removed, leaving the viscous gluten behind.

glutinous rice   Sweet or sticky rice with a high starch content and opaque creamy color; often served at celebrations and rituals; in both long and short grain varieties.

glycerin, glycerine, glycerol   A sweet, clear, syrupy liquid used to retain moisture in certain kinds of confectionery, such as cake icing, and to sweeten and preserve foods.

gnocchi (NYOHK-kee)   Small Italian dumplings made from **choux** paste, **semolina flour,** or puréed potatoes, poached in water, and served covered with cheese or other sauce or in a soup.

goats' milk cheese   See **chèvre.**

gobi (gō-BEE)   Cabbage in Indian cooking; cauliflower, *phul gobi.*

gobō (gō-bō)   Japanese for burdock root.

gochu jang (go-choo jahng)   Hot fermented chile paste, the staple seasoning in Korean food.

gohan   Japanese for rice.

goi cuon (goy koon)   Vietnamese salad of varied herbs rolled in rice wrappers and served with bean sauce.

goi-ga (goy-gah)   Vietnamese salad of poached chicken with shredded cabbage, carrot, and grapefruit, sprinkled with sesame seeds and served with **nuoc mam** dipping sauce.

goi tom thit (goy tohm tit)   Vietnamese salad of pork and shrimp, served with shrimp chips and **nuoc mam** dipping sauce.

golden buck   In British cooking, poached eggs on toast with **Welsh rarebit.**

golden oak mushroom   See **shiitake.**

goma   Japanese for sesame seeds.

goober   Peanut; the term derives from an African word for the peanut.

gooseberry   A thorny shrub whose tart fruit, mostly small and green or larger and purple, but sometimes white or yellow, is especially popular in France and England for pies, compotes, or preserves; gooseberry sauce is a traditional accompaniment to mackerel in France.

goosefish   See **monkfish.**

gordita (gor-DEE-tah)   In Mexican cooking, cornmeal and potato dough flavored with cheese, fried in lard, and served with ground pork and **guacamole.**

Gorgonzola (gor-gon-ZŌ-lah)   An Italian blue cheese from whole cows' milk, either raw or pasteurized, from the village of the same name near Milan; shaped in twenty-five-pound drums, it has a rough reddish rind and creamy white interior streaked with blue; milder and less salty than **Roquefort,** it is one of the great blue cheeses, but made from a different mold than most.

Gouda (GOO-dah, HOW-dah)   A round whole-milk cows' cheese from the town of the same name near Amsterdam; creamy yellow and firm, its taste becomes more pronounced with age. Gouda is sometimes flavored with **cumin** or **caraway** seeds; young cheeses are covered with yellow wax, older cured cheeses with black wax.

gougère (goo-jhayr)   In French cooking, a savory ring of **choux pastry** flavored with cheese, often eaten as a light meal with red wine.

goujonette (goo-jhoh-net)   In French, fillet of sole cut into strips, floured or breaded, and deep-fried, to resemble little fishes or "gudgeons."

goulash   See **gulyás.**

gourmand (goor-manh)   French for one who appreciates fine food and drink, a gastronome; in English the term has come to mean glutton, but this association is foreign to France.

goût (goo)   French for taste in both senses—flavor and discriminating style.

graham flour   Whole-meal flour made from unbolted wheat; invented in 1840 by the American social reformer Sylvester Graham, who also advocated vegetarianism and sexual abstinence; the crackers sold in supermarkets today under his name, which include among their ingredients sugar, salt, and preservatives, would horrify him.

grana (GRAH-nah)   Italian for a hard granular cheese sometimes eaten when young as table cheese but more often aged and used grated on pasta or minestrone or in cooking; dry, crumbly, and long-lasting, several of this type, such as **Parmesan,** are separately entered.

granada (grah-NAH-dah)   Spanish for pomegranate.

granadilla   See **passion fruit.**

granchio (GRAHN-kyō)   Italian for crab.

Grand Cru (granh krü)   For French **Burgundy** wine, the highest classification, including thirty vineyards in all; their individual appellations usually exclude the name of the **commune.**

Grand Marnier (granh maahr-nyay)   A French liqueur with a **Cognac** base, flavored with bitter orange peel.

grand' mère, à la (ah lah granh mayr)   In French cuisine, garnished with sautéed pearl onions, potatoes cut into olive shapes, parsley, lemon juice, and browned butter.

grandville (grahn-vee)   A classic French white wine sauce with truffles, mushrooms, and shrimp.

granita (grah-NEE-tah)   Italian fruit ice or sweetened coffee to which no **Italian meringue** is added, so that its ice crystals intentionally form a grainy texture.

grappa (GRAHP-pah)   Italian **marc.**

gratin de, au gratin, gratiné (gra-tinh deu, ō gra-tinh, gra-tee-nay) In French, topped with a crust of breadcrumbs and sometimes grated cheese and browned in the oven or under a grill.

Graves (grav) A wine region on the left bank of the Garonne River southwest of Bordeaux producing mostly dry white wines; the best reds are sold under their estate names and, except for **Château Haut-Brion,** were omitted from the 1855 classification; an excellent sweet wine similar to **Sauternes,** usually named *Cérons,* is also produced in Graves.

gravlaks, gravlax (GRAHV-lahks) Scandinavian raw salmon fillets cured for a day or so in sugar and salt and seasoned with dill.

grecque, à la (ah lah GREK) French for vegetables, particularly Greek ones such as artichokes and mushrooms, stewed in olive oil, lemon juice, water, and seasonings.

green onion See **scallion.**

green sauce See under **mayonnaise.**

green tea Unfermented tea whose leaves are minimally processed, yielding a pale tea that is healthful and soothing; green tea is widely drunk in the Orient, especially in Japan.

gremolada (grem-ō-LAH-dah) In Italian cooking, a mixture of chopped parsley, garlic, and grated lemon zest sprinkled over **osso buco** as an aromatic garnish; sometimes spelled *gremolata.*

Grenache (gre-nash) A grape variety, productive and good in quality, planted extensively in southern France, the Rioja region of Spain, and California.

grenadine (gre-na-deen) Pomegranate syrup; used to color and flavor cocktails.

grenouille (gren-noo-yuh) French for frog; *cuisses de grenouille,* frog legs.

gribiche (gree-beesh) A French sauce for chilled fish, based on mayonnaise with capers, chopped gherkins and herbs, and hard-boiled egg whites.

griglia, alla (ah-lah GREE-yah) Italian for grilled.

Grigson, Jane (1928–90) English foodwriter whose newspaper columns and books on charcuterie, vegetables, fruit, and other subjects, show her deeply humanistic attitude towards food.

grill To cook over flames or embers or under a broiler in intense direct heat.

grillade (gree-yad) French for grilled meat; grilling or broiling.

Grimod de la Reynière, Alexandre Balthazar Laurent (1758–1838) (GREE-MŌ deu lah RAY-NYAYR) French gastronome, critic, and author of the *Almanach des Gourmands,* with a mordant sense of humor; he organized a jury to taste and approve the meals sent by willing tradesmen seeking favorable publicity.

grissino (grees-SEE-nō) Italian for breadstick.

grits See **hominy.**

groats Hulled grain, usually broken up or coarsely ground, as with grits (see **hominy**).

groseille (grō-zay) French for currant; *groseille à maquereau* means **gooseberry,** the traditional French garnish for mackerel.

groundnut Peanut.

grouper Several varieties of fish, all members of the **sea bass** family; the lean, firm, moist meat can be cooked in a wide variety of ways.

grouse A large family of wild game birds, prepared in various ways, depending on age and species; one bird usually serves one person.

gruel A thin cereal, usually oatmeal, cooked in milk or water.

grunt Stewed fruit topped with dumplings; an early American dessert similar to **slump.**

Gruyère (grü-yayr) A cows' milk cheese, cooked and pressed, from the valley of the same name in French-speaking Switzerland; originally of skimmed or partially skimmed milk but now made with whole milk; the pale yellow cheese with a golden brown rind is made in rounds of over a hundred pounds and aged; those for the export market are made less salty and with little holes; an excellent table or cooking cheese with fine melting properties.

guacamole (gwah-kah-MŌ-lay) In Mexican cooking, avocado mashed with onion, chilies, lime juice, seasonings, and perhaps tomato, and served as a dip, filling, or sauce.

guajillo (gwah-HEE-yō) A long, thin, dried chili pepper, reddish brown and smooth, very hot, about 4 inches long and 1 inch wide; it is sometimes called **cascabel** because it resembles the tail, rattle, and bite of a rattlesnake, but should not be confused with that chili.

guajolote (gwah-hō-LŌ-tay) Mexican for wild turkey.

guarnito (gwahr-NEE-tō) Italian for garnished.

guava (GWAH-vah) A tropical shrub whose odiferous berrylike fruit is made into pinkish orange jams and jellies; a poor traveler, this delicious fruit is inadequately appreciated outside its native habitat.

güero (GWAYR-ō) A greenish yellow chili pepper, about 4 inches long and 1 inch wide, and pointed; it is fairly hot, with some variation, and is generally used fresh and toasted or canned, but never dried; also called Californian pepper or sweet green pepper.

Gugelhupf (GOO-gel-hupf) Austrian dialect for **Kugelhopf.**

guisantes (gwee-SAHN-tays) Spanish for peas.

guiso, guisado (GWEE-sō, gwee-SAH-dō) Spanish for stew, stewed.

gül (guhl) Turkish for rose or rosewater.

gulai (goo-lī) In a spicy coconut sauce, in Indonesian and Malaysian cooking.

gulyás (GOO-lahsh) A Hungarian stew of beef or sometimes veal or pork, onions, potatoes, and dumplings, seasoned with plenty of **paprika;** it varies widely according to the region and individual, from delicate to hearty. The English spelling is *goulash.*

gum arabic, gum tragacanth Vegetable gums used as emulsifiers and thickeners in certain processed foods such as ice cream, candy, and commercial sauces.

gumbo A thick **Creole** soup or dish thickened with **okra** or **filé powder;** the word *gumbo* is derived from an African word for **okra.**

Gumpoldskirchen (GUM-polts-keer-shen) An Austrian town south of Vienna known for its fine white wine, which is pale, clean, fruity, and pleasing.

gung Thai for shellfish; *gung foi,* prawns, *gung narng,* shrimp, and *gung ta lay,* lobster.

gung Vietnamese for ginger.

Gurke (GOOR-keh) German for cucumber.

gwaytio (gwī-tyō) Thai soup with large rice noodles; *gwaytio neua nam,* a robust beef noodle soup.

gye tang (gay tahng) Korean spicy crab stew, with onions, chilies, and zucchini, served with rice.

gyro (YEER-Ō) See **kebab.**

gyūniku (gyoo-nee-koo) Japanese for beef.

haricot

haba (HAH-bah) Spanish for **fava** or broad bean or, in South America, lima bean; *habas secas* are dried beans.

habañero (hah-bah-NYAYR-ō) A very hot green chili pepper, smooth-skinned and oval, smaller than the **jalapeño;** sometimes available in yellow and red.

hachée (ash-ay) A classic French sauce of chopped shallots and onions reduced in vinegar, mixed with **demi-glace** and tomato purée, and flavored with **duxelles,** capers, diced ham, and parsley.

hacher (ash-ay) In French, to chop or mince; *hachis* means hash.

Hackbraten (HAHK-brah-ten) German for meat loaf.

haddock A small variety of **cod,** usually sold fresh or smoked but not salted.

haggis (HAG-is) A traditional Scottish dish of sheep's stomach stuffed with chopped lamb's liver and heart, onions, black pepper and oatmeal, well steamed like a pudding; celebrated by the Scots poet Robert Burns.

Hahn German for cock.

hǎi shēn (hī shen) Chinese for a spineless marine creature, called a sea cucumber or sea slug; a delicacy relished for its gelatinous texture and saved for special occasions.

hake A small variety of **cod.**

hakusai (hah-koo-sī) Japanese for Chinese cabbage.

haldi (HAHL-dee) Turmeric, in Indian cooking.

half-mourning See **demi-deuil, à la.**

halibut A large flatfish of the **flounder** family.

hallacas (ah-YAH-kahs) Cornmeal mixed with meat, vegetables, and spices, wrapped in banana leaves, and steamed like tamales; from South America.

Hallgarten (HAL-gar-ten) A village in the german Rheingau producing very good full-bodied white wines.

halvah See **helva.**

hamaguri (hah-mah-goo-ree) Japanese for hard-shell clams.

Haman's ears See **Hamantaschen.**

Hamantaschen (HAM-un-tahsh-un) Triangular pastries stuffed with poppy seeds and apple, apricot, or prune filling, traditionally eaten for the Jewish holiday of Purim.

Hammelfleisch (HAM-mel-flīsh) German for mutton.

hamud (hah-MOOD) In Egyptian cooking, a lemony chicken soup, sometimes served as a sauce for rice.

Handkäse (HAHNT-kay-zeh) A pungent acid-curd cheese from Germany made from skimmed cows' milk, in small round or oblong shapes; originally made by hand. In Hesse, the cheese is served "mit Musik"—onion relish— which produces flatulence, hence the name.

Hangtown fry A dish, apparently from the California Gold Rush, of breadcrumbed oysters, fried bacon, and beaten eggs cooked together like an omelet until set.

happy cakes See **banh xeo.**

hard-ball stage Sugar syrup that has reached a temperature of 250–268° F (121–130° C) and that forms a firm ball between the fingers when immersed in cold water.

hard-crack stage Sugar syrup that has reached a temperature of 300–320° F (150–160° C) and that, when immersed in cold water, forms brittle threads and sheets that break easily between the fingers.

hard sauce Butter creamed with sugar and flavored with liquor; served with dessert puddings such as **plum pudding.**

hardtack A hard cracker that was often used for military rations because of its excellent keeping qualities; also known as ship biscuit and pilot biscuit.

hare   A large wild cousin of the rabbit, relished for its dark rich meat with gamy flavor; hare is usually hung, skinned and drawn, marinated, and then roasted or stewed; see also **jugged hare.**

hareng (a-renh)   French for herring.

haricot (a-ree-kō)   French for bean, either fresh (*frais*) or dried (*sec*); *haricot blanc*, white kidney bean, fresh or dried; *haricot de mouton*, mutton stew with turnips and potatoes but no beans at all; *haricot flageolet*, pale green bean, usually fresh in France and rare in the United States; *haricot rouge*, red kidney bean, fresh or dried; *haricot vert*, green string bean.

harina (hah-REE-nah)   Spanish for flour.

harira (hah-REE-rah)   A rich and spicy Moroccan soup of meat, usually lamb, beef, or chicken, chickpeas and noodles, rice, or flour, with lemon, tomatoes and other vegetables. Made in many variations and eaten during Ramadan to break the day-long fast. Sometimes spelled *hareera* or *hereera*.

harissa (hah-REE-sah)   A popular Tunisian sauce of dried chile peppers and garlic thinned with olive oil and lemon juice; colored red and extremely hot.

haroset (hah-RŌ-set)   Paste of chopped apples, raisins, nuts, and red wine, traditional in the Passover seder, symbolizing mortar for buildings.

hartgekocht (HART-geh-kōkht)   German for hard-boiled.

Hase (HAH-zeh)   German for hare; *Hasenpfeffer* is a hare stew flavored with pepper and other spices and braised in red wine.

Haselnuss (HAH-zel-noos)   German for hazelnut.

hash   Chopped meat, often with vegetables, usually combining leftovers, seasonings, and gravy; from the French word *hacher*, meaning to chop.

hashi (hash-ee)   Japanese for chopsticks.

hassoo (hah-SOO)   In Tunisia, a thick winter soup filled with little lamb meatballs.

hasty pudding   See **Indian pudding.**

Hattenheim (HAT-en-hīm)   A village in the German Rheingau whose vineyards produce excellent white wine.

Hauptgerichte (HOWPT-geh-rish-teh)   German for main course.

Hausfrauen Art (HOWS-frow-en art) German for housewife's style, meaning with sour cream and pickles.

hausgemacht (HOWS-geh-mahkt) German for homemade.

Haut-Brion, Château (ō-bree-onh) A very famous red Bordeaux wine, ranked a first growth in the 1855 classification (the only **Graves** included) because of its superlative quality.

Haut-Médoc (ō-may-dohk) The southern and more elevated half of the French Médoc, north of Bordeaux, including **Margaux, Saint-Julien, Pauillac,** and **Saint-Estèphe;** its wines are superior to those from the Bas-Médoc to its north.

Havarti (hah-VAHR-tee) A Danish cheese made from partially skimmed cows' milk, semihard and containing many small holes; pale and mild, sometimes flavored with herbs, its flavor grows sharper with maturity.

haw mok Thai fish dish with green curry paste, coconut milk, chilies, **lemongrass,** and onions, wrapped in banana leaves and steamed.

hazelnut See **filbert.**

head cheese Meat from a pig's or calf's head and other scraps boiled, molded into a loaf, and served in its own jelly with condiments.

heavy syrup Two parts sugar to one part water, dissolved; this is a *sirop à trente* with a density of 30 degrees on the Baumé scale. A light syrup has an approximately equal sugar-to-water ratio.

Heilbutt (HĪL-boot) German for halibut.

heiss (hīs) German for hot.

helado (heh-LAH-dō) Spanish for ice cream.

helles Bier (HEL-es BEER) German light beer.

helva (HEL-vah) Turkish sweet of flour, butter, nuts or sesame seeds, and sugar or honey, served soft and warm or stiffened into a slab.

Hendel (HEN-del) Chicken, in Austrian dialect.

Henne (HEN-neh) German for hen.

Henry IV (ENH-REE KAT-ruh) Garnished with artichoke hearts filled with potato balls and **béarnaise** sauce mixed with meat glaze—a classic French garnish.

hermetical seal Airtight closure of a casserole or container with bread dough or flour and water paste, designed to keep steam inside during cooking.

Hermitage (ayr-mee-tajh) A celebrated Rhône wine from a large steep slope south of Lyons; most of this full-bodied, richly colored and flavored wine is red, from the Syrah grape; the white wine is pale gold, dry, and also full-bodied, if not so fine.

herring A flavorful and nutritious fish, until recently abundant in the Pacific and Atlantic Oceans and very important economically; herring is particularly appreciated in northern Europe and, with its high fat content, lends itself to smoked or pickled preparations (separately entered).

herring rollmop Filleted herring rolled around a pickle or onion, marinated, and served as an appetizer.

Herve (ayrv) A whole-milk cows' cheese, soft, rich, and pungent, made in three-inch cubes with a reddish brown rind; named for the town of Herve, near Liège, Belgium.

hervir (ayr-VEER) In Spanish, to boil.

Hessia A region in western Germany delineated on the north and east by the Rhine, on the west by the Nahe, and on the south by the Pfalz, which produces a large quantity of white wine; the best, from the Riesling grape, comes from particular towns along the Rhine, while the rest, from the Sylvaner grape, is quite ordinary.

hibachi (hih-bah-chee) An Americanized word for a Japanese small open charcoal grill; in Japan, a heater rarely used for cooking.

hickory A tree native to North America whose nut was eaten by the Indians and which we still eat, especially the **pecan;** the word hickory comes from the Algonquin Indian language.

hígado (HEE-gah-dō) Spanish for liver.

hígado a la italiana (ee-GAH-dō ah lah ee-tal-YAHN-ah) A Cuban dish of liver "Italian-style," with onions and peppers, but unknown in Italy.

higo (HEE-gō) Spanish for fig.

hijiki (hee-jee-kee) Asian seaweed with a nutty flavor, usually dried, reconstituted, and cooked for garnishes and salads.

Himbeer (HIM-bayr) German for raspberry.

Himmel und Erde (HIM-mel uhnt AYR-deh) Apples and potatoes with onions and sausage or bacon (literally "heaven and earth"); a very popular German dish.

hinojo (ee-NŌ-ho) Spanish for fennel.

hirame (hee-lah-may) Japanese for flounder.

Hirn (heern) German for brains.

Hirsch (heersh) German for stag, venison.

hiyashi (hee-yah-shee) Japanese for cold, chilled; used with another word.

hochepot (ōsh-pō) A thick French stew, sometimes more of a soup, made from less desirable cuts of meat and winter vegetables; the English and Scottish *hotch-potch, hodge-podge,* and *hot pot* are all derivatives.

Hochheim (HŌHK-hīm) A town in the northeast corner of the German **Rheingau** producing distinctive and characteristic Rhine wine even though situated on the Main River; hock, designating Rhine wine to an Englishman, is derived from its name.

hock See **Hochheim.**

hodge-podge See **hochepot.**

hoecake Jonny cake, originally cooked over an open fire, using the hoe as a griddle, when kitchen equipment was less readily available than now; early American in origin.

hói sìn jiāng (hī shen jung) In Chinese cooking, a thick, rich, dark brown sauce made from fermented soy beans, garlic, sugar, and salt, and used to flavor sauces and marinades; it is a Cantonese version of **sweet bean sauce.**

hoisin sauce See **hói sìn jiāng**.

hoja santa (Ō-hah SAHN-tah) Anise-flavored culinary herb used in southeastern Mexico and around Mexico City.

hollandaise (ō-lanh-dez) In classic French cuisine, a thick emulsion sauce of reduced vinegar whisked with egg yolks, into which melted butter is gradually beaten. It is then flavored with lemon juice and kept warm in a **bain-marie;** one of the basic sauces, it is used primarily with fish, eggs, and vegetables; in modern cooking there are many shortcuts in technique and ingredients.

Holsteiner Katenschinken (HŌL-shtī-ner KAHT-en-shink-en) German for smoked raw ham.

Holsteiner mit Spiegelei; Holstein Schnitzel (HŌL-shtīn-er mit SHPEE-gel-ī) German for veal chop garnished with a fried egg and smoked salmon.

homard (ō-maahr)   French for lobster.

hominy   Corn kernels with the bran and germ removed either by a lye bath, as for whole kernels in lye hominy, or by crushing and sifting, as for pearl hominy; hominy grits, a Southern favorite, are often served as porridge for breakfast or as starch for dinner seasoned with cheese; the word *hominy* is American Indian in origin.

hongroise, à l' (ah l'onh-gwaz)   In French cuisine, meat garnished with cauliflower flowerets, glazed with **Mornay** sauce, paprika, and sautéed potatoes cut into olive shapes.

Honig (HŌ-nig)   German for honey.

hoogli   See **ugli fruit.**

Hoppelpoppel (HOHP-el POHP-el)   German for scrambled eggs with potatoes and bacon.

hoppin' John   A dish of rice and beans—usually black-eyed or cowpeas—cooked with bacon; a staple of African-American cooking in the southern United States and Caribbean, traditional for New Year's Day.

hops   Ripe conical female flowers of the hop vine, used in brewing to impart a bitter flavor to beer, in order to balance the sweetness of the malt; in continental Europe the young male shoots of the hop vine are eaten as a vegetable.

horchata (or-CHAH-tah)   A Spanish summer drink, usually of chufa nuts, pumpkin seeds, or almonds.

horehound   A fragrant Old World herb of the mint family used to flavor candy and medicine; also spelled hoarhound.

hōrensō (hor-en-sō)   Japanese for spinach.

hornear (or-nay-AR)   In Spanish, to bake.

horno (OR-nō)   Spanish for oven; *al horno* means baked.

hors d'oeuvre (OHR-D'EUV-ruh)   Light and stimulating finger food eaten before the main meal (in French, literally "outside the works") as an appetizer; the term is often misspelled: when used as a collective noun it has no final *s*, but a group of specific appetizers takes the plural *s*.

horseradish   A vegetable related to mustard, whose pungent root is grated and mixed with vinegar, then folded into a cream or tomato sauce and served as a condiment or sauce; the tender leaves can be used for salad; native to southeastern Europe.

Hospices de Beaune (hōs-pees deu bōn) A fifteenth-century charitable hospital in Beaune, France, endowed and maintained with some forty **Côte de Beaune** vineyards; at the auspicious annual auction the wine, all very good, often sets Burgundy prices for that year.

hot dieu (hōp deeyoo) Vietnamese for **annatto** seeds, used for their orange color and mild flavor.

hotch-potch See **hochepot** and **Lancashire hot pot.**

hot cross bun A British yeast roll, round, slightly sweetened, with spice and dried fruit added, and traditionally cut or iced with a cross; eaten on Good Friday or during Lent.

hot pot See **hochepot.**

houria (hoo-REE-ah) Tunisian carrot salad, puréed or chopped with **harissa**, mint, capers, and **vinaigrette.**

huachinango (HWA-chih-NANG-ō) Red snapper in Mexican Cooking.

huā jiāo (wha jow) Hot peppercorns from Sichuan, reddish brown in color; when roasted, crushed, and added to salt as a dipping sauce they become *huā jiāo yen.*

huckleberry A small black berry, similar to the blueberry but seedier, tarter, and darker in color, lacking the blueberry's silver sheen; the low shrub grows wild in North America, was praised by Thoreau, and chosen by Mark Twain for the name of his greatest fictional character.

huevo (WAY-vō) Spanish for egg; *huevo a la flamenco,* eggs baked on a bed of peas, peppers, onions, tomatoes, ham, and sausage; *huevo asturian,* scrambled eggs with eggplant, tomatoes, and **fava** beans; *huevo pasados por agua,* soft-boiled eggs; *huevo rancheros,* tortillas "country style," that is, with eggs and a hot spicy sauce; *huevo revueltos,* scrambled eggs.

Huhn (hoon) German for chicken, hen, fowl.

huile (weel) French for oil.

huitlacoche (WEET-lah-KŌ-chay) A fungus that grows on green corn cobs, making a favorite Mexican stuffing for **quesadillas** or soup; the fungus makes the kernels grow large, black, and deformed, but tastes delicious.

huître (WEE-truh) French for oyster.

hull To husk or remove the outer covering of a seed or fruit, as of a nut, or the interior pith, as of a strawberry.

Hummer (HOOM-er) German for lobster.

hummus (HOOM-uhs) Chickpeas mashed to a paste with lemon juice and garlic, flavored with **tahini,** and eaten with **pita** bread as an appetizer throughout the Middle East.

hún tún (whun tun) Chinese for wonton: a pastalike dough wrapper.

hunkar begendi (hyuhn-KYAHR beh-yen-DEE) "The sultan approved," a Turkish dish of cubed lamb braised with onions and tomatoes, and served on creamed roasted eggplant.

huǒ guō (whō gwō) Chinese for Mongolian hot pot; see also **shuàn yáng ròu.**

hush puppies Deep-fried cornmeal dumplings, sometimes flavored with chopped onions, usually eaten as a savory accompaniment to fried fish; from the southern United States.

hyssop (HIS-up) Perennial herb of southern Europe and the Middle East, used fresh or dried in savory dishes and liqueurs for its minty and somewhat bitter flavor.

Indian pudding

ice   See **water ice.**

ice cream   A frozen dessert of cream that is sweetened, flavored variously, and beaten during freezing to keep ice crystals from forming; a custard base is frequently, though not necessarily, used for rich flavor and smooth texture.

icing   A confectionery mixture made of sugar, egg white, butter, flavorings, etc., used to cover or decorate cakes and other pastries; the various types, both cooked and uncooked, differ according to purpose.

icing sugar   British for **confectioners' sugar.**

Idaho potato   See **potato.**

idli   (ID-lee)   Indian steamed rice cake, sweet or spicy, using the same sweet or savory ingredients as for **dosa** but a different method; usually eaten with **sambal** for breakfast, in southern India.

igname   (ee-nyam)   French for yam.

ijja   (EU-jah)   An Arab omelet, related to the Spanish **tortilla**, with many varied ingredients as filling and egg as binder; firm, thick, and cake-like, it is turned out of the pan and cut in wedges to be eaten hot or cold; also spelled *eggah.*

ika   (ee-kah)   Japanese for squid.

ikan   (ee-kan)   Indonsian for fish; *ikan asam manis,* fish in a piquant sweet and sour sauce; *pepes ikan,* fish marinated and baked with coconut.

Île de France (EEL deu FRANHS)   The region around Paris, the original Frankish kingdom, famous for its fine produce, cheeses, bread, pastry, game, meat, and fish; the Île de France also lays claims to the culinary creations of Paris's many fine restaurants.

île flottante (eel flō-tanht)   A French dessert of meringue "islands" on a sea of custard; also sponge cake sliced, sprinkled with liqueur, spread with jam, nuts, and dried fruit, reshaped and covered with **crème Chantilly,** with custard or fruit purée poured over all.

imam bayıldı (ee-MAHM bī-eul—DEU)   A cold Turkish vegetable dish of eggplant sautéed in olive oil with onions, tomatoes, garlic, and parsley; the name in Turkish means "the priest fainted."

imbottito (eem-boh-TEE-tō)   Italian for stuffed.

impanato (eem-pah-NAH-tō)   Italian for breaded.

impératrice, à l' (ah l'imh-payr-a-trees)   In the style of the empress; for desserts, this means rice pudding with candied fruit and cream.

impériale, à l' (ah l'imh-payr-ryal)   In French cuisine, garnished with truffles, **foie gras,** cocks' combs and kidneys, sweetbreads, and Madeira sauce.

Indian fig   See **prickly pear.**

Indian pudding   Cornmeal pudding sweetened with molasses and spiced, made by early English settlers with English methods; also called **hasty pudding.** The word Indian indicates corn.

indienne, à l' (ah l'inh-dyen)   In French cooking, served with boiled rice and sauce flavored with curry powder.

infuse   To steep or soak herbs, spices, or vegetables in a liquid to extract their flavor.

Inglenook   A distinguished California vineyard in the Napa Valley that concentrates on **varietal wines.**

inhame (een-YAM-ay)   Portuguese for yam.

injera (IN-jah-rah)   An Ethiopian flatbread made from *teff,* a type of **millet;** the bread is light, spongy, slightly fermented, eaten with **wot.**

insalata (een-sah-LAH-tah)   Italian for salad.

interlard   To lard: to thread strips of pork fat or **lardons** through meat or other flesh in order to baste it during cooking.

involtine (een-vōl-TEE-nay)   Italian for scallops of meat, usually veal, or fish, pounded thin, stuffed, and rolled up; veal birds.

iota   See **jota.**

Irish coffee   Coffee laced with Irish whiskey, usually flavored with sugar, spices, and cream.

Irish Mist   A liqueur made with Irish **whiskey** flavored with heather honey.

Irish moss   See **carrageen.**

Irish soda bread   A traditional Irish bread, usually baked in free-form rounds, whose leavening agent is baking soda with buttermilk rather than yeast.

Ischlertörtchen (EESH-ler-TERT-shen)   In German, a biscuit spread with jam.

isinglass (Ī-zin-glas)   Gelatin, obtained from the air bladder of sturgeon and other fish, which is pure and transparent.

Ismaîl Bayaldi (EES-mīl bī-YAL-dee)   A classic French garnish, originally from Turkey, of sliced fried eggplant, crushed tomatoes, rice **pilaf**, and sauce **portugaise;** related to **imam bayıldı.**

Italian meringue   Meringue made by whipping hot sugar syrup into stiffly beaten egg whites; used to frost pastries, to lighten pastry and buttercreams, in soufflés, and in sherbets.

italienne, sauce (sōs ee-tal-yen)   A classic French sauce of finely chopped mushrooms with diced ham and chopped parsley.

ivoire, sauce (sōs ee-vwaahr)   *Sauce suprême* (see under **suprême de volaille**) with meat glaze, colored ivory.

à la jardinière

jack See **Monterey Jack.**

Jäger, Jäger Art (YAY-ger) German for hunter's style—with mushrooms and usually in a wine sauce.

jaiba (HĪ-bah) Mexican for crab.

jalapeño (hah-lah-PAY-nyō) A green chili pepper, very hot, about 2½ inches long, generally used fresh.

jalebi (jah-LAY-bee) An Indian dessert sweet; **besan** batter is pressed through a pastry bag in tubular coils, deep-fried, and dipped in rosewater syrup; also spelled *jellabies.*

jalousie (jha-loo-zee) In French cooking, a **feuilletage** pastry strip with a sweet filling, whose top layer is cut into parallel strips like a Venetian blind (hence its name).

jambalaya (jahm-bah-LĪ-yah) A dish from **Cajun** cuisine of rice with ham, shellfish, sausage, chicken, and beans, seasoned with **Creole** vegetables and spices; the ingredients vary widely.

jambon (jhamh-bonh) French for ham.

jamón (hah-MŌN) Spanish for ham.

japonaise, à la (ah lah jha-pō-nez) In French cuisine, garnished with Chinese or Japanese artichokes and potato croquettes.

jardinière, à la (ah lah jhaahr-dee-nyayr) In French cuisine, "in the style of the gardener's wife": garnished with various fresh vegetables cooked and arranged separately around the main piece of meat or poultry.

Jarlsberg (YAHRLZ-bayrg) A Norwegian hard cows' milk cheese, made from partially skimmed milk, nutty and sweet, made in large wheels, and similar to **Emmental.**

jarret (jhaahr-ray) French for knuckle or hock.

Jerez de la Frontera (hayr-EZ day lah frohn-TAY-rah) A city in southern Spain whose outlying vineyards produce sherry (the name is an Anglicization of *Jerez*).

jerky Preserved meat, usually beef and originally sometimes buffalo, that is cut into thin strips and dried in the sun; used by the American Indians and early settlers as a staple for its keeping powers.

jeroboam (jayr-oh-BŌ-um) A large wine bottle with the capacity of six ordinary bottles (about ⅘ of a gallon); named for the first king of the Hebrews.

Jerusalem artichoke A tuberous vegetable of the sunflower family, native to North America, whose knotty root is a versatile and nutritious foodstuff; also called sunchoke; "Jerusalem" is a corruption of the Italian *girasole,* meaning "sunflower."

jeyuk sun (jay-ook sun) In Korean cooking, pork strips marinated and stir-fried with sliced potatoes, garnished with egg strips and chilies, onions, and **sesame** seeds.

jhinga (JING-ah) Shrimp or prawn in Indian cooking; also spelled *ginga.*

jī (jee) Chinese for chicken; *jī ròu* designates chicken meat.

jiāng (jung) Chinese for sauce; the word also means ginger root.

jiāng yóu (jung yō) Chinese for soy sauce in light, medium, and dark grades; light soy sauce, saltier and thinner, is used with seafood and chicken; dark soy sauce, thick, rich, and strong, is best with red meat roasts, stews, and barbecues.

jícama (HEE-kah-mah) A root vegetable, crisp and slightly sweet, that resembles the turnip; used both raw and barely cooked in Mexican and Asian cooking.

jigger A volume measure of 1½ ounces for making cocktails.

jitomate (hee-tō-MAH-tay)   Mexican word for tomato; not to be confused with **tomatillo.**

Johannisberg (yō-HAHN-is-bayrg)   A German village in the Rheingau that produces fine wine; that from the Schloss Johannisberg, overlooking the Rhine, deserves its venerable reputation.

Johannisberg Riesling   A fine white grape variety from Germany cultivated increasingly in California.

John Dory   A saltwater fish found mainly in European waters, especially the Mediterranean, with two black spots surrounded by yellow rings on either side of the body, said to be the fingerprints of St. Peter (hence its French name, *Saint-Pierre*); its delicate, white flavorful flesh is valued in many recipes, either in fillets or chunks, as for **bouillabaisse.**

johnny cake, jonny cake   A hearth- or pancake of cornmeal, sometimes mixed with other grains, cooked in the ashes or in a griddle or pan; the name is often said to be derived from Shawnee and the cake originally from Rhode Island, but what is certain is that early American settlers adapted the native cornmeal to a familiar cooking method.

Joinville, à la (ah lah jhwinh-vee)   Garnished with finely diced shrimp, truffles, mushrooms, and bound in **sauce normande.**

jollof (JOL-uf)   A West African dish of fried beef or chicken pieces with onions, chilies, tomatoes, and rice, in many variations; like a **risotto.**

jon (jawn)   Korean for pancakes or sometimes fritters; *pa jon*, a scallion pancake, commonly sold as a street snack.

jota (YŌ-tah)   A robust Italian soup of beans with sauerkraut, potatoes, and bacon cooked slowly; *jota* comes from Trieste, its unusual spelling a holdover from the Austro-Hungarian influence (the Italianized spelling is *iota*).

judía (hoo-DEE-ah)   Spanish for kidney bean, string bean; *judías verdes* are green string beans.

jugged hare   Hare (or other furred game) that is stewed in an earthenware pot or jug to which some of the animal's blood is added, to thicken the sauce just before serving.

jujube (JOO-joob)   The fruit of a tropical Asian plant, sometimes called Chinese date, which is picked ripe, dried, and used to sweeten cough medicines; also the name of a candy.

julienne (jhü-lyen) Vegetables or other foodstuffs cut into fine matchsticks; a clear consommé garnished with sautéed vegetables cut into matchsticks.

juniper An evergreen tree whose purple berries flavor gin, marinades, sauerkraut, and game dishes.

junket Milk curds formed with **rennet** and served as a custardlike dessert.

Jurançon (jhür-anh-sonh) An unusual and renowned wine from the foothills of the Pyrenees in southwestern France, possessing a gold color and a sweet, spicy taste.

jus (jhüs) French for juice; *au jus* means meat served with its natural juices; *jus de viande* means gravy.

kale

ka (kah) Thai for **galangal**.

k'ab al-ghzal (kab al-HRAZL) "Gazelles' horns," crescent pastries filled with almond paste, from Morocco.

kabak tatlısı (kah-BAHK TAHT-leu—seu) A Turkish dessert of pumpkin slices slowly cooked until tender, served in syrup topped with crushed walnuts.

Kabeljau (KAH-bel-yow) German for cod.

Kabinett (kah-bee-NET) Superior or special reserve unsweetened wine, usually estate-bottled and from the German Rheingau.

kabocha (ka-bō-cha) Japanese for pumpkin, squash.

kabu (kah-boo) Japanese for turnip.

kadaif See **kunaifa**.

kadın budu (kah-DEUN boo-DOO) "Ladies' thighs," a Turkish dish of lamb and rice meatballs first poached, then battered and fried.

kadın göbeği (kah-DEUN geu-BAY-ee) "Ladies' navels," a Turkish dish of dimpled balls of batter, deep-fried and soaked in syrup.

Kaffee (KAH-fay) German for coffee; afternoon coffee in Germany can include elaborate cake and sandwiches, a social occasion not unlike the English tea.

Kaffir lime (KAF-er) A member of the citrus family whose fruit has bumpy, nubbly skin; much used in the cooking of southeast Asia, especially Thailand, its zest, juice, and especially leaves, chopped and added to dishes at the last moment.

kafta (KAHF-tah) In Arab cooking, ground meat flavored with cinnamon or other spices and shaped into balls; the Turkish is *köfta*, the Indian *kofta*.

kahlúa (kah-LOO-ah) A Mexican coffee-flavored liqueur.

kahve (KAH-veh) Turkish coffee, very strong, aromatic, and foamy on top.

kai (kī) Thai for egg; *kai kwan*, eggs stuffed with pork and seafood and deep-fried.

k'ak bil yuyu (KAHK bil YOO-yoo) Tunisian doughnuts of orange-flavored egg dough deep-fried and honey dipped; eaten with Arab coffee.

kakadi (KAH-kah-dee) Cucumber in Indian cooking.

kake (kah-kay) Japanese for noodles; used with another word.

kaki (kah-kee) Japanese for **persimmon**; several European languages, including French, have borrowed the word *kaki* for persimmon; it also means oyster in Japanese.

Kalamata See under **olive.**

Kalb (kalp) German for veal; *Kalbschnitzel,* veal cutlet cooked simply in butter; *Kalbshaxe,* veal shanks or knuckles, very popular in Bavaria.

kalbi jim (gal-bee CHIM) Beef or pork ribs, braised with chestnuts and mushrooms in a spicy sauce; a Korean dish.

kale A loose, green leafy vegetable of the cabbage family, highly nutritious; its hardiness in frost and snow makes it a winter staple in cold rural areas, where it appears in such country dishes as **colcannon** and kailkenny.

kalt German for cold.

kamaboko Japanese fish paste or sausage in many varieties.

kambing Indonesian for lamb.

kampyō Japanese for dried gourd shavings.

kang kung (kahng kuhng) Laotian soup of melon, dried shrimp, mushrooms, ginger, and chicken stock.

kani (kah-nee) Japanese for crab.

Kaninchen (kah-NEEN-shen) German for rabbit.

kanom (kah-nohm) Thai for cake, cookie; *kanom mo kaeng,* baked custard squares; *kanom klug,* coconut pancakes.

kanten Japanese for **agar-agar** seaweed.

kăo (kow) In Chinese, to roast or bake.

kao (kow) Generic Thai term for rice or grain; *kao nieo,* sticky rice; *kao pad,* fried rice.

Kapaun (kah-POWN) German for capon.

kapee (kap-ee) Thai for shrimp paste.

Kaper (KAH-payr) German for caper.

karashi (kah-rah-shee) Japanese for mustard.

karela (kah-RAY-lah) **Bitter melon,** a popular vegetable in Indian cooking.

Karfiol (kar-FYŌL) Cauliflower, in Austrian dialect. See also **Blumenkohl.**

kari (KAH-ree) In Indian cooking, curry, seasoned sauce; also the aromatic leaves of the *kari* plant.

kari-kari (KAH-ree KAH-ree) Philippine oxtail stew flavored with garlic and onion, the sauce thickened with crushed peanuts and rice flour.

Karotte (kah-ROHT-teh) German for carrot.

Karpfen (KAR-pfen) German for carp—a very popular fish in Germany and traditional for Christmas Eve.

Kartoffel (kar-TOHF-el) German for potato; *Kartoffelbrei,* mashed potatoes, *Kartoffelklösse,* dumplings, and *Kartoffelpuffer,* potato pancakes.

Käse (KAY-zeh) German for cheese; *Käseteller,* cheese plate; *Käsetorte,* cheesecake.

kasha Hulled, crushed, and cooked groats, usually **buckwheat,** used in Russian cooking.

Kasnudeln (KAHZ-nood-eln) German noodles stuffed with savory meat and cheese filling or fruit and poppy seed filling for dessert.

Kassler Rippenspeer (KAHS-ler RIP-en-shpayr) Cured and smoked pork loin served on a bed of sauerkraut, mashed potatoes, and apples or red cabbage and potato dumplings, with a red wine and sour cream gravy; a great favorite in Germany.

Kastanie (kah-STAHN-yeh) German for chestnut.

Katenschinken (KAT-en-shink-en) German smoked country ham, originally from Schleswig-Holstein; *Katenwurst,* smoked sausage from the same area; the word *Katen,* peasant hut or cottage, where these meats were originally cured.

katsuo-bushi (kat-soo-ō-boo-shee) Japanese dried bonito flakes, essential in making **dashi.**

kau muong (kow muong) Vietnamese for water spinach, with heart-shaped leaves and hollow stems; eaten stir-fried or wilted in salads and soups, its taste is mild yet tangy.

kayısı (KĪ-yeu—seu) Turkish for apricots.

kaymak (KĪ-mak) Turkish clotted cream made from buffalo milk, very thick, for spreading on bread or making desserts.

kdra See **qdra.**

kebab (keh-BAHB) In Turkish cuisine, pieces of seasoned and marinated meat, usually lamb, grilled over or under a fire. In *shish kebab,* meat cubes are threaded on a skewer or sword (*şiş* or *shish*), often with vegetables; the Russian version, from the Caucasus, is *shashlyk.* For *döner kebab,* long thin strips of meat turning on a spit; the Greek word for this rotating spit is *gyro,* the Arab *shwarma.*

kedgeree See **kitcheri.**

kéfir (KAY-feer) Fermented milk, slightly effervescent and alcoholic, widely consumed in the Middle East and Russia; the *kéfir* bacteria sours the milk (usually cows'), making it thick, frothy, and healthful.

kefta (KEF-tah) Moroccan for **kafta.**

kejenou (KAY-jay-noo) Chicken and shrimp braised in an earthenware pot with onions, tomatoes, chilies, spices, and rice and served in individual ramekins; from the Ivory Coast.

Keks (kayks) German for biscuit.

kelapa (keh-lah-pah) Indonesian and Malaysian for coconut; *kelapa sayur,* vegetables simmered in spicy coconut milk.

Kellerabfüllung See **Original-Abfüllung.**

Kelerabzug   See **Original-Abfüllung.**

kelp   See **konbu.**

kesar   (KAY-sahr)   **Saffron** in Indian cooking.

kesksou   (KES-koo)   Algerian for **couscous.**

ketchup   Savory sauce or condiment, Chinese in origin, made from a variety of foodstuffs, such as mushrooms, anchovies, or oysters, pickled in brine; our commercially manufactured tomato ketchup is a sorry comedown; also spelled *catchup, catsup,* and *katsup.*

Key lime pie   A pie originally made from a variety of lime grown on the Florida Keys that is no longer commercially cultivated; the pie has a pastry or graham-cracker crust with an egg yolk, **condensed milk,** and lime-juice filling, with a meringue topping.

kheer   (keer)   Indian rice pudding made with milk, sweet spices, and almonds; also spelled *khir.*

khira   (keer-ah)   Indian for cucumber; also spelled *kheera.*

khoresh   (koh-RESH)   Thick sauce, almost like a stew, with small pieces of meat, vegetables, and fruit and mild spices; eaten with rice in Persian cooking.

khoshaf   (HŌ-shahf)   In Middle Eastern cooking, dried fruit salad, usually of macerated apricots, raisins, almonds, and pistachios.

khoya   (KOY-ah)   Fresh milk condensed to a thick paste by boiling and simmering, used for sweet dishes such as **kulfi** in Indian cooking.

khubz   (hoobz)   Arabic for bread.

khudar   (HOO-dar)   Arabic for vegetables.

kibbeh   (KIH-bee)   **Bulghur** and ground lamb, onions, and pine nuts, deep-fried or served raw; its origin is Lebanese and it has many variations.

kidney   A pair of organs embedded in white fat, those from veal or lamb considered best; excellent for various culinary preparations trimmed of exterior membrane and interior gristle, then sautéed or broiled quickly or braised slowly in stews or meat pies.

kielbasa   (KEEL-bah-zah)   Polish sausage made of pork, sometimes beef or veal, flavored with garlic, smoked, and cooked; its links are very long.

Kiev, chicken à la   See **chicken Kiev.**

kiku (kee-koo) Japanese edible chrysanthemum.

kikurage (kee-koo-rah-gay) Japanese for **cloud ear** or **wood ear** mushroom, usually dried.

kim chee A pungent Korean condiment of pickled shredded vegetables, including Chinese cabbage, radishes, cucumbers, greens, onions, garlic, and chili peppers, seasoned with fermented shellfish and salt; the condiment varies widely in its strength and is especially common in winter, when fresh vegetables are unavailable; also spelled *keem chee* and *kim chi.*

king Thai for ginger.

king crab A large variety of **crab** living in northern Pacific waters and growing up to twenty pounds; the meat is usually sold cooked and frozen; also called Alaska king crab and Japanese crab.

king salmon See **salmon.**

Kipferl (KIP-fayrl) A German crescent-shaped roll, sweeter and doughier than a **croissant.**

kippered herring, kipper Herring that has been split, lightly salted, dried, and smoked to preserve it; a favorite breakfast dish in Britain.

Kir (keer) See **cassis.**

Kirsch (keersh) German for cherry.

Kirschwasser (KEERSH-vah-ser) A German colorless liqueur distilled from the fermented mash of wild cherries, especially those grown in the French Alsace and the German Black Forest; often used as a flavoring in confectionery and pastry; sometimes called simply *Kirsch.*

kissel (KIS-sel) A Russian and Baltic berry pudding, often made with puréed strawberries, thickened with potato flour or cornstarch; also used as a dessert sauce.

kitcheri (KIH-cher-ee.) Kedgeree; cooked rice, lentils, and spices, of Hindi origin; when the English anglicized this Indian dish they often served it with leftover fish, hard-boiled eggs, and curry, which is how it survives as a breakfast dish in England today.

kited fillet Fish cut through along the backbone and filleted but left attached at the belly.

kiwano A spiky, bright orange fruit that, despite its comic-book looks, is an ancient fruit native to Africa; the green pulp, gelatinous and juicy, with lots of white seeds, tastes bland; also called *horned melon.*

kiwi   A small tree of Chinese origin whose plum-shaped fruit is covered with a thin layer of brownish fuzz; once peeled, the soft green interior with small black seeds radiating from a pale green center is entirely edible, tasting somewhere between a strawberry and melon; also called Chinese gooseberry, but recently marketed as kiwi.

Klopse   (KLOHP-seh)   German ground meatballs usually containing two or three kinds of meat; *Königsberger Klopse* are poached meatballs of pork with veal or beef, flavored with anchovies and served with a lemon, sour cream, and caper sauce; from the Slavic northeast.

Klösse   (KLEUS-eh)   German dumplings or meatballs; the singular is *Kloss.*

Kloster Eberbach   See **Steinberg.**

kluay   (kloo-ay)   Thai for banana; *kluay tord*, fried bananas.

Knackwurst   (KNAHK-voorst)   German sausages similar to hot dogs but thicker.

knädlach   (KNED-lakh)   Jewish dumplings of **matzo** meal, egg, ground almonds, and chicken fat dropped into chicken broth; spelled variously.

knead   To work dough with the fingers and heels of the hand in order to distribute ingredients uniformly, develop the gluten, and produce an even texture ready for rising.

knish   Chopped chicken livers or **kasha** wrapped in a pastry of mashed potatoes, flour, and chicken fat; traditional Jewish dish from Eastern Europe.

Knoblauch   (KNOB-lowkh)   German for garlic.

Knödel   (KNEU-del)   German for dumpling.

Kobe gyū   (kō-bay gyoo)   Japanese steer raised and pampered to an impeccably high standard for its delectably tender meat which, in accordance, is exorbitantly expensive.

kofta   See **kafta.**

Kohl   (kōl)   German for cabbage; *Kohlrouden* is cabbage stuffed with ground meats and braised.

kohlrabi   (kōl-RAH-bee)   A vegetable in the cabbage family whose stem swells just above the ground into a bulbous knob; this bulb, the long stems, and the leaves are edible and taste like cabbage and turnip, which together give it its name; favored in central and eastern Europe and Asia.

koi-kuchi shōyu (koy-koo-chee shō-yoo)   Japanese dark soy sauce, thicker and heavier but less salty than light soy sauce (*usu-kuchi shōyu*).

Kompott (kohm-POHT)   German compote of stewed fruit.

konafa   See **kunaifa**.

konbu (kon-boo)   Japanese dried kelp, essential in making **dashi;** sometimes spelled *kombu;* should be soaked and scored before use and can be reused.

Konditorei (kohn-dee-tor-Ī)   German for a pastry shop, where coffee and hot chocolate are offered.

kong (kohng)   Thai for snack.

Königenpastete (KEU-ni-gen-pas-TAY-teh)   German for pastry filled with meat and mushrooms or other savory fillings.

konnyaku (kon-yah-koo)   Literally, "devil's tongue jelly" in Japanese; a translucent cake made from arum root.

Kopfsalat (KŌPF-sah-laht)   German for lettuce salad, head of lettuce.

korma (KOOR-mah)   Minced vegetables or meat in Indian cooking; by extension, a dish braised with yogurt or cream, usually rich and spicy but not necessarily hot; also spelled *qorma*.

Korn   German for grain, cereal; the word means the dominant grain in a specific region, whether rye, wheat, or barley—not necessarily corn.

kosher   According to Jewish dietary laws, the *kashruth*, as set forth in the *Talmud*.

Kotelett (koh-teh-LET)   German for cutlet, chop.

Krabbe (KRAH-beh)   German for **crab,** the plural *Krabben* often means shrimp.

Krakauer (KRAHK-ow-er)   German for Polish ham sausage.

Krapfen (KRAH-pfen)   Sweet Bavarian fritters, similar to doughnuts.

Kraut (krowt)   German for plant, herb, greens; on a menu the word usually means cabbage.

kreatopita (kray-ah-TŌ-pee-tah)   A Greek meat pie wrapped in **phyllo** dough.

Krebs (krayps) German for **crab,** crayfish.

Kren German for **horseradish;** *Krenfleisch,* top round of beef boiled, sliced, and served with bread, gherkins, and horseradish, from Bavaria.

kreplach (KREP-lakh) Small dough turnovers with savory filling, often served in soup, eaten during the Jewish celebration of Succoth.

Kreuznach (KROYTS-nakh) A German town on the Nahe River, west of the Rhine, that is the center of the valley's wine industry; a good wine school is located there.

Kronsbeer (KRŌNS-bayr) A berry similar to the cranberry.

krupnik (KRUHP-nik) Mushroom barley soup, from eastern Europe.

kuài zi (kwī tseu) Chinese for chopsticks.

kubecake (KOOB kayk) Coconut rum ball, sweet and gingery, sold by street vendors in West Africa; potently flavored but not cakelike.

Küche (KÜ-she) German for kitchen, cooking.

Kuchen (KOO-khen) German for cake, tart, pastry.

kudamono (koo-dah-mō-nō) Japanese for fruit.

kugel (KOO-gel) A baked casserole or pudding, associated especially with the Jewish holiday of Hanukkah.

Kugelhopf (KOO-gel-hohpf) A German yeast cake, sometimes made from **brioche** dough, flavored with currants steeped in brandy and baked in a special fluted mold strewn with almonds; now a specialty of Alsace, it is originally from Austria where it is called *Gugelhupf,* each region having its traditional molds.

kulibyaka (koo-lee-BYAH-kah) A Russian pie filled with layers of salmon or fish, rice or kasha, herbs, mushrooms, onion, etc., oval in shape, large or small in size; French *haute cuisine* has adapted it as *coulibiac.*

kulfi (KUL-fee) Indian ice cream, made from **khoya,** cream, starch, sugar, nuts, and rosewater; served frozen hard in squares, textured with lumps of cream and nuts.

kulich (KOO-lish) A tall cylindrical Russian cake in the shape of a priest's hat, flavored with fruit, almonds, and saffron; this is the Russian Orthodox ceremonial dessert for Easter, decorated with the letters *XB*, signifying "Christ Is Risen," and traditionally served with **paskha.**

kulikuli (KOO-lee-KOO-lee) An African biscuit or ring made of peanut paste, fried and eaten as a snack or **rusk.**

Kümmel (KÜ-mel) German for caraway seed, much used with cabbage, stew, and pastry; also the liqueur flavored with caraway.

kumquat A small oval citrus fruit, native to China, eaten whole, either fresh or preserved in syrup, and often used as a garnish; its rind is sweeter than its pulp; the name means "golden orange" in Cantonese.

kunaifa (KNAH-fee) Middle Eastern pastries made from **phyllo,** similar to **baklava;** called *kadaif* in Turkey and Greece.

kuri (koo-ree) Japanese for chestnuts.

Kutteln (KOO-teln) German for tripe.

kuy tieu (kwee tyoo) Traditional Cambodian Khmer soup of noodles, sliced pork, bean sprouts, fried garlic, and cilantro.

kvass (kvahs) A fermented Russian drink similar to beer, made from yeast, rye, and barley; it is used to flavor **borsch, chlodnik,** and other soups; sometimes spelled *kwas.*

kyinkyinga (chin-CHING-ah) West African meatballs skewered with sweet peppers, grilled, and sprinkled with roasted crushed peanuts; often sold on the street.

kyūri (kyoo-ree) Japanese cucumber.

lettuce

la chuoi (la chooee)   Vietnamese for banana leaves, used for steaming dumplings, coconut rice, fish, and other foods, also for lining steamers.

laban (LUH-ban)   Arabic for yogurt, especially in Syria and Lebanon; *laban zabadi* in Egypt. In North Africa *laban* means milk.

labna (LUB-nah)   Strained yogurt in the Middle East; also spelled *labni*, *lubni*, or *labneh*; sometimes salted, spiced, shaped into balls, and rolled in olive oil; eaten with bread for breakfast, an Arab favorite.

Labskaus (LAHBS-kows)   German "seaman's stew" from Hamburg, of pickled pork or beef cooked with onions and potatoes, sometimes with pickled fish, beets, or gherkins as garnish.

Lachryma Christi (LAH-kree-mah KREE-stee)   A white wine from the vineyards on Mt. Vesuvius near Naples, Italy, pale, gold, and fairly dry; the name means "tears of Christ"; a sparkling white wine with the same name is made elsewhere in Italy.

Lachs (lahks)   German for salmon.

lacón con grelos (lah-KÓN kon GRAY-lōth)   Cured pork shoulder with turnip tops—a famous dish from Galicia in Spain.

lactic acid   The acid in sour milk produced by bacterial starter culture, which turns lactose (milk sugar) into lactic acid, causing the coagulation of the milk and the first step in the cheesemaking process; lactic acid is also present in rested muscle tissue and acts as a natural preservative in slaughtered meat. Many milk products, such as **buttermilk, sour cream, kéfir,** and **yogurt,** are made by a lactic culture.

Lafite, Château (sha-tō lah-feet)   A great Bordeaux vineyard, from Pauillac in the Haut-Médoc, which fully deserves its fame; ranked a first growth in 1855, it is owned by the Rothschild family; the wine is full-bodied and long-lived, with remarkable bouquet and depth—perhaps the greatest red wine of all.

lager   Bottom-fermented beer that has been aged; most American beers are lager.

lagniappe (lan-yap)   In New Orleans, a **Creole** word meaning a little something extra, a bonus, such as a thirteenth roll.

lahm   Arabic for lamb.

lahmejune (lah-meh-JOON)   Armenian pizza; open **pita** dough topped with finely chopped lamb, tomatoes, peppers, onions, and herbs; also spelled *lahma bi ajeen* and other ways; the Turkish version is *lahmacun*.

lait (lay)   French for milk; *au lait*, with milk.

laitue (lay-tü)   French for lettuce.

là jiāo jiàng (lah jow jung)   Chinese for hot chili sauce; a condiment made from chili peppers, vinegar, and seasonings; red in color, red hot in taste.

laksa (lahk-sah)   Malaysian dish of rice noodles in a spicy fish and shrimp soup rich with coconut milk; bean sprouts, shredded cucumber, and greens may be added, and **sambal** may be served on the side.

Lambrusco (lahm-BROO-skō)   A slightly effervescent red wine, fruity, fragrant, and pleasant, made near Modena from the *lambrusco* grape.

lamb's lettuce   A plant indigenous to Europe, whose dark green, nutty-flavored leaves are used for winter salads; it is prized by the French; also called corn salad and *mâche*.

lampone (lahm-PŌ-nay)   Italian for raspberry.

lamprey (LAM-pree)   A salt- or freshwater fish similar to the **eel;** its fatty flesh is eaten in various ways, most often stewed.

Lancashire (LANK-ah-shur)   A creamy white cows' milk cheese from England, cooked and pressed yet still soft and crumbly; true farm-house Lancashire has a full flavor and excellent melting qualities for **Welsh rarebit** and other dishes, but travels poorly or not at all; the factory-made variety is a pale comparison.

Lancashire hot pot   A traditional English stew of secondary cuts of lamb, especially neck, stewed with layered potatoes and onions, lamb kidneys and oysters often included; a relative of the French **hochepot.**

Landjäger (LAHNT-yay-ger) A smoked sausage from Swabia in Germany.

langouste (lanh-goost) French for rock or spiny lobster, as it is called in the United States; called saltwater crayfish or crawfish in Britain; found in the Mediterranean and Pacific, its claws are small, so most of the meat comes from the tail; when cooked its color is paler than lobster red; the Spanish word for this crustacean is *langosta.*

langoustine (lanh-goo-steen) French for a small lobster, a saltwater crayfish; also called Dublin Bay prawn (British), Norway lobster, and *scampo* (Italian).

langue (lanhg) French for tongue.

langue-de-chat (LANHG-deu-SHA) French for a long, thin cookie shaped like a cat's tongue, hence the name; light and dry, these cookies often accompany simple desserts and sweet wines.

Languedoc (LANH-ge-DŌK) A region in southeastern France along the Mediterranean, a former province, with wonderful produce and an excellent gastronomic tradition; some of its specialties are **cassoulet, confit, brandade** de morue, **Roquefort,** Bouzigues oysters, and other seafood, to name just a few.

languedocienne, à la (ah lah LANH-ge-DŌ-SYEN) In French cuisine, meat or poultry garnished with eggplant rounds, *cèpes,* and tomatoes *cancassés,* all sautéed in oil, with chopped parsley.

laos Indonesian for **galangal.**

lapin (la-pinh) French for rabbit; *lapin de garenne,* wild rabbit; *lapin en gibelotte,* rabbit stew with onions, mushrooms, and **lardons,** in white wine sauce.

Lapsang Souchong See **Souchong.**

lard Rendered pork fat, excellent for flaky pastry because of its solidity and for deep-frying because of its high smoke point and purity; as a saturated fat high in cholesterol, however, it has become less popular. See also **interlard.**

lard de poitrine fumé (laahr de pwah-treen fü-may) French for bacon.

larder (laahr-day) In French, to lard, to interlard.

lardo (LAR-dō) Italian for salt pork; *lardo affumicato* is bacon.

lardon (laahr-donh)   French for lardoon; larding fat cut into long strips and threaded through lean cuts of meat by a special larding needle in order to moisten the meat as it cooks; the term also includes pork or bacon, diced, blanched, and fried, used to flavor and moisten braised dishes and stews.

largo   A long, thin chili pepper, pale yellow green in color, fairly hot; often used in Mexican soups and stews.

lasagne (lah-ZAH-nyeh)   Large flat ribbons of Italian pasta about 4½ inches wide, baked in layers with sauce, cheese, or other filling; *lasagne* is usually made with egg and often puréed spinach as well to color it green.

lassi (LAH-see)   Refreshing Indian yogurt drink, salted or sweet.

lassoon (lah-SOON)   Garlic in Indian cooking.

latkes (LAHT-kez)   Potatoes grated and fried in pancakes, traditionally eaten at the Jewish festival of Hanukkah.

Latour, Château (sha-tō la-toor)   A great and renowned Bordeaux vineyard in Pauillac in the Haut-Médoc; ranked a first growth, it deserves its place next to Margaux and Lafite; the wine is robust, deep-colored, and long-lived.

latte (LAHT-tay)   Italian for milk.

lattuga (lah-TOO-gah)   Italian for lettuce.

Lauch (lowkh)   German for leek.

lauro (LOW-rō)   Italian for bay leaf.

La Varenne, François Pierre de (lah vaahr-en)   (c. 1615–78)   Seventeenth-century chef and author of *Le Cuisiner Français* (1651), a landmark cookbook which, breaking with the Middle Ages, began the culinary tradition of the golden age; La Varenne set up a system of ready stocks, **liaisons** (**roux** first appeared in his book), **forcemeats,** and herb and spice mixtures to be drawn upon as needed.

lavash (lah-VAHSH)   Armenian thin flat wheat bread, often baked in large sheets; used to scoop up food or spread and rolled up as a kind of sandwich.

laver (LAY-ver)   Thin, black seaweed used in Japanese cooking and called **nori** in Japan; in Wales it is often called laverbread.

leavening   Any agent that produces gas in dough or batter by means of **fermentation,** thus raising and lightening it. **Yeast, baking powder,**

and **baking soda** are all common forms of leavening; beaten egg whites, although they do not involve fermentation, are another kind of leavening.

Leber (LAY-ber) German for liver.

Leberkäs (LAY-ber-kays) Meat loaf or pâté of mixed ground meats, from Bavaria.

Leberknödelsuppe (LAY-ber-KNEU-del-zoo-peh) Soup of clear meat broth with liver dumplings, from Bavaria.

Leberwurst (LAY-ber-voorst) A German smoked sausage made from ground pork liver and (usually) pork or veal meat.

Lebkuchen (LAYB-koo-khen) German spiced honey cake traditionally eaten at Christmas.

leche (LAY-chay) Spanish for milk; the word can also mean custard.

lechecillas (lay-chay-THEE-lahth) Spanish for sweetbreads.

lechón asado (lay-CHŌN ah-THAH-dō) Spanish for roast suckling pig.

lechuga (lay-CHOO-gah) Spanish for lettuce.

Leckerli (LEK-er-lee) Swiss rectangular biscuit, flavored with cinnamon, honey, dried citrus peel, and almonds; from Basel.

leek An ancient member of the lily family, originating in the Mediterranean; its flavor, more subtle than that of other onions, lends itself to soups, stews, and braises; because the leek lacks a well-defined bulb, dirt gets well down into its leaves, necessitating careful washing.

lees The sediment that settles in the wine barrel before bottling.

legumbres (lay-GOOM-brayth, lay-GOOM-brays) Spanish for vegetables; *legumbres secos,* dried vegetables.

legume (lay-GYOOM) The seed pod of leguminous plants whose peas or beans are eaten fresh (sprouted or not) and dried for their high protein and carbohydrate value; legumes are an important staple food crop in much of the world.

légumes (lay-güm) French for vegetables.

legumi (lay-GOO-mee) Italian for vegetables.

Leicester (LES-ter) An English whole-milk cows' cheese, cooked and pressed, made in large cylinders; it has a hard brownish red rind and a yellow, flaky but moist interior; similar to **Cheddar,** English farmhouse Leicester has a tangy, rich flavor.

lekach (LAY-kakh) A honey and spice cake, traditional for the Jewish holiday of Rosh Hashanah.

lemon balm A Mediterranean herb whose leaves, faintly lemon-scented, are used in salads, compotes, drinks, tea, and in the making of **Chartreuse.**

lemon curd Lemon juice, sugar, butter, and egg yolks mixed together and cooked slowly until the yolks thicken (but do not curdle); used for pastries and breads.

lemongrass A type of grass with long, tapered, fibrous leaves and small tender white bulb; much used in Southeast Asia, where lemons do not grow, to impart its subtle but distinct flavor to curries, soups, and other dishes. Lemongrass (sometimes two words) can flavor indirectly, like bay leaf, when the stalk is removed before eating the dish, or more pungently, when the thicker bulb is finely chopped or ground to a paste before being added to stir-fries, braises, and raw dishes. For storage, lemongrass can be frozen or dried.

lemon thyme See **thyme.**

lemon verbena An herb whose lemon-scented leaves flavor teas and salads; native to South America.

lengua de ternere (LENG-wah day TAYR-nay-ray) Spanish for calf's tongue.

lenguado (len-GWAH-dō) Spanish for sole.

lenticchie (len-TEEK-kyay) Italian for lentils.

lentil A legume that originated in Southwest Asia; high in nutrients, it has been a staple in the Middle East and Central Asia for millennia and is cultivated in many varieties.

lepre (LAY-pray) Italian for hare; *lepre in salmi* is **jugged hare.**

lesso (LES-sō) Italian for boiled, especially boiled meat.

levée, pâte See **pâte levée.**

leveret (lev-ray) French for young hare.

Leyden (LĪ-den) A hard Dutch cheese similar to **Edam,** made from partially skimmed cows' milk; the curd is cooked, flavored with **cumin, caraway,** and spices, molded, and pressed.

liaison (lyay-sonh) In French cuisine, binding or thickening a soup or sauce by means of egg yolk, blood, or starch such as flour (see **beurre manié** and **roux**), arrowroot, cornstarch, or tapioca.

lichi, lichee See **lychee.**

licorice (LIK-er-is, LIK-er-ish) A plant, native to the Middle East, whose name derives from the Greek for "sweet root"; the ancients used the root for medicinal purposes, while today its anise flavoring is used primarily for candy; before sugar cane, strips of the raw root were chewed as a kind of candy.

licuado (lee-KWAH-dō) Spanish for fruit drink, especially citrus.

Liebfraumilch (LEEB-frow-milsh) A catchall name for Rhine wine, almost all very ordinary; the name means "milk of the Blessed Mother."

Liederkranz A pasteurized cows' milk cheese invented by a Swiss immigrant in the United States and named after a choral society ("wreath of song"); it is a soft, mild, surface-ripened cheese shaped in rectangles.

liégeoise, à la (ah lah lyejh-waz) "In the style of Liège," in Belgium; garnished with **juniper berries.**

lier (lee-ay) In French, to blend.

lièvre (LYEV-ruh) French for hare.

lights The lungs of an animal, used in the United States for pet food but in other countries combined with other organs and meat in stews, pâtés, etc., for human consumption.

li jiàng (lee jung) Chinese oyster sauce, consisting of oysters, salt, and seasonings concentrated into a thick paste; used mostly in Cantonese cooking.

Lillet (lee-lay) French apéritif with a fairly dry white wine base flavored with herbs and brandy.

lima (LEE-mah) Spanish for lime; the Mexican *lima agria,* a sour lime from the Yucatán.

limande (lee-manhd) French for lemon sole.

Limburger (LIM-boor-ger) A pasteurized cows' milk cheese, originally Belgian but now German; soft, surface-ripened, creamy yellow, dense, with a strong and characteristic smell.

lime, limette (leem, lee-met) French for lime.

limon (lee-monh) French for lime; lemon is *citron.*

limón (lee-MŌN) Spanish for lemon; but in the Caribbean, *limón* means lime, and *limones franceses* means lemon.

limone (lee-MŌ-nay) Italian for lemon.

limousine, à la (ah lah lee-moo-seen) "In the style of Limousin," garnished with red cabbage.

limun immallah (lee-MOON ih-MAH-lah) Moroccan preserved lemons; fresh lemons pickled in salt and their own juice, sometimes flavored with spices and herbs, and ripened for a month to a year; their distinct taste and texture is idiomatic to Moroccan cooking.

lingua di bue (LEEN-gwah dee BOO-ay) Italian for ox tongue.

lingue di passero (LEEN-gway dee pahs-SAY-rō) Very thin, flat, eggless pasta; In Italian, literally, "sparrows' tongues."

linguiça (leen-GWEE-sah) Portugese pork sausage flavored with garlic; similar to *chouriço* (see under **chorizo**).

linguine (leen-GWEE-nay) Thin flat eggless pasta, in Italian literally "little tongues."

Linse (LIN-seh) German for lentil; *Linsensuppe*, lentil soup with sausage.

Linzertorte (LIN-tser-tor-teh) An Austrian tart of ground hazelnut pastry filled with raspberry jam and covered with a latticework crust, named after the city of Linz.

Liptauer (LIP-tow-er) A ewes' milk cheese, originally German, now made in Hungary; soft, dense, rindless, and strong, it is made in small blocks.

litchi See **lychee.**

littleneck See **quahog.**

Livarot (lee-va-rō) A French whole-milk cows' cheese from the town of the same name in Normandy, made in one-pound discs; the cheese is soft, even-textured, and tangy in flavor, with a hard, shiny surface; colored yellow or dyed deep red with **annatto,** it is a fall or winter cheese.

lobster A family of marine crustaceans, including the saltwater **crayfish,** rock or spiny lobster, Spanish lobster, and American or Maine lobster; its delicate, lean, flavorful meat—concentrated in the large tail and sometimes the claws—its coral (roe), and tomalley (liver) all are prized in cooking.

loc lac (lōk lahk) Cubed beef in a spicy marinade of garlic, pepper, and soy sauce; a Cambodian dish.

locro (LŌ-crō)   A South American vegetable stew that uses different ingredients in different countries, but is always served hot with rice.

locust bean   See **carob.**

loganberry   A hybrid cultivar of the blackberry, developed by Judge James Logan in California; the fruit is darker, larger, and more pro-lific than the raspberry and milder in flavor; excellent for cooking.

loin   A cut of beef from the hindquarter, between the **rib** and **round;** the full loin contains the tenderest cuts within the **sirloin** and **short loin.**

Loire (lwaahr)   The longest river in France, flowing northwest from near Lyons to the Atlantic at Nantes; there are many diverse vineyards in its valley, mostly white and some quite fine, including **Pouilly-Fumé, Sancerre, Vouvray, Saumur,** and **Muscadet.**

lokma (LŌK-mah)   Turkish round fritters in syrup.

lolla rossa   A variety of salad green with frilly edges and splashed pink, with a bitter edge to its flavor; excellent as a garnish and in salad.

lombo, lombata (LOHM-bō, lohm-BAH-tah)   Italian for loin; the Spanish word is *lomo.*

London broil   A cut of beef from the **flank**—one thin, flat muscle that is usually either braised or broiled and sliced on an angle; other cuts from different sections of beef are sometimes loosely called London broil; unheard of in London, United States only.

longanzia (lohn-GAHN-thyah)   A large Spanish pork sausage flavored with garlic, marjoram, and pimiento.

longe de veau (lonhjh deu vō)   French for loin of veal.

lonza (LOHN-zah)   Italian for loin; the word often means cured loin of pork.

loquat (LŌ-kwat)   A plum-shaped golden fruit from a small Oriental tree, sometimes called the Chinese or Japanese medlar; because it ripens in March, it was very popular in Europe before air travel, as it is the first fruit to ripen in spring; now that fresh fruit is flown from the other side of the globe, the bland but juicy loquat is mostly used in jams and jellies.

Lorraine (lohr-ren)   A region in northeastern France (a former duchy) bordering on Germany, Luxembourg, and Belgium; its excellent cui-sine and wines, like Lorraine's political history, show the influence of Germany, with many distinguished dishes using pork, veal, geese, **crayfish,** apples, eggs and cream, and pastries.

lorraine, à la (ah lah lohr-ren)   Garnished with braised red cabbage balls and olive-shaped potatoes sautéed in butter, in classic French cuisine.

lotte (loht)   French for **monkfish.**

lotus root   Root of a plant in the water lily family that in cross section has a beautiful starlike pattern; thin slices of the peeled root, crisp but juicy, go well in Asian stir-fries and salads.

loup (loo)   French for sea bass; the word also means wolf.

lovage (LUV-aj)   An herb once popular but little used today, whose unusual and strong celery flavor seasons meat stews and stocks; its leaves, stems, roots, and seeds can all be used; it is indigenous to the Mediterranean and resembles overgrown celery in appearance.

lox   Salmon, usually from the Pacific Ocean, cured (but not smoked, as it used to be) with salt, then soaked in water to remove some of the salt; often eaten with cream cheese on **bagels;** see also **nova.**

lubina (loo-BEE-nah)   Spanish for sea bass.

luganeaga (loo-gah-nay-AH-gah)   Italian mild, fresh pork sausage flavored with **Parmesan** cheese, made in long tubes without links.

lumaca (loo-MAH-kah)   Italian for snail; the plural is *lumache.*

lumpia (lum-PEE-ah)   In Philippine cooking, a thin pastry wrapper enclosing a savory filling, either fresh and wrapped in a lettuce leaf or deep-fried like a **spring roll.**

lutefisk (LOO-teh-fisk)   In Scandinavian cooking, dried cod soaked in a lye bath of potash, eaten with cream sauce or pork drippings; a Christmas tradition and an acquired taste.

lychee (LEE-chee)   The fruit of a small tree, also called the Chinese plum, often used in Oriental cuisine; the exterior of the nutlike fruit is a thin red scaly shell; the soft, white, fleshy interior surrounds a stone; the fruit is eaten fresh, dried, canned, or preserved in syrup both as a fruit dessert and as an accompaniment to savory foods; spelled variously.

Lyonerwurst (LEE-ō-ner-voorst)   German ham sausage flavored with garlic.

lyonnaise, à la (ah lah lee-onh-nez)   With onions; *lyonnaise* sauce in classic cuisine, chopped onions sautéed in butter, reduced with white wine and vinegar, **demi-glace** added, and strained; the city of Lyons, located near Beaujolais, where the Rhône and Saône Rivers flow together, has a renowned gastronomic tradition. The French spelling is Lyon (no *s*).

mushroom

ma uon (mah oowan) "Fat horses," a Thai snack of chopped pork, chicken, and crab steamed in banana leaf cups; *ma ho*, "galloping horses," is another snack of orange or other fruit topped with a contrasting spicy pork and peanut mixture.

maafe (MAH-fee) A West African chicken and peanut stew with chilies, tomatoes, and spices.

ma'amoul (mah-MOOL) Middle Eastern small stuffed pastries, traditional for Easter, with many different fillings.

ma'amrra (MAHM-rah) Moroccan for stuffed.

maasa (MAH-sah) Fritter of **millet** and rice, raised with yeast and lightly sweetened; served as a snack, light meal, or for breakfast with porridge; from Mali.

maatjes herring See **Matjes herring.**

macadamia nut Nut from a tree native to Australia but now cultivated mostly in Hawaii; usually shelled and roasted before purchase, the round nut is white, sweet, and high in fat, making it prized as a dessert nut.

macaroni See **maccheroni.**

macaroon A small, light, round cookie made of almond paste, sugar, and egg whites; in Italy, where they probably originated, these pastries are called *amaretti*.

maccarèllo (mak-kah-REL-lō) Italian for mackerel.

maccheroni   Italian for macaroni, tube-shaped pasta; except in Naples (where it is spelled *macaroni*), Italians spell this type of pasta thus. In eighteenth-century England, young dandies who on their return from Italy affected continental dress and style were called *macaronis;* hence the line "stuck a feather in his hat and called it macaroni."

mace   A spice made from the lacy covering of the **nutmeg** seed, dried to an orange brown color and usually powdered; mace tastes like nutmeg with a hint of cinnamon and is used more widely in savory dishes than nutmeg.

macédoine   (ma-say-dwahn)   French for a mixture of fruits or vegetables served hot or cold; its name refers to the racial variety of Macedonia.

macerate   To steep food in liquid; usually refers to fresh fruit steeped in liqueur.

mâche   (mash)   French for **lamb's lettuce.**

machi   (mah-CHEE)   Fish or seafood in Indian cuisine; also spelled *machchi.*

Mâcon   (ma-konh)   A town in southern Burgundy on the Saône River and the center of its wine trade; Mâcon wines are red, white, and rosé, strictly limited according to grape variety; Mâconnais is the large wine-producing region encompassing Mâcon.

Madeira   A Portuguese island in the Atlantic famous for its fortified wines, which are 18–20 percent alcohol; aged and blended in **soleras** like **sherry,** the special character and longevity of Madeira comes from the long and gradual heating process called *estufa;* Madeira wines range from very dry to very sweet, so they are suitable for **apéritif** and dessert wines as well as for cooking; specific types of Madeira are separately entered.

madeleine   (mad-len)   A small French cake made of flour, sugar, butter, and eggs baked in a special shell mold; its origin is uncertain, but the town of Commercy is famous for *madeleines,* Louis XV favored them, and Proust gave them immortality with the beginning of *A la Recherche de temps perdu.*

madère   (ma-dayr)   A classic French sauce of **demi-glace** flavored with **Madeira.**

maderisé   (ma-dayr-ee-zay)   French for wine that is partially spoiled by oxidation; a maderized wine has acquired a brownish color and the special aroma of **Madeira** due to the effects of excessive heat.

madrilène, à la (ah lah ma-dree-len) "In the style of Madrid," in French cooking, flavored with tomato.

mafalde, mafaldine (mah-FAL-day) Long Italian pasta strips with fluted edges, in medium and narrow widths.

maggiorana (mah-jor-AH-nah) Italian for marjoram.

magnum A double-sized wine bottle that helps exceptional Bordeaux or Burgundies mature to their fullest, but not advantageous to the development of other wines.

magret, maigret (ma-gray, may-gray) French for breast of duck cooked rare.

maguey (mah-GAY) Species of several large succulent plants, misleadingly called cacti; in Mexico, used to wrap food in its leaves, to produce tequila and other alcoholic drinks, and to harbor an insect larva considered a delicacy. Not available in the United States.

mahammer (mah-HAM-er) Braised and browned in Moroccan cooking.

mahi mahi Hawaian name for dolphin (no relation to the porpoise mammal "dolphin," despite confusion); its flesh is usually skinned and cut into steaks or fillets that are versatile in cooking: rich, sweet, moist, firm, with a large flake.

mahleb (MAH-leb) Middle Eastern spice from the kernel of the black cherry; golden-brown, aromatic, and ground to flavor rolls and sweet breads.

mahshi (MAH-shee) Arab for stuffed.

maiale (mī-YAL-ay) Italian for pork; suckling pig is *maigletto*.

maigre (MAY-gruh) A French adjective denoting thin, lean, low-fat; food suitable for fast days, as prescribed by the Roman Catholic Church. At first only vegetable dishes were allowed during Advent, Lent, and days before important feasts; gradually, butter, milk, eggs, and cold-blooded animals, including fish and eventually waterfowl, were allowed, with many dispensations. The Italian word is *magro*.

maionese (mī-yō-NAY-say) Italian for mayonnaise; the Spanish word is *mahonesa*.

maison (may-sonh) In French, literally "house"; designates a dish made in a restaurant's own style, such as *pâté maison*.

maître d'hôtel (ME-truh D'Ō-TEL) French for the person in charge of a restaurant dining room, who must command every aspect of service to

patrons; originally, in royal or noble households, it was a position of great importance; the informal *maître d'* is often used today. *Maître d'hôtel* butter is seasoned with chopped parsley and lemon juice.

maize   Corn; the French word *maïs* (mah-ees) actually means sweet corn, while the Spanish word *maíz* means dried corn.

mak kam (mah kam)   Thai for tamarind.

makeua taet (MAHK-oo-ah tet)   Thai for tomato.

makhan (mah-KOON)   Butter, in Indian cooking.

makholi (mah-GŌ-lee)   Korean for rice wine.

maki (mah-kee)   Japanese for rolled; used with another word.

mako   See **shark.**

makrut (mak-rood)   Thai for **Kaffir lime.**

Málaga (MAH-lah-gah)   A sweet, heavy, dark **sherry** from the region north of the southern Spanish city of the same name, where it is blended.

malagueta (mah-lah-GWAY-tah)   A hot chili pepper used in African and Caribbean cooking.

malai (mah-lī)   Cream (all kinds), in Indian cooking.

malakor (MAL-ah-kor)   Thai for papaya.

malanga (mah-LAHN-gah)   A root vegetable from tropical America, similar to (and often confused with) **taro;** of many varieties, *malanga amarilla* (yellow) and *blanca* (white) are common; in Puerto Rico, it is called *yautia.*

Malbec (mal-bek)   A French red-wine grape variety used for some better Bordeaux wines; faster-maturing than **Cabernet.**

Malmsey (MAWLM-see)   The English name for Malvasia, a grape variety producing very sweet, heavy, golden **Madeira** that turns amber with age; the wine, originally Greek, is produced elsewhere, but that of Madeira is the most famous.

malsouka (mahl-SOO-kah)   In Tunisian cooking, thin pastry leaves used for **brik,** much like **warqa.** *Tajin malsouka,* a lamb variation of **bastilla.**

malt   Germinated barley used in brewing and distilling; malt extract, highly nourishing, is used to make food for children and invalids. In a malted milk, the malt powder is dissolved in milk, and other flavorings, such as chocolate, are sometimes added. Malt vinegar is popular in Britain.

maltagliati (mal-tah-LYAH-tee) "Badly cut" flat Italian pasta about ½ inch thick and cut on the bias; used mainly for bean soups.

maltaise (mal-tez) A classic French sauce of **hollandaise** flavored with grated orange zest and **blood orange** juice; the cold sauce *maltaise* is **mayonnaise** similarly flavored.

Malvasia See **Malmsey.**

Malzbier (MALTS-beer) Dark, sweet, malty German beer, low in alcohol.

mamé (mah-may) Japanese for bean.

mamey See **mammee.**

mammee (ma-MAY) A tall tropical tree that grows in Central and South America; its round fruit, with smooth orange pulp, is eaten fresh and in ice creams.

mamuang (mah-MOHNG) Thai for mango.

manao (mah-now) Thai for lime.

manche (manhsh) French for the projecting bone on a chop; a *manchette* is a frill used to cover the bone; for *manche à gigot* see **gigot.**

Manchego (mahn-CHAY-gō) A pale, golden, dense ewes' milk cheese from Spain; the curd is molded, pressed, salted in brine, and cured; the rind has a greenish black mold that is sometimes brushed off and replaced with a thin smearing of olive oil. *Manchego* also means in the style of La Mancha.

mandarine (manh-da-reen) French for tangerine.

Mandel (MAHN-del) German for almond; the Italian word is *mandorla.*

mandoline (manh-dō-leen) French for a tool, "strummed" as if playing the musical instrument, used to cut vegetables evenly and quickly into thick or thin, furrowed or smooth slices.

mange-tout (manhjh-too) French for a pea or bean, such as the snow pea or sugar snap, whose pod and seeds are literally "eaten whole."

mango A tropical evergreen tree, probably of Indian origin, whose fully ripened fruit is perhaps the most luscious of all fruits; varying in size, shape, and color, in the United States it is usually a deep green to orange color and pear shaped, with smooth orange flesh; mangoes are eaten fresh or cooked in preserves and chutneys, still green.

manicotti (mah-ni-COHT-tee) Flat circular sheets of Italian pasta stuffed variously and baked in a sauce.

manié See **beurre manié.**

manioc See **tapioca.**

manjar (MAHN-har, MAHN-jhar) **Blancmange;** a pudding, custard, or creamed dish in Spanish and Portuguese cooking, sometimes with chicken.

Manteca (mahn-TEK-ah) A spun-curd cows' milk cheese from southern Italy wrapped around a pat of butter; *manteca,* fat, lard, or butter in Italian and Spanish; this small cheese is also called *Burro, Burrino,* or *Butirro,* locally.

mantecado (mahn-te-KAH-dō) Spanish for rich vanilla ice cream with whipped cream folded in.

mantequilla (mahn-te-KEE-yah) Spanish for butter.

mantı (MAHN-teu) Turkish meat-filled ravioli topped with yogurt and sprinkled with dried mint and **sumac.**

manzana (mahn-SAH-nah) Spanish for apple.

Manzanilla (mahn-sah-NEE-yah) An extremely dry pale Spanish **sherry** with a special, almost bitter, taste; drunk mostly in Spain, especially in Seville; *manzanilla* also means camomile, camomile tea in Spanish.

manzo (MAHN-zō) Italian for beef.

maple syrup Syrup made from the sap of sugar maples and certain other maple trees in northeastern North America. The trees are tapped with a spigot set into the tree trunk. The sap begins to run in late winter in a natural process not entirely understood by scientists, but recognized by the American Indians and certain animals; the sap is boiled down into syrup and even further into maple sugar.

maprao (mah-prow) Thai for coconut.

maquereau (mak-ayr-ō) French for mackerel.

maraschino (mah-rah-SKEE-nō) A liqueur made from the sour *marasca* cherry and its crushed stones, originally from Yugoslavia and now from Italy as well. American maraschino cherries are cooked in artificially colored syrup and flavored with imitation liqueur—a far cry from the original.

marbled A term used to describe meat, especially beef, that has small flecks of fat throughout the muscle tissue. Such meat is generally considered high quality for its juiciness and flavor when cooked. Marbled pastry has light and dark dough swirled together so that it resembles marble stone.

marc (maahrk) French for pomace: usually grape or sometimes apple skins and seeds remaining after the juice has been pressed; *eau de vie de marc* (often shortened to *marc*) is the strong brandy distilled from these residual solids; known in Italy as **grappa.**

marcassin (maahr-kas-sinh) French for young wild boar.

marchand de vin (maahr-shanh deu vinh) A classic French sauce for grilled meats, similar to **Bercy** or **bordelaise**: red wine is flavored with chopped shallots and parsley and well reduced; butter is then beaten in. The name means wine merchant.

Marcobrunn (MAHR-kō-BROON) A well-known vineyard from the German **Rheingau** producing one of the very best white wines.

maréchale, à la (ah lah maahr-ay-shal) In French cuisine, small cuts of meat or poultry, egg-and-bread-crumbed, fried in butter, and garnished with sliced truffles, asparagus tips, or green peas.

marée (maahr-ay) French for all saltwater fish and shellfish.

Marengo, à la (ah lah ma-reng-ō) Chicken pieces browned in olive oil, braised with tomatoes, garlic, and brandy, and garnished with fried eggs, crayfish, and sometimes croûtons. This famous French dish was devised by Napoléon's chef Dunand after the defeat of the Austrians at Marengo in 1800, when no other food could be found.

margarine A butter substitute, originally made from animal fats and now from vegetable fats, developed in 1869 by a French chemist. Similar in cost and calories to butter, but with no cholesterol and less saturated fat, *margarine* is now questioned by health food purists for its preservatives and hydrogenated oils.

Margaux (maahr-gō) A wine-producing **commune** in the French **Haut-Médoc;** a first-growth wine (see **classed growth**) and one of the world's very finest red wines.

Marguéry (maahr-gayr-ee) A classic French sauce of **hollandaise** flavored with oyster liquor and garnished with poached oysters.

Maribo (MAR-ee-bō) A semihard pasteurized cows' milk cheese from the Danish island of Lolland; the large oblong cheeses have a yellow wax coating, a white paste with small holes, and a flavor that grows quite strong with age.

Marie Louise (maahr-ee loo-weez) A classic French garnish of artichoke hearts filled with mushroom purée and **soubise;** named for Napoléon's second wife.

marignan (maahr-ee-nyanh) A boat-shaped French pastry made of rich yeast dough soaked in rum-flavored syrup, brushed with apricot jam, and filled with **crème Chantilly.**

marigold A plant with bright golden flowers used fresh or dried as an herb or dye.

Marille (mah-RIL-leh) German for apricot.

marinade A liquid, including seasonings and acid (vinegar or wine), in which food is steeped before cooking in order to flavor, moisten, and soften it.

marinara, alla (ah-lah mar-ee-NAR-ah) Literally "sailor style"; in Italian a loose term often meaning a simple tomato sauce flavored with garlic and herbs, usually served with **fettucine** or other pasta.

marinière, à la (ah lah maahr-ee-nyayr) Literally "sailor style" in French; seafood cooked in white wine with chopped shallots, parsley, and butter and garnished with mussels; *moules marinière* is the classic example.

marinierter Hering (mar-i-NEER-ter HAYR-ing) German for pickled herring.

mariquita (mar-ee-KEE-tah) Spanish for chip, as in plantain or potato chip.

mariscos (mah-REES-kōs) Spanish for shrimp or scallops; shellfish; seafood; *mariscada,* a shellfish soup.

marjolaine (maahr-jhō-len) A famous French pastry created by **Fernand Point** of almond and filbert **dacquoise** layered with chocolate, praline, and buttercream. *Marjolaine* also means sweet marjoram.

marjoram, sweet marjoram An herb in many varieties, originally Mediterranean, from the mint family; it is used in diverse savory dishes.

marmalade Citrus fruit jam, usually from bitter **Seville oranges** with the rind included, stewed for a long time and reduced to a thick preserve. Marmalade is indispensable to a proper British breakfast. The word derives from the Roman quince and honey preserve, *melimelum* ("honey apple").

marmelade (maahr-muh-lad) French for a thick sweetened fruit purée (or occasionally onion), reduced to a jamlike consistency; not to be confused with **marmalade.**

marmite (maahr-meet) French for a large covered pot, usually earthenware but sometimes metal, for cooking large quantities of food. *Marmite* is a brand name for a type of yeast extract. See also **petite marmite.**

Maroilles (maahr-wahl) A soft, uncooked cows' milk cheese, invented a thousand years ago by the monks at the Abbey of Maroilles in Flanders; square with a reddish rind and pale yellow interior, it is ripened up to six months with regular washings of the rind in brine; the flavor is creamy, rich, and tangy, the aroma attractively strong; also called *Marolles.*

marqa (MAHR-kah) In Tunisian cooking, with ragoût or sauce.

marquise (maahr-keez) French for a fruit ice with whipped cream folded in.

marron (maahr-onh) French for a cultivated chestnut used as a vegetable, for stuffings, and for pastry; *marrons glacés*—whole peeled chestnuts poached for a long time and glazed in a thick syrup—are a choice delicacy.

marrow A large summer squash similar to zucchini.

marrow bone A large beef or veal bone cut into short segments and poached or braised to solidify the rich and nutritious interior marrow, which is then scooped out and spread or diced; marrow is prized in such recipes as **osso bucco** and sauce **bordelaise.**

Marsala (mar-SAH-lah) An Italian **fortified** dessert wine, 17–19 percent alcohol, from the Sicilian city of the same name. The wine is a deep amber color, usually dry but sometimes sweet, roughly comparable to **sherry;** it is an important ingredient in **zabaglione.**

marshmallow A confection made from egg whites, sugar, and gelatin, originally flavored with the root of the marshmallow plant.

Marzenbier (MARTS-en-beer) A strong, medium-colored German beer traditionally brewed in March (hence its name) and drunk in spring and summer; any remaining beer is consumed at festivals such as Oktoberfest.

marzipan A paste of ground almonds, sugar, and egg white shaped and often colored to resemble fruits, vegetables, animals, etc.; the tradition of these decorative confections is very old, dating at least to the Middle Ages.

masa (MAH-sah) In Mexican cooking, a dough of dried cornmeal and water, used in making **tortillas** and other preparations; *masa harina,* corn meal.

masala (mah-SAH-lah) Spice or a blend of spices, in Indian cooking; see also **garam.**

mascarpone (mahs-kar-PŌ-nay) A soft cows' milk cheese made near Milan; the curd made from the cream is beaten or whipped into a thick, velvety cheese with a rich sweet flavor; it is served with fruit and pastries like cream, layered with **Gorgonzola** to make *Torta Gaudenzio,* and used in various other ways, occasionally savory but mostly sweet.

masfouf (mahs-FOOF) In Tunisia and Algeria, a sweet **couscous** with raisins, nuts, and butter eaten as a snack; there are also savory *masfouf couscous* dishes of vegetables and perhaps meat, eaten as a meal. Also spelled *mesfouf.*

masitas de puerco fritas (mah-SEE-tas day PWAYR-kō FREE-tas) Fried pork chunks, a traditional Cuban dish.

mask To cover food with sauce before serving.

masoor (mah-SOOR) Red lentils in Indian cooking; also spelled *masur.*

masquer (mas-kay) In French, to mask.

massa (MAH-sah) Portuguese for pastry or paste; *massa de pimentao,* a red pepper paste used as a marinade for meat.

massepain (mas-pinh) French for **marzipan.**

Mastgeflügel (MAHST-geh-flü-gel) Specially raised grain-fed poultry from the Vierlande region southeast of Hamburg, Germany, of fine quality.

mastic A resinous substance from a tree that grows around the Mediterranean, used to make chewing gum and to flavor bread, pastries, puddings, and liqueur.

matan (MAH-tan) Goat in Indian cooking; in the west, lamb is usually substituted.

matelote (mat-lōt) A French fish stew (usually of freshwater fish) made with red or white wine.

matignon (ma-tee-nyonh) **Mirepoix** cooked in butter, for stuffing or garnish.

Matjes herring (MAHT-yes) High-quality, lightly salted young "virgin" herring that have not yet spawned; very popular in Germany, the Netherlands, and Scandinavia.

matoutou (mah-too-TOO) A spicy crab dish from the Caribbean, traditional for Easter.

matsutake (mat-soo-tah-kay) Japanese "pine" mushrooms.

mattar (mah-TAHR) Peas in Indian cooking; *mattar pilau,* a spicy dish of fresh peas and rice.

matzo, matzoh (MAHT-soh) Flat unleavened bread eaten during Passover to symbolize the Jews' hurried flight from Egypt, when there was no time for the bread to rise; *matzo* meal is used in other dishes such as **knädlach** and **gefilte fish.**

Maultaschen (MOWL-tahsh-en) Ground veal, pork, and spinach wrapped in noodle dough and served in gravy or broth for Maunday Thursday; from Swabia, in Germany.

mayonnaise (mī-yohn-nez) The classic French **emulsion** of egg yolks seasoned with vinegar and mustard, with oil added very gradually to form a thick sauce; there are many variations of this basic cold sauce and many explanations, none certain, as to the name's derivation. *Mayonnaise verte,* flavored and colored green with finely minced herbs such as spinach, sorrel, watercress, parsley, chervil, and tarragon; the herbs may be **blanched** first.

May wine A white-wine spring punch, lightly sweetened and flavored with the herb **woodruff** and served chilled in a bowl with strawberries; originally German.

mazamorra morada (mah-sah-MOR-rah mor-AH-dah) "Purple pudding," from Peru and Ecuador, made with purple corn, various fresh and dried fruits, and cornstarch.

mchicha (m'SHEE-kah) Leafy green vegetable, like spinach, much used in Tanzanian cooking in soups, salads, and stews; *machicha na nazi,* with coconut.

mead Ancient drink of fermented honey, often flavored with herbs.

meat birds Scallops or slices of meat filled with a savory stuffing, rolled up and secured (usually with string), browned in fat, and braised; also called olives. The French term is *oiseaux sans tête,* the Italian *olivetti.*

mechoui See **mishwi.**

médaillon (may-dī-yonh) French for small round "medallion" or scallop of meat, such as beef, lamb, veal, or even a slice of **foie gras.**

medlar See **loquat.**

Médoc (may-dohk) French wine-producing region north of Bordeaux bounded on the east by the Gironde River and on the west by the Atlantic Ocean; red wines so labeled come from the northern part, the *Bas-Médoc,* and are good though not as fine as those from the **Haut-Médoc** in the southern part of the region.

mee Indonesian for noodles; *mee goreng,* fried noodles; *mah mee,* noodle soup with shrimp, pork, vegetables, and spices; *mee siem,* sautéed rice noodles with spicy minced pork, onions, and bean sprouts, garnished with shredded omelet; also spelled *mie.*

Meerrettich (MAYR-ret-tish) German for horseradish.

meetha See **mithai.**

megadarra Arab lentils and rice with onions, served hot or cold with yogurt; a very old and favorite dish.

Mehlspeise (MAYL-shpī-zeh) A flour-based German dish, especially popular in Bavaria—**dumplings,** pancakes, and **Strudel** are examples; in Austrian dialect this word means pudding.

mejillone (may-hee-YŌ-nay) Spanish for mussel.

mejorana (may-hor-AH-nah) Spanish for marjoram.

mela (MEL-ah) Italian for apple.

melagrana (mel-ah-GRAH-nah) Italian for pomegranate.

mélanger (may-lanh-jhay) In French to mix; the word *mélange* means mixture or blend.

melanzana (mel-ahn-ZAH-nah) Italian for eggplant; the Greek word is *melidzanes.*

Melba toast Very thin slices of toast, named for Dame Nellie Melba, the great Australian soprano; **pêche Melba** was also created for her by **Escoffier.**

melocotón (meh-lō-kō-TŌN) Spanish for peach.

Melton Mowbray pie An English pork pie encased in a pastry "coffin" or crust, served cold; an old and traditional convenience food that is easily transportable; named after the Leicestershire town.

melokhia See **mulukhiya.**

Mendocino (men-dō-CHEE-nō) A wine-producing county in northern California, near Ukiah, with especially good **Zinfandels.**

menestra (meh-NETH-trah, meh-NES-trah) Spanish for stew.

menthe (menht) French for mint; *crème de menthe,* a mint-flavored liqueur, either green or colorless.

menudo (meh-NOO-dō) Spanish for tripe stew.

mercimek çorbası (mayr-jee-mek CHOR-bah—seu) Turkish lentil soup, usually red lentils *(suzme).*

merguez See **mirqaz.**

merienda (mayr-YEN-dah) Spanish for afternoon tea or snack, to tide appetites over to late dinner.

meringue Pastry made of stiffly beaten egg whites with sugar, shaped variously, and baked in a slow oven. For *meringue italienne* see **Italian meringue.**

merlan (mayr-lanh) French for whiting; the Italian word is *merlango.*

Merlot (mayr-lō) A red-wine grape variety, productive and early-ripening, that yields soft, fruity, and graceful wines; Merlot combines well with the more astringent, later-maturing, and longer-lived **Cabernet;** widely planted in Bordeaux, California, parts of Switzerland, and northern Italy.

merluza (mayr-LOO-thah) Spanish for hake; the Italian word *merluzzo* means cod.

mero (MAYR-ō) Spanish for rock bass.

mesclun (mes-klunh) A Provençal mixture of young salad greens whose seeds are sown together, traditionally including wild **chicory, mâche,** curly **escarole,** dandelion, **rocket,** and other tender lettuces; *mesclun* comes from the Niçoise dialect word for mixture.

mesquite (mes-KEET) A scrub tree that grows wild in the southwestern United States and Mexico, whose wood is used for grilling food.

metate (may-TAH-tay) A sloping slab of porous volcanic rock standing on three legs and used to grind corn and spices in Mexican cooking; similar to a **molcajete;** the stone that is rolled over the surface for grinding is called a *mano.*

methi (MAY-thee) **Fenugreek** in Indian cooking.

Methuselah   An oversized bottle of Champagne, holding up to eight regular bottles, named after the biblical patriarch said to have lived 969 years; spelled variously.

Mettwurst (MET-voorst)   German smoked pork sausage with red skin and a coarse texture.

Meunier (meu-nyay)   A fine grape variety, a subvariety of the **Pinot** Noir; planted extensively in Champagne, Alsace, and California.

meunière, à la (ah lah meu-nyayr)   Lightly dredged with flour, sautéed in butter, and served with melted butter and sliced lemon; in French *meunière* means "in the style of the miller's wife."

Meursault (meur-sō)   A village in the French **Côte d'Or** of Burgundy that produces a large quantity of distinguished white wine.

Mexican saffron   See **safflower.**

mezzani (met-TSAH-nee)   Italian pasta in a long narrow tube.

mezze (MEH-zeh)   Middle Eastern **hors d'oeuvre,** that is, food eaten before or outside the regular meal, such as nuts, cheese, pickled vegetables, smoked meats, salads; the Turkish word is *meze*, the Greek *mezedes.*

m'hanncha (m'HAHN-shah)   "The snake," a coiled cake of layered **warqa** filled with almond paste and aromatic with cinnamon, from Morocco.

mi-chevre (MEE SHEV-ruh)   Half goats' cheese, that is, from mixed goats' and other (usually cows') milk; such cheeses should be at least ¼ goats' milk.

microwave oven   An oven that works on the principle of electromagnetic radiation; these high-frequency waves penetrate the food being cooked to a depth of two inches and heat the water inside very quickly and efficiently but without browning the outside; for this reason some microwave ovens include browning elements.

midollo (mee-DOHL-lō)   Italian for marrow.

midye (MEE-dyay)   Turkish for mussels.

mie (mee)   The crumb or soft interior part of a loaf of bread; *pain de mie* is sandwich bread. See also **mee.**

miel (myel)   French for honey; in Italian the word is *miele.*

mien (meen)   Vietnamese for mung bean noodles, cellophane noodles.

migas (MEE-gahth, MEE-gahs) Spanish for breadcrumbs.

mignonette (mee-nyoh-net) In French cuisine, coarsely ground white pepper; originally, this seasoning included various other spices, such as nutmeg, coriander, cinnamon, ginger, clove, and red pepper. A *mignonette* is also a **médaillon** of lamb.

mi jiú (mee jō) Chinese rice wine, yellow in color.

mijoter (mee-jhō-tay) To simmer in French.

Mikado French for Japanese style.

mikan (mee kahn) Japanese for tangerine.

milanaise, à la (ah lah mee-lah-nez) A classic French garnish of julienne of tongue, ham, mushrooms, and truffles with spaghetti, tomato sauce, and **Parmesan** cheese.

mille-feuille (meel foy) See **pâte feuilletée;** the Italian term is *mille foglie* or *pasta sfoglia.*

millet A grain native to Africa and Asia. Millet has been cultivated in dry, poor soil for millennia as an important high-protein staple, but in the United States it is used mostly for animal fodder; it has no **gluten.**

miloukia See **mulukhiya.**

milt Fish sperm, prepared like roe, and sometimes euphemistically called roe or spleen.

Milzwurst (MILTS-voorst) Veal sausage from Bavaria.

mimosa A garnish of finely chopped hard-boiled egg yolk, sometimes including the white as well, that resembles the mimosa flower; also a drink of Champagne and orange juice, usually served with brunch.

mince British for chopped meat.

mincemeat A preserve of chopped mixed foodstuffs much changed over the centuries. In fifteenth-century England it included small furred and feathered game, meat, spices, and gradually more fruit; in present-day England it consists mainly of fresh and dried fruits, nuts, spices, rum or brandy, with suet being the only vestige of meat. Mincemeat is cured and served in a piecrust for a traditional Christmas dessert.

minestra (mee-NES-trah) Italian for soup or sometimes pasta served as the first course; *minestrina* means a thinner soup, while *minestrone* (literally, a "big soup," or meal in itself) means a thick vegetable soup in a meat broth with pasta, **Parmesan,** and various vegetables, depending on the region and season.

mint   An aromatic herb, Mediterranean in origin, that includes **basil, marjoram, oregano, peppermint, rosemary, sage, savory,** and **thyme** (all separately entered) in its large family. Common garden mint is spearmint or one of its many close relatives; it has wide culinary uses from mint julep to accompaniments for lamb (see **mint sauce**) to flavoring liqueurs, but has never been favored by the French except to garnish desserts.

mint julep   **Bourbon** and fresh **mint** cocktail, traditionally served in a silver julep cup; associated with Kentucky.

mint sauce   British sauce of chopped and lightly sugared fresh mint in vinegar, served with roast lamb; not to be confused with American commercial mint jelly, which is apple jelly flavored with mint and now usually dyed bright green.

Mirabeau   (meer-a-bō)   A French garnish of anchovy fillets laid in a criss-cross pattern, pitted olives, tarragon, and anchovy butter; for grilled meat.

mirabelle   (meer-a-bel)   A small golden plum with a highly aromatic perfume, grown almost exclusively in Europe; used in stews, preserves, tarts, and a colorless **eau de vie** from Alsace.

mirasol   A mild chili pepper from Peru.

mirchi   (MEER-shee)   Chili peppers, in Indian cooking; *lal mirchi,* red peppers.

mirepoix   (meer-pwah)   In French cooking, a mixture of diced vegetables—usually carrot, onion, celery, and sometimes ham or pork belly—used to flavor sauces and other preparations; see also **brunoise.**

mirin   (meer-in)   Japanese rice wine, syrupy and sweet, used for cooking.

mirliton   See **chayote.**

miroton   (meer-ō-tonh)   A French stew of meat with onions in brown sauce; the classic *sauce miroton,* a **demi-glace** with sautéed onion rings, sometimes flavored with tomato purée and mustard.

mirqaz   (mayr-GEZ)   North African sausage; in Algeria a spicy lamb mixture, in Tunisia more often beef; also spelled *merguez.*

mise en place   (meez enh plas)   A French term, literally "put in place," meaning that the preparation is ready up to the point of cooking.

mishmishiya (mish-mish-EE-yah) Arab stew of lamb and apricots, with almonds, spices, and herbs.

mishwi (MISH-wee) Arabic for grill and, by extension, food that is grilled or spit-roasted. Often refers to whole lamb spit-roasted over embers and basted with herbed garlic butter, so that the outside is crisp and the inside tender and juicy; traditionally eaten with the fingers. The term can refer to other grilled meats, poultry, or vegetables. Also spelled *mechoui*.

miso (mee-sō) Japanese fermented bean paste made from soybeans and grain—a high-protein staple used extensively and in many different forms; *miso-shiru* is a soup thickened with red bean paste, often eaten for breakfast and sometimes with other meals.

Mission-Haut-Brion, Château La (sha-tō lah mee-syonh-ō-bree-onh) An excellent first-growth wine of Pessac, Graves; an immediate neighbor of **Haut-Brion** and an exceptional red Bordeaux.

misto (MEES-tō) Italian for mixed.

mithai (mee-TĬ) Indian sweets or desserts; sweet taste is *meetha*.

mitsuba (mee-ts-bah) Japanese green resembling its cousin parsley, sometimes called trefoil for its three-part leaves; used fresh in salads and garnishes.

Mittagessen (MIT-tahg-es-en) German for midday dinner, lunch; traditionally a substantial meal, the main one of the day.

mixed grill Various grilled meats, such as lamb chops, kidneys, bacon, and sausages, served with grilled mushrooms, tomatoes, and fried potatoes; the French *friture mixte* and Italian **fritto misto** are equivalents, including foods appropriate to those countries.

mizuna Bitter green with spiky leaves, from the mustard family, usually sautéed, steamed, or braised, or mixed into **mesclun** in small amounts.

mocha Originally, a very fine variety of coffee from the town of Mocha in Yemen, often blended with Java; today this is more likely to be a Mocha-style bean from Africa; *mocha* often means coffee-flavored and sometimes, more loosely, coffee- and chocolate-flavored.

mochi-gome (mō-chee-gō-may) Japanese glutinous rice, used for special dishes such as red rice and sweet rice cakes (*mochi*); *mochiko* is the flour made from it.

mochomos (mō-CHŌ-mōs) In Mexican cuisine, cooked meat, shredded and fried crisp.

mock turtle soup   A clear soup made from a calf's head and often garnished with calf brains, originally intended to spare the expense and trouble of using real turtle. In Tenniel's illustration for *Alice in Wonderland,* the mock turtle is a calf beneath a turtle's shell with mock tears rolling down its cheeks.

mode, à la   (ah lah MŌD)   In French cuisine, a large cut of braised beef with vegetables; in the United States, pie or other pastry served with ice cream.

moelle   (mō-el)   French for beef marrow.

moghlai   (MŌG-lī)   In Indian cuisine, Moghul-style or Muslim, rich and spicy.

Mohn   (mōn)   German for poppy; *Mohnbeugel, Mohnkipferl,* and *Mohnstrudel* are popular poppy-seed pastries.

Möhre, Mohrrübe   (MEUR-eh, MOHR-rü-beh)   German for carrot.

Mohr im Hemd   A chocolate pudding, from Austria, literally, "moor in a shirt"; *Mohrenkopf* is chocolate meringue with whipped cream.

mojo   (MŌ-hō)   Spanish for sauce; the Mexican is **mole,** the Portuguese *moljo; mojo crillo,* a pungent Creole garlic sauce from Cuba, made with lard, olive oil, citrus, and onion; often served with **yuca,** pork, and chicken.

moka   French for **mocha.**

molasses   The syrup remaining from sugarcane juice after sucrose crystallization, during the manufacture of sugar; the process is repeated three times, each yielding a lower grade of molasses with more impurities and darker color from the high heat; **blackstrap** is the third grade, rich in flavor.

molcajete y tejolote   (mōl-kah-HAY-tay ee tay-hō-LŌ-tay)   Mexican mortar and pestle, made of heavy, porous stone, and balanced on three legs; indispensable for grinding spices.

mole   (MŌ-lay)   In Mexican cooking, a mixture or sauce, from the Aztec word for chili sauce; *mole* **poblano** *de guajolate,* a festive Mexican specialty of wild turkey (or pork or chicken) in a rich dark subtle smooth sauce of powdered **mulato, ancho,** and **pasilla** chilies simmered with vegetables, seasoning, and a little chocolate.

molee   (MŌ-lee)   Indian curry dish of coconut milk, green chilies, and fresh ginger.

Molinara (mō-lee-NAR-ah) A fine Italian red-wine grape variety, used for **Valpolicella** and **Bardolino.**

moljo (MŌL-hō) Sauce in Portuguese; the Spanish is **mojo,** the Mexican **mole.**

mollusk, mollusc A class of shellfish: an invertebrate with a soft, un-segmented body, with a single or double shell; includes scallops, clams, oysters, mussels, squid, octopus, whelks, and one land-dweller, the snail.

Monbazillac (monh-ba-zee-yak) A soft, sweet, golden dessert wine, not unlike **Sauternes,** produced east of Bordeaux in the Dordogne.

Mondeuse (monh-deuz) A good French red-wine grape variety, extensively grown in the Savoie and Upper Rhône regions and, to a lesser extent, in California.

monégasque, à la (ah lah mō-nay-gask) In the style of Monaco; a salad of **nonats,** tomatoes, and rice; also refers to numerous other preparations.

Monferrato (mon-fayr-AH-tō) A major Italian wine-growing region south of the Po Valley in the Piedmont; none of its many wines bears its name.

Mongolian hot pot See **shuàn yáng ròu.**

monkey bread A curious sweet bread, sometimes called bubble bread, made of separate clumps of dough piled and baked in a tube pan. Currants are sometimes added; no relation to the monkey "bread" that is the fruit of the **baobab** tree.

monkfish A voracious and odd-looking fish whose tail contains firm white flesh similar in flavor to lobster; the meat can be prepared in numerous ways but should be cooked longer than that of most other fish; also called goosefish, anglerfish, and *lotte.*

monopole (mō-nō-pōl) A French wine-label term meaning that the entire vineyard belongs to one proprietor.

monosodium glutamate (MSG) A type of salt long used in Oriental cooking as a taste intensifier and enhancer. MSG was chemically isolated in 1908, but scientists do not fully understand how it works; often found in excessive amounts in Chinese restaurant food and instant and canned soups.

Montasio (mon-TAH-zyō) A firm, whole-milk cows' cheese from north-eastern Italy; this pale yellow cheese with a smooth rind and scattered

holes is made in large wheels; it is cooked, pressed, salted, and cured up to two years; when young it makes a mild and nutty table cheese, and when aged it makes a brittle and pungent grating cheese.

Mont Blanc (monh blanhk)   A classic French dessert of chestnut purée sweetened, flavored with vanilla, mounded, and masked with **crème Chantilly;** the Italian version, *Monte Bianco*, includes chocolate and rum; named for the Alpine peak.

monter (monh-tay)   In French, to whip egg whites or cream to give volume; *monter au beurre* means to enrich a sauce with a little butter.

Monterey Jack   A semihard cooked cows' milk cheese first made in Monterey, California in 1892; a **Cheddar**-type of cheese, the whole-milk version, aged for three to six weeks, is pale, creamy, and bland, while the skimmed-milk version, matured for at least six months, is harder and stronger.

Montilla (mohn-TEE-ya)   A Spanish wine from the villages of Montilla and Moriles, very similar to **sherry** and until recently sold as such, but now with its own appellation; Montilla, which is not fortified, makes an excellent **apéritif** or table wine, chilled.

Montmorency (monh-mohr-enh-see)   A variety of sour cherry that lends its name to a classic French duck dish.

montone (mon-TŌ-nay)   Italian for mutton.

Montpensier (mohn-penh-syay)   A classic French garnish of green asparagus tips and sliced truffles, sometimes with artichoke hearts and Madeira sauce.

Montrachet (monh-ra-shay)   A celebrated vineyard in the **Côte de Beaune** of Burgundy, straddling the **communes** of Puligny and Chassagne, whose dry white wine—made entirely from the **Chardonnay** grape—is one of the finest in the world; it lends its name to neighboring vineyards as well. *Montrachet* is also the name of a fresh goats' milk cheese, mild and creamy, usually shaped in logs and sometimes covered with vegetable ash or herbs.

Montreuil (monh-troy)   In French cooking, with peaches; also fish poached in white wine, served with large potato balls and shrimp sauce.

montrouge (monh-roujh)   With mushrooms in cream.

moo   Thai for pork; *moo daeng*, roast red pork.

moong dal   See **mung bean.**

moo shu (moo sheu) In Chinese cooking, shredded pork stir-fried with scallions, **cloud ears,** and egg, then rolled up in pancakes.

moqueca (mō-KAY-kah) Brazilian seafood stew, usually from white fish and shellfish, with a rich tomato, green pepper, onion, and herb sauce.

Morbier (mohr-byay) A hard, uncooked cows' milk cheese with a delicate flavor, from the Franche-Comté of France; it is made in large rounds with a yellowish thin rind and an even paste marked by a traditional horizontal streak of ash between morning and evening milk layers.

morcilla negra (mor-THEE-yah NAY-grah) Spanish blood sausage made with pork, garlic, spices, and pig's blood, the best coming from Asturias; *morcilla blanca,* a sausage containing chicken, bacon, hard-boiled eggs, and parsley.

morcón (mor-KŌN) Philippine beef roulade filled with vegetables, sausages, and hard-boiled eggs, braised and sliced into decorative rounds.

morel (mor-EL) A wild fungus with a spongelike hollow cap, prized for its fine nutty flavor; this mushroom appears in springtime but can be dried successfully for other seasons; morels are never eaten raw.

morello cherry Variety of sour cherry excellent for cooking and making liqueurs.

morille (MOHR-EE-yuh) French for **morel.**

Mornay (mohr-nay) **Béchamel** sauce with butter, grated **Parmesan** and **Gruyère** cheeses, possibly with egg yolks beaten in—a classic French sauce.

moros y cristianos (MOR-ōs ee krees-TYAH-nōs) "Moors and Christians," a Cuban dish combining black beans and white rice; named for the expulsion of the Moors from Spain in 1492.

mortadella (mor-tah-DEL-lah) A large Italian sausage of ground pork with white cubes of fat, **pistachio** nuts, wine, and **coriander;** the best are from Bologna but should not be confused with American baloney.

morue (mohr-ü) French for salt cod; see also **brandade.**

moscada (moh-THKAH-dah, moh-SKAH-dah) Spanish for **nutmeg.**

Moselle (mō-ZEL) A river in western Germany on whose banks, between Trier and Koblenz—where it flows into the Rhine—are

many vineyards; Moselle wine, in its characteristic green bottle, comes from the **Riesling** grape. Some of these wines, especially those from the *Mittel-Mosel* or central section, are exceptionally fine, distinguished by their delicacy, fragrance, and spiciness. The German spelling is *Mosel*.

Most   German for fruit juice; cider; **must.**

mostarda di frutta (moh-STAHR-dah dee FROOT-tah)   Various fruits preserved in a syrup flavored with mustard; traditionally eaten with bread or cold meat, like chutney; from Cremona in Lombardy.

mouan (mwan)   Cambodian for chicken.

moulage (moo-lajh)   French for molding, as in molding a dessert; *moule* is mold.

moule (mool)   French for mussel.

moulokhia   See **mulukhiya.**

mountain oyster   Testicles of a bull, pig, or lamb, usually breaded and fried; sometimes called prairie oyster or Rocky Mountain oyster; this American slang term is as much descriptive as euphemistic.

moussaka, mousaka (moo-SAH-kah)   A Balkan dish, varying from one region to another, of vegetables layered with minced or ground meat, perhaps with a white sauce or cheese; the Greek version, with eggplant, lamb, tomatoes, and white sauce, is most familiar abroad.

mousse (moos)   A sweet or savory French dish, usually cold, lightened with beaten egg whites or cream; from the French word for froth or foam; can also refer to Champagne bubbles.

mousseline (moos-leen)   A French dish or sauce with whipped cream or egg whites folded in; it often designates **hollandaise** or **mayonnaise** with whipped cream added. The term can also mean a "little mousse" in a small mold or in spoonfuls, especially for seafood preparations. See also **mousse.**

mousseux (moos-seu)   French for sparkling or effervescent wine (literally "foaming"); does not include **Champagne,** which is considered a separate category.

moutarde de Meaux (moo-taahrd deu mō)   Mustard from the French town of Meaux made with partly crushed seeds, giving it a pleasantly grainy texture.

mouton (moo-tonh)   French for mutton.

Mouton-Rothschild, Château (sha-tō moo-tonh rōt-sheelt) An extraordinary Bordeaux wine from **Pauillac** in the **Haut-Médoc,** classified in 1855 as a second growth but unquestionably a great wine; it is large, robust, slow-developing but remarkably long-lived; from the **Cabernet Sauvignon** grape.

moyashi (mō-yah-shee) Japanese for bean sprouts.

Mozzarella (mohts-ah-REL-lah) A Italian white spun-curd cheese originally made from buffalo milk; the uncooked curd is kneaded into a smooth mass from which small pieces are cut off (*mozzare* in Italian) and shaped into single cheeses, which are salted in brine. Mozzarella ripens fast, has a fresh, slightly acidulated flavor, and is sometimes smoked; it is widely imitated with cows' milk for pizza and other uses.

MSG See **monosodium glutamate.**

mtori (muh-TOR-ee) Puréed plantain soup with beef stock, onion, and tomato, from the Kilimanjaro region of Tanzania.

muesli (MÜS-lee) Swiss breakfast dish of rolled oats with fruit and nuts, devised by the health food advocate, Dr. Bircher-Benner.

muffin A round individual pastry, either flat or raised, often served with butter. An "English muffin" (unknown in England) is a flat yeast bread baked on a griddle, while its American counterpart is a raised quick bread made of any kind of flour and often including nuts or fruit, baked in a deep mold in the oven.

muhallabia (moo-hah-lah-BEE-yah) A Middle Eastern pudding similar to **balouza** but, with rice, milk, and garnish of nuts, more elegant.

mujadarra Arab lentils and rice with onions, served hot or cold with yogurt; a very old and favorite dish.

mukh (mook) Arabic for brains, very popular in the Middle East.

mulard (mü-laahr) French for a crossbreed duck bred for its meat and sometimes for its liver; as a hybrid it cannot reproduce.

mulato (moo-LAH-tō) A dried chili pepper, large, brown, and pungent.

mulberry A tree originating in China and cultivated for the silkworms that feed upon its fruit (white berries only); a relative of the fig, it was known in ancient Greece and Rome and is still most appreciated in the Middle East; its berries are white, deep red, or black and are formed like raspberries without the central cone.

Müllerin Art (MÜL-er-in art) "In the style of the miller's wife"—dredged in flour and fried in butter—the German version of **à la meunière.**

mullet The name of several unrelated fish; the Mediterranean red mullet is the most distinguished, its liver and roe as prized as its flesh; the American striped and silver mullet, whose roe is used in **taramosalata,** are related to the European gray mullet.

mulligatawny An anglicized soup of East Indian origin; chicken or lamb poached in broth, flavored with curry and other spices, and served with rice, cream, lemon, and the diced meat.

mulling A process in which wine, ale, or cider is warmed, sweetened, and spiced for punch.

mulukhiya (moo-loo-KEE-yah) "Jew's mallow," a mucilaginous vegetable whose green leaves go into an ancient Egyptian soup by the same name, enjoyed throughout the Middle East. The spinach-like leaves are added to meat, duck, rabbit, or poultry broth and served with chopped vegetables, chunks of meat, and rice on the side. Frozen *mulukhiya,* found at Middle Eastern shops, substitutes well for fresh in the United States. Also spelled *miloukia, melokhia,* and *moulokhia.*

Münchner Literally, from Munich; used to designate the dark malty beers popular there.

mung bean A variety of bean usually dried and used for **bean sprouts.**

Munster (MUHN-sterh) A French pasteurized whole-milk cows' cheese first made by Benedictine monks in the Munster Valley of the Vosges mountains. The round cheese has a smooth orange rind and a pale yellow, fairly soft paste with cracks; its delicate salty flavor grows tangy with age. Alsatians eat their favorite cheese with rye or caraway bread, which complements it perfectly. There is also a German Münster cheese.

Murazzano (moo-rah-TSAH-nō) A soft uncooked cheese from northwest Italy, made with a mixture of milks, mostly ewes'; the cylindrical cheese has no rind and a dense white paste that grows pale yellow with age.

mûre (mür) French for blackberry or mulberry.

murgh (moorg) Chicken in Indian cooking; *murgh tandoori,* skinned chicken marinated in yogurt and spices, then roasted in a hot **tandoor** oven; *murgh moghlai,* chicken moghul-style, in a rich saffron sauce.

murol (mü-rōl) A hard cows' milk cheese, uncooked but pressed, from the Auvergne in France; the wheel-shaped cheese has a pinkish rind with a hole in the center.

Muscadet (mü-ska-day) A light, dry, fresh white wine from the lower Loire Valley; Muscadet tastes best drunk young and accompanies the seafood of neighboring Brittany exceptionally well.

Muscat A grape whose many varieties are used for wine, raisins, and table grapes; it ranges widely in color, yield, and quality, but all types have the characteristic musky flavor; planted widely with different names, depending on the location.

Muschel, Jakobsmuschel (MOOS-kul, YAH-kōps-moos-kul) German for scallop, named for St. James, the apostle, whose emblem was the shell.

mush Cornmeal porridge; an American version of **polenta,** which can be sliced and fried.

mushi (moo-shee) Japanese for steamed; *mushimono* means steamed food.

mushroom The fruiting body of a fungus whose spores, if given the proper conditions, sprout up virtually overnight. Gastronomes for millennia have prized edible mushrooms for their delicate flavor and meaty texture, but their cultivation has been understood only since the early eighteenth century. In addition to the common field mushroom, many wild mushrooms (separately entered) can be gathered by those with the knowledge to distinguish between edible and poisonous species.

Musigny (mü-see-nyee) An extraordinary red Burgundy wine from the Côte de Nuits; a **Grand Cru,** with great delicacy and refinement.

Muskatnuss (moos-KAHT-noos) German for **nutmeg, mace.**

muskmelon A melon with netted skin, sometimes called nutmeg melon because of its resemblance to the spice, and orange or pale green flesh; the fruit that Americans call cantaloupe is really a muskmelon, while the true cantaloupe (not cultivated in the United States) has rough, scaly, or segmented—but never netted—skin. Muskmelons and cantaloupes have a separation layer in their stems, unlike **winter melons,** so that they cannot be harvested into frost.

müsli See **muesli.**

musli (MOOS-lee) A Tunisian dish of lamb braised with potatoes and peppers, garnished with lemon slices.

muslin bag   A bag filled with a **bouquet garni,** spices, or other flavorings and tied tightly, used for infusing liquids; it can be removed without leaving any solids.

mussel   A bivalve **mollusk** with a blue black shell and a beard that attaches to rock or other solid objects (and should be removed before cooking); long popular in Europe in many preparations such as **Billy Bi** and **à la marinière,** mussels are gaining acceptance in the United States.

must   Grape juice not yet fermented into wine.

mustard   A plant related to cress, radish, horseradish, and turnip and sharing their pungent taste: its name means "burning must." Mustard seeds were eaten by prehistoric man, spread by the Romans, and today are consumed more than any spice but pepper; the black, brown, and yellow varieties are dried, crushed, powdered, moistened, and mixed with many seasonings. Young mustard greens make a refreshing spring vegetable, and mustard oil is important in Indian cooking. See also **Dijon.**

mutton   The flesh of mature male sheep (over one year in age), dark red in color and rich in flavor; high-quality mutton is hard to find and generally unappreciated by Americans.

myrtille   (meer-teel)   French for bilberry, whortleberry, blueberry.

Mysost   (MÜ-sohst)   A hard uncooked Norwegian cheese made from cows' milk whey; it is dark brown and sweet, usually firm and dense, and is made in several varieties; see also **Gjetöst.**

sauce Nantua

naan (nahn)   Indian flatbread baked on the side of a **tandoor** oven until puffed; sometimes flavored with savory or sweet ingredients; from the Punjab; also spelled *nan*.

nabe (nah-bay)   Pot in Japanese; *nabemono* means one-pot communal cooking.

nacho (NAH-chō)   In Mexican cooking, a small **tortilla** chip topped with melted cheese and chilies.

Nackenheim (NAHK-en-hīm)   A German wine-producing town overlooking the Rhine south of Mainz; the fruity white wines, from the **Riesling** and **Sylvaner** grapes, are of high quality.

naeng myon (NAHNG myen)   A cold noodle soup, a popular Korean one-dish summer meal, assembled at table; it includes buckwheat noodles in cool beef broth with vegetables and seasoning on top, finished with hard-boiled egg.

naganegi (nah-gah-nay-gee)   Japanese for long onion, for which the leek can be substituted.

nage, à la (ah lah najh)   In French cuisine, cooked in a **court bouillon** of white wine, carrots, onions, shallots, and herbs; *nage* means swimming.

Nahe (NAH-he)   A German river flowing into the Rhine at Bingen; the Nahe Valley wines, from **Riesling** and **Sylvaner** grapes, produce a lot of good white wine.

nam (nahm)   Thai for water; *nam cha*, tea; *nam chuang*, syrup; *nam katee*, coconut milk; *nam prik*, Thai hot sauce, a basic condiment, containing shrimp, garlic, chilies, **nam pla,** and lime juice.

ñame (NYAH-may)   Spanish for **yam;** also called *igname.*

naméko (nah-may-kō)   In Japanese cooking, a mushroom appreciated for its slippery texture; usually canned.

nam pla (nahm plah)   Thai fish sauce, salty, fermented, and pungent, used as a condiment and seasoning throughout southeast Asia; related to **nuoc mam** and **patis.**

Nantua, sauce (NANH-tü-ah, SŌS)   In classic French cuisine, **béchamel** sauce reduced with cream, beaten with crayfish butter, and garnished with crayfish tails; *à la Nantua* is a garnish of crayfish tails with Nantua sauce and sliced truffles.

Napa   A valley northeast of San Francisco whose vineyards produce some of California's best wines, especially **Cabernet Sauvignon,** Pinot Noir, Pinot Chardonnay, and **Chenin Blanc.**

napoleon   A dessert of **puff pastry** strips spread with **crème patissière** and stacked in layers, the top often iced; this pastry is not French.

napoletana, alla (ah-lah nah-pōl-lay-TAH-nah)   A meatless spaghetti sauce made with tomatoes, onion, garlic, and olive oil, in the style of Naples.

napolitain (na-pōl-lee-tinh)   In French cuisine, originally a large ornamental cake—probably created by **Carême,** who delighted in such creations—of stiff almond pastry layers spread with different jams, piled high, and elaborately decorated; now it usually means a smaller-scale **génoise** filled with jam and spread with **Italian meringue** and more jam.

napolitaine, à la (ah lah na-pōl-lee-ten)   In French cuisine, "in the style of Naples": veal scallops dipped in beaten eggs and breadcrumbs mixed with grated **Parmesan,** fried, and garnished with spaghetti, tomato sauce, and Parmesan—a classic preparation.

napper (nap-pay)   In French, to coat or mask with sauce.

naranja (nah-RAHN-hah)   Spanish for orange; *naranja agria* is a **Seville orange.**

nasi   Indonesian for rice; *nasi goreng,* fried rice cooked with various spices and ingredients, usually including chilies, garlic, onions, and shrimp paste and sometimes also meat, chicken, or shellfish; popular throughout Malaysia and Indonesia; when noodles replace the rice it is called *bami goreng* (or *bakmi goreng*); *nasi kuming,* "yellow rice," cooked in coconut milk with turmeric.

nasturtium A plant whose blossoms and young leaves are eaten in salads and whose buds and seeds are pickled like **capers.**

nasu (nah-s) Japanese for eggplant.

natillas (nah-TEE-yahth) A soft runny Spanish custard, made from ewes' milk, sweetened and flavored with lemon and cinnamon; from the Basque country.

natural A term that is used by commercial producers to imply that no pesticides or additives have been used or that there has been no adulteration of any kind; however, the word has been given no specific legal definition.

nature (na-tür) French for plain, ungarnished; the Italian is *naturale,* the German *natur;* when used with wine the term means that nothing—in particular, sugar—has been added.

Naturschnitzel (NA-toor-shnit-sel) German for unbreaded veal cutlet.

navarin (na-vaahr-inh) A French mutton stew with small onions and potatoes; in spring, when the dish is called *navarin à la printanière,* it is made with young vegetables such as carrots, turnips, new potatoes, and peas.

navarraise (na-vaahr-rez) French tomato sauce flavored with garlic and chopped herbs.

navel orange A nearly seedless orange variety with a characteristic protuberance at the blossom end (hence its name), a thick skin, distinct segments, and sweet, flavorful flesh; best for salads and desserts, as its juice, when exposed to the air, turns bitter.

navet (na-vay) French for turnip; the Spanish word is *nabo,* the Italian *navone.*

navy bean A variety of common bean, small and white, widely used in dried bean dishes such as **cassoulet** and **Boston baked beans.**

neapolitan ice cream Ice cream of various flavors, layered in a brick mold.

Nebbiolo (neb-BYŌ-lō) A red-wine grape variety that produces some of Italy's finest wines; it grows best in northern Italy and yields robust, full-bodied wines.

Nebuchadnezzar (NEB-oo-kad-NEZ-er) A wine bottle, usually for Champagne, that holds 20 regular bottles; named for the superannuated biblical patriarch.

neck See **chuck.**

négi (nay-gee) Japanese for leek, scallion, onion.

négresse, négresse en chemise (nay-gres enh she-meez) French for chocolate mousse topped with whipped or iced cream; sometimes called by the Spanish term *negrítas.*

negus (NAY-gus) An English wine punch flavored with sugar, lemons, and spices; served warm.

nem Spicy Thai sausage.

Nesselrode A pudding of custard, whipped cream, and chestnut purée mixed with candied fruits, piled in a **charlotte** mold, and frozen; apparently invented by Mouy, chef to Count Nesselrode, the nineteenth-century diplomat and chancellor of Russia.

nest See **yàn cài.**

nettle A prickly weed used in northern countries as a green similar to spinach; picked young and cooked, its sting disappears.

neua (NOO-ahr) Thai for meat.

Neuchâtel (neu-sha-tel) A well-known white wine produced on the northern shore of Lake Neuchâtel in Switzerland, from the **Chasselas** grape; it is pleasant and refreshing though unremarkable.

Neufchâtel (neu-sha-tel) A soft uncooked cheese from the town of the same name in Normandy; made in many shapes from pasteurized cows' milk, either skimmed or whole and sometimes enriched with cream; eaten fresh when delicate or ripe when pungent.

new American cuisine A recent development in fashionable American restaurants, highly influenced by **nouvelle cuisine;** this style of cooking emphasizes American ingredients in imaginative new dishes usually made by classic techniques, albeit lighter and fresher.

Newburg A thick cream sauce for lobster meat, enriched with egg yolks and flavored with **sherry** and **cayenne pepper;** named after a Captain Wenberg who had the sauce made for him at Delmonico's restaurant in New York.

New England boiled dinner A Yankee **pot-au-feu** of corned beef and salt pork, possibly a chicken, cabbage, potatoes, carrots, and other vegetables, cooked together in one pot and usually served with mustard or horseradish.

New England clambake A traditional method of cooking seafood learned from the Indians: a pit is dug in the beach, layered with hot rocks, then covered with generous amounts of seaweed, clams, lobsters, chicken, unhusked corn (silk removed), potatoes, etc.; the food cooks by the heat of the steaming seaweed around it.

ngo (ngoh)   Vietnamese for coriander.

ngu vi huong (ngoo vee hoong)   Vietnamese for five-spice powder, usually including cloves, cinnamon, fennel seed, licorice, and star anise.

ni (nee)   Japanese for braise, simmer; *nimono* is braised or simmered food.

niçoise, à la (ah lah nee-swahz)   A classic French preparation of tomatoes chopped and sautéed in olive oil with garlic, capers, sliced lemon, anchovies, and black olives; the popular *salade (à la) niçoise* contains, in addition to many of these ingredients, a variety of vegetables (usually including French beans and potatoes), seafood, especially tuna, and herbs.

Nieren (NEER-en)   Kidneys in German.

Nierstein (NEER-shtīn)   An important wine-producing town in the German Rheinhessen, with many good or fine white wines, mostly from the **Riesling** grape.

niku (nee-koo)   Japanese for meat.

nimboo (nim-BOO)   Lemon, lime, in Indian cooking.

ninjin (neen-jeen)   Japanese for carrot.

níspola (NEES-pō-lah)   Spanish for persimmon.

niú ròu (nyō rō)   Chinese for beef.

nivernaise, à la (ah lah nee-vayr-nez)   In French cuisine, "in the style of Nivernais": garnished with glazed carrots and turnips cut into olive shapes, onions, braised lettuce, and boiled potatoes.

noble rot   A mold (*Botrytis cinerea*) that develops on grapes in certain regions, withering the grapes but concentrating the sugar and flavor; grapes so affected produce very fine—and expensive—wine; the French term is *pourriture noble,* the German *Edelfäule.*

nocchette (nohk-KET-tay)   Small Italian pasta "bow ties" for soup.

noce (NŌ-chay)   Italian for nut, walnut; *noce moscata* means nutmeg; *nocciòla* means hazelnut.

Nock (nohk)   German for dumpling; in Austrian dialect, the word is *Nockerl.*

Noël, bûche de   See **bûche de Noël.**

nogada (nō-GAH-dah)   In Mexican cooking, walnut sauce; traditionally served with **poblano** chilies stuffed with shredded pork and garnished with pomegranate seeds—a celebrated dish.

noisette (nwah-zet)   French for hazelnut, or food that is shaped or colored like a nut. The word also means a cut of meat from the rib, usually of lamb, trimmed, rolled, tied in a small round, and served in an individual portion. *Noisette* potatoes are shaped like hazelnuts and browned in butter; *beurre noisette* is brown butter sauce.

noix (nwah)   French for nut, walnut; *noix muscade* is nutmeg.

nok (nohk)   Thai for bird.

Nøkkelost (NEU-kel-ohst)   A Norwegian cheese based on the Dutch **Leyden** and similarly flavored with **cumin** or **caraway.**

nom krourk (nuhm kroork)   In Cambodia, little pancakes of rice flour and **scallions** with **shrimp** and coconut milk.

nonat (nō-na)   French for a very small Mediterranean fish, usually deep-fried or served as an **hors d'oeuvre.**

nonpareille (nonh-paahr-ay)   French for small pickled capers from Provence—a superior variety "without equal."

nopales (nō-PAH-les)   In Mexican cooking, the fleshy oval joints of the *nopal* cactus, eaten with scrambled eggs or in salad; *nopalitos* are cactus leaves eaten in salad.

noques (nōk)   French for the Alsatian version of **gnocchi;** in Austria, *noques* are made into a sweet, light dessert similar to **snow eggs.**

noquis (NŌ-keeth)   Spanish for **gnocchi.**

nori   In Japanese cooking, thin black sheets of seaweed, used either toasted or untoasted for wrapping **sushi,** rice balls, and crackers, and for coating food to be deep-fried.

normande (nohr-manhd)   In French cuisine, fish **velouté** with mushrooms and oyster liquor, thickened with egg yolks and cream, and enriched with butter—a classic sauce; the garnish *à la normande* consists of oysters, mussels, crayfish, **goujonettes,** shrimp, mushroom caps, and truffle slices with **fleurons,** in *sauce normande.*

Normande (nohr-manhd)   Normandy, the French province renowned for its butter, cream, cheese, apples, seafood, and salt-meadow sheep; cider is drunk here instead of wine, and **Calvados** is the local brandy.

norvégienne (nohr-vay-jhyen) "Norwegian style," a classic French sauce of hard-boiled egg yolks mashed and seasoned with vinegar and mustard and beaten with oil for a mayonnaiselike texture; *omelette à la norvégienne* is **baked Alaska.**

Norway lobster See **Dublin Bay prawn.**

nostrale, nostrano (nō-STRAH-lay) Italian for native or homegrown.

nougat (noo-gah) In French cuisine, a confection of roasted nuts (usually almonds or walnuts) with honey or syrup; there are many varieties. *Nougatine,* a vague term, can mean almond brittle or nougat combined with chocolate.

nouilles (noo-yuh) French for noodles.

nouvelle cuisine (noo-vel kwee-zeen) Literally "new cooking," this movement beginning in the 1970s features fresher, lighter food in innovative combinations, served in small portions with striking presentations, but otherwise cooked by classic French techniques.

nova Cold-smoked salmon, originally from Nova Scotia and now probably, but not necessarily, from the Pacific; in American Jewish tradition eaten like **lox** with cream cheese and **bagels.**

Nudeln (NOO-deln) German for noodles.

nuez (nwez) Spanish for nut, walnut; the plural is *nueces.*

Nuits-Saint-Georges (nwee sinh jhorjh) A town in the Côte de Nuits whose vineyards produce excellent red Burgundies.

nuoc mam (nuhk mahm) Vietnamese fermented fish sauce (anchovies), salty and pungent, related to **nam pla** and **patis**; an essential ingredient, highly nutritious; *nuoc mam cham* is the dipping sauce.

Nuss (noos) German for nut, walnut.

nutmeg The oval seed of the tropical nutmeg tree, native to the Moluccas, which is dried, ground, and used to flavor a wide variety of sweet and savory dishes. Connecticut is known as the Nutmeg State because Yankee peddlers sold wooden "nutmegs" to unsuspecting customers. See also **mace.**

nyama (NYAH-mah) Beef; *n'dizi ya na nyama,* a plantain and beef stew with coconut; from Tanzania.

nymphes à l'aurore (nimhf ah l'ō-rohr) In French cuisine, frog legs poached in white wine and served in a pink **chaud-froid** sauce with aspic, a favorite dish of Edward VII of England.

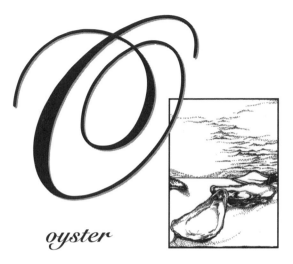

oyster

oats Grain traditional to cold climates where other grains cannot grow. Rolled oats are hulled oats ground into a meal, then steamed to gelatinize some of their starch (thus reducing spoilage), rolled into flakes, and dried; rolled oats are quicker to prepare as oatmeal than other kinds of oats, even if they have lost much of their texture. Steel-cut oats, sometimes called Scottish or Irish oats, are whole groats steamed and cut into pieces.

Obst (ōbst) German for fruit; *Obsttorte* is an open mixed fruit tart, glazed, and perhaps garnished with almonds, whipped cream, or meringue; *Obst-suppe nach Hamberger Art* is a soup of puréed fruits, from Hamburg.

oca (ŌK-ah) Italian for goose.

ocha (ō-chah) Japanese for **green tea.**

ocopa (ō-KŌ-pah) A South American dish of new potatoes in a sauce of chile peppers, onions, garlic, olive oil, and **feta.**

octopus A marine mollusk whose flavorful but tough meat is appreciated mainly by Oriental and Mediterranean cultures, often smoked, marinated, or stewed.

oeil d'anchois (oy d'anh-shwah) Literally "eye of anchovy" in French, this **hors d'oeuvre** is a raw egg yolk surrounded by anchovies and chopped onions.

oenology (ee-NOL-oh-jee) The science of winemaking.

oeuf (euf) French for egg; *oeufs brouillés* means scrambled eggs; *oeufs en cocotte*, poached in a casserole; *oeufs à la coque*, soft-boiled; *oeufs* *durs,* hard-boiled; *oeufs en gelée,* poached and chilled in aspic; *oeufs mollets,* soft-boiled; *oeufs au plat* or *sur le plat,* fried or baked; *oeufs pochés,* poached; *oeufs pochés bénédictine,* poached and served on a creamed salt-cod base (not eggs Benedict); *oeufs à la poêle,* fried.

oeufs à la neige   See **snow eggs.**

offal   So-called variety meats, consisting of organs or trimmings that the butcher removes from the skeletal meat. Offal includes brains, heart, sweetbreads, liver, kidneys, lungs, pancreas, spleen, tripe, tongue, headmeat, tail, blood, skin, feet, horns, and intestines. Offal can also mean inedible waste or carrion.

oie   (wah)   French for goose; *oison* is a gosling.

oignon   (oy-nyonh)   French for onion; *oignon clouté* is an onion studded with cloves.

oiseau   (wah-zō)   French for bird; *oiseaux sans tête,* meat birds, a meat scallop stuffed, rolled up, and cooked.

oja   See **ujjah.**

okra   A tropical plant of the mallow family, native to Africa and brought to the southern United States with the slave trade; its unripe seed pod, star-shaped in cross section, is used as a vegetable and a thickener for soups and **gumbos** because of its mucilaginous texture. Its West African name, *okro,* extends to various soups and stews using okra, especially combining smoked or salted seafood, meat, and vegetables.

Öl   (eul)   German for oil.

øl, öl   (eul)   Beer in Scandinavian countries.

oleo   See **margarine.**

olio   (Ō-lyō)   Italian for oil; in Italy, *olio* means olive oil—*olio d'oliva.*

olive   The fruit of the olive tree is never eaten raw but cured when green and unripe or black and ripe. Of many types, *kalamata* are large Greek unpitted olives, purple to black in color, with a pungent full flavor. The French *niçoises* are small, salty, with stems on; French *picholine* olives are larger, briny, and green. Among Italian olives, *Gaeta* are dry and wrinkled, *Liguria* tart.

olive oil   Tree indigenous to the Mediterranean whose fruit is pressed for oil that is low in monounsaturated fat. With a fairly low burning point, it imbues much of the region's food with its character. Colored green to gold, dark or pale, top-quality oil, cold-pressed from the first pressing and unrefined, has low acidity (under 1%). Laws vary from country to country, but extra-virgin is best, followed by superfine, fine, pure (also called virgin), and blends. Newly marketed "light" olive oil has little flavor, the same nutritional profile, and a higher smoke point.

olives, meat See **meat birds.**

Olivet (ō-lee-vay) A French whole- or partially skimmed-milk cows' cheese similar to **Camembert,** from Orléans; it is eaten very fresh or matured for a month, when it develops a delicate blue rind and is called *Olivet Bleu.*

olivette di vitello (ō-lee-VET-tay dee vee-TEL-lō) Italian veal scallops filled with a savory stuffing, rolled up, and braised; veal birds.

olla podrida (Ō-yah pō-DREE-dah) A Spanish stew, literally "rotten pot," made from many different meats (mainly pork) and vegetables, including cabbage, chickpeas, and tomatoes; similar to the **cocido** of Madrid; *olla* means stewpot and lends its name to other hearty dishes.

oloroso (ō-lor-Ō-sō) A type of Spanish **sherry** matured in **soleras** like **fino** but without **flor** yeast; its color is dark—deep gold to amber— its alcoholic content higher than *fino,* and it has a rich flavor and intense, characteristic bouquet; *olorosos* range from nearly dry to very sweet.

omelette (ōm-let) French for omelet: eggs beaten and cooked in butter in a special flat pan until set, often filled or flavored with a wide variety of other ingredients.

oolong (oo-long) A partially fermented, amber-colored tea, mostly from Taiwan—a cross between black fermented tea and green unfermented tea.

Oporto (ō-PORT-ō) A city in Portugal near the mouth of the Douro River; the fortified wine **port,** whose name comes from that of the city, must by law be shipped from Oporto or the town across the river.

Oppenheim (OHP-pen-hīm) A town in the German Rheinhessen whose many vineyards produce good white wines (although not as distinguished as those of its northern neighbor, **Nierstein**).

orange, sauce (sōs ohr-anhjh) In French cuisine, **demi-glace** flavored with orange and perhaps lemon juice and julienne of orange zest.

orange flower water Liquid distilled during the extraction of essential oil from bitter orange blossoms and used as a flavoring; before **vanilla** was discovered it was the principal flavoring extract and remains so in the Middle East.

orange pekoe A superior grade of black tea from India or Ceylon with leaves slightly larger than **pekoe;** the name no longer refers to the flavor of the tea, but rather to leaf size.

orecchiette (or-ek-KYET-tay) Eggless pasta in the shape of "little ears"; originally from Apulia, in Italy's heel, and usually made commercially; the traditional sauce for *orecchiette* is broccoli with anchovies and cheese; often misspelled.

oregano (or-AY-gah-nō) Wild **marjoram,** an herb especially popular in Italian cooking as well as Greek and Middle Eastern cooking; oregano is very similar to marjoram but more pungent; the Italian word is *origano,* the French *origan.* Mexican oregano is another unrelated herb.

Oregon grapes See **barberry.**

organic Refers to produce grown without artificial or chemical fertilizers or pesticides and therefore favored by the health movement.

orgeat (ohr-jha) French for a syrup or drink originally made from barley and later from almonds, flavored with **orange flower water.**

orientale, à l' (ah l'or-yenh-tal) In French cuisine, dishes seasoned with saffron or curry, sometimes in a garnish of tomatoes stuffed with rice.

Original-Abfüllung (or-EE-gee-nal AHB-fül-ung) German for **château-bottled.**

Orloff, veal See **veal Orloff.**

ormer See **abalone.**

ortolan (ohr-tō-lanh) French for a small bird, the European bunting, prized for its flavor; though once prolific in southern France, it is now nearly extinct; it is plucked and often boned but not drawn, and its entrails are considered delicious.

Orvieto (or-VYAY-tō) A town in Umbria in central Italy whose white wine of the same name is light, pleasant, and popular.

orzo (OR-zō) Rice-shaped pasta; in Italian the word means barley.

Oscar, veal See **veal Oscar.**

oseille (ō-zay) French for sorrel.

osso buco, ossobuco alla milanese (OHS-sō BOO-kō ahl-lah mee-lah-NAY-say) In Italian cooking, veal shanks or shin bones (literally "bone with a hole"), preferably from the hind, slowly braised with onions, garlic, carrots, celery, possibly tomatoes, stock, and white wine, and traditionally garnished with **gremolada** before serving; the morsels of marrow are removed with a special implement. In Milan, **risotto** accompanies the *oss bus,* as it is called in local dialect. The plural form is *ossi buchi.*

ost (ohst) Cheese in Scandinavian languages.

ostra (OTH-trah) Spanish for oyster; *ostion* is another kind of oyster, eaten cooked; the Italian word is *òstrica.*

ot (eu) Vietnamese for chile peppers; *ot kho,* dried red Chinese chilies; *tuong ot,* prepared chile sauce.

oursin (oor-zinh) French for **sea urchin.**

ouzo (OO-zō) A sweet anise-flavored liqueur from Greece.

ovos moles (Ō-vōs MŌ-lays) In Portuguese cooking, egg yolks and sugar mixed together and used as a sauce or filling; in Aveiro, the mixture is molded into fanciful shapes, cooked in rice water, and eaten sprinkled with cinnamon.

Oxford and Cambridge pudding English apricot tart masked with meringue.

Oxford sauce Virtually the same as **Cumberland sauce.**

oxidation When applied to wine, the process of exposing the wine (usually white) to the air. This generally causes it to darken, as well as robbing it of its freshness.

oxtail Tail of beef, excellent for stews and soups because of the gelatin rendered from the high proportion of bones; ox simply means steer.

oyster A bivalve marine **mollusk** prized since ancient times and cultivated since the Romans; eaten raw or cooked (only until its edges curl) in preparations as various as **Hangtown fry, angels on horseback,** and *à la normande;* Marennes and Belon (French), Colchester and Whitstable (English), and Blue Point and Olympia (American) are choice varieties.

oyster mushroom An Oriental mushroom that grows both wild and cultivated and is available fresh, dried, and canned; the clusters, with

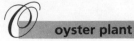

gray oval caps and white stems, are sold in plastic pouches; the taste is peppery when raw, mild when cooked.

oyster plant　See **salsify.**

oyster sauce　See **li jiàng.**

oysters Rockefeller　Oysters on the half shell, resting on a bed of rock salt, each topped with a spoonful of puréed seasoned spinach, quickly browned; originally from Antoine's in New Orleans and named for John D. Rockefeller; apparently first made with watercress rather than spinach.

pain

paan (pahn) Betel leaves, sometimes stuffed with spices and nuts, and used as a digestive in Indian cooking.

pachadi (PAH-chah-dee) Vegetables and yogurt with mustard seeds in Indian cooking.

Pacific rim Cooking styles of countries or regions in the Pacific that have recently become popular; these are often **fusion cuisine** and combine traditional techniques with exotic ingredients and Asian influences.

paella (pah-AY-ah) A Spanish dish of short-grain rice cooked with a variety of meats and fish (usually **chorizo,** chicken, rabbit, and shellfish) and an assortment of vegetables, including garlic, scallions, peas, and tomatoes, flavored with **saffron,** and served in the pan in which it is traditionally made; the exact ingredients vary widely according to region, season, and pocketbook; originally from **Valencia.**

pagello (pah-JEL-lō) Italian for red snapper.

paglia e fieno (PAH-lyah ay FYAY-nō) Italian "straw and hay" fettucine, the yellow and green colors coming from egg and spinach pasta dough; usually served in a cream sauce with ham or sausage, peas, and perhaps mushrooms.

paillarde de veau (pī-yaahrd deu vō) French for grilled veal scallop.

paillettes (pī-yet) French for pastry straws; *paille* means straw in French.

pain (pinh) French for bread, loaf; *pain mollet,* soft bread; *pain grillé,* toast; *petit pain,* a roll; *pain perdu,* French toast as made in France, usually sweetened and spiced with cinnamon, so-called ("lost bread") because it is made with stale bread; *pain de mie*, sandwich bread; *pain de Gênes*, Genoa cake, a rich almond pound cake.

pain à l'anglaise   See **bread sauce.**

pak   (pahk)   Thai for greens, leafy vegetable; *pak chee*, coriander; *pak chee farang*, parsley; *pak kard hom*, lettuce; *pak sod*, a salad of mixed raw vegetables.

pak choy   See **bai cai.**

pakora   (pah-KOR-ah)   Fritters in Indian cuisine.

palacsinta   (pal-ah-SHIN-tah   Hungarian for **crêpe;** the word in Austrian dialect is *Palatschinke.*

palak   (PAH-lahk)   Spinach in Indian cooking.

Palatinate   See **Rheinpfalz.**

palaver   (pah-LAH-ver)   A thick stew from West Africa of spinach with chicken or meat and various vegetables.

pallet knife   A flexible, wide-bladed knife without a sharp edge; used for spreading butter, icing, filling sandwiches, and other soft mixtures.

palm   A large family of trees and shrubs, usually tropical, many of whose parts are edible: dates are its fruit, coconut its seed or nut, palm hearts its new buds or shoots, sago a starch from its trunk, and, in addition, palm oil and wine.

palmier   (pal-myay)   A French pastry made from strips of **pâte feuilleté** sprinkled with sugar, folded, sliced, and baked, which forms a palm-leaf shape as the pastry puffs out.

paloise   (pal-wahz)   In French cuisine, "in the style of Pau": classic **béarnaise** sauce but with mint in place of tarragon.

palombe   (pal-omhb)   French for wild pigeon or dove; in Spanish *palombacco* means squab or young pigeon.

palourde   (pal-oord)   French for clam.

pamplemousse   (pamh-pluh-moos)   French for grapefruit.

pan   (pahn)   Spanish for bread; *pan tierno*, fresh bread; *pan duro*, stale bread.

panaché   (pa-na-shay)   French for mixed or multicolored; used to describe salad, fruit, or ice cream; also means plumed.

panade (pa-nad) A French peasant soup of water, stock, or milk thickened with bread; also a thick paste made with flour (see **roux**), breadcrumbs, or other starch, possibly thickened with eggs, and used to bind fish and meat **mousses** and **forcemeats;** from the Spanish word for bread, *pan.*

panais (pan-nay) French for parsnip.

panato (pah-NAH-tō) In Italian cooking, fried in breadcrumbs.

pancake A thin batter cake cooked on a griddle or pan and appearing in almost every cuisine the world over. See also **crêpe.**

pancetta (pahn-CHET-tah) Italian bacon that is sometimes rolled into a solid round; used in **battuto.**

pancit (pan-seet) In Philippine cooking, pasta in the form of noodles, often stir-fried with chopped meats, shrimp, and vegetables, or in the form of dough-wrappers stuffed like **wontons.**

pan de Spagna (pahn day SPAH-nyah) Italian sponge cake, often soaked in liqueur and filled with jam or cream.

pandorato (pahn-dor-RAH-tō) In Italian cooking, "gilded bread": bread dipped in an egg and milk batter and deep-fried; sometimes with a savory stuffing.

pandowdy An early American dessert, probably from New England, of sliced apples mixed with cider, brown sugar or molasses, spices, and butter, covered with biscuit dough, and baked.

pan-dressed Refers to a whole fish that has been scaled and gutted, with head and fins removed; usually for sautéing or deep-frying.

pane (PAH-nay) Italian for bread; *panino* is a roll or biscuit; in French *pané* means breadcrumbed; see also **panade, panure,** and **pain.**

paneer (pah-NEER) In Indian cooking, fresh milk curds, made from boiled milk curdled with lemon juice, that have been drained and compressed; used like fresh unripened cheese or tofu; also spelled *panir.* Another word for these curds is *chenna.*

panetière (PAN-eh-TYAYR) In French, a cupboard with open latticework for storing bread; it is either suspended from the ceiling to keep away pests or set on a sideboard. The term can refer to an edible case, as of pastry, to enclose food.

panettone (pah-net-TŌ-nay) A light Italian yeast cake containing **sultana** raisins and candied citron peel, baked in a domed shape and eaten for breakfast; originally from Milan, *panettone* is traditional for Christmas.

panforte (pahn-FOR-tay) Italian for fruit cake.

pan-fry To sauté: to cook in a skillet in a small amount of fat, as opposed to **deep-frying.**

panna (PAHN-nah) Italian for cream; *panna montata* is whipped cream.

pannequet (pan-kay) Small French pancake or **crêpe** filled with a sweet or savory mixture and folded in quarters.

Pannerone (pan-nayr-Ō-nay) An uncooked whole-milk cows' cheese from Lombardy, usually unsalted; the cheese is pale straw-colored with many holes, delicate and creamy in taste with a slight tang; it matures quickly; also called White **Gorgonzola** and *Gorgonzola Dolce,* rather misleadingly.

Pannhas (PAHN-hahs) In German cooking, a kind of mush made from **buckwheat** flour cooked in broth left over from cooking sausages; this Westphalian specialty, similar to Pennsylvania German **scrapple,** is a traditional part of the fall pig slaughter.

panucho (pah-NOO-chō) In Mexican cooking, a small **tortilla** puffed up, the pocket filled with a savory stuffing, then fried until crisp.

panure (pa-nür) In French, golden breadcrumb crust.

panzanella (pahn-zah-NEL-lah) A rustic Italian salad of vegetables and herbs with stale bread soaked in water and squeezed dry, or perhaps fried in olive oil; from Tuscany.

panzarotti (pahn-zah-ROHT-tee) Italian pastry crescents stuffed with cheese and deep-fried.

papa (PAH-pah) Spanish for potato; also called *patata*; *papa seca,* freeze-dried potatoes from the Andes, an ancient method of preservation. *Chuno* is another method in which the potatoes are naturally freeze-dried in the high altitude and cold climate.

papa dzules (PAH-pah-TSOO-lays) Literally "food for the lords," which the Mayans supposedly gave the Spaniards. This Mexican Yucatán specialty consists of **tortillas** filled with hard-boiled egg yolk, tomato sauce, pumpkin seed sauce, and green pumpkin seed oil.

papain (pah-PAY-in) An enzyme derived from the **papaya** and used, diluted in sugar and salt, as a meat tenderizer. South American Indians have for centuries wrapped fresh papaya leaves around meat for the same purpose.

papaw, pawpaw (PAW-paw)   A small tree native to North America whose fruit has yellowish skin and smooth, creamy flesh with sweet, fragrant flavor. American Indians and settlers appreciated it, but today it is ignored. The name is easily confused with the **papaya** (no relation); another name for the fruit is **custard apple,** to confuse it further.

papaya (pah-PĪ-yah)   A tall tropical plant native to America; its large pear-shaped fruit has a thin skin that turns yellow when ripe, a smooth yellow or orange flesh, and many black seeds resembling peppercorns; the unripe papaya can be cooked as a vegetable like squash; the sweet ripe fruit is eaten in many ways, like melon, and even the leaves can be boiled like spinach; see also **papain** and **papaw.** The plural of papaya is papaya.

papillon (pa-pee-yonh)   A French "butterfly"-shaped pastry cookie made from **feuilletage.**

papillote (pa-pee-yōt)   In French cuisine, a paper frill used to garnish the end of the rib bone on chops and crown rib roasts; *en papillote* means an individual portion of fish, poultry, or meat that is wrapped in paper (usually parchment) with seasonings and liquid to moisten it, cooked in the oven, and served while still in the puffed-up paper, slit at table to release the aromatic steam.

papos de anjo (PAH-pōs day AHN-hō)   Literally "angel's breasts" in Portuguese; small yellow egg cakes served with syrup.

pappad (PAH-pahd)   Crisp thin Indian flatbread, roasted, grilled, or fried, made from mung beans or lentils; sometimes called *pappadam.*

pappardelle (pap-par-DEL-lay)   Long flat egg noodles, ⅝ inch broad, cut with a crimped edge; they are the traditional accompaniment to hare cooked in a rich wine sauce; from Tuscany.

paprika   A spice made from sweet red pepper, dried and powdered; widely used in Hungarian cooking and essential to **gulyás;** different types of paprika vary in strength.

paprikás csirke (pahp-ree-KAHSH SHEER-kuh)   Hungarian dish of chicken braised with onions and garlic, with plenty of **paprika** and sour cream; *paprikás,* a favorite Hungarian dish, is also made with meat and fish.

paquette (pa-ket)   French for fully developed lobster roe about to be laid, turned from bright orange to dark greenish black—considered a great delicacy; *paquette* also means the female lobster carrying such roe.

paratha (PAH-rah-tah)   In Indian cuisine, flaky whole-wheat flatbread fried in **ghee** on a griddle, sometimes stuffed with spicy meat or vegetables.

parboil   See **blanch.**

pareve (PAR-uh-vuh)   Food containing no meat or milk and therefore, by Jewish **kosher** law, suitable to be eaten with either.

parfait (paahr-fay)   A French **mousse**like dessert, originally a coffee cream, but now any fruit, nut, or flavored syrup into which whipped cream is folded, then chilled or frozen; in the United States a parfait is served in a tall narrow glass filled with ice cream, layered with sauce, with whipped cream on top.

parga (PAHR-gah)   Spanish for red snapper.

parihuela salvaje (pahr-ee-WAY-lah sal-VAH-hay)   Mixed fish and shellfish with **chorizo** in a spicy tomato sauce, a **Creole** dish from South America.

Paris-Brest (paahr-ee brest)   A French pastry ring of **pâte à choux** topped with sliced almonds and filled with crème praliné (see **praline**) or **crème Chantilly** and fresh strawberries.

parisienne, pommes à la (pohm ah lah paahr-ee-zyen)   In French cuisine, potatoes cut into small ovals and sautéed in butter; there are various other *parisienne* preparations, including a white-wine reduction sauce with shallots.

Parker House roll   A yeast-bread roll folded into two halves before baking, named for the Parker House hotel in Boston, where the roll was first created in the nineteenth century.

Parmentier, Antoine-Augustin (1737–1813) (paahr-menh-tyay)   A French pharmacist and agronomist who, when fed potatoes as a prisoner of war, realized their potential importance. Parmentier spent his life promoting the scorned tuber, eventually persuading Louis XVI to serve it at court. Parmentier's name is attached to many potato dishes.

Parmesan   See **Parmigiano Reggiano.**

parmesane, à la (ah lah paahr-meh-zan)   In French cuisine, with grated Parmesan cheese; see **Parmigiano Reggiano.**

Parmigiano Reggiano (par-mee-JAH-nō rej-JAH-nō)   A cooked, pressed, partially-skimmed cows' milk cheese shaped in large squat cylinders; protected by law, this very old and famous **grana** cheese comes from designated areas in northern Italy. Its rind is smooth and golden, its paste pale straw-colored, dense, and grainy, with tiny holes radiating from the center; sweet, mellow, and fragrant, it is eaten young as a table cheese or very old and sharp as a grating cheese.

parrilla (pahr-REE-ah) Spanish for grill; *parrillada di pescado* is mixed seafood grill with lemon.

parsley An herb known to the ancient Greeks and Romans for its medicinal properties but now used for culinary purposes; it grows in several varieties, among them the curly-leaf, most popular in the United States, and the more pungent flat-leaf, popular in Europe, especially in the Mediterranean, where it originated.

parson's nose See **pope's nose.**

partridge A fall game bird with delicate white flesh, cooked in various ways depending largely on age; a single bird serves one.

pasilla (pah-SEE-yah) A long, thin, dark brown chili pepper, very hot and about 6 inches long.

paskha (PAHS-kah) A traditional cake for Russian Orthodox Easter (*paskha* means Easter) made of cream cheese, dried fruits, and nuts, and shaped in a high four-sided pyramid marked with the letters *XB* for "Christ is Risen"; usually served with **kulich.**

passata (pahs-SAH-tah) Italian for purée.

passatelli in brodo (pahs-sah-TEL-lee een BRŌ-dō) Parmesan, eggs, and breadcrumbs mixed to a paste and pressed through a tool to form strands that are cooked and served in meat broth; from Romagna in Italy.

passer (pas-ay) In French to strain through a sieve or tammy cloth.

passion fruit A climbing vine or shrub, native to Brazil, whose unusual blossom is considered symbolic of Christ's passion; the egg-sized fruit turns deep purple and wrinkled with ripeness; its ochre flesh, lemony and intense, is eaten raw with the seeds or squeezed and bottled for juice.

pasta (PAHS-tah) Italian for dough or paste, as well as the whole family of noodles; *pasta all'uovo*, egg pasta; *pasta ascuitta*, "dry" or plain pasta, possibly stuffed or sauced, as opposed to *pasta in brodo*, which is pasta cooked in soup; *pasta frolla*, short pastry; *pasta sfoglia*, puff pastry.

pasta e fagioli (PAHS-tah ay fah-JŌ-lee) A robust Italian soup of pasta, white beans (some of which are puréed to thicken it), and salt pork.

pastel (PAHTH-tel, PAHS-tel)   Spanish for pie, cake, pastry, **pâté;** a *pastelería* is a pastry shop.

pastèque (pas-tek)   French for watermelon.

pasteurization   The process of heating food high and long enough to kill microorganisms and prevent or slow fermentation; used especially for milk; named after the French chemist Louis Pasteur (1822–95).

pasticcio (pahs-TEE-chō)   In Italian cooking, a pie, either savory or sweet, but often of layered pasta with a savory filling; a *pasticcerìa* is a piece of pastry or pastry shop.

pastilla   See **bastilla.**

pastillage (pas-tee-yajh)   French for a mixture of sugar, water, and **gum tragacanth** that forms a paste that can be molded into fantastic shapes; though little used today, in centuries past it was used extensively for elaborate table ornamentation; **Carême** excelled in architectural *pastillage.*

pastina (pahs-TEE-nah)   Small Italian pasta for soup.

pastis (pas-tees)   A potent anise-flavored liqueur popular in southern France; usually mixed with water which turns its green color cloudy; see also **Pernod.**

pastitsio (pas-TEET-syō)   Greek macaroni baked in a dish with ground meat, onion, tomato sauce, and cheese.

pastrami (pas-TRAH-mee)   Beef, usually shoulder, first pickled in spices and then smoked; of Rumanian origin and now associated with Jewish cooking.

pastry bag   A cone of paper or cloth with an open tip, sometimes fitted with a specially cut tip; soft smooth foods, such as whipped cream, icing, puréed potatoes, and **pâte à choux,** are forced through it to make even and decorative shapes.

pastry blender   A simple kitchen tool—parallel stiff metal wires on a handle—for cutting fat into flour.

pastry comb   Confectioner's tool with serrated edges for making designs on the iced or chocolate tops and sides of cakes and pastries; also called cake comb.

pastry cream   See **crème patissière.**

pasty   See **Cornish pasty.**

patata (pah-TAH-tah) Italian and Spanish for potato; *patate fritte* are fried potatoes; *patate lesse*, boiled potatoes; *patate stacciate*, mashed potatoes.

patate (pa-tat) French for sweet potato.

pâte (pat) French for pastry, paste, pasta, dough, or batter; the word is often confused with **pâté**. See following entries.

pâte à choux (pat ah shoo) French for cream puff pastry; a simple paste made by stirring flour into boiling water and butter; eggs are then mixed in; upon cooking, the eggs puff up the dough, making a cavity, so the inside of the pastry is generally filled with flavored cream, as in **éclairs, profiteroles,** etc.; spelled both *pâte à chou* and *choux*.

pâte à croissant (pat ah kwah-sanh) **Croissant** pastry dough.

pâte à foncer (pat ah fonh-say) See **foncer.**

pâte brisée (pat ah bree-zay) Pie dough, short pastry, literally "broken" pastry in French.

pâte d'amandes (pat d'a-manhd) French for almond paste, **marzipan.**

pâte feuilletée (pat foy-eh-tay) French for flaky or puff pastry; it is made by enclosing butter within the **détrempe** or elastic dough and then folding and turning it many times to produce *mille feuille*, a "thousand leaves" or thin layers; during baking the steam from the melted butter pushes the layers up to make the delicate puff of pastry.

pâte levée (pat leh-vay) French for raised or leavened dough.

pâte sucrée (pat sü-kray) French for sweet pastry for pie dough and pastry shells, very high in fat (butter for best flavor) and low in moisture to form a crumbly base that will not become soggy when filled.

pâté (pa-tay) French for a rich mixture, usually savory, of meat, poultry, game, seafood, or vegetables cooked in pastry (*pâté en croûte*) or earthenware dish (*pâté en terrine*); *pâté de foie gras*, smooth, rich, and well seasoned, is a typical example; *pâté de compagne* has a coarse, crumbly texture. *Pâté* can also mean pastry, pie, pasty, or patty, but should not be confused with **pâte.**

patis (pa-tees) Philippine fermented fish sauce, salty and pungent.

pâtissier (pa-tees-syay) French for a pastry chef or cook; a *pâtisserie* is a piece of pastry or a pastry shop.

pâtissière, crème See **crème pâtissière.**

patlıcan (paht-lee-jahn) Turkish for eggplant.

pato, pata (PAH-tō, PAH-tah) Spanish for duck, either drake or female.

paton (pa-tonh) In French, one recipe or "pad" of **pâte feuilletée,** of optimal size for handling.

patty pan A variety of round summer squash with a scalloped edge, usually white, sometimes yellow.

Pauillac (pō-yak) A wine-producing town in the **Haut-Médoc** of Bordeaux, where some of the greatest vineyards lie, including Château **Lafite, Latour,** and **Mouton-Rothschild.**

paupiette (pō-pyet) French for a thin slice or scallop of meat filled with savory stuffing, rolled up, and braised; see also **meat birds** or **olivette** and **scallop.**

pavé (pa-vay) A French dish such as a savory **mousse** or **pâté** chilled in a square mold and garnished; a square cake, often sponge, spread with buttercream and garnished; the name means paving stone and designates a square or rectangular shape.

pavo (PAH-vō) Spanish for turkey.

payasam (PĪ-yah-sahm) An Indian pudding of mung beans, peas, and coconut milk.

paysanne, à la (ah lah pī-zan) "Peasant style": with vegetables—most often carrots, onions, and potatoes—and diced bacon.

peanut Not a true nut but the seed of a leguminous bush indigenous to Brazil and brought to North America as a result of the slave trade; highly nutritious, peanuts are a staple in Africa and an important crop in India and China. The oil, with a high burning point and light flavor, is important for cooking.

pearl barley Hulled and polished **barley,** small and round like pearls, usually eaten in soups or like rice.

pecan The nut of a tall tree native to the Mississippi Valley and a member (with the walnut) of the hickory family; an important dessert nut in the United States but uncommon elsewhere; the name is of American Indian origin.

pêche Melba (pesh MEL-bah) In French cuisine, skinned peaches poached in vanilla-flavored syrup, served on vanilla ice cream with raspberry purée; created by **Escoffier** for Dame Nellie Melba, the great Australian coloratura soprano.

pechuga de pollo (peh-CHOO-gah day PŌ-lō)   Spanish for chicken breast.

Pecorino Romano (pek-or-EE-nō rō-MAH-nō)   A cooked and pressed whole-milk ewes' cheese, originally made outside Rome but now made mostly in Sardinia. This ancient **grana** cheese is round, white, or very pale straw-yellow, and dense, with a yellow brown rind. Aged at least eight months, its flavor is sharp, salty, and intense. There are other types of *pecorino* (from *pecora*, meaning ewe), but this is the most famous and finest.

Pecorino Siciliano (pek-or-EE-nō see-chee-LYAH-nō)   A hard uncooked Italian cheese made from whole ewes' milk, with a flavor made more pungent by the addition of peppercorns; a **grana** cheese, it is often used for grating.

pectin   A jellylike substance found in certain fruits—especially apples, currants, quinces, and citrus—and other plants. Pectin causes fruit to set when it is cooked at a high temperature (220° F/105° C at sea level) with sugar and acid in jelly making.

ped (pet)   Thai for spicy, hot, peppery, pungent.

Pedro Ximénez (PAY-drō hee-MEN-eth)   A Spanish grape variety, said to be (but probably not) the **Riesling** grape brought from the Rhine Valley; **sherry, Montilla,** and **Málaga** wines are made from it.

peixe (PAY-shay)   Portuguese for fish, singular and plural.

Peking duck   See **Bei jīng kǎo yā**.

pekoe (PEE-kō)   A superior grade of black tea from India and Ceylon whose leaves are slightly smaller than that of **orange pekoe** and that brews dark, though not necessarily strong.

Pellkartoffeln (PEL-kar-tohf-eln)   German for potatoes boiled in their skins.

pemmican   Preserved meat, often buffalo or venison, dried, pounded, mixed with melted fat and sometimes berries, and pressed into cakes; used by the American Indians and early settlers on expeditions as a high-energy convenience food.

penne (PEN-nay)   Italian for quill-shaped pasta, that is, tubes cut on the diagonal.

pepe nero (PAY-pay NAY-rō)   Italian for black pepper; red pepper is *pepe rosso.*

peperonata (peh-payr-ō-NAH-tah)   Italian for sweet peppers, tomatoes, onions, and garlic cooked in olive oil and served cold; an Italian **pipérade.**

peperoncino (peh-payr-ōn-CHEE-nō)   Italian for a hot red chili pepper, fresh or dried.

peperoni (peh-payr-Ō-nee)   Italian for green or red sweet bell peppers; also an Italian sausage of pork and beef highly seasoned with hot red peppers.

pepino (peh-PEE-nō)   Spanish for cucumber; also a melon from South America with striped purple and yellow skin and delicate flavor.

pepita (peh-PEE-tah)   Spanish for fruit seed; in Mexican cooking this means pumpkin seed.

pepitoria, en (en peh-pee-TOR-ya)   A Spanish sauce, usually for chicken, of almonds, garlic, herbs, saffron, and wine; probably of Arab origin.

pepper (black)   The fruit of a vine native to India, which has been fermented and dried; white pepper, used in pale foods for aesthetic reasons, has a milder taste because the black outer skin of the fully ripened berry has been removed before drying. This type of pepper is not related to the *Capsicum* family, to which **cayenne, paprika, chili,** and **sweet red** and **green bell peppers** belong.

pepper (chili or red)   See **chili.**

pepper (sweet bell)   A mild member of the fiery *Capsicum* family native to tropical America; the unripe green fruits turn red, yellow, orange, or deep purple when mature.

pepperpot   A soup or stew made from tripe and highly seasoned, originally from Philadelphia and probably derived from the German **Pfefferpothast.** The West Indian version of pepperpot contains *cassareep* (**cassava** juice), meat, and seafood, as well as vegetables.

pera (PAYR-ah)   Italian and Spanish for pear.

perch   The name given to various fresh- and saltwater fish, many of them unrelated.

perdrix (payr-dree)   French for partridge; *perdreau* is a young partridge; *perdiz* is the Spanish word.

peregrinos (payr-eh-GREE-nōth, payr-eh-GREE-nōs)   Spanish for scallops.

Périgord, périgourdine (payr-ee-gohr)   A French **demi-glace** sauce with truffle essence and chopped truffles; *à la périgourdine* means garnished with truffles—for which Périgord is famous—and sometimes **foie gras.**

Perilla (payr-EE-yah)   A cows' milk cheese from Spain similar to **Tetilla;** firm in texture, mild in flavor.

perilla leaf   Broad-leafed plant in the mint family, in both red and green varieties, used as a vegetable either whole or shredded, as a wrapper, and as a garnish; also called beefsteak plant, *shiso,* or *tia to.*

periwinkle   A small sea snail popular along the French and British seashores but largely ignored on the American Atlantic coast.

perlant (payr-lanh)   French for a wine that is slightly and naturally sparkling but not deliberately vinified so.

Perlwein (PAYRL-vīn)   German for a wine that is slightly sparkling and intentionally vinified so.

pernice (payr-NEE-chay)   Italian for partridge; the Spanish word is *perdiz.*

Pernod (payr-nō)   Brand name of an anise-flavored liqueur, originally **absinthe,** now used for **pastis.**

perry   Pear cider.

persil (payr-seel)   French for parsley; *persillade* is chopped parsley—perhaps mixed with chopped garlic—added to a dish before serving; *persillé* means sprinkled with parsley and also designates top-quality beef marbled with fat.

persimmon   The fruit of a tree native to the United States and China, though the Chinese varieties are, through cultivation, sweeter and larger; the deep orange fruit ripens in mid to late fall but until then it is unpleasantly astringent; known as *kaki* to the rest of the world, we call it by its American Indian name. Sharon fruit is a less astringent type of persimmon developed in Israel.

pesca (PES-kah)   Italian for peach (the plural is *pesche*); *pesca noce* is nectarine.

pescado (peth-KAH-dō, pes-KAH-dō)   Spanish for fish; *pescado a la sal* is whole fish baked in rock salt; *pescadilla* is a small fish.

pesce (PAY-shay)   Italian for fish; *pesce persico,* perch; *pesce spada,* swordfish; *pesce San Pietro,* John Dory.

pesto (PES-tō)   A sauce from Genoa of crushed basil, garlic, pine nuts, and **Parmesan** or **Pecorino** in olive oil; it is a robust sauce for minestrone and pasta (which in Italy is invariably **trenette**).

Petersilie (pay-tayr-ZEEL-yeh) German for parsley.

pétillant (pay-tee-yanh) French term for effervescent, slightly sparkling wine; the French equivalent of **frizzante** (Italian) and **Perlwein** (German) and deliberately vinified so (unlike **perlant**).

petite marmite (peu-teet maahr-meet) In French cuisine, a clear consommé served from the earthenware **marmite** in which it is cooked; lean meat, marrow bones, a whole chicken, and vegetables flavor the broth, which is served with **croûtes** spread with marrow or sprinkled with grated cheese.

petit four (peu-tee foor) A very small cake or cookie, often elaborately garnished; also a sweetmeat served at the end of a dinner (in French, literally "little oven").

petit pain See **pain.**

petit salé See **salé.**

Petit-Suisse (peu-tee swees) A French pasteurized cows' milk cheese, sometimes enriched with cream, made into a fresh, mild cheese shaped in small cylinders; it was invented by a Swiss cowherd and a farmer's wife in France in the nineteenth century.

Petit Syrah The name used in California for the **Syrah** grape.

pétrissage (pay-tree-sajh) French term for kneading the dough.

petto (PET-tō) Italian for breast, chest, brisket; *petti di pollo* are chicken breasts.

pez (payth, pays) Spanish for fish (singular); the plural is *peces.* The Portuguese is *peixe.*

pez espada (peth eth-PAH-dah, pez es-PAH-dah) Spanish for swordfish.

pezzo (PET-sō) Piece, chunk in Italian.

Pfannkuchen (PFAHN-koo-khen) German for pancake.

Pfeffer (PFEF-fer) German for pepper.

Pfefferkuchen (PFEF-fer-koo-khen) A German spice cake, similar to gingerbread, originally from Nuremberg; a traditional Christmas dessert.

Pfefferpothast (PFEF-fer-poht-hahst) A German stew of beef ribs and onions in gravy, liberally seasoned with pepper and lemon; from Westphalia.

Pfifferling (PFIF-fer-ling) German for **chanterelle.**

Pfirsich (PFEER-zish) German for peach.

Pflaume (PFLOW-meh) German for plum.

pheasant A fall game bird with colorful plumage whose flesh, properly hung, is relished at the table; though a bit smaller, hen pheasants are considered slightly plumper and more succulent than cocks; plenty of moisture must be provided to prevent the meat from drying out during cooking.

pho (feu) Vietnamese one-dish meal of noodles in meat broth with bean sprouts, herbs, chicken, pork, or seafood, preserved cabbage, scallions, chilies, and sauces; served in one bowl at breakfast or any other time; *pho bo,* Hanoi soup, with beef stock, is the favorite; *pho ga,* with ginger and chicken, is another version.

phyllo (FEE-lō) Very thin sheets of dough, made from flour and water, layered, and filled with savory or sweet foods; in Greek the word means "leaf," and *phyllo* is, in fact, similar to the French **mille-feuille.**

piacere, a (ah pyah-CHAYR-eh) Italian for cooked "to please"; as you like it.

piaz (pee-AHZ) Onion, in Indian cooking.

pib, pibil (peeb) In Mexican cooking, a pit used in the Yucatán for barbecuing that allows the meat to smoke partially while cooking.

picada See **sope.**

picadilla (pee-kah-DEE-yah) Spanish for ground, minced, or shredded meat.

picadillo (pee-kah-DEE-yō) In Spanish cooking, a hash made of ground beef sautéed with chopped vegetables and savory seasonings.

picarones (pee-kah-RŌ-nays) A Peruvian yeast pastry of puréed squash or sweet potato mixed with dough, deep-fried, and served warm in a spicy sweet syrup.

piccalilli (PIK-ah-lil-ee) A vegetable pickle, probably Anglo-Indian, prepared with vinegar, mustard, and other spices.

piccante (pee-KAHN-tay) Italian for piquant, spicy, sharp; the Spanish word *picante* emphasizes hot, spicy flavor.

piccata (pee-KAH-tah) Italian for veal scallop.

pichón (pee-CHŌN) Spanish for a squab bred for the table.

pickerel See **pike** and **walleye.**

Pickert (PEE-kayrt) German for peasant bread of potato or wheat flour, from Westphalia.

Picón See **Cabrales.**

picpoul See **Folle Blanche.**

pí dàn (pee dahn) Chinese thousand-year-old eggs: duck eggs preserved in a clay casing made of ashes, lime, salt, and strong tea, rolled in rice husks, and buried for three months; the yolks turn greenish brown, the whites deep aubergine; also known as hundred-year-old eggs.

pièce montée (pee-es monh-tay) French for an ornamental centerpiece of **pastillage,** often inedible and very elaborate, that usually adorned the table at important banquets in the past. **Carême's** emphasis on *pièces montées* revealed his passion for architecture as well as for display.

piémontaise, à la (ah lah pyay-monh-tez) A classic French garnish of **risotto timbales** mixed with grated white truffles.

pierna de cordero (PYAYR-nah day kor-DAYR-ō) Spanish for leg of lamb; *pierna de puerco* is a fresh ham.

Piesport (PEES-port) A village in the German **Moselle** Valley that produces many fine white wines that are fruity and delicate.

pigeonneau (pee-jhoh-nō) French for a young squab bred for the table.

pignoli (pee-NYŌ-lee) Italian for **pine nuts;** the French word is *pignons.*

pike A freshwater fish whose sweet white flesh is used in many fine dishes, such as the renowned **quenelles** *de brochet;* Izaak Walton called the pike "choicely good."

pil pil (PEEL peel) In Spanish cuisine, a dish simmered in an earthenware casserole, from the Basque word for "shake."

pilau, pilav, pilao (PEE-lahf, PEE-low) Persian dish of long-grain rice sautéed in a little fat and simmered in flavored liquid until the grains are swollen yet separate; pieces of meat, poultry, or vegetables can be added. *Pilaf* is the Turkish version of the basic technique. Many other rice dishes come from it, such as **polo,** *pelau* (Provence), **purloo** and **pullao.**

pilot biscuit See **hardtack.**

Pilsener **Lager** beer; strictly speaking *Pilsener* is only the very fine beer brewed in Pilsen, Czechoslovakia, but the term is now used generally for any high-quality lager of the same style; pale golden and lower in alcohol and calories than ordinary American beer.

Pilz (peelts) German for mushroom.

piment doux (pee-menh doo) French for sweet pepper.

pimienta (pee-MYEN-tah) Spanish for black pepper; *pimiento* means capsicum red pepper, either sweet *(pimiento dulce)* or hot.

piña (PEE-nyah) Spanish for pineapple, so named for its visual resemblance to the pine cone; *piña colada,* a cocktail of fresh pineapple juice and light rum, originally from the Caribbean but now made widely and in many variations.

Pineau de la Loire (pee-nō deu lah lwaahr) A white grape variety, whose proper name is **Chenin Blanc,** that produces many of the best white wines of Touraine and Anjou as well as of Saumur and California.

Pineau des Charentes (pee-nō day shaahr-anht) A French **apéritif** wine made from new wine with Cognac added, then matured in oak; it is high in alcohol, sweet, and has a distinctive bouquet.

pine nut The seed of certain pine trees that comes from the pine cone, a multiple fruit, used in savory and sweet dishes, especially in Mediterranean countries.

Pinkel A German smoked sausage of groats, raw bacon, and onions

piñón (pee-NYŌN) Spanish for pine nut; the plural is *piñones.*

Pinot (pee-nō) A family of wine grapes including the Pinot Noir, the variety from which fine red Burgundy is made, *Pinot Blanc,* possibly Pinot Chardonnay, as well as *Pinot Gris* and *Pinot Meunier.* The Tyrol, northern Italy, and California also have many vineyards planted with Pinot grapes.

pintade (pinh-tad) French for guinea hen; a young chick is a *pintadeau;* the Spanish word is *pintada.*

pinto bean A variety of common bean, splotched red, used in many Latin American stewed dishes.

pinzimonio (peen-zee-MŌ-nyō) An Italian dipping sauce of oil, salt, and pepper for raw vegetables.

pipérade (pee-payr-ad) In French cuisine, tomatoes cooked in olive oil with green bell peppers and onions, with lightly beaten eggs and sometimes ham or bacon added; this Basque specialty has many variations.

pipián (pee-pee-AN) In Mexican cooking, a deep red sauce for chicken made of sesame and pumpkin seeds ground with spices and sometimes peanuts or almonds.

piquante (pee-kanht) A classic French sauce of chopped shallots reduced with white wine and vinegar, **demi-glace** added, strained, then garnished with chopped gherkins, parsley, chervil, and tarragon.

piquín (pee-KEEN) A dark green chili pepper, very small and very hot.

pirão (pee-ROW) In Brazil, a paste of flour (**manioc,** cornmeal, or another) mixed with coconut milk and **dendê.**

piri-piri (PEE-ree-PEE-ree) A Portuguese sauce made from hot red chili peppers and olive oil; the chili pepper gives its name to the sauce.

pirinç (peu-RINCH) Turkish for raw rice.

piroshki (pee-ROSH-kee) In Russia, small turnovers or dumplings filled with a savory or sweet stuffing; *pirogi* are large pastries cut into servings; the spellings vary, the fillings are infinite.

Pischingertorte (PISH-ing-er-TOR-teh) An Austrian torte made of round wafers filled with chocolate hazelnut cream, covered with chocolate icing.

piselli (pee-ZEL-lee) Italian for peas; *piselli alla romana* are peas cooked with butter, onion, and ham.

pissaladière (pees-sa-la-dyayr) A French pizzalike tart from Nice, made with anchovies, onions, black olives, and perhaps tomatoes arranged in a decorative pattern.

pissenlit (pees-enh-lee) French for **dandelion** leaves; the name ("piss in bed") alludes to the plant's diuretic capabilities; wild dandelion greens are best eaten before flowering or after frost.

pistachio A deciduous tree, native to Asia, cultivated since ancient times for its nuts; their delicate flavor and green color make them useful in savory and sweet dishes, especially **pâtés** and stuffings, ice cream, and pastries.

pisto (PEETH-tō) A Spanish vegetable dish of chopped tomatoes, red or green peppers, zucchini, and onions stewed together, with many variations; this dish is associated with La Mancha.

pistou, soupe au (soop ō pees-too) A rich Provençal vegetable soup, made with white beans, **mange-touts,** and **vermicelli,** garnished with crushed basil and garlic in olive oil; *pistou* is the French version of **pesto.**

pita (PEE-tah) Middle Eastern flat white pocket bread; also spelled *pitta.* The Turkish is *pide.*

Pithiviers (pee-tee-vyay) A French pastry dessert, named for the town where it originated, consisting of a large round of puff pastry filled with almond paste and traditionally decorated with a pinwheel or rosette pattern.

pizza Literally pie in Italian, the word usually denotes an open-faced tart on a yeast dough base spread with all manner of savory foods; originally from southern Italy.

pizzaiolo (peets-ī-Ō-lō) Italian fresh tomato sauce with herbs and garlic, often served with meat dishes.

pla (plah) Thai for fish.

plaice A European member of the **flounder** family; its fine-textured and delicate white flesh is eaten fresh or sometimes smoked.

plancher (planh-shay) In French, to **plank**.

plank To bake or broil food, especially fish, on a board of hardwood that seasons the food on it—a technique early settlers learned from the American Indians.

plantain (PLAN-tin, not PLAN-tayn) A fruit closely related to the banana, but whose higher starch and lower sugar content require that it be cooked for savory or sweet dishes; a staple food in Latin America, the plantain is usually larger than the banana but is sometimes short and fat, with green skin ripening to yellow and black.

plátano (PLAH-tah-nō) **Plantain,** much used in Caribbean cooking; semiripe plantains, *plátano pintones,* ripe plantains, *plátano maduros,* and green plantains, *plátano verdes. Plátano a la tentación,* very ripe plantains baked with brown sugar, wine or rum, and cinnamon; a rich Cuban dish usually served with savory food.

play cheu (plī cheu) Cambodian for fruit.

pletzlach (PLETS-lahkh) Apricot or plum pastry squares, traditional for Passover.

pleurotte See **oyster mushroom.**

Plinz (pleents) Austrian pancake, fritter.

plover (PLUH-ver) A shore bird particularly valued in Europe for its delicious eggs; the lapwing and golden plover are favorite species.

pluck The heart, liver, and lungs of an animal.

plum duff In British cooking, a restrained version of **plum pudding** made with dried raisins or currants; the word "duff" comes from dough.

plum pudding   A British steamed dessert of various dried fruits (excluding plums) and suet, often flamed with brandy; traditional for Christmas.

plum sauce   See **suan mei jiāng.**

pluvier   (plü-vyay)   French for plover.

poach   To cook food gently in liquid held below the boiling point.

poblano   (pō-BLAH-nō)   A large, dark green chili pepper, mild but varying in flavor; it is about 5 inches long, 3 inches wide, and triangular in shape; sometimes available canned; when ripened and dried it becomes the **ancho** chili.

pocher   (pō-shay)   In French, to **poach.**

pochouse,   (pō-shooz)   See **matelote.**

podina   (pō-DEE-nah)   Mint in Indian cooking.

poêler   (pwah-lay)   In French cooking, to cook food with a little butter or other fat in a tightly closed pot; *poêle* means both frying pan and stove.

point, à   (ah pwinh)   French for just right or to the perfect point; with reference to steak, *à point* means rare; with reference to fruit and cheese, it means at the peak of ripeness.

Point, Fernand   (1897–1955) (fayr-nanh pwinh)   Magnanimous *chef-patron* of La Pyramide in Vienne, near Lyons; at this celebrated restaurant he trained many of the finest chefs of the next generation, ensuring the continuity of French cuisine; at the same time, because of his emphasis on simplicity, Point is often called the father of **nouvelle cuisine.**

poire   (pwaahr)   French for pear.

poireau   (pwaahr-ō)   French for leek.

pois   (pwah)   French for pea; *pois cassés* are split peas; *pois chiches*, chickpeas; *petits pois*, spring peas; *petits pois princesse*, snow peas; *pois à la francaise*, peas braised with lettuce, spring onions, parsley, butter, a pinch of sugar, and a little water.

poisson   (pwah-sonh)   French for fish; a *poissonnier* is a fish chef in a large restaurant kitchen or a fishmonger.

poitrine de porc   (pwah-treen deu pork)   French for pork belly; *poitrine* can mean chest, breast, or brisket.

poivrade (pwah-vrad)   A French sauce, usually for game, of **mirepoix** cooked in butter with game trimmings, reduced with crushed peppercorns and herbs, moistened with the marinade and vinegar, **demiglace** and game essence added, then strained and finished with butter.

poivre (PWAH-vruh)   French for pepper; *grain de poivrade* is peppercorn; *poivré*, pungent or spicy; *poivron* or *poivre de la Jamaïque*, allspice; see also **poivrade.**

Pökel (PEU-kel)   German for pickle.

pokeweed   A leafy plant, usually considered a weed, that grows wild in the eastern United States; only the young leaves and shoots are edible, and they are cooked like spinach and asparagus.

polenta (pō-LEN-tah)   An Italian cornmeal pudding eaten as a peasant porridge or more often cooled, sliced, and fried, grilled, or baked with various other foods; polenta is a specialty of Venice and northeastern Italy, where natives hold it in special regard; Marcella Hazan has written that "to call polenta a cornmeal mush is a most indelicate use of language."

pollack   A member of the **cod** family.

pollame (pōl-LAH-may)   Italian for poultry.

pollo (PŌL-lō)   Italian and Spanish for chicken; in Italian, *pollo ruspante* means free-range chicken; *pollastrino*, spring chicken. In Spanish, *pollo a la chilindrón*, chicken braised in a sauce of sweet red peppers, tomatoes, onions, and a little garlic and ham.

polo (PŌ-lō)   In Persian cuisine, rice cooked with other ingredients.

polonaise, à la (ah lah pō-lō-NEZ)   In French cuisine, "Polish style": vegetables, especially cauliflower or asparagus, cooked and sprinkled with chopped hard-boiled egg, breadcrumbs, parsley, and melted butter.

polpetta (pōl-PET-tah)   Italian for meat patty, croquette; *polpettone* is meat loaf, *polpetta* is meatball.

polpo, polipo, polipetto (PŌL-pō)   Italian for squid or octopus; in Spanish the word is *pulpo* or *pulpetto;* in French, *poulpe.*

Polsterzipfel (PŌL-ster-zip-fel)   An Austrian jam-filled turnover.

pomace (poh-mus)   The fruit pulp remaining after all of the juice has been pressed out; refers particularly to apple or grape pulp in the making of cider or wine.

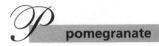

pomegranate A small tree native to the Middle East with a gold or red fruit whose interior chambers hold many edible seeds embedded in pith; the crimson juice in the seed sacs is refreshingly acid and is used for various savory and sweet dishes, especially in the Middle East, as well as for **grenadine;** the many seeds of the fruit probably account for its part in ancient fertility rites.

pomelo (POH-meh-lō) The largest member of the citrus family, native to Malaysia and similar to the grapefruit, with a thick coarse skin; it is fibrous and sweet, with a dry pulp; also called shaddock, after Captain Shaddock, an English ship commander who is said to have brought the seed from the East Indies to Barbados in 1696. Also spelled *pummelo.*

Pomerol (poh-mayr-ōl) A wine-producing area in Bordeaux, just northwest of **Saint-Emilion,** whose velvety wines have a fullness, warmth, and depth of flavor; *Château Pétrus* is the finest among them.

Pommard (poh-maahr) A **commune** in Burgundy between **Beaune** and **Volnay,** producing a quantity of red wine especially popular in the United States and England; the best, estate-bottled wines, are excellent, the lower range is less good than its reputation.

pomme (pohm) French for apple.

pomme de terre (pohm de tayr) Potato (literally "apple of the earth"); often abbreviated to *pomme,* especially for certain potato preparations, such as *pommes frites,* but not to be confused with apple; *pommes frites* are French fried potatoes, as are *pommes Pont-Neuf,* originally sold on the *Pont Neuf* over the Seine River in Paris.

pommes Anna (pohm AN-nah) A French dish of layered potato slices baked with butter in a special casserole; brown and crisp on the outside, soft on the inside.

pommes château In French cuisine, potatoes cut into small ovals and sautéed in butter.

pommes paille (pohm pī) Deep-fried potato "straws."

pomodoro (pō-mō-DOR-ō) Italian for tomato (literally "golden apple"), so named because the first tomatoes in Europe, in the sixteenth century, were yellow.

pompano (POHM-pah-nō) A silvery fish found off the southeastern U.S. coastline in the Atlantic Ocean and Gulf of Mexico; its rich white meat is a delicacy that can be cooked in many ways; often **en papillote** with shrimp and crab.

Pont-l'Evêque (ponh l'eh-vek) A soft, uncooked, and unpressed cheese made from whole or partially skimmed raw cows' milk, from Normandy; this washed-rind cheese has a rich creamy texture and taste, a full aroma, and a square golden rind.

Pont-Neuf See **pomme de terre.**

poo Thai for crab; *poo cha,* steamed and fried crab cakes.

poor knights of Windsor Sliced stale bread soaked in sherry, dipped in egg batter, fried in butter, and served with sugar and cinnamon; a British version of French toast.

popcorn Certain varieties of corn with a high protein content and specific moisture content; with dry heat the corn kernel explodes, and the endosperm swells into the light and crisp snack we know as popcorn.

pope's nose The tail piece of a bird; also known as "parson's nose."

popone (pō-PŌ-nay) Italian for melon.

popover A puffed-up hollow muffin made from an eggy batter very much like that of **Yorkshire pudding,** baked in muffin tins, and served with butter; American in origin.

poppy seed The dried seed of the poppy plant, much used in breads and pastry as well as in Middle Eastern and Indian cooking.

porchetta (por-KET-tah) Italian for roast suckling pig; the Spanish is *porcella.*

porcino (por-CHEE-nō) Italian for a wild mushroom, the French *cèpe* or **boletus;** the plural is *porcini.*

porgy A saltwater fish related to the **bream;** bony but with delicate moist flesh, the porgy is best barbecued or fried.

porridge A cereal or grain, usually oatmeal, cooked in water or milk to a thick puddinglike consistency; it may or may not be flavored with salt, sugar, butter, and various other ingredients.

pòrro (POR-rō) Italian for leek.

port A sweet fortified dessert wine from Portugal's upper Douro Valley, shipped from Oporto (hence the name); brandy is added to partially fermented grape juice, arresting fermentation and producing a strong, sweet wine that is then matured. *Vintage port* is wine from exceptional years that is unblended, bottled young, and then aged for at least a dozen years. *Tawny port* is blended with wine from several years, aged in oak in Oporto to give it a rounder flavor and

softer color, then bottled and shipped ready for sale. *Ruby port* is kept in wood for a shorter time to retain its color and can be blended or not. *White port* is made similarly but from white grapes. As *porto,* drunk as an apéritif in France.

porter   A very dark and strongly flavored British **lager** beer in which the malt is toasted before brewing; porter is usually higher in alcohol than lager beer.

porterhouse   A superior cut of beef from the **short loin** next to the T-**bone,** with a large portion of the **filet mignon** and **strip loin.**

porto, au   (ō POR-tō)   A classic French sauce of **demi-glace** and **port;** when *à l'anglaise* it is a reduction of port, orange and lemon juice and zest, shallots, and thyme, strained and mixed with veal stock.

portobello mushroom   A variety of cultivated white field mushroom allowed to develop fully and renamed as a marketing ploy; its large size, earthy flavor, and firm texture work well for grilling and sautéing and as a meat substitute. Also spelled portabella, but portabello or portobella are both incorrect.

Port-Salut   (por-sal-ü)   An uncooked, pressed, pasteurized cows' milk cheese from France, originally made on a small scale by Trappist monks, using unpasteurized milk (this type of cheese is now called *Entrammes*), but now factory-produced; similar to its cousin **Saint-Paulin.**

portugaise   (por-tü-gez)   A classic French sauce of chopped onions cooked in butter or oil, with chopped tomatoes, tomato sauce, meat glaze, garlic, and chopped parsley; the garnish *à la portugaise* is stuffed tomatoes with **château potatoes** and *portugaise* sauce.

posset   (POS-set)   An old-fashioned British punch made of milk, eggs, wine or ale, lemon juice, spices, and sugar, with whipped cream folded in; a remedy for colds as far back as the Middle Ages, posset is akin to **syllabub** or our latter-day **eggnog.**

postre   (PŌTH-tray, PŌS-tray)   Spanish for dessert.

potage   (pō-tajh)   French for soup, especially a thickened vegetable soup, but not as hearty as **soupe;** the Spanish word *potaje* means a thick soup or stew; *potage Saint-Cloud,* a soup of green peas and lettuce puréed; served with **croûtons.**

potato   Starchy tuber cultivated by the Incas in hundreds of varieties. Types today tend to be floury (best for boiling) or starchy (best for baking). Of the latter, the russet Burbank, developed by Luther

Burbank, is the quintessential Idaho. New potatoes are young, freshly dug poatoes of any variety whose sugar has not yet turned to starch. **Sweet potato** and **yam** are botanically unrelated. See also **Parmentier.**

potato flour Flour ground from cooked potatoes, used in thickening gravies and soups and in breads, where it keeps the crumb moister than wheat flour.

pot-au-feu (pō-tō-feu) In French cuisine, meat and vegetables cooked together in water; the resulting broth is served first, followed by the meat and vegetables as the main course; this classic provincial dish can contain several different meats.

pot de crème (pō deu krem) A small, individual covered cup that holds custard, mousse, and similar desserts; the top keeps a skin from forming on custards.

potée (pō-tay) Originally any food cooked in an earthenware pot, now usually a thick French soup of pork and vegetables—often potatoes and cabbage.

potiron (pō-teer-onh) French for pumpkin.

pot liquor, potlikker The broth remaining after greens and vegetables have been cooked; it is nutritious and an essential part of southern African-American cooking, usually served with cornbread or **corn pone.**

potpie Meat or poultry and perhaps vegetables, cut up and baked with gravy in a deep dish covered with pie crust; American in origin and ranging in quality from the ridiculous to the sublime.

pot roasting A method of braising food (usually large cuts of meat) slowly in a tightly covered pot; the food is browned in a little fat and cooked with some stock or other liquid and vegetables over low heat until tender.

potted shrimps In British cooking, small shrimps shelled, warmed in **clarified butter,** seasoned with **mace** or **nutmeg,** and preserved in the butter for a few days; served as an **hors d'oeuvre** with brown bread.

Pouilly-Fuissé (pooy-yee fwee-say) A popular French white wine from southern Burgundy, just west of **Mâcon,** made from the **Chardonnay** grape; it is dry, clean, fresh, and fruity, with a lovely bouquet.

Pouilly Fumé (pooy-yee fü-may) A French white wine produced from the **Sauvignon Blanc** grape in the village of Pouilly-sur-Loire; dry,

pale, fresh, with a slightly "smoky" *(fumé)* quality; similar to its neighbor **Sancerre** but no relation to **Pouilly-Fuissé.**

poularde (poo-laahrd)   French for a fat hen or chicken—a "roaster"—over four pounds in weight.

poule-au-pot (pool-ō-pō)   **Pot-au-feu** including a sausage-stuffed chicken, made famous by Henri IV's perhaps apocryphal remark that he wanted every household in France to have *poule-au-pot* on Sunday; the chicken is a plump hen, even though *poule* means stewing chicken.

poulet (poo-lay)   A young spring chicken—a "fryer" or "broiler"—weighing up to about four pounds; *poule* means a stewing chicken, one that is too old for other treatment; *poulet d'Inde,* a turkey.

Pouligny-Saint-Pierre (poo-lee-nyee sinh pyayr)   A French goats' milk cheese, uncooked and unpressed, from Berry; soft, crumbly, and pyramid-shaped.

poultry   All domestic fowl, excluding game birds.

pound cake   Cake traditionally made with one pound each of flour, butter, sugar, and eggs.

pourriture noble (poor-ee-tür NŌ-bluh)   French for **noble rot.**

pousse (poos)   French for rise, as in a first rise for yeast pastry.

poussin (poo-sinh)   French for a very young chicken.

Powidl (PŌ-vee-dl)   A special Austrian plum preserve used for pastries and puddings.

pozole (pō-ZŌ-lay)   A thick Mexican soup, almost a stew, made of pork, hominy, and large white dried *cacahuazintle* corn kernels, and served with a hot chili sauce.

pra ram long song   Thai dish of sliced beef and greens simmered with onions and spices in coconut milk.

praline (pra-leen)   Almonds, or in America often pecans, in a caramel syrup or coating; in French cooking, praline is usually crushed and added to confections; named after the seventeenth-century French *maréchal* du Plessis-Praslin, duc de Choiseul, whose chef created this preparation; the adjective is *praliné.*

prawn   A crustacean similar to the shrimp, strictly speaking, but the term is used loosely for any large shrimp.

Preiselbeer (PRĪ-sel-bayr)   German for a red berry similar to the cranberry.

Premier Cru (preu-myay crü) For French **Burgundy** wine, the next to highest classification of vineyards, usually including the name of the vineyard's **commune** as well as the name of the vineyard itself. For *Premier Cru* wines from **Bordeaux,** see **classed growth.**

pre-salé (pray sa-lay) French for lamb and mutton from coastal Normandy that graze on saltmarsh meadows (hence the name), giving their flesh a special salty flavor much prized.

preserved lemons See **limun immallah.**

pressure cooker A covered pot that, because it is under pressure, can cook food above the boiling point, saving time and energy. Pressure cookers are suitable for any food cooked by moist heat, such as soup, stock, stew, pudding, and preserves, but generally not for meat. A safety valve keeps the cooker from exploding in case of malfunction.

pretzel A crisp, savory kind of biscuit made from a flour and water paste that is formed into a rope and twisted into a knot, sprinkled with coarse salt, and baked; the pretzel is associated with German cooking but goes back to the Romans; the characteristic knot represents folded arms, perhaps originally for prayer.

prezzemolo (PRET-say-MŌ-lō) Italian for parsley, which in Italy is the flat-leafed variety.

prickly pear An edible cactus, native to Mexico, with a spiny exterior and soft interior flesh, brilliant and variously colored, eaten fresh or sometimes cooked; the fruit is shaped like a pear and tastes rather sweet and mild; also called Indian fig; even when debarbed, beware of needles.

prik (pik) Thai chilies of all sorts; *prik thai,* black pepper; *saus prik,* bottled chile sauce.

primavera, alla (ah-lah pree-mah-VAYR-ah) In Italian, literally "spring style"; dishes so garnished, especially pasta, include raw or blanched spring vegetables—the Italian version of **à la printanière.**

prime Top-quality beef graded by the U.S. Department of Agriculture—the top 10 percent of beef cattle, available mostly in restaurants and special outlets, but not generally sold in retail markets.

primeur (pree-meur) French for early or forced fruit or vegetables; also first or new wine, as in *Beaujolais Nouveau.*

princesse, à la (ah lah prinh-ses) A classic French garnish of asparagus tips with sliced truffles in cream sauce; also artichoke bottoms stuffed with asparagus tips, served with **noisette** potatoes.

pringar (PREEN-gar)   In Spanish, to baste.

printanière, à la (ah lah prinh-ta-nyayr)   In French, literally "spring style"; the classic garnish consists of new carrots, turnips cut into olive shapes, peas, small green beans, and asparagus tips.

prix fixe (pree feeks)   French for set price for complete meal, as opposed to *à la* **carte.**

processed cheese   Cheese produced by a technique developed in the early twentieth century: green and aged cheeses, often of different varieties and qualities, are finely ground and blended. Emulsifiers are mixed in before the cheese is pasteurized to arrest ripening, and it is packaged in plastic while still hot. Certain kinds of acid, salt, preservatives, coloring, spices, water, and other additives may also be used.

profiteroles (prō-fee-tayr-ōl)   In French cuisine, small puffs of **choux** paste often filled with whipped cream or **crème patissière** and piled high in a dish with chocolate sauce poured over; or as an **hors d'oeuvre**, stuffed with something savory or flavored with cheese.

prosciutto (prō-SHOO-tō)   Fresh Italian ham cured by salting and air-drying but not generally by smoking; the name implies that it is *crudo* (uncooked), although *prosciutto cotto* (cooked) is also made; ham from Parma, where pigs are fed the **Parmigiano** whey, is especially fine and somewhat sweet in flavor.

provençal (prō-venh-sal)   From **Provence;** the classic sauce consists of chopped tomatoes sautéed in olive oil with garlic, parsley, and a pinch of sugar; the garnish *à la provençale* is small tomatoes with stuffed mushrooms and parsley.

Provence (prō-venhs)   A region in southeastern France on the Mediterranean; garlic and olive oil are the basis of its pungent cuisine, and the region abounds with herbs, vegetables, and seafood, not unlike its neighbor, Italy.

Provolone (prō-vō-LŌ-nay)   A cooked and kneaded spun-curd cheese made from cows' milk, originally from southern Italy; Provolone is made in many versions, shapes, and sizes, and is matured either briefly or up to two years; when two to three months old, its color and flavor are buttery and pale; when aged and pungent, used for grating.

prugna (PROO-nyah)   Italian for plum; *pruna* and *prugna secca,* prune.

prune (prün)   French for plum; *pruneau* means prune.

puchero (poo-CHAYR-ō) Spanish for pot; *puchero de gallina* is a special dish of braised stuffed chicken with a sauce of chicken livers; in the Mexican Yucatán, *puchero* is a hot pot including various meats, vegetables, legumes, and even fruit, with the broth served first, followed by the solids.

pudding A vague culinary term which in Britain usually means dessert, but can also mean a savory dish, because of its derivation from *boudin*, meaning sausage.

pudim flan (POO-deem flahn) The Portuguese version of caramel custard, richer and thicker than the Spanish.

pudina (poo-DEE-nah) **Mint** in Indian cooking.

puerco (PWAYR-kō) Spanish for pig, pork.

puerro (PWAYR-ō) Spanish for leek.

Puffer (POO-fer) German for pancake, fritter.

puff pastry See **pâte feuilletée.**

puit d'amour (pwee d'a-moor) In French, literally "wishing well": a small round pastry filled with pastry cream, jelly, or fruit.

Puligny-Montrachet (poo-lee-nyee monh-ra-shay) A village in the Burgundian **Côte de Beaune** which, with its neighbor Chassagne-Montrachet, produces excellent dry white wine, almost all from the **Chardonnay** grape.

pullao (poo-LOW) Indian rice dish, also spelled *pilau* or *pilao*; see **pilau.**

pullet A young hen under one year old.

pulpeta (pool-PAY-tah) Spanish for meat loaf.

pulse The edible seeds, often dried, of leguminous plants such as peas, beans, lentils, and chickpeas; respected by the ancients and virtually all cultures since for their nutritional importance.

Pultost (POOL-tohst) A Norwegian cooked cows' milk cheese, soft and rindless, often flavored with caraway and eaten year-round.

pummelo See **pomelo.**

pumpernickel A dark, coarse-textured, slightly sour bread made from unbolted **rye** flour; originally from Westphalia, Germany.

purée (pü-ray) French for food that is mashed, very finely chopped, or pushed through a sieve to achieve a smooth consistency.

puri (POO-ree)   Indian wholewheat bread deep-fried in **ghee** and puffed; also spelled *poori.*

purloo (per-LOO)   Rice cooked with vegetables and seasonings, from the Carolinas and southern United States, but derived from **pilaf.**

purslane   A once-popular herb with small fleshy leaves, now considered a weed except by the French, who eat it fresh in salad and boiled or sautéed like spinach; in its native India it is used more widely.

Puter (POO-ter)   German for turkey.

puttanesca (poo-tah-NES-kah)   Italian pasta sauce "in the style of a prostitute," that is, quick, pungent, and satisfying: with garlic, anchovies, black olives, capers, parsley, and tomatoes.

Puy, lentilles de (lenh-teey deu pwee)   Small, dark green **lentils,** from the French town of Puy, considered the best type of lentil because of their flavor; they also hold their shape well in cooking.

pyramide (peer-a-meed)   The generic French term for **chèvre,** or fresh goats' milk cheese, uncooked and unpressed, shaped in a small truncated pyramid; this type of cheese is very white, soft, crumbly, and delicate in flavor, becoming sharper if allowed to mature; it is sometimes covered with vegetable ash to keep it from drying out.

quail

qarawah bil hummus (KAH-rah-wah bee HUH-mus) In Arab cooking, calves' feet with chickpeas, widely eaten.

qdra (KUH-drah) A Moroccan **tajin,** often with chicken, cooked with **samneh,** onions, pepper, saffron, and lemon juice; with many variations.

quadrucci (kwah-DROO-chee) In Italian cooking, "little squares" of egg pasta for chicken or meat broth.

quaglia (KWAH-lyah) Italian for quail.

quahog (KŌ-hog) A large hard-shelled North Atlantic clam found off the New England coast; firm and meaty, usually eaten raw, like the medium-size "cherrystones" or small "littlenecks," or in chowder; the very large ones with heavy shells are particularly good for chowder or stuffed with a breadcrumb mixture.

quail A small migratory game bird (two or three per serving) relished for its delicious flavor; there are many varieties the world over, but since wild quail are becoming scarce, those that we eat today are mostly farm-bred; cooked without hanging.

Quark (kvark) A soft, runny, acid-curd cows' milk cheese from Germany made from skimmed or partially skimmed milk; *Quark* is a type of cottage cheese and is eaten with fruit or salad or used in cooking; originally Central European and also spelled *Quarg* or *Kvarg;* known as *Topfen* in Austria and widely used in such pastries as *Topfen Schnitten* and *Topfen Strudel.*

Quartirolo (kwar-teer-Ō-lō)   A soft, uncooked, pressed, whole-milk cow's cheese from Lombardy in Italy; similar to **Taleggio** but cured in caves where it acquires a mushroomy flavor; square, with a thin washed rind, the paste is smooth, pale, and creamy; still made by traditional small-scale farmhouse methods.

quasi de veau bourgeoise (ka-zee deu vō boor-jhwahz)   In French cuisine, veal chump or hind end braised in a casserole with pork, calf's foot, and vegetables.

quatre-épices (ka-tr'ay-pees)   A French mixture of "four spices": finely ground ginger, clove, nutmeg, and white pepper; a descendant of the elaborate spice mixtures used to flavor savory and sweet food in the Middle Ages.

quatre-quarts (KA-truh-KAAHR)   A classic French pound cake, made of "four quarters"; that is, equal parts of egg, butter, flour, and sugar.

queen of puddings   A British breadcrumb and custard pudding base baked with strawberry or raspberry jam covering, then topped with meringue and lightly browned in the oven.

Queensland nut See **macadamia nut.**

queijo (KAY-hō)   Portuguese for cheese.

quenelle (keh-nel)   A light dumpling made of seafood, chicken, game, or veal forcemeat bound with eggs; although quenelles were once quite large, now they are usually small ovals, like light **mousselines,** poached in simmering water or broth and served with a creamy or buttery sauce.

quesadilla (KAY-sah-DEE-ya)   A Mexican **tortilla** turnover filled with a savory stuffing and toasted or fried.

queso (KAY-thō, KAY-sō)   Spanish for cheese; *queso blanco* is the fresh, smooth, rindless cows' milk cheese made throughout Latin America; it is an acid-curd cheese made from whole or partially skimmed milk, pressed, salted, and eaten fresh with fruit or matured for two or three months.

quetsch (kvech)   A variety of plum made into tarts and other confections but best known for the clear colorless **eau de vie** or liqueur distilled from it in Alsace.

queue de boeuf (KEU de BEUF)   French for **oxtail.**

quiche (keesh)   A French custard tart, usually savory, from Alsace and Lorraine; in the United States it has come to mean *quiche lorraine,* which is filled with eggs, cream, bacon, and (more recently) **Gruyère,** but the variations are infinite; from the German word *Kuchen.*

quick bread Any bread or muffin made with a quick-acting leavening agent, usually **baking powder** or **baking soda.**

quimbombo (keem-BOHM-bō) **Okra,** much used in Cuban and Caribbean cooking and showing its African roots; from the Bantu word, *quingombo,* for okra.

quince A tree indigenous to Persia, whose fruit may be the golden apple of antiquity; popular throughout the temperate world until the last century or so, especially for pies and preserves (because of its high amount of **pectin**), it is now largely ignored except in the Middle East; long, slow cooking and generous amounts of sugar bring out the quince's mellow flavor and golden color. The plural is quinces.

quinoa (KEEN-wah) The seed of a South American plant used as a staple, like grain, since the Incas; light in texture, it is cooked like rice but should be rinsed first to remove any residual *soponin* covering, a natural bitter substance; when cooked, quinoa's tiny pearls reveal the spiral germ.

Quitte (KVIT-eh) German for **quince;** *Quittengelee* is quince marmalade.

R

rice

raan Indian roast leg of lamb in spicy yogurt marinade, Kashmiri-style.

rabadi (RAH-bah-dee) Thickened, reduced milk, in Indian cooking.

rábano (RAH-bah-nō) Spanish for radish.

rabattage (ra-ba-tajh) French for deflating the dough in yeast pastry-making.

rabbit A small member of the hare family, both wild and domesticated, whose flesh can vary in flavor depending on its age and diet; leaner and sweeter than chicken, rabbit is cooked in similar ways.

rabbit, Welsh See **Welsh rarebit.**

râble de lièvre (RA-bluh deu LYEV-ruh) French for **saddle** of hare.

rabri (RAHB-ree) Sweetened milk boiled until condensed and thickened into a cream, flavored with rosewater and sprinkled with pistachios; an Indian dish.

Rachel (ra-shel) In French cuisine, garnished with bone **marrow** and accompanied by **bordelaise** sauce; for **tournedos.**

racine (ra-seen) French for root vegetable.

rack A cut of lamb or veal from the rib section, with tender and flavorful meat; can be kept whole, cut into seven rib chops, or made into crown roast.

racking Drawing off clear wine from one barrel or vat to another, leaving the sediment.

Raclette (ra-klet)   Type of Swiss cheese whose name comes from the French verb *racler,* to "scrape"; half a large wheel of cows' milk cheese is placed near the fire, melting the rich, buttery cheese, which is scraped onto a plate and eaten with boiled potatoes *en chemise* (in their jackets), pickled onions, and gherkins. A specialty of the Valais region of the Swiss Alps; see also **walliser.**

radicchio (rah-DEEK-kyō)   Chicory with red leaves, used for garnishing or for salad; the leaves and root can be cooked too.

radis (ra-dee)   French for radish.

rafano (rah-FAH-nō)   Italian for horseradish.

raffinade (ra-fee-nad)   French and German for refined sugar.

rafraîchir (ra-fresh-eer)   In French, to "refresh" boiling vegetables by plunging them into cold water to halt cooking and retain color; to chill.

ragoût (ra-goo)   A French stew of meat, poultry, or fish, which may contain vegetables; a *ragoût* literally "restores the appetite."

Ragoût fin (ra-GOO FINH)   In German cooking, a delicate combination of organ meats such as sweetbreads and brains, cooked with mushrooms in a winy cream sauce; often served in a puff pastry shell.

ragù alla bolognese (rah-GOO ah-lah bō-lō-NYAY-say)   An Italian meat sauce from Bologna and not a stew or **ragoût** as commonly thought; often used for pasta. Ground beef and sometimes pork and ham are sautéed in butter and oil with chopped vegetables and simmered with milk, white wine, and tomatoes.

Ragusano (rah-goo-ZAH-nō)   A spun-curd cows' milk cheese from Sicily, cooked, kneaded, and sometimes smoked; rectangular in shape; delicate and sliceable table cheeses are matured for three months, firm, sharp grating cheeses up to twelve months.

Rahm   German for cream.

raidir (ray-deer)   In French, to sear.

raie (ray)   French for skate.

raifort (ray-for)   French for horseradish.

Rainwater   A general term for a very pale dry **Madeira** developed by an American in the early nineteenth century.

raisin (ray-zinh) French for grape; *raisin sec* is raisin; *raisin de Corinthe,* **currant.**

raita (RĪ-tah) In Indian cooking, vegetables, raw or cooked, or sometimes fruits mixed with yogurt, to accompany spicy dishes.

rajas (RAH-hahs) **Poblano** or other chili strips, fried with onions and sometimes potatoes or tomatoes, in Mexican cooking.

rajma (RAHJ-mah) Red kidney beans, in Indian cooking.

rallado (rah-YAH-dō) Spanish for grated.

ramen (rah-men) Japanese soup noodles.

ramequin (ram-kinh) French for a small flameproof dish, a ramekin; also a small cheese tart.

ramp A wild leek—an Appalachian spring delicacy—that looks like a scallion but tastes stronger; an acquired taste.

rampion A plant, cultivated or wild (but rarely eaten nowadays), whose leaves are eaten like spinach and whose roots, also either raw or cooked, taste like **salsify.**

ranchero (rahn-CHAY-rō) Spanish for country style; *salsa ranchero* combines tomatoes, **serrano** chilies, garlic, and onion into a hot and spicy sauce known best in **huevos rancheros,** but also served with meat.

rapa (RAH-pah) Italian for turnip.

rape A member of the Brassica (cabbage) family whose seeds yield an oil used for salad and frying (mostly in India and increasingly in Europe) and for blending in margarine; it is sometimes confused with its cousin *colza* (see **canola oil**). The young leaves and shoots can be braised as a vegetable but are mostly used for fodder; in southern Italy the tender leaves and stems are best appreciated, especially as a robust accompaniment to **orecchiette.** See also **broccoli rabe.**

rapé (rah-PAY) Spanish for monkfish, angler.

râper (ra-pay) In French, to grate, especially cheese; the adjective is *râpé.*

rapeseed oil See **canola oil.**

rapini See **broccoli rabe.**

rarebit See **Welsh rarebit.**

ras gulas (rahs GOO-lahs)   Indian cream cheese balls made from **paneer** and semolina; they are slowly simmered in cardamom syrup until they puff up and become spongy.

ras malai (ras MAL-ī)   Indian dessert balls similar to **ras gulas,** but served in **rabri.**

rasher   British for a slice of bacon.

ratafia (rah-TAF-yah)   A liqueur flavored by infusion with the kernels of certain fruits, such as peaches and apricots; a favorite homemade Victorian cordial. In Britain the word also means **macaroon.**

ratatouille (ra-ta-TOO-yah)   A vegetable stew from Provence of diced eggplant, tomatoes, zucchini, green peppers, onions, and garlic all cooked in olive oil; there are many variations, and it can be eaten hot or cold.

räuchern (ROY-shayrn)   In German, to smoke; smoked is *geräuchert.*

Rauenthal (ROW-en-tal)   A village in the German **Rheingau** that produces perhaps the best Rhine wines: fruity, elegant, with a characteristic spiciness.

ravanèllo (rah-vah-NEL-lō)   Italian for radish.

rave (rav)   French for turnip; *petite rave* is a radish.

ravigote (ra-vee-gōt)   A classic French cold sauce of **vinaigrette** with capers, chopped onions, and herbs; as a classic sauce served hot, it is a reduction of white wine and vinegar with **velouté**, shallot butter, and herbs.

ravioli (rah-VYŌ-lee)   Small pasta squares filled with spinach, **ricotta,** and herbs rather than meat; see also **agnolotti.**

raw   Uncooked, fresh; in reference to milk products, the word means unpasteurized.

ray   See **skate.**

raya (RĪ-yah)   Spanish for skate.

Reblochon (reu-blō-shonh)   An uncooked, lightly pressed cows' milk cheese made in the Haute-Savoie of France and across the Italian border. Originally made with the undeclared second milking (concealed from the owner after his quota had been collected), while the milk was still warm, it is a rich, soft, and delicately fruity cheese shaped in a disc and with a golden rind.

recette (reu-set)   French for recipe.

rechauffé (reu-shō-fay)   French for food that is reheated or made with leftovers.

récolte (ray-kōlt)   French for harvest, crop, vintage.

red beans and rice   A Louisiana specialty of red beans (sometimes kidney beans) and rice, cooked with ham hock; there are many variations. Louis Armstrong signed his letters, "Red beans and ricely yours."

redeye gravy   Ham gravy made with ice water or sometimes coffee and perhaps a little brown sugar; served in the South for breakfast with **grits** and biscuits.

red flannel hash   Cooked beets fried with bacon, potatoes, and onions, and often served with corn bread; rustic American fare.

red herring   Herring salted strongly to a deep red color.

red mullet   See **mullet.**

red snapper   A saltwater fish from the Gulf of Mexico, usually marketed at about five pounds but sometimes much larger; there are many types of snapper, but the rosy red snapper, with white, succulent, sweet meat, is a choice delicacy cooked in many ways, often stuffed whole.

reduce   To boil down a liquid to thicken its consistency and concentrate its flavor, as in a reduction sauce. **Escoffier** was the first chef to thicken sauces by reduction rather than with flour or other starch.

réduire (ray-dweer)   In French to **reduce.**

Réforme, à la (ah lah ray-form)   Lamb chops breadcrumbed, fried, and garnished with **julienne** of ham, truffles, carrots, and hard-boiled egg whites, with a **poivrade** sauce; created by **Alexis Soyer** for the Reform Club in London.

refried beans   Cooked **pinto** beans, mashed and fried with garlic, often for a **tortilla** filling; of Mexican-American origin. See also **frijoles.**

régence, à la (ah lah ray-jhenhs)   Garnished with **quenelles, truffles, foie gras,** and cockscombs, if for sweetbreads or chicken, or with oysters and roe, if for fish—a classic French garnish.

Regensburgerwurst (RAY-gens-boor-ger-voorst)   A short, fat German sausage of pork and beef.

Reh (ray) German for venison; *Rehrücken* is saddle of venison and also an oblong chocolate cake garnished with almonds.

reiben (RĪ-ben) In German, to grate or rub; a *Reibschale* is a mortar.

reine, à la (ah lah REN) French for "queen's style," garnished with chicken in some form; named after Louis XV's queen.

Reis (rīs) German for rice.

relâcher (reu-lash-ay) In French, to thin a sauce or purée with liquid; literally, to relax or loosen.

relevé (reu-lev-ay) French for highly seasoned.

religieuse (reu-lee-jhyeuz) French for nun because the pastry resembles the hooded habit; a small cream puff tops a large one, each filled with **crème pâtissière,** glazed, and decorated with **buttercream.**

relleno (rel-LAY-nyō) Spanish for stuffing, stuffed.

rémol (RAY-mōl) Spanish for **brill.**

remolacha (reh-mō-LAH-chah) Spanish for beet.

rémoulade (ray-moo-lad) **Mayonnaise** seasoned with mustard, anchovy essence, chopped gherkins, capers, parsley, chervil, and tarragon—a classic French sauce.

remuage (reu-mü-ajh) In making **Champagne,** the daily shaking and turning of the bottles, nearly upside down, to bring the sediment down to the cork before the *dégorgement* (see **dégorger**).

Renaissance, à la (ah lah reu-nes-sanhs) Various spring vegetables arranged separately around a large roast—a classic French garnish.

render To melt fat, thus clarifying the drippings to use in cooking or flavoring.

rennet The stomach lining of an unweaned calf, kid, or lamb, containing rennin and other enzymes that coagulate milk; in cheesemaking, rennet extracts are used to curdle milk. There are also vegetable rennets with the same property.

renverser (renh-vayr-say) In French, to unmold or turn out onto a serving dish.

repollo (reh-POHL-lō) Spanish for cabbage.

repos (reu-pō) French for repose or rest, as for the resting of dough in pastrymaking.

res (rays)   Spanish for beef.

resserrer (reu-sayr-ay)   In French, to "tighten" or pull a sauce together by thickening it.

Rettich (RET-ish)   German for radish.

revenir (reu-ven-eer)   In French, to brown, as for meat *(faire revenir).*

Rheingau (RĪN-gow)   A white-wine district in Germany where the Rhine flows east-west for twenty miles between Mainz and Rüdesheim; the southern-facing slopes produce the finest German wines, mostly **Rieslings,** which are separately entered.

Rheinpfalz (RĪN-pfalts)   A wine-producing region in Germany, also known as the Palatinate, west of the Rhine and northeast of Alsace-Lorraine; the vineyards are on the slopes of the Harz mountains.

Rhine (rīn)   A major river flowing northwest to the North Sea through western Germany; along her slopes and those of her tributaries, especially the Nahe and the Moselle, most German wine is produced; spelled *Rhein* in German.

Rhône (rōn)   A major river flowing west from Switzerland through Lake Geneva and south through France into the Mediterranean; along her slopes many wine grapes are grown, most notably those in France between Lyons and the sea, for Rhône wines.

rhubarb   Native to southeastern Russia, this leafy vegetable is cultivated for its thick reddish stalks, which are used in pies and compotes and occasionally in savory sauces. The leaves are poisonous, but the astringent stalks are made palatable for "fruit" desserts with lots of sugar and brief cooking.

rib   A section of beef from the top forequarter comprising the most tender steak and roast cuts, including the **Delmonico, rib-eye,** rib steak, and **rib roast.**

ribes (REE-bays)   Italian for gooseberry, currant.

rib-eye steak   A cut of beef from the **rib** section, virtually the same as a **Delmonico** except that the rib-eye has been further trimmed of fat.

ribollita (ree-bōl-LEE-tah)   A hearty Italian soup of white beans, vegetables, bread, cheese, and olive oil, from Florence; usually served reheated, hence the name.

rib roast   A cut of beef from the forequarter, between the **chuck** and **loin;** this seven-rib cut is often divided into three parts, the first cut of which, partially boned, becomes the "prime ribs" of a standing rib roast.

rice A grain native to India and probably the world's most important food crop, especially in Asia where it has been cultivated for millennia. The thousands of varieties divide into long-grained rice, which separates into distinct kernels when cooked, and short-grained rice, which is higher in starch, wetter, and stickier when cooked. In the milling process, removal of the hull produces *brown rice.* Removal of the bran and most of the germ produces *unpolished rice.* To reduce spoilage, removal of the outer aleurone layer produces *polished rice,* which is then coated with a thin layer of vitamins (which should not be rinsed off). *Converted rice* (parboiled) has been steamed and dried before milling for higher nutritional content and easier processing. "Instant" rice grains have been partially cooked and split open, with flavor and nutritional loss. See also **wild rice.**

rice Used as a verb, to force cooked fruits or vegetables, especially potatoes, through an instrument with small perforations in it, so that the food resembles grains of rice; the tool is called a ricer.

rice wine Distilled from fermented rice and made in many varieties, qualities, and strengths, rice wine is far less common in China than it used to be. **Saké, sherry, Scotch whisky,** or dry **vermouth** can be substituted for rice wine in cooking.

Richelieu, à la (ah lah REE-she-LYEU) Garnished with stuffed tomatoes and mushrooms, braised lettuce, **château** potatoes, and veal stock—a classic French garnish for meat.

ricotta (ree-KOHT-tah) Literally "recooked" in Italian, ricotta is strictly speaking not a cheese; ricotta is made from the leftover whey from other cheeses, either ewes' or cows' milk, and is sometimes enriched with milk or cream. As the whey is heated, the cloudy top layer is skimmed off and drained to make the cheese. Bland, slightly sweet, and dry, ricotta is eaten fresh or cooked in pasta and vegetable dishes and sweet desserts.

Riesling (REES-ling) A superlative white-wine grape variety probably native to the Rhine Valley, where it has been cultivated since the Romans; the grape has been transplanted to many other countries where it continues to distinguish itself. It is fortunately subject to **noble rot.**

rigaglie (ree-GAL-yay) Italian for giblets.

rigatoni (ree-gah-TŌ-nee) Italian fat-ribbed **macaroni,** commercially made.

rigodon (ree-gō-donh) A **brioche** custard tart filled with bacon, ham, nuts, or puréed fruit, served either warm or cold; a specialty of Burgundy.

rijstaffel (RĪS-tahf-el) Literally "rice table," this is the elaborate colonial Dutch version of the Indonesian rice table, with dozens of side dishes. The various offerings in the buffet include meat and seafood dishes, savory fried and steamed foods, **satés,** sauces, vegetable salads, rice, fruit, and chili dishes—hot and cool, spicy and bland—in profusion.

rillettes (ree-yet) In French cuisine, pork cubed and cooked with its fat and herbs, then pounded in a mortar and potted; goose and rabbit are sometimes prepared similarly. *Rillauds* and *rillons* are the same but are not pounded.

Rind (rint) German for beef; *Rinderbraten* is roast beef, *Rinderbrust* is brisket of beef, *Rindertalg* is beef suet, *Rindswurst* is beef sausage.

riñones (ree-NYŌ-nayth) Spanish for kidneys.

Rioja (ree-Ō-hah) A wine region in northern Spain where light, dry, and refined red wines and more ordinary white wines are made.

ripièno (ree-PYAY-nō) Italian for stuffed or filled; stuffing.

Ripp German for rib; *Rippenbraten* is roast loin, *Rippenspeer* is ribs of pork, *Rippenstück* is a chop.

ris de veau (ree deu vō) French for veal sweetbreads; *ris d'agneau* are lamb sweetbreads.

rishta (REESH-tah) In Arab cooking, fresh egg noodles, like Italian pasta. In Tunisia, a peasant soup of chicken, chickpeas, and thin flat noodles.

riso (REE-zō) Italian for rice; *risi e bisi* is a very thick soup of rice and spring peas cooked in broth with onion, parsley, and **Parmesan**—a Venetian specialty.

risotto (ree-ZOHT-tō) Italian for short-grain rice cooked in butter with a little chopped onion to which stock is gradually added as it is absorbed; all manner of savory foods can be added; **Arborio rice** gives the proper texture, tender and creamy but never sticky; *risotto milanese,* flavored with **saffron,** a classic accompaniment to **osso buco.**

rissoler (ree-zō-lay) In French to brown in hot fat; *rissolé* refers to food, such as potatoes, that has been fried thus; a *rissole* is a puff-pastry turnover or fritter that is stuffed, often with ground meat, and deep-fried.

riz (reez) French for rice; *riz à l'impératrice*, rice pudding flavored with vanilla, crystallized fruit soaked in **Kirsch,** and custard cream.

riz au djon-djon (rees ō jonh-jonh) Haitian dish of rice cooked with tiny flavorful black mushrooms.

roast To cook food by baking it in hot dry air, either in an oven or on or near a fire or hot stones; by extension, the noun *roast* is a large piece of meat that has been roasted.

Robert (rō-bayr) A classic French sauce of sautéed onions reduced with white wine and vinegar, **demi-glace** added, and finished with mustard.

Robiola (rō-BYŌ-lah) A soft, uncooked, and unpressed cheese from northern Italy; in Lombardy, cows' milk is used and the cheeses are shaped in rectangles, while in Piedmont either ewes' or goats' milk is used, perhaps mixed with cows', and the cheeses are shaped in discs. *Robiola* is named for its reddish thin rind; the interior paste is smooth and even.

robusta (rō-BOO-stah) A type of coffee bean, hardy, prolific, and high in caffeine, but with a flavor inferior to that of **arabica;** used mostly for commercial blends and instant coffee.

Rock Cornish game hen A crossbreed of a Plymouth hen and a cock from Cornwall which, when fresh, can be deliciously succulent, although the gamy flavor is long since bred out; usually shortened to Cornish hen.

rocket See **arugula.**

rockfish A large family of saltwater fish in the Pacific, sometimes mistakenly called red snapper or rock cod; the firm, lean, delicate flesh is versatile and is especially appreciated by the Chinese.

rodaballo (rō-dah-BAL-lō) Spanish for turbot.

roe Fish or shellfish eggs, ranging from the humble cod all the way to beluga **caviar;** the male **milt** is sometimes, rather euphemistically, called soft roe.

roebuck Male roe deer; venison.

Roggenbrot (ROHG-en-brōt) German for rye bread.

roghan josh (RŌ-gahn JŌSH)   Rich and spicy Muslim lamb dish from Northern India, red in color; served with rice.

rognons (rō-nyonh)   French for kidneys; *rognonnade de veau* is saddle of veal with kidneys attached. In Italian the word is *rognoni*.

rognures (rō-nyür)   French for trimmings, especially in making **pâte feuilletée,** useful for certain kinds of pastry; also called *demi-feuilletage.*

roh (rō)   German for raw; *Rohkost* means raw vegetables or **crudités.**

rohat lokum (rō-HAHT lō-KOOM)   Turkish for "Turkish delight," the luxurious confection flavored with **mastic,** orange- or rosewater, and almonds or pistachios.

Rohwurst (RŌ-voorst)   German sausage cured and smoked by the butcher, eaten uncooked.

rojak (rō-jak)   Malaysian salad of cucumbers, pineapple, chilies, and shrimp paste.

rolé (rō-LAY)   Italian for a slice of meat stuffed and rolled; *rollatini* are small rolls; in Spanish the word is *rollo*.

rollmop   See **herring rollmop.**

roly-poly pudding   A British nursery pudding of suet or biscuit-dough crust, spread with jam, rolled up, and baked or steamed.

romaine lettuce   A variety of lettuce with long, thick central stems and narrow, green leaves; also called cos lettuce.

Romanée-Conti (rō-ma-nay kohn-tee)   An exceedingly fine, rare, and celebrated red Burgundy wine from the **Côte d'Or,** made from the **Pinot Noir** grape.

Romano   See **Pecorino Romano.**

Romanoff, strawberries   See **strawberries Romanoff.**

romarin (rō-maahr-inh)   French for **rosemary.**

Rombauer, Irma (1877–1962)   Author of *The Joy of Cooking,* first privately printed in 1931 and enlarged with her daughter, Marian Rombauer Becker, in 1936. Its many successive editions and comprehensive coverage have made it indispensable to American cooks.

romesco, salsa (rō-METH-kō, THAHL-thah)   Classic Spanish sauce for fish, from Catalonia, of crushed tomatoes, chilies, garlic, hazelnuts, and almonds, with olive oil and vinegar.

Roncal (rōn-KAL) A ewes' milk cheese from the Navalle Valley in Spain, similar to **Manchego** but smaller and harder; the texture is close-grained, the flavor pungent.

ropa viejo (RŌ-pah VYAY-hō) "Old clothes," a classic Cuban dish of beef hash in tomato sauce; the beef is first used to make broth, hence the name.

Roquefort (rōk-for) An ancient and celebrated French blue cheese made from the milk of Larzac sheep; the curd from the raw, uncooked milk is molded, salted, and injected with *Penicillium roqueforti,* then matured for three months in limestone caves in the southwestern town of Roquefort-sur-Soulzon, whose fissures naturally provide the proper humidity and ventilation. The six-pound round cheeses have a thin orange rind, an ivory paste with blue green veining (*persillage*), and a salty and sharp but still creamy taste that is unique.

roquette (rō-ket) French for rocket; **arugula.**

rosbif (rōs-beef) French for roast beef.

rosé (rō-zay) French for wine made from black grapes with some of the skins included during fermentation, thus producing its characteristic color; rosé is best drunk young and served well chilled. The Italian word for rosé is *rosato.*

rose hips The fruit of certain roses, which turn red with ripeness; used for making syrup and jelly; high in vitamin C.

rosemary A shrub native to the Mediterranean, whose needlelike leaves are used fresh and dried as an herb, especially with pork, lamb, veal, and game. Its name means "dew of the sea," although often mistakenly thought to mean "rose of the Virgin Mary." To the ancient Egyptians it symbolized death, to the Greeks and Romans it also meant love.

Rosenkohl (RŌZ-en-kōl) German for Brussels sprouts.

rosewater An extract distilled from water steeped with rose petals, which impart their essential oil; this extract is used as a flavoring in the Middle East, the Balkans, and India.

Rosine (rō-ZEE-neh) German for raisin.

rosmarino (rōz-mah-REE-nō) Italian for **rosemary.**

Rossini A classic French garnish of **foie gras,** sliced truffles, and **demiglace,** usually for **tournedos;** named after the composer and gastronome Gioacchino Rossini (1792–1868).

rossl (ROH-sel)   Fermented beets, traditional for Passover **borsch.**

Rostbraten (ROST-brah-ten)   In northern Germany, roast beef; in Bavaria and Austria, a thin steak quickly cooked with onions and gravy.

Rostbratwurst (ROST-braht-voorst)   German ham sausage seasoned with caraway and nutmeg, roasted over a wood fire.

Rösti (REU-stee)   Potatoes grated and fried in a pancake, from Switzerland.

roti (RŌ-tee)   Bread (generic) in Indian cooking; also another word for **chapati.** In Guyana and the Caribbean, a wheat pancake with curried meat or fish filling; of Indian origin.

rôti (rō-tee)   French for roasted, a roast; a *rôtisserie* is a broiling device with a motorized spit for roasting large pieces of meat and birds; a *rôtisseur* is the cook responsible for roasting in a large kitchen.

Rotwein (RŌT-vīn)   German for red wine.

rouelle (roo-el)   French for a round slice of meat.

rouennaise (roo-enh-nez)   **Bordelaise** sauce with a reduction of red wine and shallots, finished with puréed raw duck livers—a classic French sauce.

rouget (roo-jhet)   French for red mullet.

rouille (roo-eey)   A spicy red pepper and garlic **mayonnaise** from Provence, served with fish soups.

roulade (roo-lad)   French for a rolled slice of meat or piece of fish filled with a savory stuffing; the term can also mean a sheet of sponge cake or the like spread with a suitable filling, rolled up, and perhaps garnished.

Roulade (roo-LAH-deh)   German for stuffed rolled beef.

rouleau (roo-lō)   French for rolling pin.

round   A cut of beef from the hindquarter, comprising the hind leg; the top and bottom round, eye of round, and top sirloin (sirloin tip) are lean subdivisions that can be further cut into steaks or left whole and braised or roasted.

roux (roo)   French for a mixture of flour and butter or other fat, usually in equal proportions, cooked together slowly and used to thicken sauces and soups. A *white roux* is heated long enough to cook the flour but not color it and is used for **béchamel** and **velouté**

sauces; a *blond roux* is allowed to color slightly during cooking; a *brown roux,* which may use a clarified fat other than butter, is cooked slowly for a long time so that it acquires a rich flavor and mellow brown shade to color the sauces it thickens. The word *roux* means reddish or reddish brown.

rowanberry (RŌ-an-bayr-ee)   The fruit of the mountain ash, which ripens in the fall. The berries are used to make a bright red, tart jelly often served with lamb, venison, and other game; in Alsace an **eau de vie** is made from the berries.

royale (rwah-yal)   French for unsweetened custard, possibly flavored, cooked in a mold and then cut into decorative shapes; used to garnish clear soups.

royale, charlotte   See **charlotte.**

royal icing   Icing used for pastry-writing, decorating, and glazing Christmas or wedding cakes; made from confectioners' sugar, egg white, and a little lemon juice.

royan (rwah-yanh)   French for fresh sardine.

roz   Moroccan for rice.

Rübe (RÜ-beh)   German for turnip, **rape;** *Weisserübe* is turnip, *Roterübe* is beet, *Gelberübe* is carrot.

ruchetta (roo-KET-tah)   Italian for rocket; see **arugula.**

Rücken (RÜ-ken)   German for saddle.

rucola (ROO-kō-lah)   Italian dialect for rocket; see **arugula.**

Rüdesheim (RÜ-des-hīm)   A small town on the western end of the **Rheingau,** opposite the mouth of the Nahe, on whose steep slopes excellent **Riesling** wines are produced.

rue   An herb used by the ancients for medicinal purposes but now used only as a flavoring for **grappa.**

Rugelach (ROO-ge-lukh)   A rich pastry in a rolled crescent shape, traditionally filled with raisins and cinnamon and baked for Hanukkah.

rugola   See **arugula.**

Rührei (RÜ-rī)   German for scrambled eggs.

rump   A cut of beef from the **round,** usually braised or roasted; unboned, it is a standing rump roast, while boned, it is a rolled rump roast.

ruote (roo-Ō-tay)   Italian wheel-shaped pasta.

rusk   Bread sliced and baked again slowly until crisp and golden brown, such as **zwieback.**

russe, à la (ah lah RÜS)   French term for food served sequentially course by course, hot from the kitchen, as opposed to all of the dishes for a service being laid out on the table in a large and elaborate display (*service à la francaise*); this Russian style of service gradually overtook the older French style in the early nineteenth century and survives today, greatly simplified.

russe, charlotte   See **charlotte.**

russet potato   See **potato.**

rustica, alla (ah-lah ROO-stee-kah)   An Italian spaghetti sauce of **anchovies, garlic, oregano,** and **Pecorino** cheese.

rutabaga (ROO-tah-BAY-gah)   A yellow or Swedish turnip; the British term is swede.

ruz   Arabic for rice.

rye   A grain native to central Asia and invaluable because of its hardiness in poor soils, in cool climates, and at high altitudes; it has long been the favored flour of northern and eastern Europe. Because it does not form **gluten** well, rye and wheat flours are often mixed together for bread. In the United States it is also used to make **whiskey** and for fodder. See also **pumpernickel.**

ryōri (ryō-ree)   Japanese for food, cooking.

saucisse

sa lach dia (shah lat dyah) Vietnamese "table salad," a presentation of herbs, sliced fruits, and vegetables in the middle of the table, with rice cakes; an important part of the Vietnamese meal, served with meat and dipping sauce.

saag (sahg) Greens or spinach in Indian cooking.

Saankäse (ZAHN-kay-zeh) A cooked, pressed, hard Swiss cheese made from cows' milk from two successive milkings; it is made into large orange discs, aged up to five years, and prized as a dessert or grating cheese for its mellow fragrant flavor.

Saar (zahr) A German tributary of the **Moselle** River whose vineyards produce white wine that is legally Moselle but with an austere quality of its own.

saba Japanese for mackerel.

sabayon (sa-bī-yonh) The French version of **zabaglione,** in which various wines or liqueurs can be substituted for **Marsala.**

sablé (sa-blay) French shortbread from Normandy whose high sugar and butter content account for its "sandy" texture; shaped into various forms and thicknesses; *pâte sablée* is similar to **pâte sucrée.**

sabzi (SAHB-zee) Mixed vegetables, in Persian cooking.

saccharin A noncaloric sugar substitute, far sweeter than sugar but with a bitter aftertaste; discovered over a century ago and now reported to be a carcinogenic agent.

Sachertorte (ZAKH-er-tor-teh) A rich chocolate cake containing many eggs, a layer of apricot jam, and chocolate icing. Created by Franz

Sacher (of the Sacher Hotel in Vienna) for Prince Metternich in 1832.

sach krourk (sahch kroork) Cambodian for pork.

sack The Elizabethan English word for **sherry.**

sacristain (sa-kree-stinh) French for a strip of **pâte feuilletée** sprinkled with cheese or chopped almonds and sugar, twisted into a spiral, and baked; so named for its resemblance to a corkscrew (the *sacristain* is responsible, among other things, for uncorking the communion wine).

saddle A cut of meat extending along the hindquarters from the end of the ribs to the legs on both sides.

sadza (SAHD-zah) Dumpling of maize or red millet flour, served with stews or roasts, fish, or vegetables, the national dish of Zimbabwe; *sadza ndiuraye*, a spicy stew including beef, potatoes, cabbage, tomatoes, and chilies.

safflower A thistlelike plant, also called Mexican saffron, whose seeds yield oil and whose flowers yield an orange dye; the oil is light in flavor and high in polyunsaturates with a high smoke point.

saffron The deep orange dried stigmas of a particular crocus, which must be gathered by hand, hence the spice's exorbitant price; since ancient times and in many cultures it has been used as a medicine, aphrodisiac, dye, and spice; it colors and flavors such classic dishes as **risotto milanese, paella, bouillabaisse,** and **kulich.**

Saft (zahft) German for juice, syrup; gravy, sauce.

sage A perennial herb with gray green leaves, used since ancient times for medicinal and culinary purposes; it is used especially, though with discretion, in cooking pork and goose.

Sage Derby (DAR-bee, not DER-bee) A **Derby** cheese flavored and marbled with sage; aged nine months or more, it is flaky and mild and considered one of England's most distinctive cheeses; also called Derby Sage.

sago (SAY-gō) A starch extracted from the stem of an Asian palm tree and used for thickening puddings and occasionally soups; similar to **tapioca,** sago is formed into pearl-like beads.

Sahne (ZAH-neh) German for cream; *Sahnenkäse* means cream cheese; *Sahnenkuchen* is a cream tart or cake.

saignant (sa-nyanh) French for rare, as in meat; literally, "bleeding."

saigneux (sa-nyeu) French for neck of veal or lamb.

Sailland, Edmond See **Curnonsky.**

Saint-Cloud, potage See under **potage.**

Sainte-Maure (sinht mohr) A French goats' milk cheese, uncooked and unpressed, from the town of the same name in Touraine, also Poitou; cured for three weeks, the cheese is log-shaped with a white soft smooth paste and a white bloomy rind.

Saint-Émilion (sinht-ay-meel-yonh) A small town in the Dordogne Valley of Bordeaux celebrated for its many fine red wines, especially the rich full châteaux wines. Saint-Émilion is also the varietal name of the **Trebbiano** grape in Cognac.

Saint-Estèphe (sinht es-tef) A wine **commune** at the northern tip of the **Haut-Médoc** producing solid, full-bodied, robust wines, less delicate than some of its neighbors; aside from its **classed growths,** its *crus bourgeois* are also excellent.

Saint George's agaric A wild field mushroom, found in Europe in spring and autumn.

Saint-Germain (sinh-jhayr-minh) In French cuisine, with fresh peas; *potage Saint-Germain* is a thick purée of fresh peas.

Saint-Honoré, gâteau See **gâteau Saint-Honoré.**

Saint-Jacques See **coquille Saint-Jacques.**

Saint John's bread See **carob.**

Saint-Julien (sinh-jhü-lyinh) A wine **commune** in the **Haut-Médoc** of Bordeaux, just south of **Pauillac,** overlooking the Gironde River; its red wines are of consistently fine quality, well-balanced and smooth.

Saint-Malo (sinh-ma-lō) A classic French white sauce for fish, flavored with mustard, shallots, and anchovy essence.

Saint-Marcellin (sinh-maahr-sel-linh) An uncooked and unpressed French cheese from the Isère Valley, made in farmhouses from goats' milk and in factories from mixed milk; ripened for two weeks, it is disc-shaped with a smooth paste and a delicate bloomy rind.

Saint-Nectaire (sinh-nek-tayr) An unpasteurized cows' milk cheese, uncooked and pressed, from the French Auvergne; the flat rounds are cured up to two months for a dark pinkish rind and a creamy smooth interior, with good melting properties.

Saint-Paulin (sinh-pō-linh) A French uncooked, pressed cows' milk cheese made from whole pasteurized milk; it is large and round, with a smooth yellow rind and an even mild paste; a descendant of *Port-du-Salut* and similar to **Port-Salut,** *Saint-Paulin* is widely made.

Saint-Pierre (sinh-pyayr)   French for **John Dory.**

saisir (seh-zeer)   In French, to sear.

sakana (sah-kah-nah)   Japanese for fish.

saké (sah-kay)   Japanese rice wine, sweet or dry, usually drunk warm in small cups and also used for cooking; *sake* (without the accent mark) means salmon.

salamander   A gas oven with a top element for quickly glazing or browning dishes, used in restaurant kitchens.

salambo (sal-amh-bō)   A French oval **choux pastry** filled with kirsch-flavored **crème pâtissière** and glazed with caramel.

salami (sah-LAH-mee)   An Italian sausage, infinitely variable in ingredients, seasoning, shape, and method, and long made in many countries other than Italy. Salami is usually made of pork meat and fat, sometimes with beef, veal, or other meats, fairly highly seasoned, and cured as long as six months; its name derives from its being salted.

salata khudar mishakal (sah-LAH-tah khoo-DAHR mis-SHAH-kul)   In the Middle East, mixed vegetable salad, with vegetables chopped and dressed with **vinaigrette.**

Salbei (ZAL-bī)   German for sage.

salchicha (sahl-CHEE-chah)   Spanish for sausage.

salé (sal-ay)   French for salted or pickled; *petit salé*, salt pork; *salaison*, salting; the Italian word for salt is *sale* (no accent mark), the Spanish *sal.*

saleem (sah-lim)   A liquid dessert with thin **tapioca** noodles, from Thailand.

salep (SAH-lep)   In Turkey and Greece, a root used to make a sweet, refreshing milk drink of the same name; the Arab word is *sahlab.*

Salisbury steak   A patty of lean beef broiled and seasoned; devised by the nineteenth-century dietician Dr. James H. Salisbury to avoid supposedly unhealthy fermentation in the digestive tract.

Sally Lunn   A rich, sweet yeast bun or bread supposedly named after the woman who first sold them in Bath, England, in the late eighteenth century.

salmagundi (SAL-mah-GUN-dee) A British mixed dish, really a *salade composée,* including greens, chopped meats, hard-boiled eggs, pickles, anchovies, onions, and perhaps other vegetables, all carefully arranged and dressed.

salmi A stew made from leftover or partially roasted feathered game, in a wine sauce; also spelled *salmis.*

salmon (SA-mun; the L is not pronounced) A noble fish that is spawned in fresh water before migrating to the sea, returning several years later to its original upstream waters to spawn, thus completing its life cycle. Salmon meat ranges from very pale to deep orange red, depending on species and habitat. In the United States, the *king* or *chinook* salmon is largest; the *coho* salmon is smaller and paler-fleshed; the *sockeye* turns deep red before spawning and is considered choice for canning. The northern Pacific and Atlantic Oceans provide feeding grounds for marine salmon, in addition to landlocked salmon. The firm, rich, flavorful meat—before spawning—lends itself to varied culinary preparations, simple or elaborate; cured salmon is a great delicacy; the specific types are separately entered.

salmonete (thahl-moh-NAY-tay) Spanish for red mullet.

salmon trout See **sea trout.**

salpicão (sahl-pee-KOW) Portuguese for smoked ham roll.

salpicon (sal-pee-kōnh) In French cuisine, one or more ingredients cooked separately, cut into fine dice, and bound with a sauce; often used as a filling or garnish, like **mirepoix; allumettes** cut across into small cubes make *salpicon.*

salpicón (thal-pee-KŌN, sal-pee-ŌN) In Spanish cooking, a mixed salad of cooked seafood, or possibly meat, with vegetables.

salsa (SAHL-sah, THAAL-thah) Italian and Spanish for sauce; this is also the general name for hot sauces in Mexican-American cooking; see also **sugo.** *Salsa mexicana cruda,* literally "fresh Mexican sauce," made of tomatoes, onions, and chilies (preferably **serranos**), chopped and mixed together with water; much used in Mexican cooking, with regional variations.

salsify (SAHL-si-fee) A plant whose long white tapered root is eaten boiled or sautéed; also called oyster plant, its resemblance in flavor to oyster requires a vivid imagination; scorzonera, with its black-skinned root, is very similar.

saltare (sal-TAR-ay)   In Italian, to sauté, literally "to jump."

salteña (sahl-TAY-nyah)   A Bolivian **empanada** with cheese fillings.

saltimbocca (sal-teem-BŌK-kah)   Italian veal scallop with a sage leaf and a thin slice of **prosciutto** laid on top, braised in butter and **Marsala** or white wine; this dish, whose name means "jump in the mouth," comes from Rome.

saltpeter, saltpetre   Potassium nitrate; used in small quantities to preserve meat, saltpeter gives flavor and imparts a reddish color.

salumeria (sal-oo-mayr-EE-ah)   Italian delicatessen.

salvia (SAL-vyah)   Italian for **sage.**

Salz (zalts)   German for salt; *Salzegebäck* is a salty biscuit, or pretzel.

samak (sah-MAK)   Arabic for fish.

samaki wa nazi (sah-MAH-kee wah NAZ-ee)   Tanzanian fish curry with coconut.

sambal (SAHM-bahl)   A very hot and spicy side dish, often a sauce, several of which accompany the main dish; from Indonesia and Southeast Asia.

sambar (SAHM-bar)   Vegetarian dish from southern India of peas or lentils and vegetables, often with rice; *sambar* spice is a very hot spice mix with mustard oil. Also spelled *sambhar*.

sambuca (sahm-BOO-kah)   Italian liqueur flavored with elder and licorice.

samosa (sah-MŌ-sah)   A triangular savory pastry filled with vegetables or meat spiced with curry or chilies; from India and Pakistan.

samneh (SAHM-neh)   In Arab cooking, fresh sweet butter that is cooked, clarified, salted, and aged, or sometimes washed and kneaded with spices and herbs and then aged; often, but erroneously, described as rancid. Also called *smen*.

samphire (SAM-fir)   A plant that grows wild along the rocky Mediterranean and European coastline; its crisp leaves are eaten fresh in salads, cooked as a vegetable, and pickled; also called sea fennel and *herbe de Saint Pierre* (its name is a corruption of the latter).

samsa (SAM-sah)   Tunisian pastry triangles of **brik** leaves stuffed with ground almonds, geranium or rosewater, and orange zest; then deep-fried, brushed with lemon syrup, and sprinkled with sesame seeds.

Samsø (SAHM-seu) A whole-milk cows' cheese from the Danish island of Samsø; cooked and pressed, the large, round, firm cheese is golden yellow with scattered holes and a nutty, mild, but not bland taste; widely used in Denmark.

sanbusak (sahn-BOO-zahk) A Middle Eastern tartlet of minced meat with pine nuts, onions, and cinnamon in a thin yeast dough, popular in Syria, Lebanon, and Egypt.

Sancerre (sanh-sayr) A town perched on a hill overlooking the Loire Valley in central France; its white wine is agreeably fresh and flinty, not unlike the **Pouilly-Fumé** produced nearby, also from the **Sauvignon Blanc** grape.

sanchocho (sahn-CHŌ-chō) South American soup of beef or sometimes another meat or seafood with vegetables; a type of boiled dinner.

Sangiovese (sahn-jō-VAY-say) A very good Italian red-wine grape planted widely in Tuscany; vinified especially for **Chianti.**

sangría (thahn-GREE-ah, sahn-GREE-ah) Spanish punch, literally "bleeding," of red wine, a little brandy, soda water, sugar, and sliced orange or lemon and other fruit; a cool refreshing drink for warm weather.

sangue, al (ahl SAHN-gway) Italian for rare, as for steak.

San Pedro (thahn PAY-drō) Spanish for **John Dory.**

San Simon (thahn THEE-mōn) A cows' milk cheese from northwest Spain, semihard, rather bland, pear-shaped, and often smoked.

santen (sahn-ten) Indonesian for coconut.

Saône (sah-ōn) A tributary of the Rhône River, joining it at Lyons, France, where the **Beaujolais** is said to be the third river.

sapsago See **Schabzieger.**

saracen corn See **buckwheat.**

Sarah Bernhardt In French cuisine, garnished with purée of **foie gras;** after the celebrated actress.

sardine A young herring, pilchard, or sprat varying widely in species and treatment; usually brined, cooked, and canned in oil, but excellent cooked fresh.

sashimi (sah-shee-mee) Literally "fresh slice," in Japanese this really means raw fish expertly sliced according to the particular variety and served with garnishes, condiments, and sauces.

satay   See **saté.**

saté (sa-TAY)   In Indonesian cooking, pieces of meat or seafood marinated in a spicy sauce, skewered, and grilled; usually served with a peanut sauce; also spelled *satay.*

sauce   From the Latin word meaning salted, sauce includes all liquid seasonings for food and a few that are not liquid; **Carême** organized the many French sauces into families with four mother sauces: **espagnole, velouté, allemande,** and **béchamel,** with emulsified sauces, such as **mayonnaise,** forming the fifth group. *Saucier* means the chef responsible for sauces in a large kitchen.

saucisse (sō-sees)   French for fresh sausage; *saucisson* is a cured sausage, usually large; see also **salami.**

Sauerbraten (ZOWR-brah-ten)   In German cooking, top round of beef marinated in red wine and vinegar, beer, or buttermilk, then braised, and sometimes served with dried fruit and nuts or other spicy or fruity accompaniments; *sauer* means sour.

Sauerkraut (ZOWR-krowt)   Shredded white cabbage pickled in brine and flavored with juniper berries—a classic accompaniment to a wide variety of German dishes.

sauge (sōjh)   French for **sage.**

saumon (sō-monh)   French for salmon.

Saumur (sō-mür)   A French town and wine region on the south bank of the Loire River producing a variety of wines, including sparkling wines.

saunf (sownf)   Fennel in Indian cooking.

saus prik   See **prik.**

sauter (sō-tay)   To cook food quickly in butter or other hot fat, stirring to brown it evenly; in French, *sauter* means literally "to jump"; a *sauté* is a dish that has been cooked thus; *sauteuse,* a shallow sauté pan with sloping sides; *sautoir,* a shallow pan with straight sides.

Sauternes (sō-tayrn)   A French village south of Bordeaux whose five surrounding townships produce the white dessert wine of the same name. Sauternes grapes are late-harvested for their high sugar content and **noble rot,** resulting in a very sweet but natural wine: fruity, intense, buttery, golden, and long-lived. Sauterne (without the final *s*) is altogether unconnected—a meaningless California term for medium sweet white wine.

sauvage (sō-vajh)   French for wild, uncultivated, undomesticated.

Sauvignon Blanc (sō-vee-nyonh blanhk)   An excellent white-wine varietal grape, widely planted in **Graves, Sauternes** (with the **Semillon** grape), the **Loire** Valley (where it is known as *Blanc Fumé*), and California.

savarin (sa-va-rinh)   A ring-shaped **baba** filled variously with **crème Chantilly, crème pâtissière,** or fresh fruit; this French pastry is named after **Brillat-Savarin.**

Savoie, biscuit de   See **biscuit de Savoie.**

savory   Food that is not sweet; in Britain, where it is spelled *savoury,* it is the last dinner course after **pudding,** consisting of sharply flavored salty little dishes intended to cleanse the palate for port—a custom favored by Victorian and Edwardian gentlemen. Savory is also an herb in the mint family known since Roman times and used traditionally with beans, meat, and poultry.

savoyarde, pommes à la (pohm ah lah sav-wah-yaahrd)   In French cuisine, "in the style of Savoie"; potatoes cooked **à la dauphinoise,** but with **bouillon** instead of milk; *savoyarde* generally means with cheese and potatoes.

saya-éndō (sah-yah-en-dō)   Japanese for snow pea.

sayur (sah-yoor)   Indonesian dish of vegetables in broth or stew.

Sbrinz (zbrints)   A whole-milk cows' cheese made immediately after milking, cooked, and pressed; it is an ancient cheese, originally Swiss but now made elsewhere. Hard, grainy, and yellow, Sbrinz is aged six to twelve months or longer and mostly used as a flavorful grating or cooking cheese or slivered into curls to accompany wine.

scald   To heat a liquid, usually milk, to just below the boiling point, when small bubbles form around the edge. For vegetables and fruit, to scald means to **blanch.**

scallion   A young, undeveloped onion, sometimes called spring onion or green onion.

scallop   A **mollusk** with an edible adductor muscle; in Europe, the pink roe is also eaten; also, a **collop** or **escalope** of meat—a thin slice possibly flattened by pounding.

scaloppina di vitello (scah-lop-PEE-nah dee vee-TEL-lō)   Italian for veal scallop, properly cut across the grain from a single muscle, top round, so that there are no separations.

Scamorza (skah-MOR-zah)   A whole-milk cows' cheese, sometimes mixed with ewes' milk; this spun-curd cheese is similar to **Mozzarella** but firmer; the cheeses are tied near the top in pairs with string or raffia, hence their name, which means "beheaded" in southern Italian dialect.

scampi (SKAHM-pee)   Italian for saltwater crayfish found in the Adriatic and a favorite dish in Venice; pale in color and quite large, similar to the **Dublin Bay prawn, langoustine,** and **Norway lobster.**

scarola (skah-RŌ-lah)   Italian for **escarole.**

Schabzieger (SHAHB-tsee-ger)   A Swiss skimmed-milk cows' cheese, uncooked but hard, sometimes called *sapsago* in the United States; it is flavored with blue melilot clover to give it a pungent flavor and green color and is shaped in truncated cones.

Scharzhofberg (SHAHRTS-hōf-bayrg)   A German vineyard on a steep slope in Wiltingen on the **Saar,** whose **Rieslings** yield a very fine white wine with bouquet, depth, freshness, and austerity.

Schaum (showm)   German for froth, foam, mousse; *Schaumrollen* are puff-pastry rolls filled with whipped cream; a *Schaumschlager* is a whisk or beater; *Schaumwein* is sparkling wine or Champagne.

scheena   See **tfina.**

Scheibe (SHĪ-beh)   German for slice.

Schiava (SKYAH-vah)   A very fine red-wine grape extensively planted in the northern Italian Adige; also used as an eating grape.

Schinken (SHINK-en)   German for ham.

Schlächter (SHLEK-ter)   German for butcher; a *Schlachtplatte* is a plate of various cold meats and sausages.

Schlag, mit (mit SHLAHG)   In German, with cream; *Schlagobers* and *Schlagsahne* both mean whipped cream.

Schlegel (SHLAY-gel)   German for drumstick.

Schlesisches Himmelreich (SHLEH-see-shes HIM-mel-rīkh)   Salted pork belly and dried fruits stewed together and served with dumplings; in German, literally "Silesian heaven."

Schmalz (shmalts)   German for melted fat, grease, or lard; *Schmaltzgebackenes,* food fried in lard or fat. In Yiddish, the word means rendered chicken fat.

Schmand (shmahnt)   German for sour cream.

Schnapps (shnaps) A German version of **akvavit.**

Schnitte (SHNIT-teh) German for a cut or slice, chop, or steak; *Schnittlauch* means chive.

schnitz, apple See **apple schnitz.**

Schnitzel (SHNIT-sel) German for a cutlet, slice, scallop, chop, steak; see also **Wiener Schnitzel.**

Schokolade (shō-kō-LAH-deh) German for chocolate.

Schrotbrot (SHRŌT-brot) German for wholewheat bread.

Schulter (SHOOL-ter) German for shoulder.

Schwamm (shvahm) German for mushroom.

schwarma See **kebab.**

Schwärtelbraten (SHVAYR-tel-brah-ten) German for roast leg of pork cooked with sauerkraut and dumplings and served with a sour cream sauce; from Silesia.

Schwarzfisch (SHVARTS-fish) German for carp.

Schwarzsauer (SHVARTS-zowr) A stew of goose giblets and blood stewed with dried apples, prunes, and pears.

Schwarzwald (SHWARTS-vahlt) German for Black Forest.

Schwarzwälder Kirschtorte (SHARTS-vel-der KEERSH-tor-teh) A rich chocolate cake made with cherries, **Kirschwasser,** and whipped cream from the Black Forest.

Schwein (SHVĪN) German for pork; *Schweinebauch,* pork belly; *Schweinbraten,* roast pork, a very popular dish cooked variously according to region.

scone (skohn, *not* skōn) A traditional Scottish cake of white flour, sometimes mixed with wholewheat flour, oatmeal, or barley, and combined with buttermilk and baking powder; the dough is usually shaped into a round and quartered or dropped onto a greased girdle (griddle) and turned.

score To make cuts, usually parallel, in the surface of food to help it cook evenly.

scorzonera See **salsify.**

Scotch broth Scottish vegetable soup made with lamb and barley.

Scotch whisky Whisky distilled in Scotland from barley malt dried over peat fires, either blended (malted and unmalted) or single-malt; the

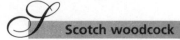

latter comes only from malt made by one distillery and has a smokier flavor. Whisky means "water of life" in Gaelic. That made outside Scotland is spelled whiskey (with an *e*).

Scotch woodcock   A British **savory** of creamy scrambled eggs on toast with anchovies.

scrapple   Pork scraps, including meat, offal, and fat, boiled together, chopped, seasoned, and thickened with buckwheat and cornmeal; this Pennsylvania German specialty is derived from the Westphalian **Pannhas.**

scrod   A marketing term for young **cod** under 2½ pounds; schrod (spelled with an *h*) indicates that the fish is young haddock.

scungilli   (skoon-JEEL-lee)   Italian for **whelk.**

sea bass   See **black sea bass.**

sea cucumber   See **hăi shēn.**

sea fennel   See **samphire.**

seafood   Edible saltwater fish or shellfish.

sea kale   A perennial vegetable of the mustard family that grows cultivated and wild, especially on the coasts of England, France, and northern Europe; the tender stalks are white and delicate and are cooked like asparagus.

sea moss   See **dulse.**

sear   To cook the surface of food, especially meat, over intense high heat, in order to brown the exterior; searing does not "seal in" the juices, as is commonly thought, but it does affect flavor.

sea slug   See **hăi shēn.**

sea trout   A brown **trout** in its marine cycle, from Atlantic waters; also called the salmon trout (but no relation to seatrout), its succulent pink flesh comes from its diet of crustaceans.

seatrout   See **weakfish.**

sea urchin   A spiny marine creature; the French relish it most cut in half, the pink or orange roe scooped out and eaten raw with a little lemon juice—a delicacy also eaten in Japan, where it is called *uni.*

seaweed   Marine vegetation, dried and processed, appreciated for its texture, flavor, and high nutritional value, especially in the Orient; sometimes called sea vegetable. Different kinds of seaweed, separately entered, are made into gelatin, used in making soup stock and for wrapping **sushi,** drunk like tea, or simply eaten as a vegetable.

sec (sek) A wine term meaning dry, as opposed to sweet; the exception is in describing **Champagne,** where *sec* has come to mean sweet; the feminine is *sèche*. The Italian word is *secco*, the Spanish *seco*.

sedano (seh-DAH-nō) Italian for celery.

sediment The solid deposit that a wine naturally leaves in the bottle as it ages. In bottles of red wine, especially big or old ones, the sediment should be allowed to settle and then left behind when the wine is **decanted;** in white wines, the clear crystals are tasteless and harmless cream of tartar.

seehk kebab (SEEK keh-BAHB) Indian-style shish **kebab.**

Seezunge (ZAY-tsung-eh) German for sole.

sel French for salt.

selchen (ZEL-shen) In German, to smoke or cure; *Selchfleisch* is smoked meat, often pork loin.

self-rising flour White flour to which baking powder (and salt) has already been added for convenience; used, especially in Britain, for making cakes, biscuits, and other baked goods; not appropriate for doughs that use yeast or eggs as leavening or that do not rise at all.

selle (sel) French for saddle.

Sellerie (ZEL-eh-ree) German for celery.

Seltzer water Naturally effervescent mineral water, or water made to resemble it, from the German village of Selters near Wiesbaden.

semifreddo (seh-mee-FRED-dō) Italian for a chilled or frozen mousse-like dessert, including cream, custard, cake, and fruit; the Spanish version is *semifrío*.

semilla (theh-MEE-yah, seh-MEE-yah) Spanish for seed.

Semillon (seh-mee-yonh) An exceptional white grape variety extensively planted in southwestern France and Australia, also grown in California. Often combined with **Sauvignon Blanc,** it is used for **Sauternes** and **Graves.** Like the **Riesling** grape, it is subject, fortunately, to **noble rot.**

semit (SEH-mit) In Egyptian cooking, large yeast bread rings covered with sesame seeds, crusty on the outside, soft inside, sold on the street; the Turkish version is *simit*.

Semmel (ZEM-mel)   German for breakfast roll; a *Semmelkloss* is a bread dumpling.

semolina (seh-mō-LEE-nah)   The coarsely milled endosperm of wheat or other flour, from which the bran and germ have been removed; **durum** semolina, made from a special kind of hard wheat, is excellent for (commercial) pasta because it has few loose starch granules to soften the dough; other types of semolina are good for **gnocchi** and **couscous.**

sen mee   Thai rice vermicelli noodles; *sen mee nam gup* is noodle and pork soup.

Senf (zenf)   German for mustard.

Sercial (sayr-syal)   A type of **Madeira,** pale and dry; an excellent **apéritif** wine comparable to a **fino** sherry, named after the white grape variety.

Serra (SAYR-rah)   A ewes' milk cheese, sometimes combined with goats' milk, from the mountainous region of Portugal called *Serra da Estrela;* the disc-shaped cheese is creamy white with a runny center and yellow rind, but with aging it becomes pungent, hard, and crumbly.

serrano (sayr-RAH-nō)   A very hot green chili pepper, about 1½ inches long and ½ inch wide; usually cooked fresh but also available pickled and canned.

serrucho (thayr-ROO-chō)   Swordfish, from the Spanish word for saw.

serviette (sayr-vyet)   French for napkin; food served in a folded napkin is *à la serviette.*

sesame   A plant native to Indonesia and East Africa and known to the ancient Egyptians, Greeks, and Romans; in Middle Eastern cooking sesame seeds are used raw, either for oil or **tahini,** while in Far Eastern cooking they are first roasted, yielding a darker, stronger taste, and used mostly for flavoring, rather than frying.

sesos (THAY-thōs)   Spanish for brains.

seviche   See **cebiche.**

Seville orange   A bitter orange whose skin is used widely in making **marmalade;** through the Moors, Europeans got to know the bitter orange before the sweet, which explains why many of their dishes and drinks are flavored with its juice or oils from the zest; see also **bigarade.**

sfogliata (sfō-LYAH-tah) Italian for puff pastry.

sgombro (S'GOHM-brō) Italian for mackerel.

shabu-shabu (shah-boo-shah-boo) In Japanese cuisine, meat and vegetables cooked at table in stock, served with a seasoned sesame sauce; not unlike **sukiyaki.**

shad A member of the **herring** family; though there are numerous species, American shad alone is *Alosa sapidissima*—"shad most delicious." This fish migrates from saltwater up rivers on the eastern coast of the United States for spawning, a welcome harbinger each spring. Shad flesh has a distinctive, rich, sweet flavor, and removing the rows of tiny bones increases the pleasure of eating it. The roe is a great delicacy, poached, broiled, or sautéed to enhance its nutty flavor, often complemented with bacon and lemon.

shaddock See **pomelo.**

shahi tukri (SHAH-ee too-KREE) "Toast of the shah," Indian bread pudding made with cream, **ghee,** saffron, cardamom, pistachios, and rosewater.

shakshouka (shak-SHOO-kah) In Tunisian cooking, a mixture of sweet peppers, tomatoes, and garlic stewed in olive oil with beaten egg added at the last minute. Also spelled *chouchouka.*

shallot A member of the onion family whose bulbs form small clusters; the French favor its subtle, delicate taste and use it often in their cooking.

shandy In England, beer mixed with lemon soda—a refreshing summer drink; *shandygaff* is beer with ginger beer.

shao (sow) Chinese for braising.

sharbat (SHAR-baht) A fruit punch or flavored drink, from which the word **sherbet** is derived; the drink appears throughout India and the Arab world.

shark Although prolific and similar to **swordfish** in flavor and texture, shark (especially mako and dogfish) is not particularly popular in the United States, probably because of its voracious reputation; its dense, lean, delicate flesh takes well to baking, broiling, and marinating.

shark's fin See **yú chì.**

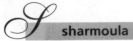

sharmoula (shar-MOO-lah) A Moroccan marinade for fish that combines chopped coriander and parsley leaves, garlic, cumin, lemon juice, paprika, and sometimes hot chili pepper; a Tunisian version is a sweet-and-sour sauce of raisins and onions. Also spelled *charmoula.*

sharon fruit See **persimmon.**

shashlyk See **kebab.**

she-crab soup A springtime soup from South Carolina, made with the meat and roe from female blue crabs, mixed with cream and flavored with Worcestershire sauce and sherry.

shellfish Any kind of seafood with a shell, including **mollusks** and **crustaceans.**

shell steak A cut of beef from the **strip loin,** a boneless and tender steak.

shepherd's pie Cooked ground meat, usually lamb or beef, in a gravy and covered with a layer of mashed potatoes.

shepherd's purse A wild green in the mustard family, eaten in Europe.

sherbet A frozen mixture much like **water ice,** made with sweetened fruit juice or purée or another flavoring, such as coffee or liqueur, and sometimes including beaten egg white or **Italian meringue** to keep ice crystals from forming during freezing; *sorbet* is the French word for sherbet. American sherbet, especially in the Midwest, sometimes contains milk.

sherry A fortified blended wine, strictly speaking from a specified area around the city of Jerez in southern Spain, from whose name the anglicized word "sherry" comes. The young wine, from several grape varieties, is kept in oak casks where it is **fortified,** worked on by **flor** yeasts, blended in **soleras,** and perhaps sweetened and colored with a dose of reserve sherry into several different categories such as **fino, amontillado,** and **oloroso.** In California and other countries the term *sherry* is used more loosely.

shiitake (shee-tah-kay) A Japanese mushroom, dark brown with an earthy flavor, available both fresh and dried; cultivated widely in the Orient and now also in the United States; the woody stem is usually discarded; sometimes called golden oak mushroom in the United States.

shimofuri (shee-mō-foo-ree) In Japanese, to blanch; the name refers to the white color.

shio (shee-ō) Japanese for salt.

ship biscuit See **hardtack.**

shirataki (shee-ra-tah-kee) Japanese translucent noodles made from **konnyaku.**

shirred eggs Eggs cooked in a shallow dish, either on the stove or in the oven, perhaps with a sauce.

shirumono (shee-roo-mō-nō) Japanese soup of all kinds, including thick and thin (*suimono* means thin soup).

shish kebab See **kebab.**

shiso See **parilla leaf.**

shōga (shō-gah) Japanese for fresh ginger root.

shoofly pie A pie with a molasses and brown sugar filling, of Pennsylvania German origin; supposedly so sweet that you have to shoo away the flies.

short loin A cut of beef from the hindquarter, between the **rib** and **sirloin,** comprising the **porterhouse, T-bone,** and **club steak.**

shortbread A rich pastry made from butter, flour, cornstarch, and sugar mixed together, shaped in fingers or rounds, and baked until golden; traditional in Scotland for New Year's Day.

shortening Any fat, usually butter, lard, or vegetable fat, used in baking; shortening lends its name to rich pastries such as **shortbread,** shortcake, shortcrust, and shortening bread.

shortening bread A **quick bread** from the American South using **shortening;** often called shortnin' bread.

shorva Soup in Indian cooking.

shōyu (shō-yoo) Japanese for **soy sauce.**

shred To cut into narrow strips.

shrimp A small decapod crustacean of many species, usually marine—a miniature version of the **lobster;** the family includes the tiny shrimp from cold northern waters, the rock shrimp off the warmer southeastern American coastlines, and the saltwater **crayfish.** Commercially marketed shrimp are sorted—and priced—by size and usually flash-frozen on board immediately after they are caught, either peeled or not, raw or cooked; when thawed, shrimp should have a resilient texture and fresh smell. Shrimp are cooked in innumerable ways around the world from earthy peasant dishes to *haute cuisine* creations.

shrub A fruit drink, sometimes alcoholic—a distant relative of the fruit **sherbet.**

shuàn yáng ròu (sooahn yahng rō) Mongolian hot pot: pieces of lamb (and sometimes other meats) cooked in a communal pot of simmering stock that is placed in the middle of the table; it is served with sauces, and the rich stock is consumed afterward; a kind of Chinese **fondue.**

shurba (SHOR-bah) Arabic for soup; the Turkish is *çorba,* the Persian *shourba.*

shwarma (SHWAHR-mah) See **kebab.**

sild, sill Scandinavian for herring.

silver dollar cakes See **banh can.**

silverside British term for a cut of beef from the crown of the **rump.**

simmer To cook food in liquid just below the boiling point.

Simmons, Amelia The author of *American Cookery,* published in Hartford, Connecticut, in 1796; it was the first cookbook written by an American for Americans using native produce and methods.

Simon, André Louis (1877–1970) A French-born wine connoisseur and gastronome who spent his adult life in London writing about his enthusiasms; he also formed a book collection of considerable distinction and founded the Wine and Food Society.

singer (sinh-jhay) In French, to sprinkle or dust, as with flour or sugar.

Single Gloucester A nearly extinct English cheese made from part skimmed and part whole milk of the rare Gloucester breed (now being revived); half as large as **Double Gloucester** and milder in taste.

sippet A small piece of bread to dip in soup; a piece of toast.

sirloin A cut of beef from the hindquarter, between the **short loin** and **round.**

sirloin tip See **round.**

sirop à trente See **heavy syrup.**

şiş kebab See **kebab.**

skate A diamond-shaped relative of the **shark,** often very large, with edible wings that are usually skinned and trimmed before cooking; skate is most often poached, fried, or sautéed, and in classic French cuisine, served with **beurre noir;** also called ray.

skim To remove the top layer from a liquid, as cream from milk or scum from stock.

skim milk, skimmed milk Milk with nearly all of its cream removed by centrifugal force, leaving .5 percent butterfat; low-fat milk, slightly richer, contains 1 percent butterfat. The skimming also removes vitamins A, D, E, and K, so these nutrients are usually added later.

skirt steak Cut of beef, the diaphragm muscle from the flank, long, flat, and thin; flavorful but tough if cooked improperly.

slivovitz (SLEEV-oh-vits) Plum brandy from Eastern Europe, dry and slightly bitter.

sloe The fruit of the blackthorn—a wild European plum, small, dark, and astringent; used for flavoring sloe gin and, when touched by frost, for preserves.

slump A dessert of cooked fruit baked with a dumplinglike top, served with cream; popular in eighteenth- and nineteenth-century America. Louisa May Alcott named her home in Concord, Massachusetts, "Apple Slump."

smelt A small silvery fish, called sparling in Britain, that migrates between fresh- and saltwater unless landlocked; eaten whole or gutted, most often floured and fried.

smen See **samneh.**

smetana (SME-tah-nah) Russian for sour cream.

smitane (smee-tan) A classic French sauce of chopped onions sautéed in butter, sour cream added, cooked, strained, and flavored with lemon.

Smithfield ham Ham from hogs fattened in the past on peanuts, today on corn. It is cured, salted, smoked, and aged, but not cooked, by traditional methods in the Virginia town of the same name.

smoke To cure meat over burning wood chips by means of the steady low heat and chemical components in smoke; there are many variations of this prehistoric technique, often used in combination with salt curing.

smörgåsbord (SMEU-yahs-bor) A profusely varied buffet of open sandwiches, pickled fish, meats, vegetables, eggs, and salads served in Scandinavian countries as **hors d'oeuvres** or as the meal itself.

smørrebrød (SMEU-breu) Literally "buttered bread" in Danish, an open-faced sandwich made with all kinds of fish, meat, and vegetable fillings with various sauces, artfully presented.

smothered   Braised; in southern cooking, meat—often chicken—that is cooked in a closed pot with a gravy or sauce.

snail   A land-dwelling gastropod **mollusk** appreciated by gastronomes since the Romans; usually canned already prepared for the table; *escargots* (in French) are often served *à la bourguignonne*—fattened on Burgundian grape leaves and bathed in a rich garlic and parsley butter sauce—as well as in other ways.

snap bean   String bean.

s'ngao mouan   (sngow mwahn)   A Cambodian spicy chicken soup with lemongrass, basil, scallions, and lime.

snow eggs   Meringue shaped like eggs with spoons, poached in sweetened milk, drained, and served with custard sauce made from the milk; a classic dessert known in French as *oeufs à la neige.*

snow peas   Peas that are undeveloped and have thin, flat pods; bred to be eaten whole, as their French name *mange-tout* ("eat-all") implies; much used in Chinese cookery.

Soave   (SWAH-vay)   An Italian white wine produced around Verona, dry, pale, fresh, and clean. This wine, which is sold in distinctive tall green bottles, is best drunk young.

soba   (sō-bah)   Japanese buckwheat noodle.

sockeye salmon   See **salmon.**

soda   See **baking soda.**

sodium bicarbonate   See **baking soda.**

soffrito   See **battuto** and **sofrito.**

sofrito   (thō-FREE-tō)   In Spanish cooking, a mixture of chopped vegetables—tomatoes, onions, garlic, and other herbs—cooked together in olive oil, perhaps with diced sweet peppers, ham, and **chorizo,** or other flavorings; the *sofrito,* which can be made ahead, is a base for many sauces and stews. The Italian *soffrito,* made from cooking the **battuto,** is essentially the same thing.

soft-ball stage   Sugar syrup that has reached a temperature of 234–239° F (113–115° C) and that forms a soft ball between the fingertips when immersed in cold water.

soft-crack stage   Sugar syrup that has reached a temperature of 270–290° F (135–140° C) and that forms brittle threads between the fingertips when immersed in cold water.

soft-shell crab   A blue crab caught while molting, when its new shell is so thin that it is edible; a "buster," a Chesapeake specialty.

sògliola (SŌ-lyō-lah)   Italian for sole.

sole   A flatfish family that includes the flounder and many other varieties (see **flounder**); Dover sole is the common sole of European waters, whose white and delicate but firm flesh has inspired many culinary creations. Although there are few true soles in the United States, many types of flounder are called sole to make them more marketable.

solera (sō-LAYR-ah)   The method by which **sherry** and other fortified wines are blended and matured to achieve consistency.

sole Véronique (sōl vayr-on-eek)   In French cuisine, sole poached in white wine and served with **velouté** sauce, garnished with skinned and seeded white grapes; chicken is prepared similarly.

solyanka (sōl-YAHN-kah)   Russian stew of freshwater fish with pickled cucumbers, onions, olives, vinegar, sour cream, and dill; also made with meat or game; the name refers to the brined ingredients.

som (sohm)   Thai for orange (in color); *som tam* is green papaya and shrimp salad.

somlah kako (sohm-law kah-kō)   A Cambodian Khmer stew of various vegetables and green papaya, with chicken, preserved fish, and lemongrass.

somlah machou (sohm-law mah-choo)   A Cambodian spicy soup of shrimp, tomatoes, and fried garlic.

sommelier (sohm-mel-yay)   French for wine steward, wine waiter.

Sonoma   A California wine-producing county just north of San Francisco and east of the Napa Valley; various wines are grown here, especially reds.

sonth (soonth)   Dried ground ginger in Indian cooking.

sooji (soo-jee)   Semolina, farina in Indian cooking.

sookha dar (SOO-kah dahl)   Coriander seeds in Indian cooking.

sopa (THŌ-pah, SŌ-pah)   Spanish for soup.

sope (SŌ-pay)   In Mexican cooking, a small round of **tortilla** dough cooked and filled with a savory stuffing; *sopes* can be eaten as a first course or appetizer. Also called *garnacha* or *picada*.

sorbet (sor-bay)   French for **sherbet.**

sorghum (SOR-gum)   A grain similar to **millet** and used in Asia and Africa for porridge, flour, beer, and molasses, but in the United States mostly for forage; it is a drought-resistant staple crop in East Africa, where it originated, and in Asia; an African bread called *durra,* flat because sorghum has no **gluten,** is made from a variety of the grain.

sorrel   A leafy green plant similar to spinach, whose name, derived from the German word for "sour," is appropriate; especially popular in France, this lemony-tasting green is used in salads or cooked for purées, soups, and sauces, often to complement fish; of the many varieties, wild sorrel is highest in oxalic acid and is sometimes called lemon grass, not to be confused with **lemongrass.**

Sosse (ZOHS-seh)   German for sauce.

sotanghon (sō-tahn-gōn)   Cellophane noodles in Philippine cooking.

soubise (soo-beez)   Chopped onions sautéed in butter with **béchamel** and strained; *soubise* can also be a purée of onions and rice finished with butter and cream—a classic French sauce named for the prince de Soubise, a friend of Louis XV.

Souchong   A black tea from India or Ceylon with large, coarse leaves that make a pale but pungent brew; Lapsang Souchong is a variety with a smoky, dark flavor.

soufflé (soo-flay)   In French cuisine, a sweet or savory pudding made with a white sauce, basic flavoring ingredients, egg yolks, and beaten whites, which cause it to puff up during baking; *soufflé* means blown or puffed up.

soupe   In French cuisine, a hearty and robust peasant soup, usually based on vegetables; not to be confused with **consommé** or **potage.**

sour mash   See **bourbon.**

sourdough   Dough for various baked goods, especially bread, leavened with a fermented starter culture kept from a previous dough rather than with fresh yeast.

sous chef (soo shef)   French for second chef; literally, "under chef."

soused   Pickled in brine or vinegar; usually describes fish.

soutirage (soo-tee-rajh)   French wine term for **racking.**

souvlakia (soov-LAH-kyah)   In Greek cooking, meat marinated in olive oil, lemon juice, and herbs, then skewered and grilled; Greek shish **kebabs.**

soybean A bean extremely important to Asia for its nutritive value (very high in minerals and protein) and for its uses in various forms (fresh, dry, sprouted, and processed in innumerable ways). The seeds yield **soy milk,** flour, and oil (highly unsaturated), all of which can be processed into many useful products. See also **tōfu.**

soybean curd See **tōfu.**

Soyer, Alexis (1809–58) A colorful French chef who gained renown in England through his food served at the Reform Club in London, his books, and his philanthropic efforts in Ireland and the Crimea. He introduced the gas oven, a great improvement over coal.

soy milk A nutritious vegetable product made from dried **soybeans** that are soaked in water, crushed, and boiled; various other products, such as soy cheese, made when a coagulant forms curds and whey from the milk, come from soy milk.

soy sauce A condiment widely used in Chinese and Japanese cooking (where it is known as *shōyu*), made from naturally fermented soybeans and flour; some commercial brands, however, are chemically fermented and contain additives that attempt to make up for lost color, flavor, and body; Chinese soy sauce (**jiāng yóu**) comes in light, medium, and dark grades, depending on their use; Japanese soy sauce is lighter, sweeter, and less salty than Chinese soy sauce. Some types of soy sauce are separately entered.

spaghetti squash Variety of winter squash whose flesh when cooked and combed separates into long strands, suitable for sauce.

spaghettini Thin spaghetti, "little strings" in Italian.

spanakopita (SPAH-nah-KŌ-pee-tah) Greek spinach pie wrapped in **phyllo** dough.

Spanferkel (SHPAHN-fayr-kel) German for suckling pig.

Spanische Windtorte (SHPAH-nish-eh VINT-tor-teh) An Austrian meringue shell—not unlike the French **vacherin**—elaborately decorated with swirls, filled with berries, and served with whipped cream.

spareribs A cut of pork from the breast section, usually grilled or barbecued.

Spargel (SHPAHR-gel) German for asparagus; the white blanched asparagus are favored in Germany, rather than the green, and in spring much is made of their season.

sparling See **smelt.**

spatchcock   Old English way of cooking small birds, by splitting them down the backbone, spreading them, and flattening them, for quick grilling.

spätlese (SHPAYT-lay-zeh)   A German wine term meaning late-picked—after the regular harvest, when these riper grapes yield a bigger, sweeter, natural wine (which is also more expensive).

Spätzle (SHPAYTS-leh)   German for noodle or dumpling from Swabia, small and handmade, usually pressed through a colander.

Speck (shpek)   German for bacon, lard.

spelt   A type of wheat eaten as food in ancient times but now used mostly as livestock fodder.

Spencer steak   See **Delmonico.**

spèzie (SPET-tsyay)   Italian for spices.

spezzatino (SPET-tsah-TEE-nō)   Italian for stew; literally, "cut into little pieces."

Spickgans (SHPIK-gahns)   German for smoked goose, usually the breast—a great delicacy.

spiedo (SPYAY-dō)   Italian for spit for roasting meat; *spiedino* means skewer or brochette.

Spiegelei (SHPEE-gel-ī)   German for fried egg; literally "mirror egg."

Spiess (shpees)   German for skewer; *Spiessbraten* is meat roasted on a spit.

split pea   A pea of several varieties, generally green or yellow, that is dried and hulled; mostly used for soup and, in Britain, for "pease" pudding or porridge.

sponge   A bread dough mixture based on yeast that is set aside, covered, to develop bubbles and flavor before the remaining ingredients are added and the bread completed. Also a name for an airy gelatin or **mousse** dessert.

sponge cake   A cake whose texture is lightened with separately beaten egg whites but little or no shortening; it contains some sugar and flour but no leavening other than eggs.

spoom   See **spuma.**

spoon bread   A moist and unsweetened southern American dish made from white cornmeal and eggs, eaten at various meals; although called "bread," the consistency of spoon bread is more like that of pudding; also called batter bread.

spotted dick, spotted dog   A British steamed suet pudding with raisins—a traditional nursery food.

sprat   See **brisling.**

Springerle (SHPRING-er-leh)   German cookies, pale yellow and anise-flavored, sometimes molded into very large and elaborate figures; traditional for Christmas and originally from Swabia.

spring-form pan   A cake pan whose bottom is removed by means of a spring or hinge on the sides, rather than by inverting the cake.

spring onion   See **scallion.**

spring roll   See **chūn juǎn.**

spritzig (SHPRITS-ish)   German for sparkling, effervescent, as for wine.

sprout   A dried bean that, with proper moisture and warmth, germinates; mung, alfalfa, and soybeans are favorite varieties for sprouting, and they can be eaten raw or lightly cooked.

spuma (SPOO-mah)   In Italian cooking, a fruit or **water ice** with **Italian meringue** folded in halfway through the freezing process, as in a **sherbet.** *Spuma* means foam, froth, or mousse. *Spumone* is a mousse-like ice cream lightened with whipped cream or beaten egg whites.

spumante (spoo-MAHN-tay)   Italian for sparkling, as for wine.

squab   A young pigeon about to leave the nest. Squabs are full-grown at about four weeks but still unfledged; most squabs are domesticated, that is, bred for the table, and their meat is tender, all dark, but not gamy.

squid   A marine **mollusk** with a long body and ten arms, highly nutritious and with little waste; most appreciated by Mediterranean and Oriental cultures; squid can be cut into diamonds or rings or stuffed whole to be cooked in various ways, sometimes in sauces flavored and colored with its ink.

Stachelbeere (SHTAHK-ul-bayr-eh)   German for gooseberry.

Stampfkartoffeln (SHTAHMPF-kar-tohf-eln)   German for mashed potatoes.

Stange (SHTAHNG-eh)   German for stick; *Stangen* and *Stangerl* are stick-shaped pastries, sweet or savory; *Stangenspargel* means asparagus spears.

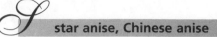

star anise, Chinese anise   See **ba jiao.**

star fruit   See **carambola.**

steak and kidney pudding   British beef and kidney pieces, flavored with onions, mushrooms, and possibly oysters, steamed in a suet crust (or baked for steak and kidney pie).

steam   To cook by steam heat, thus preserving most of the food's nutrients; food can be steamed over boiling water or, wrapped in leaves, foil, or other protection, directly in hot coals or boiling water.

steep   To soak or infuse in liquid.

Steinberg   (SHTĪN-bayrg)   A famous old vineyard in the **Rheingau,** located in the *Kloster Eberbach* monastery and created in the twelfth century by the same Cistercian monk who established the *Clos de Vougeot* in Burgundy; its several wines have exceptional body, power, and depth.

Steinbutt   (SHTĪN-boot)   German for turbot.

Steinpilz   (SHTĪN-peelts)   German for *cèpe* or **boletus** mushroom.

stew   To cook food slowly in a small amount of liquid at low heat in a closed container in order to make the food—usually meat—tender and allow the flavors to mingle; to **braise.**

Stilton   An uncooked cows' milk cheese (now rarely from pasteurized milk) injected with the *Penicillium roqueforti* mold and aged for about six months to make one of the world's great blue cheeses. Stilton is made in Derbyshire, Nottinghamshire, and Leicestershire in large cylinders with a brownish crust. The paste is creamy with a variable blue-green veining, moist and slightly crumbly, but not dry or salty. There is also a White Stilton.

stir-fry   To cook quickly in a small amount of very hot fat, constantly stirring, to give the food a crisp yet tender texture; a method much used in Chinese and Asian cooking with the **wok.**

stock   Broth in which meat, game, poultry, fish, or vegetables have been cooked; stock is usually seasoned, strained, degreased, concentrated, and used as the foundation for soups and sauces—what the French call *fond de cuisine;* meat stock usually contains gelatin, from veal and other bones, and can be white or brown.

Stollen   (SHTOHL-len)   German for fruit bread filled with various dried fruits, shaped in a long loaf, and sprinkled with confectioners' sugar; traditional for Christmas and associated with Dresden.

stone crab   A variety of crab found off the southeastern Atlantic and Gulf coastlines, especially Florida, with very fine meat mostly from the claws; sold already cooked.

Stör (shteur)   German for sturgeon.

stout   British ale whose malt has been toasted before brewing to produce darker color, stronger flavor, and higher alcoholic content.

stoved   In Scottish cooking, simmered on top of the stove, as in **étouffer;** *stovies* is a potato dish cooked thus, possibly with meat drippings and onions.

Stracchino (strahk-KEE-nō)   An uncooked, unpressed cows' milk cheese, originally unpasteurized but now generally pasteurized, from Lombardy; this fresh, rindless cheese is buttery, smooth, and delicate. *Stracchino di Gorgonzola* is the original name of **Gorgonzola.** *Stracchino* cheeses were originally made with milk from cows still tired—*stracche* in the Lombardian dialect—from their long descent from the Alps.

stracciatella (strah-chah-TEL-lah)   Italian for light chicken or beef stock thickened with a paste of egg, cheese, and **semolina.**

stracòtto (strah-KOHT-tō)   Italian for pot roast or braised meat.

strasbourgeoise, à la (ah lah strahz-boor-jhwahz)   Garnished with sauerkraut, small pieces of bacon, and sautéed slices of goose liver—a classic French garnish.

strawberries Romanoff   A French dessert of strawberries macerated in orange-flavored liqueur and garnished with **crème Chantilly.**

straw mushroom   A wild mushroom cultivated in the Orient on rice straw and available in the West either canned or dried; it is small with a long thin stem and conical tan cap.

Streusel (SHTROY-zel)   German for a sprinkling, as of sugar or breadcrumbs; *Streuselkuchen* is a yeast cake topped with a cinnamon-sugar crumble.

striped bass   A western Atlantic fish that migrates from the sea to spawn in freshwater streams in autumn; its size varies greatly, but smaller fish taste better; the flesh of the striped bass is white, flaky, and firm, with a delicate flavor, making it a popular table fish that is very versatile in cooking.

strip loin   A cut of beef from the top of the **short loin,** tender and boneless, often cut into steaks.

Strudel (SHTROO-del)   Very thin pastry sheets with a sweet or savory filling, rolled up and baked; from Bavaria.

Stück (shtük)   German for piece, portion.

stufa (STOO-fah)   Italian for stove; *stufato* means stew.

sturgeon   A marine fish that spawns in rivers, sometimes growing to great age and size; its flesh is white, rich, firm, and tight in texture—almost like meat—taking well to smoking or pickling; the roe is a great delicacy; see also **caviar.**

su (soo)   Japanese for rice vinegar.

suan mei jiāng (sooahn may jahng)   Duck sauce, a Cantonese dipping sauce (literally "plum sauce") traditionally served with duck or goose and used more widely in American-Chinese cooking; it is a thick sweet-and-sour sauce made of plums, apricots, vinegar, and sugar.

subric (sü-breek)   French for a small ball of vegetable or other food, fried.

succotash   A dish of dried beans and corn derived from the Narragansett Indians' *msickquatash*. Early versions included poultry and meat as well as other vegetables; succotash today need not be reduced to lima beans and corn kernels.

sucker   See **buffalo fish.**

sucre (SÜK-ruh)   French for sugar; *sucre filé* is spun sugar.

sudado (thoo-DAH-dō, soo-DAH-dō)   Spanish for steamed.

suédoise (sway-dwahz)   Cold "Swedish" sauce of **mayonnaise** flavored with apple purée and grated horseradish—a classic French sauce.

suet   Solid lumps of fat from around the loins and kidneys of beef, lamb, and other animals, used for making pastry, pudding, and tallow.

sugar snap peas   Cultivated variety of **mange-tout** with edible pod and peas more developed than snow peas.

sugarcane   A tall grass of South Pacific origin from which raw sugar was first extracted in India around 500 B.C. To refine the sucrose, the ten- to twelve-month-old stalks are cut and pressed for their juice, which is then clarified, reduced, spun (to separate the sugar crystals from the **molasses** and other impurities), washed, and uniformly crystallized.

sugaring   See **chaptalization.**

sugo (SOO-gō) Italian for sauce; *sugo de carne* is gravy. When speaking of pasta sauce, *sugo* rather than **salsa** is the correct term. The plural is *sughi.*

suimono (soo-ee-mō-nō) Japanese for clear soup.

sukiyaki (soo-kee-yah-kee) Thinly sliced beef and a variety of vegetables cooked in a pot with suet at the table, seasoned, and served with ceremony; a relatively recent dish in Japanese cuisine.

sukuma wiki (soo-KOO-mah WIK-ee) Kenyan stew of leftover meat with onions, tomatoes, sweet peppers, and leafy greens.

sulphiting The addition of sulphur to **must** in order to delay or prevent fermentation—not necessarily an abuse in winemaking.

sultana A large golden raisin made from sweet, white, seedless grapes originally grown in Smyrna, Turkey, and named after the Turkish sultan; see also **currant.**

Sülz (zülts) German for aspic or meat in aspic, such as **head cheese.**

sumac A seasoning with a lemony, salty flavor used as a souring agent in Arab dishes; the dried seeds of the "Sicilian" sumac shrub are crushed to a reddish powder that is used to flavor meat and chicken dishes and also to make a drink; not to be confused with American sumac, which is poisonous.

summer pudding A British dessert of fresh raspberries and red currants stewed together gently, sweetened, pressed in a bread-lined bowl overnight, then turned out and served with cream; the result, though from humble origins, is exquisite.

sŭn (suan) Chinese for bamboo shoots.

sunflower A large heliotropic flower whose seeds are roasted and eaten like nuts and whose oil, extracted from the seeds, is light in flavor and mostly polyunsaturated.

sungkaya (SUNG-kī-YAH) Steamed coconut custard, a popular Thai dessert.

sunomono (soo-nō-mō-nō) Japanese for vinegared food.

sup (soop) Thin-textured Vietnamese soup without noodles, served as a first course.

supari (SOO-pah-ree) Betel nut in Indian cooking.

superfine sugar Very fine sugar crystals that dissolve quickly in liquid.

supparot (sup-pah-rōd)   Thai for pineapple.

suprême de volaille (sü-prem deu vō-lī)   The breast and wing fillet of a young chicken or other bird, lightly floured and sautéed in butter. *Sauce suprême* is a reduced chicken **velouté** with cream.

surimi (soo-ree-mee)   Japanese for making imitation crab meat made from pollock or other inexpensive fish; it is processed in sheets, rolled up, and colored to resemble crab legs; sometimes called seafood legs or other euphemisms.

sushi (soo-shee)   Vinegared rice formed into fingers or rounds, seasoned with **wasabi** or other spices, perhaps rolled in seaweed, and garnished with raw seafood or fish and sometimes a vegetable; in Japan, *sushi* is eaten as a meal; in the United States, it is also eaten as an appetizer.

süss (züs)   German for sweet; *süsse Speisen* are sweet dishes or desserts.

Suzette, crêpes   See **crêpes Suzette**.

sweat   To cook in a little fat over very low heat in a covered pot, so that the food exudes some of its juice without browning; used especially with vegetables.

swede   In England, a rutabaga or Swedish turnip; the Scottish term is turnips or neeps.

sweet bean sauce   See **tien mien jiāng**.

sweet bell pepper   See **pepper (sweet bell)**.

sweetbreads   The thymus or pancreas glands of a calf, sheep, or pig, located in the throat and chest of young animals. Veal sweetbreads are considered the best, pork inferior; the chest or heart sweetbread is larger and therefore the better of the pair. Sweetbreads are highly perishable and should be used quickly. They are soaked in **acidulated water** to whiten the tissue, **blanched** and weighted to firm them, and the membranes are trimmed before further cooking.

sweet cicely   See **cicely**.

sweet cumin   See **anise**.

sweet marjoram   See **marjoram**.

sweet potato   A root vegetable indigenous to Central America and brought by Columbus to the Old World; high in sugar, nutrients, and calories, it is often confused with the **yam,** especially in the United States; the sweet potato has a reddish skin, a texture like the familiar potato, and an affinity for similar preparations.

Swiss cheese   American-made (or foreign-made) **Emmental.**

Swiss roll   British term for jelly roll.

swordfish   A large marine fish whose dense white meat is marketed in steaks or chunks; because of its expense, mako **shark** is sometimes surreptitiously substituted; excellent for baking or broiling.

syllabub (SIL-a-bub)   An old-fashioned British drink made of rich milk or whipped cream with wine, beer, or cider, and flavored with sugar and spices; variously spelled; similar to **posset** and **eggnog.**

Sylvaner (sil-VAH-ner)   A very good white-wine grape, more productive but less distinguished than the **Riesling;** extensively cultivated in Germany, Austria, Alsace, and also grown in Switzerland, the Italian Tirol, California, and Chile.

Syrah (see-RAH)   A distinguished red-wine grape variety yielding a long-lived, deep-red wine; used for **Hermitage** and (with others) **Châteauneuf-du-Pape;** grown in the Rhône area as well as in California, Australia, and South Africa.

syrup, heavy   See **heavy syrup.**

terrine

Tabasco A fiery hot commercial sauce made of red chili peppers, vinegar, and salt, aged in oak barrels and bottled; made since the Civil War in **Cajun** Louisiana by the McIlhenny Co.

tabbouleh (tah-BOO-lee) A Lebanese dish of **bulghur** mixed with chopped tomatoes, onion, mint, parsley, olive oil, and lemon juice, eaten as a salad with lettuce leaves.

table d'hôte (TAB-luh D'ŌT) Full meal at **prix fixe.**

tacchino (tah-KEE-nō) Italian for turkey.

Tâche, La (lah tash) A small vineyard in the **Vosne-Romanée** that produces an outstanding red Burgundy: rich, velvety, and full-bodied.

taco (TAH-kō) A **tortilla** filled with shredded meat and sauce, rolled or folded, and sometimes fried; the Mexican word means "snack."

Tafelspitz (TAH-fel-shpits) Top round of beef boiled and accompanied with root vegetables, horseradish, and sauces—from Vienna.

taffy Candy made from sugar or molasses cooked down, usually with butter, nuts, and other flavorings. American taffy, especially saltwater taffy, tends to be soft and chewy, while British *toffee* is brittle.

tagliatelle (tah-lyah-TEL-lay) Long thin flat strips of egg pasta; this is the Florentine and northern name for **fettucine,** slightly wider and flatter. **Ragù bolognese** is the classic sauce for *tagliatelle.*

tagliolini, tagliarini (tah-lyō-LEE-nee, tah-lyah-REE-nee) Very thin Italian noodles, but not as thin as **capelli d'angelo;** used in soups.

tahini (tah-HEE-nee) A paste of crushed raw sesame seeds used as the basis of many Arab dishes such as **helva, hummus,** and **baba ghanoush;** spelled variously.

tahu (tah-hoo) Indonesian soft bean curd; *tahu goreng* is fried bean curd, often with spices or sauce.

tajin (TAH-jin) In Moroccan cuisine, a braised stew, with infinite variations, named for the earthenware pot with a conical lid in which it is cooked and served; also spelled *tagine*; the plural is *touajin*.

takaw (tah-kaw) Thai dessert of coconut milk and tapioca flour, with many variations.

takenoko (tah-kay-nō-kō) Japanese for bamboo shoots.

takrai (tahk-RĪ) Thai for lemongrass.

tala (TAH-lah) Deep-fried, in Indian cooking.

Taleggio (tah-LEJ-jō) An uncooked, unpressed, whole unpasteurized cows' milk cheese from Lombardy; made in squares with an orange rind and a delicate buttery paste. There is also a cooked-curd variety made from pasteurized milk, with a gray rind. *Taleggio* is a **stracchino** cheese.

Talleyrand (tal-lay-ranh) A classic French garnish of macaroni mixed with butter and cheese, truffle **julienne,** and diced **foie gras**—for sweetbreads and poultry.

tamago (tah-mah-gō) Japanese for egg.

tamale (tah-MAH-lee) Mexican dish of corn dough (*tamal*) made with lard, filled with a savory stuffing, wrapped up in a piece of corn husk, and steamed; the filling can be savory or sweet; *tamales* are traditionally for holidays and special occasions, and their history is ancient. In South America, banana leaves serve as tamale wrappers.

tamari (tah-mah-ree) Dark, thick Japanese sauce, similar to **soy sauce,** also made from soybeans; used primarily as a dipping sauce or in a basting sauce.

tamarillo Fruit native to Peru that looks like a slender plum tomato in deep red or gold, with dense, smooth flesh and small black seeds; it tastes like an intensely spicy, fruity tomato and is best cooked with a little acid and sugar and served as a vegetable with meat or in chutney and relish.

tamarind The pod or fruit of a large tropical tree native to India; when fresh, its pulp is white, crisp, and sweet-sour, but when dried it turns reddish brown and very sour; in Indian cooking it is used both as a souring agent and as a red coloring in curries, chutneys, pickles, sauces, and refreshing drinks. Also used in Middle Eastern and Vietnamese cooking.

tamatar (tah-MAH-tar) Tomato in Indian cooking.

tamis (ta-mee) French for sieve, sifter, strainer; the Spanish word is *tamiz. Tamiser* in French means to strain through a sieve or tammy cloth.

tampon (tamh-ponh) French for a bed of rice or vegetables.

tan Thai for palm sugar.

tandoor (tahn-DOOR) An Indian clay oven, usually recessed in the ground; *tandoori,* the food roasted in it at high temperatures, is first marinated in yogurt and spices.

tandoori chicken See **murgh.**

tāng (tahng) Chinese for soup.

tang (tahng) Korean for beef stock.

tangelo (TAN-jeh-lō) A hybrid citrus fruit—a cross between a grapefruit and a tangerine; there are several varieties, Minneola considered by many to be the best; see also **ugli fruit.**

tannin A chemical compound in the stems and seeds of grapes that imparts a characteristic astringency and puckery quality to wine; tannin is pronounced in young red wines, especially good claret, but gives them longevity.

tansy An herb with a rather bitter flavor, once popular in England but now largely ignored; a tansy pudding used to be traditional for Easter.

tapas (TAH-pahth) Appetizers served in Spanish bars with cocktails, in great variety and profusion.

tapénade (ta-pay-nad) French for a mixture of capers, anchovies, black olives, garlic, and perhaps tuna and other foods, thinned to a paste with olive oil; from the Provençal word for caper.

tapioca A starch extracted from the tuberous root of the **cassava** or manioc plant, native to tropical and subtropical America where Indians once ate it as a bread. Tapioca, almost pure starch—easily digestible and nutritious—is made into flour and "pearls," which are used for thickening soups, pies, and puddings. It has become a staple in India and Indochina. See also **cassava.**

taramosalata (tah-RAH-mō-sah-LAH-tah)   Greek salad of pink fish roe, usually gray mullet or carp, puréed with bread that has been moistened with a little milk, olive oil, lemon juice, and garlic; served with crusty bread.

tarator (TAHR-rah-tor)   A creamy Turkish sauce of ground nuts and breadcrumbs, flavored with garlic and lemon juice or vinegar, usually served with seafood or vegetables; many variations; a similar sauce is made in Syria and Lebanon.

taro (TAAHR-ō)   A tropical and subtropical plant valuable for its spinachlike leaves, asparaguslike stalks, and potatolike root. Its high starch content makes it an important staple in Polynesia, Africa, and Asia. In the Caribbean, its leaves are made into a spicy stew called **callaloo**; *dasheen* is another word for *taro.*

tarragon   An herb in the daisy family used widely in French cooking; it is essential to the **bouquet garni, béarnaise** sauce, and chicken is essential to *à l'estragon,* and is one of the **fines herbes.**

tart   A sweet or savory pie, usually with no top crust; a **flan.** A tartlet is a small individual tart.

tartare (taahr-taahr)   In French cuisine, *sauce tartare* is mayonnaise with hard-boiled egg yolks and garnished with finely chopped onions, chives, and capers; *boeuf à la tartare* is chopped lean beef served with capers, chopped onions, and parsley, with a raw egg.

tarte, tartelette (taahrt, taahrt-let)   French for tart, tartlet; *tartine* means a slice of bread spread with butter or jam, also a small tart. The Spanish words are *tarta* and *tartaleta.*

tarte (des demoiselles) Tatin (taahrt day deu-mwah-zel ta-tinh)   A French apple tart devised by the Tatin sisters in their restaurant near Orléans, baked upside down; the bottom of the pan is buttered and strewn with sugar, covered with sliced apples, then topped with a pastry crust; during baking the sugar on the bottom caramelizes, and the finished tarte is turned out and served.

tartufo (tar-TOO-fō)   Italian for truffle.

tasajo (tah-SAH-hō)   Jerked or salt-dried beef, from Cuba.

tasse (tas, TA-seh)   French and German for cup; the Spanish word is *taza.*

tasso (TAS-ō)   A **Cajun** pork, or occasionally beef, sausage that is highly seasoned with chili and other spices and smoked; used as a flavoring in Cajun dishes.

Tatin, tarte des demoiselles   See **tarte des demoiselles Tatin.**

tatlı (TAHT-leu)   Turkish for dessert.

Tavel (ta-vel)   A **rosé** wine from the Rhône Valley near Avignon—flavorful, strong, and celebrated.

tavuk göğsü (tah-OOK geu-SÜ)   A Turkish dessert pudding of finely shredded chicken breast, rice flour, milk, and sugar, flavored with cinnamon; akin to medieval **blancmange.**

T-bone steak   A cut of beef from the **loin,** very similar to the **porterhouse,** but containing less of the fillet.

té (tay)   Italian and Spanish for tea; the German word is *Tee.*

tejolate   See **molcajete.**

tel   Oil in Indian cooking.

tempeh (TEM-peh)   An Indonesian staple of fermented soybeans that are pressed into firm blocks, suitable for stir-frying or grilling.

tempura (tem-POO-rah)   In Japanese cooking, seafood and vegetables dredged in a light batter and quickly deep-fried in oil; served with a dipping sauce called *tentsuyu.*

tenderloin   A cut of meat, especially beef, from the hindquarter, consisting of one long, slender, and very tender muscle running through the **loin** section ending at the ribs; it is divided into **filet mignon, chateaubriand,** and **tournedos** for roasts or steaks.

tentsuyu   See **tempura.**

terasi   See **balachan.**

teriyaki (tayr-ee-yah-kee)   Japanese for poultry, fish, or meat marinated in a sweet soy-sauce preparation and grilled over charcoal so that the marinade forms a glaze.

Terlano (tayr-LAH-nō)   A well-known and excellent white wine from the Italian Tirol, in the Alto Adige Valley; dry, fruity, rounded, and soft.

ternera (tayr-NAYR-ah)   Spanish for veal.

terrapin   An edible water turtle that lives in fresh or brackish water; see **turtle.**

terrine (tayr-reen)   In French cuisine, a mixture of meat, game, poultry, or vegetables and seasonings, cooked in a dish lined with bacon or pork; the dish was originally earthenware, hence its name; see also **pâté.**

tête d'aloyau (tet d'al-wah-yō) French for rump steak.

tête de veau (tet deu vō) French for calf's head; in Italian, *testa di vitello.*

Tetilla (teh-TEE-yah) A Spanish cheese usually made from ewes' or goats' milk—soft, creamy, and bland.

Tex-Mex Style of cooking that combines elements of Texan and Mexican food, such as **chili con carne.** This indefinable style is more an American perception of Mexican food as that offered by Mexican restaurants north of the border, as opposed to authentic Mexican food found in Mexico.

tfina (TFEE-nah) A Moroccan and Algerian stew of beef and chickpeas cooked in the embers on Friday night to be eaten on the Jewish Sabbath.

thé (tay) French for tea.

thiebou dienne (tyay-BOO dyen) A rice and fish stew, the national dish of Senegal, traditionally served in a large communal bowl.

thon (tonh) French for tuna.

thousand-year-old eggs See **pí dàn.**

thyme An herb of Mediterranean origin (and in many varieties) that is an essential part of the **bouquet garni;** besides its many culinary applications, it has been used since ancient times for medicinal purposes.

Tia Maria (TEE-ah mah-REE-ah) A liqueur flavored with Blue Mountain coffee extract and spices; from Jamaica.

tia to See **perilla leaf.**

tian (tee-anh) French for a shallow casserole or, by extension, food baked in it—usually an aromatic **gratin** of chopped vegetables, perhaps with some leftover meat or seafood; from Provence.

tiède (tyed) French for lukewarm; tepid; at room temperature.

tien mien jiàng (tyen myen jung) In Chinese cooking, a thick, sweet, and salty paste made from fermented red beans, flour, salt, and water; used for flavoring sauces and marinades and as a dipping sauce, especially in northern China.

tikki (TIK-ee)   In Indian cuisine, cutlet; also spelled *tikka.*

til (teel)   **Sesame** seeds in Indian cooking.

tilapia (til-AH-pya)   Fish with mild, white, flaky delicate flesh that responds well to farming and will therefore be increasingly available; related to **John Dory** but not so fine an eating fish.

tilefish   A western Atlantic fish with firm but delicate lean flesh, usually cut into fillets or steaks; very versatile in cooking.

Tilsit (TIL-sit)   A cooked, unpressed German cheese made from raw or pasteurized cows' milk; oblong or cylindrical, it has a thin yellow rind and straw-colored paste with holes; the acidulated taste becomes more pronounced with age, and the cheese is sometimes flavored with caraway seeds; now made in several central European countries.

timbale (timh-bal)   French for a drum-shaped mold, usually metal, or the food prepared in such a mold, including rice, diced vegetables, or fish **mousseline;** also a high, round, covered pastry case, usually decorated, or the food in such a case.

timo (TEE-mō)   Italian for thyme.

tipsy parson or pudding   An old-fashioned English dessert pudding of sponge cake soaked with spirits or fortified wine and covered with custard or whipped cream; not unlike a **trifle.**

tirage (teer-ajh)   French wine term for "drawing off" wine from the cask.

tiramisù (tee-rah-mee-SOO)   A rich Italian dessert, literally "pick me up," created in the 1960s, that layers sponge cake soaked in brandy and **espresso** with **mascarpone** custard cream flavored with chocolate.

tire-bouchon (teer boo-shonh)   French for corkscrew.

tiropita (TEE-rō-PEE-tah)   A Greek cheese pie wrapped in **phyllo** dough.

tisane (tee-zan)   French for herbal tea.

toad-in-the-hole   In British cooking, meat, usually sausage, baked in batter.

tocino (tō-THEE-nō, tō-SEE-nō)   Spanish for bacon; *tocino de cielo,* literally "bacon from heaven," is a thick caramel custard dessert (not made with bacon).

toffee See **taffy.**

tōfu (tō-foo) Japanese bean curd, white, soft, and easily digestible; in one form or another it is eaten throughout the Orient and valued for its healthful properties: it is high in protein, low in calories, and free of cholesterol. *Tōfu* is made from dried soybeans processed into a "milk" that is coagulated like cheese; the molded *tōfu* curds are kept fresh in water. Of the many types, *momen* ("cotton") is the most common fresh *tōfu* in the United States as well as in Japan; *kinu* ("silk") has a finer texture; *yakidōfu* has been lightly broiled. Chinese bean curd (*dòu fu*) is drier and firmer than Japanese.

tōgarashi (tō-gah-rah-shee) Japanese for red hot chili peppers, fresh or dried.

Tokay (tō-KĪ) A famous wine from the town of the same name in northeastern Hungary, made with some proportion of grapes with the **noble rot** in varying grades and ranging in sugar and alcoholic content; the best and rarest Tokay has an incomparable rich, buttery, peach-caramel flavor. Tokay is also the name of an Alsatian grape, totally unrelated.

tom yam gung See **dom yam gung.**

Toma (TŌ-mah) An uncooked whole or partly skimmed cows' milk cheese, sometimes mixed with ewes' or goats' milk, made in the Italian Alps near the French Haute-Savoie and Swiss borders; shaped in discs, it ripens quickly to a pale supple paste or can be matured to a dense, pungent cheese. See also **Tomme.**

tomalley (toh-MAHL-ee) The liver of the lobster, colored olive green—a special delicacy.

tomatillo, tomate verde (tō-mah-TEE-yō) Mexican green tomato, enclosed within a papery husk, small and pungent; not an unripe red tomato (**jitomate**); used as the basis of an important Mexican **salsa,** with **serrano** peppers, garlic, and coriander, all chopped together, either fresh or cooked.

tomber à glace (tomh-bay ah glas) In French, to reduce liquid to a glaze.

Tomino (tō-MEE-nō) An uncooked, unpressed cows' milk cheese, usually pasteurized and sometimes enriched, from the Italian Alps; this rindless cheese ripens quickly to a delicate, fresh flavor and a soft, smooth paste, making it an excellent dessert cheese. See also **Tomme** and **Toma.**

tomme au raisin (tohm ō ray-zinh) French for cheese with grape seeds pressed on the outside.

Tomme de Savoie (tohm deu sa-vwah) An uncooked, pressed cows' milk cheese from the French Alps, with an Italian version across the border; made in eight-inch discs with a light brown rind, a pale yellow paste, and a nutty lactic flavor. *Tomme* means cheese in the Savoy dialect, and there are many varieties of it there, made from cows', goats', or ewes' milk. See also **Toma** and **Tomino.**

Tomme Vaudoise (tohm vō-dwahz) An uncooked, soft cheese made from whole or sometimes partly skimmed milk in the Swiss Alps; round or oblong, it has a thin, delicately molded white rind and a smooth, buttery, aromatic interior.

tonkatsu (ton-kat-soo) In Japanese cooking, pork marinated in a spicy sauce, dipped in egg and breadcrumbs, and fried.

tonno (TOHN-nō) Italian for tuna.

tooa (TOO-ah) Thai for peas, beans, peanuts.

Topf (tohpf) German for pot; stew or casserole.

Topfen See **Quark.**

topinambour (tō-pinh-amh-boor) French for **Jerusalem artichoke;** the Italian spelling is *topinambur.*

top round See **round.**

top sirloin See **round.**

tord Thai for fried; *tord man neua,* spicy fried meat balls.

toriniku (tor-ee-nee-koo) Japanese for chicken meat.

torrone (tor-RŌ-nay) Italian for **nougat.**

torsk Norwegian and Swedish for cod.

torta (TOR-tah) In Italian, tart, pie, or cake. In Spanish, cake, loaf, or roll of bread. In Mexico, the word can also mean a savory pudding of **tortillas** stacked like **chilaquiles.**

Torte (TOR-teh) German for tart, round cake, flan; *Tortenbäcker* is a pastry cook.

tortellini (tor-tel-LEE-nee) Small rounds of egg pasta stuffed, folded, and wrapped around the finger; almost the same as **cappelletti** but round instead of square.

tortilla (tor-TEE-yah) In Spain the word means omelet; in Mexico *tortilla* means a thin, flat, unraised pancake made of dried cornmeal flour, salt, and water—from the Aztec cuisine. The Mexican term for omelet is *tortilla de huevos.*

tortoni (tor-TŌ-nee) Ice cream topped with chopped almonds or **macaroons;** Italian-American in origin and often called *biscuit tortoni.*

tortue (tor-tü) French for turtle; *sauce tortue* is **demi-glace** with tomato purée, herbs, truffle essence, and **Madeira;** *à la tortue* means calf's head garnished with veal **quenelles,** mushrooms, olives, gherkins, calf's tongue, and brains, with *sauce tortue.*

Toscanello (tohs-kah-NEL-lō) A cooked, semihard ewes' milk cheese from Tuscany and Sardinia, made in six-pound cylinders; it has a brownish yellow rind and a pale dense paste and is aged three to four months to develop a mild or piquant taste.

tostada (tō-THTAH-dah, tō-STAH-dah) Spanish for toast; in Mexico this means a **tortilla** fried flat and then topped with all kinds of garnishes, sometimes stacked high.

tostaditas See **totopos.**

tostones (tōs-TŌ-nays) In Caribbean cooking, thin slices of **plantain** fried once, then pounded thinner and fried again; eaten like potato chips as a side dish or with **salsa.**

totopos (tō-TŌ-pōs) **Tortillas** cut into six to eight smaller triangles, fried crisp, and served with dips or as a garnish.

toulousaine, à la (ah lah too-loo-zen) Garnished with chicken **quenelles,** sweetbreads, mushroom caps, cocks' combs and kidneys, and truffle slices arranged separately, with **allemande** sauce—a classic French garnish.

tourage (too-rajh) French for repeated turns of the dough—rolling and folding—in the making of **pâte feuilletée.**

tourin (too-rinh) French onion soup made with milk instead of meat stock (as in *soupe à l'oignon*), thickened with egg yolks and cream, and sometimes served with grated cheese; from southwest France.

tourné (toor-nay) French for a vegetable that is "turned" or shaped with a knife, as with potatoes and mushrooms; also, food that has gone bad or a sauce that has separated.

tournedos (TOOR-neh-DŌ) French for thick slices from the middle of the beef fillet, sautéed or grilled.

tourte (toort) French for tart or pie, usually round and savory; a *tourtière* is a pie dish or flan case.

toute-épice (too-tay-pees) French for **allspice.**

tragacanth See **gum.**

Traminer (trah-MEE-ner)   A white-wine grape family to which the **Gewürztraminer** belongs.

trancher (tranh-shay)   In French, to carve, slice; a *tranche* is a slice, chop, or steak. The Italian word is *trancia*.

Trappiste (trap-peest)   French for a cheese made all over the world by Trappist monks—**Port-Salut** being the best known of this type—all of them with slight variations. The round cheese is semihard, with a soft rind and a dense, smooth paste with small holes.

Traub(e) (trowb, TROW-beh)   German for grape; bunch of grapes.

travailler (tra-vī-yay)   In French, to beat; to stir in order to blend or smooth.

treacle (TREE-kul)   British for a syrup similar to molasses but slightly sweeter; used in making puddings, tarts, and other desserts.

Trebbiano (treb-BYAHN-nō)   A white-wine grape much used in Italy (for White **Chianti, Soave,** etc.) and also grown in southern France and California, where it is called *Ugni Blanc.*

tree ear   See **yún ěr.**

tree oyster   See **oyster mushroom.**

trenette (tre-NET-tay)   Flat pasta similar to **fettucine,** but thicker ("train tracks"); traditional pasta for **pesto.**

trey (tray)   Cambodian for fish; *chien trey,* fried fish; *trey aing,* fish grilled over charcoal, served with raw vegetables, greens, and herbs, with pungent fish sauce containing roasted ground peanuts.

trid (treed)   In Tunisia, a primitive kind of **bastilla.**

triflach (TREE-flakh)   **Farfel** lightened with extra eggs.

trifle   A British dessert pudding of sponge cake or biscuits soaked with sherry or other liquor, topped with custard and whipped cream, usually garnished with sliced fruit.

triglia (TREE-lyah)   Italian for red mullet, a Mediterranean fish.

trigo (TREE-gō)   Spanish for **wheat.**

tripe   The first and second stomachs of ruminants (plain and honeycomb tripe, respectively); *tripe à la mode de Caen* (see **Caen**), requiring the laborious preparation of beef tripe, is the classic dish.

triple sec   French for a clear, colorless orange-flavored liqueur, such as **Cointreau** and **Curaçao.**

Trockenbeerenauslese (TROHK-en-bayr-en-ows-lay-zeh)   A very sweet wine made from raisined (nearly dry) grapes left on the vine and individually chosen from bunches—the most selective and expensive German wine produced.

Troja (TRŌ-yah)   An Italian red-wine grape, productive and widely grown for its deep color and full body; used for blending.

trota (TRŌ-tah) Italian for trout.

trotter The foot of an animal, especially a pig or sheep.

trout A game fish, primarily freshwater and related to **salmon,** with fine-textured flesh high in fat content, usually white but sometimes pink. With very small scales, a simple bone structure, and succulent flesh, it is adaptable to many culinary uses. Brook, brown, lake, rainbow, **sea trout,** and **char** are a few of the many varieties.

trouvillaise, à la (ah lah troo-vee-yez) Shrimp, mussels, and mushroom caps with shrimp sauce—a classic French garnish.

trucha (TROO-chah) Spanish for river trout.

truffle The fruiting body of a black or white fungus that grows underground, unlike other mushrooms. The dense truffle, rough, round, and with interior veining, grows in symbiosis with certain trees, especially oak, and only in particular soils and climates. Trained dogs, goats, and sows can find the scent of truffles, similar to that of boars' saliva in mating season, and sniff them out. Their exquisite aroma makes their exorbitant price worthwhile. The best black truffles, increasingly rare, come from Périgord, France; white truffles come from Alba, in northern Italy. Chocolate truffles are chocolate buttercream balls rolled in cocoa, crushed almonds, or chocolate shavings to resemble real truffles.

truite au bleu See **bleu, au.**

truss To tie poultry or game with string in order to hold its shape during cooking, to ensure even cooking, and to improve its appearance; the particular method of trussing depends on the animal, its size, and the cooking method used.

Trut-hahn, Trut-henne (TROOT-hahn, TROOT-hen-neh)   German for tom turkey or hen.

tsukemono (tsoo-kay-mō-nō) Japanese for pickled food.

tube pan A ring-shaped cake pan traditionally used for rich cakes, since the hollow center can be filled and the extensive surface coated with syrup or icing.

tubu (DOO-boo)   Korean version of **tōfu,** thick and soft, not firm like Chinese tōfu; *tubu choerim* is fried spiced bean curd.

tuile (tweel)   French for a crisp cookie, sometimes made with crushed almonds, that is placed on a rolling pin immediately after baking so that it curves when cool like a "tile" (hence its name).

tukbaege (TOOK-bay-gee)   A Korean round clay pot, an all-purpose cooking container made in various sizes.

tuk trey (tuhk tray)   Cambodian Khmer fish sauce with vinegar, lime juice, sugar, and garlic, used extensively.

tulipe (too-leep)   French for a crisp, thin, cookielike dough ruffled while still warm from the oven into a flower shape to hold dessert berries, ices, etc.

tuna   A large saltwater fish with rich meat varying in color and oiliness from one species to another and also from one part of a fish to another; *albacore* is high-quality tuna with white meat; other species yield darker flesh, **bonito** being the darkest; tuna is often brined before cooking to lighten the color. Much of the commercial catch is canned, solid ("fancy"), chunks, and flakes being the three styles, packed either in oil or water. Baking, broiling, braising, marinating, and smoking are good cooking methods for tuna; the Japanese hold it in special regard for its use in **sashimi.**

tuna   Mexican word for **prickly pear.**

Tunke (TUHN-keh)   German for sauce, gravy.

tunny   British term for **tuna.**

turban   Food, often cooked in a ring mold, served in a circle; used primarily for seafood or poultry dishes.

turbinado sugar   Partially refined sugar, light brown in color, similar to **demerara.**

turbot   An eastern Atlantic **flounder** with delicate white flesh that rivals the Dover **sole** in culinary preparations; true turbot is rarely found in the United States.

turlu (TOOR-loo)   Turkish for stew.

turmeric (TER-mer-ik)   A spice obtained from the dried and powdered rhizome of an Indian plant of the ginger family, whose bitter flavor and ochre color contribute to curries; in the Middle Ages its color made it a substitute for **saffron,** and even today turmeric is used as a dye for cloth and dairy products such as **margarine.**

turnover A pastry square or round filled with a sweet or savory stuffing, folded in half to enclose the stuffing, and baked; the turnover appears in many cultures.

turrón (toor-RŌN) A chewy Spanish candy made of toasted almonds, honey, egg whites, and sometimes other ingredients; from Alicante and traditional for Christmas.

turshi (TOOR-shee) In Middle Eastern cooking, pickled food.

turtle Land and water turtles are both edible, but the aquatic green and diamondback are especially valued for their flesh, mainly in soups and braised dishes; the expense and difficulty of preparing turtle meat and also conservation measures designed to protect the species' diminishing numbers have made turtle recipes far less fashionable than in the past. A terrapin is an edible water turtle that lives in fresh or brackish coastal water; tortoise generally means a land turtle.

Tuscany The region around Florence, Italy, producing **Chianti** and other red table wines. The Tuscan style of cooking is relatively simple, featuring olive oil, herbs, **cannelloni,** beans, game, and bread, rather than pasta (except for hare with **pappardelle**).

tutti-frutti (TOO-tee FROO-tee) Italian for mixed fruits (literally "all fruits") chopped and preserved in syrup, usually with brandy.

Tybo (TÜ-bo) A Danish cooked cows' milk cheese similar to **Samsø;** brick-shaped, supple-textured, with fairly large holes, Tybo is straw-colored on the inside with a yellow rind; its taste is mild and slightly acidulated.

tyrolienne, à la (ah lah tee-rō-lyen) Fried onion rings and tomatoes *concassées*—a classic French garnish.

tyropita (TEE-rō-PEE-tah) A traditional Greek cheese pie made with **phyllo** and **feta,** similar to **spanakopita.**

tzimmes (TSIM-mes) A casserole of **brisket of beef** with carrots, prunes or other dried fruit, and syrup, topped with potatoes and dumplings; traditional for Rosh Hashanah and Passover.

uccèllo

uccèllo (oo-CHEL-lō) Italian for bird; *uccèlli scappati* (literally "escaped birds") are veal birds skewered with bacon and sage; *uccelletti* or *uccellini* are small birds, usually skewered and roasted whole; see also **meat birds.**

uchepos (oo-CHAY-pōs) Fresh corn **tamales** from Michoacán.

udang (oo-dahng) Indonesian for shrimp; *udang goreng* is fried shrimp.

udon (oo-dōn) Japanese wheat noodle.

ugali (oo-GAH-lee) Steamed porridge made of **maize,** or occasionally **millet, cassava,** or **sorghum;** a staple food in Tanzania and East Africa, served with meat stews or vegetables, sometimes cooled and fried.

ugli fruit (OO-glee, *not* UG-lee) A hybrid cross between a grapefruit and tangerine, not to be confused with the Minneola, Orlando, and Seminole **tangelos;** grown in Jamaica where it is called *hoogli*, it has a yellowish green, thick, coarse skin and sweet orange flesh.

Ugni Blanc See **Trebbiano.**

ujja (UH-jah) A Tunisian egg dish with filling, rather like an **omelet** or **tortilla;** see also **ijja.**

umé (oo-may) Japanese for plum (actually a kind of apricot); *umeboshi* are pickled plums; *umeshu* is plum wine.

umido, in (een OO-mee-dō) Italian for stewed.

unagi (oo-nah-gee) Japanese for eel.

uovo (WŌ-vō) Italian for egg; *tuorlo d'uovo* is the yolk, *bianco d'uovo* the white; *uovo affogato* is a poached egg, *uovo molletto* is a soft-boiled egg, *uovo al burro* is a fried egg, and *uovo sode* is a hard-boiled egg.

usu-kuchi shōyu (oo-soo-koo-chee shō-yoo) Japanese for light soy sauce, clearer, thinner, and saltier than dark soy sauce (**koi-kuchi shōyu**).

uva (OO-vah) Spanish for grape; *uva espina* is gooseberry, *uva passa* or *secca* is raisin.

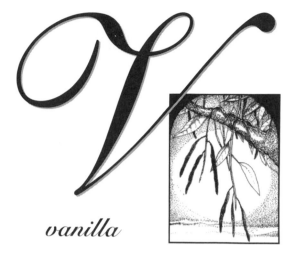

vanilla

vaca frita (VAH-kah FREE-tah)   "Fried cow," an informal but popular Cuban dish of beef first simmered for broth, then shredded and stir-fried with chopped onions.

vacherin (vash-rinh)   In French cuisine, a meringue shell made of a solid disc of meringue and separate rings stacked on the circumference to form a container; the baked *vacherin* shell is decorated with piped scrolls, then filled with ice cream, **crème Chantilly,** berries, or other fruit.

Vacherin Mont-D'Or (vash-rinh monh d'ohr)   A whole-milk cows' cheese, uncooked and unpressed, from the Swiss and French Alps; the disc-shaped cheese has a soft, creamy, rich texture with small holes and a delicate, buttery, sweet flavor. Other types of this winter cheese are *Vacherin des Beauges* and *Vacherin Fribourgeois,* and they are all often banded with spruce bark, which imparts its subtly resinous flavor.

Valdepeñas (val-day-PAY-nyahth)   Red and white table wines from La Mancha, south of Madrid, a very large quantity of which is produced; officially called *Vino Manchego;* the red is especially light, pleasant, best drunk young, and inexpensive.

Valencia (vah-LEN-thyah)   A seaport and region in eastern Spain notable for its short-grain rice and seafood, both of which grace **paella** *valenciana*. The Valencia orange, sweet and thin-skinned, is an excellent juice or dessert orange.

valenciano (vah-len-SYAH-nō)   A chili pepper similar to the **güero.**

valencienne, à la (ah lah val-enh-syen) A classic French garnish of rice **pilaf** and sweet red peppers with a tomato-flavored sauce.

Valois (val-wah) A **béarnaise** sauce with meat glaze; also a classic French garnish of artichokes and sautéed potatoes.

Valpolicella (val-pō-lee-CHEL-lah) A red wine produced in northern Italy, northwest of Verona, in five townships. The wine is soft, light, dry, and fragrant, best drunk young; it has been called the **Beaujolais** of Italy.

Valtellina (val-tel-LEE-nah) A wine-producing region in northern Italy, near Switzerland, where the **Nebbiolo** grape yields some of the country's best wine: dark, robust, and long-lived.

vanilla The fruit pod of a climbing orchid indigenous to Central America, which is picked immature, then cured in a long process. The pod and interior seeds are used to flavor desserts, and the pod can be dried and used again, immersed in vodka or sugar, which it permeates with its aroma; the synthetic vanillin is an inferior substitute.

vanner (van-nay) In French, to stir a sauce until cool, ensuring smoothness and preventing a skin from forming.

vapeur (va-peur) French for steam; to steam is to cook *à la vapeur.*

varietal wine Wine made from a particular grape, such as **Cabernet Sauvignon, Riesling,** or **Nebbiolo,** which in part gives the wine its character; depending on the location, the wine is not necessarily made entirely from the varietal.

variety meat Edible meat other than skeletal muscle, especially organs; see **offal.**

Västerbottenost (VES-ter-BOHT-ten-ohst) A pasteurized cows' milk cheese from Sweden in which the curd is scalded, pressed, and matured for eight months. The rind of this cylindrical cheese is hard, with a wax covering; the paste is firm, with small holes, and the taste is pungent.

vatapa (vah-TAH-pah) A Brazilian paste of ground nuts, dried shrimp, and coconut milk, served as an accompaniment or stuffing for **acarajé.**

veal The meat of young beef; milk-fed veal, lean and pale pink to white in color, comes from animals under three months of age; grass-fed veal (sometimes called calf or baby beef), rosy pink with cream-colored fat, is under five months of age.

veal Orloff Saddle of veal (or sometimes lamb) braised and carved in slices. Each slice is coated with **soubise** and **duxelles,** the slices are placed back together, and the whole is masked with **béchamel,** and garnished with asparagus tips; from classic French *haute cuisine.*

veal Oscar Veal cutlets sautéed and garnished with asparagus tips, crab legs or crayfish tails, and sauce **béarnaise.**

veau (vō) French for veal.

vellutata (vel-loo-TAH-tah) An Italian soup thickened with egg yolk, like the French **velouté.**

velouté (veu-loo-tay) "Velvet" white sauce based on a white **roux** with white stock, fish, chicken, veal, or vegetable; this basic classic French sauce is similar to **béchamel** but uses stock rather than milk. A soup *velouté* is a purée combined with *velouté* and finished with cream and egg yolks.

vénitienne, à la (ah lah vay-nee-tyen) "Venetian-style" in classic French cuisine: fish fillets poached in white wine, served in a reduction sauce flavored with shallots, tarragon, chervil, and a little vinegar, and garnished with croûtons in the shape of a heart.

venison Deer meat; the word used to mean any furred game.

ventre (VENH-truh) French for belly, breast.

verbena See **lemon verbena.**

Verdelho (vayr-DAY-ō) A type of **Madeira,** now quite rare, fairly dry and not unlike a **Sercial;** the name is from a grape variety.

verdura (vayr-DOO-rah) Italian and Spanish for vegetable; the Italian plural is *verdure,* the Spanish *verduras;* in French *verdure* means greenery or foliage, not green vegetables.

verjuice The juice of unripened grapes or possibly other fruit, not necessarily fermented; in the Middle Ages sour flavorings such as verjuice and vinegar were used a great deal in cooking, before citrus was common.

vermicelli (vayr-mee-CHEL-lee) Very thin pasta—literally "little worms" in Italian—often used for soups and puddings.

vermouth A white **apéritif** wine, **fortified** and flavored with herbs and spices, including wormwood flower (*Wermut* in German, hence its name); French vermouth is dry and pale, Italian vermouth sweet and amber.

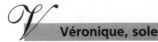

Véronique, sole   See **sole Véronique.**

verte, mayonnaise   See under **mayonnaise.**

vert-pré (vayr-pray)   A French garnish for grilled meats of straw potatoes, watercress, and *beurre* **maître d'hôtel;** also chicken or fish
masked with **mayonnaise verte;** literally, "green meadow."

vessie (ves-see)   French for pig's bladder; *poularde en vessie* is a famous
old dish from Lyons of stuffed chicken poached in a pig's bladder.

Vezzena (vet-SAY-nah)   A hard cows' milk cheese made in the Italian
Alps from partially skimmed milk; it is a scalded-curd cheese, aged
six months to a year, depending on whether it is to be used as a table
or grating cheese.

viande (vyanhd)   French for meat.

Vichy, carrots à la   See **carrottes à la Vichy.**

vichyssoise (vee-shee-swahz)   Cream of potato and leek soup, served
chilled and garnished with chives; the 1917 creation of Louis Diat,
chef of the Ritz-Carlton in New York, and named for his native
French city; often misspelled.

Victoria   In French cuisine, lobster sauce with diced lobster and truffles,
for fish; also a classic French meat garnish of tomatoes stuffed with
duxelles and artichoke quarters sautéed in butter, the pan deglazed
with veal stock and **port** or **Madeira;** also various cakes and ice
cream desserts.

viennoise, à la (ah lah vyen-wahz)   "Viennese style"—coated with egg
and breadcrumbs, fried, and garnished with sliced lemon, capers,
olives, chopped parsley, and hard-boiled egg yolks and whites (separately); a classic French garnish, used especially for veal and chicken
cutlets or fish fillets.

Vierlander Poularde (FEER-lahn-der poo-LAAHRD)   German chickens bred in the Vierlande district near Hamburg, known for their
fine quality.

vigneron (VEEN-yuh-RONH)   French for winegrower; *à la vigneronne*
means with wine, brandy, grapes, or grape leaves.

Villalón (veel-lah-LŌN)   A fresh ewes' milk cheese, originally from the
Spanish Old Castile near Portugal; white, even-textured, sharp-
flavored and salty; cylindrical in shape.

Villeroi, Villeroy (veel-rwah) A **velouté** sauce well reduced with truffle and ham essence.

vinaigrette (vee-nay-gret) A basic French sauce or dressing of oil and vinegar, usually in a proportion of three to one, with salt and pepper and perhaps some chopped herbs or mustard.

vindaloo (VIN-dah-loo) A spicy Indian dish from Goa, highly seasoned with vinegar, garlic, and curry; usually made with rich meat.

vin du pays (vinh dü pay-ee) French for local wine of a specific region, usually not well known or shipped elsewhere.

vinegar Literally "sour wine," a liquid (wine, beer, cider, etc.) turned into weak acetic acid by fermentation; the many types, some separately entered, are used for preserving and flavoring.

vine leaves Young grape leaves blanched and used to wrap small birds and savory mixtures such as **dolmas;** the leaves flavor and encase their stuffing and keep it from drying out.

vinho verde (VEE-nyō VAYR-day) "Green" young wine produced in northern Portugal, often very enjoyable and occasionally sparkling.

vin nature (vinh na-tür) Unsweetened French wine—a term used loosely.

vin ordinaire (vinh ohr-dee-nayr) Common French table wine of unknown origin but specific alcoholic content.

vintage The grape harvest of a particular year and the wine made from it.

Viognier (vee-ō-nyay) White grape variety, originally of the Rhône Valley, that produces a full-bodied, complex wine high in alcohol.

violet A plant whose flowers are crystallized as a dessert garnish; the fresh flowers and young leaves can be used in salads.

Virginia ham See **Smithfield ham.**

Viroflay, à la (ah lah vee-rō-flay) A classic French garnish of spinach balls, quartered artichoke hearts, **château potatoes,** and veal stock; also means "with spinach."

vit quay (vit whī) Vietnamese glazed duck, like **Peking duck,** but simpler, with a darker glaze, and with more aroma than the Chinese version.

vitello (vee-TEL-lō) Italian for veal; *vitello tonnato* is braised veal marinated in tuna sauce flavored with anchovies and capers with broth and a little cream, or, in the newer version, with mayonnaise; served cold—a classic dish.

volaille (vō-lī)   French for poultry, fowl, or chicken.

vol-au-vent (vōl-ō-venh)   Puff pastry cases, literally "flight of the wind" in French; either large or small round shells with a cap, used to hold savory or sweet fillings; the small shells are sometimes called *bouchées à la reine.*

Vollrads, Schloss (SHLOHS FŌL-rahts)   A celebrated vineyard in the German **Rheingau** next to *Schloss* **Johannisberg** and with its own medieval castle; the wide-ranging and numerous wines produced there, despite the complicated labeling, all reveal the vineyard's breeding and charm.

Volnay (vōl-nay)   A village in the French **Côte de Beaune,** between **Pommard** and **Meursault,** producing excellent and renowned red Burgundy wine; it is soft, delicate, and refined, with a long aftertaste.

vongola (VOHN-gō-lah)   Italian for clam.

Vorspeisen (FOR-shpī-zen)   German for appetizers, hors d'oeuvre.

Vosne-Romanée (vōn-rō-ma-nay)   A wine-producing **commune** in Burgundy with some extraordinarily fine red wines that possess exceptional bouquet, balance, and breeding.

Vouvray (voo-vray)   A white wine of the Touraine region of the Loire Valley made from the **Chenin Blanc** grape; *Vouvray* can vary greatly in character from dry, fruity, and tart, to rich, sweet, and golden, or even effervescent or sparkling. For a white wine it is extraordinarily long-lived.

watercress

Wachenheim (VAHK-en-hīm) A wine-producing town in the German **Rheinpfalz;** its fine wines are mostly from the **Sylvaner** and **Riesling** grapes.

waffle A crisp, thin cake made from a pancakelike batter and baked inside a special double-sided and hinged iron, giving it its honeycombed surface; waffles, whose history reaches far back, are eaten with sweet or savory toppings. Belgian waffles have especially large and deep pockets.

Wähen (VAY-en) Large open Swiss tart filled with vegetables, cheese, or fruit.

wakame (wah-kah-mee) Japanese seaweed of fine flavor and texture, usually bought in dried form for soups or fresh for salads.

Waldmeister (VAHLT-mīs-ter) German for **woodruff.**

Waldorf salad Chopped apples, celery, and walnuts in mayonnaise; created by Oscar Tschirky of the Waldorf-Astoria in New York before the turn of the century, although the walnuts were added later.

Walewska, à la (ah lah vah-LEF-skah) Garnished with sliced **langoustine** and truffles and glazed with **Mornay** sauce with langoustine butter; a classic French sauce named after the son of Napoléon's Polish mistress.

walleye, walleyed pike Actually a member of the **perch** family, this excellent freshwater fish, with firm, white, fine-textured flesh, lives in large North American lakes.

walliser (VAL-is-er) A generic Swiss term for **Raclette** cheese.

Walnuss (VAHL-noos) German for walnut.

walnut A tree indigenous to Asia, Europe, and North America, whose nuts have been favored since ancient times. The nut meats are eaten plain, pickled, or used in sweet and savory dishes; their oil is much esteemed for its distinctive flavor; their husks are even made into a liqueur called *brou.* In several European languages the word for walnut is also the generic name for nut, showing its dominance.

warqa (WAHR-kah) In Moroccan cuisine, a tissue-thin pastry sheet used in **bastilla,** made like the Chinese spring-roll sheet of dough; **phyllo** or **strudel** can be substituted.

wasabi (wah-sah-bee) A plant, often called Japanese horseradish though botanically unrelated, whose root is used as a spice for raw fish dishes; it comes fresh, powdered, and as a paste, and is very hot in flavor and green in color.

washed rind cheese A cheese whose rind is washed with water, brine, beer, wine, or another liquid during ripening. The purpose is to prevent the growth of certain bacterial cultures but encourage that of others and to keep the cheese from drying out.

Washington, à la A classic French garnish of corn with cream sauce.

wassail (WAH-sul, wah-SAYL) A spiced punch, traditionally some kind of beer, drunk on festive occasions, very often Christmas; the word, of Scandinavian derivation, means "to your health."

water chestnut The fruit of a long-stemmed water plant that grows inside irregularly shaped thorns beneath the floating leaves. The starchy fruit has a crisp texture and delicate taste not unlike that of boiled chestnuts and can be used in many ways. It grows all over the world but is little appreciated outside the Orient.

watercress A plant growing in shallow streams, whose crisp, deep green leaves are used as an herb, a salad green, and a garnish; a member of the mustard family, its flavor is characteristically peppery and slightly pungent.

water ice A frozen dessert of syrup and fruit juice or purée, usually with a little lemon juice or other flavoring such as coffee or liqueur; the ice is frozen smooth but without the addition of egg white, as in a sherbet; see also **sherbet, granita,** and **spuma.**

waterzooï (VAH-ter-zoy) A traditional Flemish stew, probably originating in Ghent (*à la gantoise*), made with either fish or chicken. The fish version probably came first, with perch, eel, carp, pike, and possibly other varieties of fish, cooked in white wine with herbs; in the other version chicken is poached in stock with onions, leeks, celery, and carrots, flavored with lemon juice, and finished with egg yolks and cream.

weakfish Also known as seatrout (but not to be confused with **sea trout**), this member of the **drum** family is no trout at all—nor is it weak; this marine fish has lean, sweet, delicate flesh that is versatile in cooking.

Wehlen (VAY-len) A small town on the Moselle River whose wines have become the best of the Mittel-Mosel; *Sonnenuhr*—a sundial painted on a slate outcropping in the steep vineyard slope—is the name given to the best of the fine wines.

Weinbeere (VĪN-bayr-eh) German for grape; *Weintraube* means a bunch of grapes.

Weinberg (VĪN-bayrg) German for vineyard.

Weissbier (VĪS-beer) Light frothy summer beer ("white beer") from Bavaria, served with a slice of lemon.

Weisswurst (VĪS-voorst) A small delicate German sausage stuffed with veal, flavored with wine and parsley; a specialty of Munich, it is eaten for breakfast with sweet mustard.

Weizen (VĪTS-en) German for **wheat.**

Wellington, beef See **beef Wellington.**

Welsh rarebit (RAB-it) This British **savory** consists of hard Cheddar-type cheese melted with beer or milk and seasonings, poured over toast, and briefly grilled.

Wensleydale An English uncooked, pressed cows' milk cheese made in both white and blue styles. The white, made in eight-pound flat discs and aged three to four weeks, is white, flaky, moist, and mellow, properly not yellow or sour. The blue, aged four to six months, is similar to **Stilton,** but less veined and smoother, sweeter, and nuttier.

Westphalian ham See **Westfälische Schinken.**

Westfälische Schinken (vest-FAY-lish-eh SHINK-en) German ham made from acorn-fed pigs, believed by many to rival **prosciutto, Bayonne,** and **Smithfield** hams in quality. The meat is lightly smoked, cured, but not cooked, and served in paper-thin slices with **pumpernickel** bread.

wheat   A grain of great importance because of its ability, when combined with yeast and water, to form leavened bread; the **gluten** thus developed stretches to contain the expanding air bubbles. The higher the proportion of protein to starch in the kernel, the more gluten. There are many types of wheat flour, subject to climate and season as well as variety, but in general soft spring wheat (low in gluten) is good for pastry, cakes, pies, biscuits, and cookies. Hard winter wheat (high in gluten) is good for bread. **Durum semolina** (also high in gluten) is good for pasta.

whelk   A gastropod **mollusk** similar to the **periwinkle,** appreciated in Europe, especially in Italy as *scungilli.*

whey   The watery liquid which, after coagulation, separates from the curds in the cheesemaking process; whey contains albumin, lactose, and other nutrients and can be used to make **ricotta** or **Gjetost** cheeses.

whiskey, whisky   Spirit distilled from grain such as barley, corn, or rye. See **Scotch whisky** and **bourbon.**

whitebait   Herring and sprat fry, plentiful in the Thames and Garonne Rivers and along the North Sea coast; the tiny fish are usually dipped in batter and deep-fried without being cleaned.

white butter sauce   See **beurre blanc.**

white chocolate   Cocoa butter, milk solids, and sugar; contains no cocoa solids and is therefore, strictly speaking, not chocolate at all. See also **chocolate.**

whitefish   A small freshwater fish, mainly North American, related to **trout** and **salmon,** with delicate white meat that tastes best in winter and is often smoked (see **cisco**); the roe is used as a **caviar** substitute.

white sauce   **Béchamel** or **velouté** sauce, both made from **roux,** or any of their descendants.

whortleberry   See **bilberry.**

Wiener Schnitzel   (VEE-ner SHNIT-sel)   Literally "Viennese cutlet" in German, veal **scallops** coated with layers of flour, beaten egg, and breadcrumbs, then fried in butter or lard and served without a sauce, usually with a slice of lemon; sometimes spelled as one word.

Wienerwurst   (VEE-ner-voorst)   German for **frankfurter** sausage.

Wild (vilt)   German for game.

wild leek   See **ramp.**

wild rice   A grass native to the Great Lakes region of North America and a distant cousin of common **rice**; now planted and harvested commercially rather than gathered in canoes, but still very expensive. A staple Indian food due to its high protein and carbohydrate value, wild rice is parched, hulled, and polished before cooking.

Wildgeflügel (VILT-geh-flü-gel)   German for feathered game.

Wiltingen (VIL-ting-en)   A famous town on the **Saar** River near Trier, Germany, whose steep vineyards planted with **Riesling** grapes produce superb wines in good years.

Windbeutel (VIND-boy-tel)   German for cream puff, literally "wind bag."

winkle   See **periwinkle.**

wintergreen   A creeping evergreen, native to the American northeast, with deep green, round leaves and red berries; the aromatic leaves are used as a flavoring.

winter melon   A melon with hard, smooth, or furrowed skin and white to pale green or orange flesh; lacking the perfumed aroma and separation layer in the stem of the **muskmelon,** the winter melon can be harvested into frost and allowed to travel as long as a month on the way to market. Honeydew, Casaba, Cranshaw (or Crenshaw), Santa Claus, and Canary melons fall into this category.

Wirsing (VEER-sing)   German for savoy cabbage.

witloof   See **Belgian endive.**

wok   A round-bottomed metal cooking pan with sloping sides that provide the large cooking surface suitable for most Chinese methods of cooking: stir-frying, deep-frying, steaming, smoking, and (with the top on) braising and poaching. Special ring trivets or flat-bottomed *woks* can adapt the utensil to western electric stoves.

wonton   See **hún tún.**

wood ear   See **yún ěr.**

woodruff   A perennial herb found in forests and sometimes used as a groundcover in shady gardens; its leaves, dried or fresh, are used to flavor teas, drinks, and punches, while its delicate flowers, which bloom in May, impart their scent to **May wine.**

woon sen   Thai for cellophane noodles.

Worcestershire sauce   (WUHS-ter-sher)   A highly seasoned commercial sauce, made by Lea & Perrins of Worcester, England, for 160 years and used widely as a savory condiment; the recipe, of Indian origin, includes soy sauce, vinegar, molasses, anchovies, onion, chilies and other spices, and lime and tamarind juices; the sauce is fermented and cured before bottling.

wormwood   An herb once used as a medicine against intestinal worms, hence its name; the toxic leaf gives **absinthe** its potency and anise flavor, while the more delicate flower imparts its taste (and its name) to **vermouth.**

wot   (wot)   Stew in Ethiopian cooking; *yedoro wot* is a spicy minced chicken and onion stew; *yemiser wot* is a spicy lentil stew seasoned with **berbere;** *atakilt wot* is a vegetable stew, also seasoned with **berbere.**

wu hsiang fun   (woo shahng fen)   Seasoning used in Chinese cuisine, a variable mixture of star anise, fennel seeds, Sichuan peppercorns, clove, cinnamon, and nutmeg; five-spice powder.

Wurst   (voorst)   German for sausage; a *Würstchen* is a little sausage.

Würz   (vürts)   German for spice or seasoning; *Würzfleisch* is a special beef stew with sour cream sauce, usually accompanied by dumplings or potatoes.

xérès

xató (shah-TŌ)   A Spanish winter salad from Catalonia of **Belgian endive** with red chili peppers, almonds, garlic, oil, and vinegar.

xcatic (shah-TEEK)   A long yellow green chili pepper from Mexico.

xérès (zayr-REZ)   French for **sherry.**

xia (shah)   Chinese for shrimp.

xiāng cài (shahng tsī)   Chinese for **coriander.**

ximxim de galinha (SHEEM-sheem day gah-LEE-nyah)   Chicken in a marinade of dried shrimp, chili peppers, ginger, and cashews; a classic dish in the African-Brazilian tradition.

xiè (sheh)   Chinese for crab.

x-ni-pec (shne-PEEK)   A Yucatecan version of **salsa mexicana cruda,** made with juice of the sour orange.

xoconostle (shō-kō-nōst-lay)   Mexican for green **prickly pear.**

xoi vo (soy vah)   Yellow mung beans and coconut rice, a popular breakfast or snack food in Vietnam.

yule log

yā (yah) Chinese for duck.

yakhni (YAK-nee) Indian meat or poultry stock.

yaki (yah-kee) In Japanese, to grill or broil; *yakimono* means grilled food; *yakitori* is chicken pieces and vegetables skewered, marinated in a spicy sauce, and grilled.

yam A tuberous vegetable of African origin whose high starch content has enabled it to serve as a valuable food source for millennia, especially in tropical and subtropical regions; it has white or yellow flesh and brown skin and is often confused with the **sweet potato,** especially in the United States, where a variety of sweet potato is mistakenly called yam.

yam (yahm) Thai for salad; *yam gung* is shrimp salad, sharp with citrus and chilies.

yaourt, yahourt (yah-OOR) French for **yogurt.**

yard-long beans See **Chinese beans.**

yarrow A plant native to England whose fine lacy leaves are used as an herb or for tea.

yasai (yah-sī) Japanese for vegetables.

yassa (YAH-sah) A Senegalese marinade of lemon, chili peppers, and onion, for chicken with rice.

yautia See **malanga.**

yeast A microscopic, naturally occurring fungus that induces fermentation, thus initiating the chemical process that makes bread, cheese,

wine, and beer. The many types of yeast, mainly fresh, dry, and brewer's, convert starch into gas and alcohol. **Baking powder** is a recent chemical alternative for leavening bread.

yedoro wot See **wot.**

yemas de San Leandro (YAY-mahth day THAHN lay-AHN-drō) Egg-yolk threads poured into hot syrup and twisted into sweets—a confection of Moorish origin made by the nuns of San Leandro in Seville.

yemiser wot See **wot.**

yemitas de mi bisabuela (YAY-mee-tahs day mee BEE-sah-BWAY-lah) A Mexican sweet of egg yolks, sherry, and syrup formed into balls and rolled in cinnamon sugar.

yen wo The nest of cliff-dwelling birds, considered a great delicacy in Chinese cuisine. The dried nests, either white or black, are soaked in water to restore their gelatinous texture and used to garnish soups at banquets and special occasions; very expensive, especially the white ones, so reserved for banquets.

yogurt, yoghurt, yoghourt Milk that has been fermented with a lactic culture, turning it slightly acid and custardlike in texture; although health claims for yogurt have been exaggerated, it is useful for its cooking and keeping properties; yogurt originated in the Balkans where it is still much used in cooking.

Yorkshire pudding A British savory pudding made from a batter of milk, eggs, and flour, originally baked under a roast beef on an open spit or rack to catch the drippings, puffing up in the process; the pudding is cut into squares for serving. Yorkshire sauce is port wine sauce with red currant jelly, garnished with julienne of orange zest—a classic sauce.

Yquem, Château d' (sha-tō d'ee-kem) A very great white dessert wine, awarded the unique *Grand Premier Cru* of **Sauternes** in the 1855 classification; it is very sweet, fruity, and luscious; made from grapes with the **noble rot,** it is exorbitant in price.

yú chì (ü tseu) Shark's fin; a nutritious delicacy in Chinese cuisine which, after considerable soaking and preparation, is savored for its gelatinous texture; an expensive specialty reserved for banquets.

yuca (YOO-kah, *not* YUK-ah) Spanish for yucca; see **cassava, tapioca,** and **manioc.**

yufka (YOOF-kah) In Turkish cooking, a thin circle of bread dough stretched and used for wrapping much like **phyllo,** but thicker.

Yukon gold New variety of potato with small size, yellow color, and rich (but not buttery) flavor.

yule log See **bûche de Noël.**

yún ěr (yoon er) An irregularly-shaped fungus that grows on logs, used in Chinese cooking for its interesting texture; yellow, brown, or black on one side and white on the other, the dried fungus expands greatly with soaking before cooking; also called **tree ear, wood ear,** and other names.

zucca

za'atar (ZAH-tahr) Thymelike herb that grows in several varieties in the eastern Mediterranean and North Africa, including a rarely imported one that tastes like a combination of oregano, marjoram, and thyme. Confusingly, the word also means a spice blend of the herb with **sumac** and **sesame seeds**; this is often eaten for breakfast in the Middle East sprinkled on hot flatbread brushed with olive oil.

zabaglione (zah-bī-YŌ-nay) An Italian dessert custard in which egg yolks, flavored with **Marsala** and sugar, are beaten over simmering water until they foam up into a frothy mass; also spelled *zabaione;* the French version is **sabayon.**

zafferone (zahf-fayr-Ō-nay) Italian for **saffron.**

zakuski (zah-KOOS-kee) Russian **hors d'oeuvre** starting with caviar and running the whole gamut; traditionally accompanied with vodka. However modest or grand the circumstances, the main meal of the day and any party always begin with *zakuski,* a tradition that goes back a thousand years to Scandinavia.

zampone (zahm-PŌ-nay, sah-nah-HOR-yah) A highly seasoned Italian pork sausage encased in the skin of a pig's foot; from Modena.

zanahoria (thah-nah-HOR-yah, sah-nah-HOR-yah) Spanish for carrot.

zapallo (sah-PAL-lō) A large deep yellow winter squash used in South American cooking, similar to pumpkin or butternut.

zarda (ZAHR-dah) Sweet rice **pilao** flavored with saffron and other spices, nuts, and raisins, in Indian cooking.

zarzamora (thahr-thah-MOR-ah) Spanish for blackberry.

zarzuela (thahr-THWAY-lah) A Spanish seafood stew, varying widely, in a piquant sauce flavored with wine or liqueur, all arranged spectacularly; the word means operetta and implies that the dish is a fantastic mixture.

Zeltingen (TSEL-ting-en) A wine-producing town in the central Moselle Valley producing a large quantity of fine wine, all estate-bottled **Riesling.**

zemino (zeh-MEE-nō) Middle Eastern sauce of anchovies and garlic with vinegar, sometimes sweetened with sugar, for fish; Sephardic in origin.

zènzero (ZEN-zay-rō) Italian for **ginger.**

zest The outer, colored skin of citrus fruits where the essential oils are concentrated. The French word is *zeste,* not to be confused with *ziste,* the white pith beneath the zest.

zeytin (ZAY-tin) Turkish for olives; olive oil is *zeytinyağı.* The Arab word used in much of the Middle East is *zeitoun.*

zhá (tsah) In Chinese, to deep-fry.

zhēng (tsun) In Chinese, to steam.

zhī má yóu (zeu mah yō) Chinese sesame oil, which is darker in color and stronger in flavor than western sesame oil; used more for seasoning sauces than for frying.

zhú ròu (jhō rō) Chinese for pork.

Zigeuner Art (tsi-GOY-ner art) German for gypsy style; *Zigeunerspies,* an Austrian specialty, is skewered cubes of meat, peppers, and onions grilled over an open fire.

zik de venado (SEEK day veh-NAH-dō) Venison cooked in a **pib,** then shredded and served with onions, sour oranges, hot chili peppers, and **cilantro;** from the Yucatán of Mexico.

Zinfandel (ZIN-fahn-del) A red-wine grape variety of uncertain origin but widely planted in California; its style ranges considerably from light and fruity, almost like a **Beaujolais,** to deep, strong, and intense.

zingara, à la (ah lah zinh-GAHR-ah) Gypsy style—a classic French garnish of julienne of ham, tongue, mushrooms, and truffles in a **demi-glace** flavored with tomato purée, **Madeira,** and tarragon essence; *zìngara* is the Italian word for gypsy woman.

ziti (ZEE-tee)   Large tube pasta cut into segments, in Italian cooking.

Zitrone (tsee-TRŌ-nay)   German for lemon.

zucca (ZOO-kah)   Italian for squash, pumpkin; *zucchini* means "little squashes."

zùcchero (ZOO-kayr-ō)   Italian for sugar.

zuccotto (zoo-KOHT-tō)   A dome-shaped Italian dessert of cake moistened with liqueur and filled with sweetened whipped cream, chocolate, and nuts; originally from Florence, it supposedly resembles the top of the *Duomo*.

Zucker (TSOO-ker)   German for sugar; *Zuckerrübe* means sugar beet.

Zunge (TSUNG-eh)   German for tongue.

zuppa (ZOOP-pah)   Italian soup.

zuppa inglese (ZOOP-pah een-GLAY-say)   Literally "English soup," this is a rich Italian dessert of rum-soaked sponge cake layered with custard and cream—a kind of trifle.

Zwetschge (TSVECH-geh)   Austrian for damson plum; see also **Powidl**.

zwieback   Bread slices baked again (from German "twice baked," like a **biscuit**); rusks.

Zwiebel (TSVEE-bel)   German for onion; *Zwiebelkuche* is an onion tart from Hesse, made with bacon and cream, perhaps flavored with caraway seeds—not unlike a **quiche** *lorraine; Zwiebelgrün* is a scallion.

Selected Bibliography

Algar, Ayla. *Classical Turkish Cooking.* New York: Harper Collins, 1991.

Anderson, E. N. *The Food of China.* New Haven and London: Yale Univ. Press, 1988.

Anderson, Jean. *The Food of Portugal.* Rev. ed. New York: Hearst, 1994.

————, and Hedy Würz. *The New German Cookbook.* New York: Harper Collins, 1993.

Andrews, Jean. *Peppers: The Domesticated Capsicums.* Austin: Univ. of Texas Press, 1995.

Androuet, Pierre. *Guide to Cheeses.* Rev. English ed. Nuffield, Henley-on-Thames, England: Aidan Ellis, 1993.

Ayto, John. *A Gourmet's Guide: Food and Drink from A to Z.* Oxford and New York: Oxford Univ. Press, 1994.

Barron, Rosemary. *The Flavors of Greece.* New York: William Morrow, 1991.

Battistotti, Bruno; Vittorio Bottazzi; Antonio Piccinardi; and Giancarlo Volpati. *Cheese: A Guide to the World of Cheese and Cheesemaking.* New York: Facts on File, 1984.

Bianchini, F., and F. Corbetta. *The Complete Book of Fruits and Vegetables.* New York: Crown, 1976.

Bickel, Walter, ed. *Hering's Dictionary of Classical and Modern Cookery.* London, Dublin, and Coulsdon: Virtue, 1981.

Bloom, Carole. *The International Dictionary of Desserts, Pastries, and Confections.* New York: Hearst, 1995.

Brennan, Jennifer. *The Original Thai Cookbook.* New York: Perigee, 1981.

Bugialli, Giuliano. *Giuliano Bugialli's Classic Techniques of Italian Cooking.* New York: Simon and Schuster, 1989.

Casas, Penelope. *The Foods and Wines of Spain.* New York: Knopf, 1982.

Chantiles, Vilma Liacouras. *The Food of Greece.* New York: Simon and Schuster, 1992.

Child, Julia. *The Way to Cook.* New York: Knopf, 1989.

Crewe, Quentin. *The Simon and Schuster International Pocket Food Guide.* New York: Simon and Schuster, 1980.

Dahlen, Martha, and Karen Phillipps. *A Popular Guide to Chinese Vegetables.* New York: Crown, 1983.

David, Elizabeth. *English Bread and Yeast Cookery.* New American ed. Newton, Massachusetts: Biscuit Books, 1994.

———. *French Provincial Cooking.* Rev. ed. Harper and Row, 1970.

———. *Italian Food.* Rev. ed. New York: Harper and Row, 1987.

Davidson, Alan, and Charlotte Knox. *Fruit: A Connoisseur's Guide and Cookbook.* London: Mitchell Beazley, 1991.

Davidson, Alan. *Mediterranean Seafood.* Rev. ed. Harmondsworth, England: Penguin, 1981.

———. *North Atlantic Seafood.* New York: Viking Penguin, 1980.

———. *Seafood: A Connoisseur's Guide and Cookbook.* New York: Simon and Schuster, 1989.

Del Conte, Anna. *Gastronomy of Italy.* New York, London, Toronto, Sidney, Tokyo: Prentice Hall, 1987.

Duong, Binh, and Marcia Kiesel. *Simple Art of Vietnamese Cooking.* New York: Prentice Hall, 1991.

FitzGibbon, Theodora. *The Food of the Western World.* New York: Quadrangle, 1976.

Grigson, Jane. *Charcuterie and French Pork Cookery.* London: Penguin, 1967.

————, and Charlotte Knox. *Exotic Fruits and Vegetables.* New York: Henry Holt, 1986.

————. *Jane Grigson's Fruit Book.* New York: Atheneum, 1982.

————. *Jane Grigson's Vegetable Book.* Harmondsworth, England: Penguin, 1978.

Grigson, Sophie. *Gourmet Ingredients.* New York: Van Nostrand Reinhold, 1991.

Guillemard, Colette. *Les Mots de la cuisine et de la table.* Paris: Belin, 1990.

Gupta, Pranati Sen. *The Art of Indian Cuisine.* New York: Hawthorn Books, 1974.

Hafner, Dorinda. *A Taste of Africa.* Berkeley, California: Ten Speed Press, 1993.

Harris, Jessica B. *Iron Pots and Wooden Spoons.* New York: Ballantine, 1989.

————. *The Welcome Table.* New York: Simon and Schuster, 1995.

Hazan, Marcella. *Essentials of Classic Italian Cooking.* New York: Knopf, 1995.

Herbst, Sharon Tyler. *The New Food Lover's Companion.* 2nd ed. Hauppauge, New York: Barron's, 1995.

Hess, Karen. *The Carolina Rice Kitchen: The African Connection.* Columbia: Univ. of South Carolina Press, 1992.

Jaffrey, Madhur. *World-of-the East Vegetarian Cooking.* New York: Knopf, 1981.

Johnson, Hugh. *Hugh Johnson's Modern Encyclopedia of Wine.* 3rd ed. New York: Simon and Schuster, 1991.

Kennedy, Diana. *The Cuisines of Mexico.* Rev. ed. New York: Harper Collins, 1989.

————. *Mexican Regional Cooking.* New York: Harper Perennial, 1990.

Lang, Jennifer H., ed. *Larousse Gastronomique: The New American Edition of the World's Greatest Culinary Encyclopedia.* New York: Crown, 1988.

Levy, Faye. *Faye Levy's International Jewish Cookbook.* New York: Warner, 1991.

Mallos, Tess. *The Complete Middle East Cookbook.* Boston, Rutland, Vermont, and Tokyo: Charles E. Tuttle, 1993.

Manjon, Maite. *The Gastronomy of Spain and Portugal.* New York: Prentice Hall, 1990.

Mariani, John F. *The Dictionary of American Food and Drink.* Rev. ed. New York: William Morrow, 1994.

Marks, Copeland. *The Great Book of Couscous.* New York: Donald I. Fine, 1994.

————. *The Korean Kitchen.* San Francisco: Chronicle, 1993.

Martinez, Zarela. *Food from My Heart.* New York: Macmillan, 1992.

McClane, A. J. *The Encyclopedia of Fish Cookery.* New York: Henry Holt, 1977.

McGee, Harold. *On Food and Cooking: The Science and Lore of the Kitchen.* New York: Scribner's, 1984.

O'Higgins, Maria Josefa Lluriá de. *A Taste of Old Cuba.* New York: Harper Collins, 1994.

Owen, Sri. *Indonesian Food and Cookery.* London: Prospect Books, 1986.

Passmore, Jacki. *The Encyclopedia of Asian Food and Cooking.* New York: Hearst, 1991.

Rance, Patrick. *The French Cheese Book.* London: Macmillan, 1989.

————. *The Great British Cheese Book.* London: Macmillan, 1982.

Randelman, Mary Urrutia, and Joan Schwartz. *Memories of a Cuban Kitchen.* New York: Macmillan, 1992.

Reynaldo, Alejandro. *The Philippine Cookbook.* New York: Coward-McCann, 1982.

Riely, Elizabeth. *A Feast of Fruits.* New York: Macmillan, 1993.

Robinson, Jancis, ed. *The Oxford Companion to Wine.* Oxford and New York: Oxford Univ. Press, 1994.

Roden, Claudia. *A Book of Middle Eastern Food.* New York: Vintage, 1974.

Rojas-Lombardi, Felipe. *The Art of South American Cooking.* New York: Harper Collins, 1991.

Root, Waverly. *Food.* New York: Simon and Schuster, 1980.

Rubash, Joyce. *Master Dictionary of Food & Wine.* New York: Van Nostrand Reinhold, 1990.

Sahni, Julie. *Classic Indian Cooking.* New York: William Morrow, 1980.

Saulnier, Louis. *Le Repertoire de la Cuisine.* Woodbury, New York: Barron's, 1976.

Schneider, Elizabeth. *Uncommon Fruits and Vegetables.* New York: Harper and Row, 1986.

Sharman, Fay, and Klaus Boehm. *The Taste of France: A Dictionary of French Food and Wine.* Boston: Houghton Mifflin, 1982.

Simon, André L. *A Concise Encyclopedia of Gastronomy.* Woodstock, New York: Overlook, 1981.

————, and Robin Howe. *Dictionary of Gastronomy.* 2nd ed. Woodstock, New York: Overlook, 1979.

Simonds, Nina. *Classic Chinese Cuisine.* Rev. ed. Shelburne, Vermont: Chapters Publishing, 1994.

Solomon, Charmaine. *The Complete Asian Cookbook.* Rutland, Vermont, Boston, and Tokyo: Charles E. Tuttle, 1992.

Stobart, Tom. *The Cook's Encyclopedia.* New York: Harper and Row, 1980.

————, *Herbs, Spices and Flavourings.* New York: Viking Penguin, 1987.

Tropp, Barbara. *The Modern Art of Chinese Cooking.* New York: William Morrow, 1982.

Tsuji, Shizuo. *Japanese Cooking: A Simple Art.* Tokyo, New York, and San Francisco: Kodansha International, 1980.

Wheaton, Barbara Ketcham. *Savoring the Past: The French Kitchen and Table from 1300 to 1789.* Philadelphia: Univ. of Pennsylvania Press, 1983.

Willan, Anne. *La Varenne Pratique.* New York: Crown, 1989.

Wolfert, Paula. *The Cooking of the Eastern Mediterranean.* New York: Harper Collins, 1994.

————, *Couscous and Other Good Food from Morocco.* New York: Harper and Row, 1987.

————, *Mediterranean Cooking.* New York: Harper Collins, 1994.

About the Author

Elizabeth Riely is a journalist and food historian whose articles have appeared in *Bon Appétit, Gourmet, House and Garden,* and *The New York Times,* among many other publications. She contributes regularly to *The Boston Globe.* Her cookbook *A Feast of Fruits* was published by Macmillan in 1993. Trained in music, she turned to foodwriting late. This dictionary of gastronomy brings together her interests in the arts, travel, and cooking. She lives in Newton Centre, Massachusetts, with her husband and two sons.